Praise for **YALE NEE**

"*Yale Needs Women* breaks through t
defined the Ivy League and delivers the powerful history of a group
of young women bold enough to reshape undergraduate education.
Perkins's richly detailed narrative is a reminder that gender equity has
never come easily, but instead is borne from the exertions of those who
precede us. You must read this book, not only to understand our past
but to glean critical insight into the future of our academic institutions."

—Nathalia Holt, *New York Times* bestselling
author of *Rise of the Rocket Girls*

"Just in time for the fiftieth anniversary of the first class of women to
enter Yale College, the author's own alma mater, Anne Gardiner Perkins
has written an enjoyable and lively history of this event. Through extensive archival research and in-depth interviews with forty-two of the
women who matriculated in 1969, Perkins focuses on the experiences of
five of these women, recounting both their struggles and their triumphs
as they encountered this bastion of male privilege. This beautifully
written history also provides a comprehensive view of the many social
and political changes that faced the young college women of this era as
well as pointing out contemporary problems on college campuses. *Yale
Needs Women* is an important addition to feminist history."

—Henry Louis Gates Jr., Alphonse Fletcher
University professor (Harvard University),
and host of PBS's *Finding Your Roots*

"Perkins tackles the discrimination these brave young women of Yale
faced, the tremendous sexism and racism of the time, with stories that
will make this #MeToo generation shudder and rage. But amid these

darker moments are the stories of women who shined, who triumphed, who took this opportunity for all that it was worth and showed Yale—and the rest of the country—that women of all backgrounds possess the intellectual rigor and leadership qualities required to deserve a place at this Ivy League institution."

—Donna Freitas, author of *Consent on Campus*

"Yes, Yale needed women, but it didn't really want them. From the moment they arrived in 1969, the first coeds faced a male administration and culture that regarded them as sexual objects, isolated them, and offered few female mentors. In her compelling account of the tumultuous early years, Anne Gardiner Perkins tells how these young women met the challenge with courage and tenacity and forever changed Yale and its chauvinistic motto of graduating one thousand male leaders every year."

—Lynn Povich, author of *The Good Girls Revolt*

"*Yale Needs Women* is a riveting and uplifting account of the experiences of Yale's early women coeds—first admitted in 1969. It reveals the multiple barriers faced by these pioneers as it chronicles their brave efforts to overcome them. Thanks to these champions of women's rights, with similar efforts across the country, opportunities for women have improved. The fight is not over. This inspiring book is a must-read for everyone."

—Janet L. Yellen, United States Secretary of the Treasury

"*Yale Needs Women* is a riveting—and long overdue—account of how the first 575 undergraduate women admitted to previously all-male Yale University in 1969 found themselves doing battle with 268 years of entrenched male hegemony in an Ivy League setting. Based on extensive interviews and archival research, Anne Gardiner Perkins weaves a tale of courage in the face of arrogance, frustration giving way to hard-won triumphs, and the redeeming power of shared visions and friendships. Perkins makes the story of these early and unwitting feminist pioneers come alive against the backdrop of the contemporaneous civil rights and antiwar movements of the 1970s and offers observations that remain eerily relevant on U.S. campuses today."

—Edward B. Fiske, bestselling author
of *Fiske Guide to Colleges*

"This smart, lively first book by Perkins, a higher education scholar and Yale graduate, challenges a 'sanitized tale of equity instantly achieved' when the elite university, after 268 years, admitted female undergraduates in 1969... Perkins succeeds admirably in restoring these women's fascinating voices and weaving in the larger historical context. This is a valuable contribution to the history of higher education, women, and the postwar U.S."

—*Publishers Weekly*

"This stunning, engaging work highlights the strength and courage of women who fought for their future against centuries of patriarchy. Perfect for readers interested in seeing how far women have come—and how far they still have yet to go."

—*Library Journal*, Starred Review

"Perkins (Yale class of 1981) does not sugarcoat history, the 360-degree approach she takes makes *Yale Needs Women* an engaging, entertaining, thoughtful work of popular history."

—*Booklist*

YALE
NEEDS
WOMEN

YALE NEEDS WOMEN

How the First Group *of* Girls Rewrote the Rules *of* an Ivy League Giant

ANNE GARDINER PERKINS

 sourcebooks

Published by Sourcebooks
P.O. Box 4410, Naperville, Illinois 60567-4410
(630) 961-3900
sourcebooks.com

Library of Congress Cataloging-in-Publication data is on file with the publisher.

Printed and bound in the United States of America.
SB 10 9 8 7 6 5 4 3 2 1

For my family:
Rick, Lily, Robby, Mac, Ginny, and Dear.
And in memory of my father, Tom, and brother, Robert.

CONTENTS

A Note on Terms   xiii

Prologue   xv

ONE: 268 Years of Men   1

TWO: Superwomen   26

THREE: A Thousand Male Leaders   54

FOUR: Consciousness   81

FIVE: Sex-Blind   103

SIX: Margaret Asks for the Mic   130

SEVEN: The Sisterhood   150

EIGHT: Breaking the Rules   178

NINE: The Opposition   194

TEN: Reinforcements   215

ELEVEN: Tanks versus BB Guns   238

TWELVE: Mountain Moving Day   262

Epilogue   288

Acknowledgments   299

Oral Histories and Interviews   303

Notes   309

Index   359

About the Author   375

A NOTE ON TERMS

SOME TERMS IN THIS BOOK MAY STRIKE THE MODERN ear harshly, but since this is a historical work, I have chosen to use the words used by Yale students in 1970, including "freshmen" to describe first-year students regardless of gender, "girls" and "coeds" for women, "blacks" for African Americans, "Afro-American" for African American studies, "sex" for gender, and "master" for the heads of Yale's residential colleges. Similarly, I have used "black" rather than "Black" to mirror the usage of students at the time.

PROLOGUE

WHEN I WAS FIFTY-TWO YEARS OLD, I DECIDED THAT the time had come to get my PhD. Better late than never. The idea was not entirely new. My best friend, Hazel, and I had met in our twenties, when we were both history graduate students, and I had considered getting a doctorate then. But while Hazel went on to get her PhD, I had felt pulled to different work, and after getting my master's, I'd gotten a job teaching in an urban high school. Thirty years later, I was still in education, now working on policies and programs for Massachusetts's public colleges and universities. I wanted to strengthen my thinking about the issues I worked on, and I knew that UMass Boston had a well-regarded higher education program. Once again, the doctorate beckoned.

So I began. Monday through Thursday, I worked at my job on Beacon Hill. Fridays, I went to class at UMass Boston. Weekends, I studied. My husband, Rick, did all the cooking and—let's be honest—every other household chore too. But it was exciting to be back in school again.

I never intended to write a history dissertation, though Hazel would tell you that my doing so was entirely predictable. I planned to research some practical topic, one tied more directly to my job, but in my first fall semester, I took a required course on the history of higher education. Needing a topic for the final class paper, I wondered, *What about those first women students who arrived at Yale in 1969? I bet there are some amazing stories there.* The idea was not as random as it might sound. You see, I had gone to Yale too.

I arrived as a freshman in 1977, eight years after the first women undergraduates. I studied history and wrote for the *Yale Daily News.* I covered women's ice hockey and eventually the president's beat. In my junior year, I became editor in chief. Yet throughout that whole time, I knew nothing about the women at Yale who came before me and all the challenges they faced when they got there.

Decades later, I searched for a book that would tell me about Yale's first women undergraduates, but the women were missing from histories of Yale in that era. The books focused instead on the decision to let women in, as if that were the end of the story. But what happened next? That's what I wanted to know. Here was a college that had been all male for 268 years, and then, suddenly, the first women students arrived. Historian Margaret Nash calls such moments "flashpoints" in history, times when the bright light of a sudden change illuminates all around it and everything, for a time, seems possible. In 1969, the U.S. women's movement had just begun. The Black Power movement was changing how Americans saw race. And into that moment stepped the first women undergraduates at Yale.

I took a day off from work and drove to New Haven to see what I might find in the Yale archives, and after that, there was no turning back. The story was just too compelling. I went back to the archives a second time, a third, a fourth, still more, now for a week at a time.

Eventually, I realized that if I really wanted to understand what had happened at Yale in that flashpoint of history, I needed to talk to the women who had lived through it.

The forty-two women I interviewed for this book were all wonderful—inviting me into their kitchens and living rooms and places of work, talking with me far longer than the one hour I'd proposed, trusting me with their stories. "Don't screw it up, Anne," one of them told me after we'd gotten to know one another, and she was only half kidding. But by that point, getting this history right had become as important to me as it was to her. The women who go first and speak out help shape a better world for all of us, yet all too often their stories are lost. I was not going to let that happen to this story.

I went back to the archives again and pored through box after box of documents. I read hundreds of old newspaper stories and compiled thousands of pages of notes. For me, though, the real gift of this book has been the remarkable women I came to know in writing it, the first women undergraduates at Yale. This is their story. I am honored to be the one to tell it.

Anne Gardiner Perkins
Boston, 2019

ONE

268 Years of Men

THE WOMEN CAME TO YALE IN BUSES, PEERING OUT
the large glass windows at the men who had gathered on the
sidewalk below to await their arrival. The girls from Vassar College
wore brightly colored dresses and skirts cut up above the knee. Their
hair shone from being combed and recombed on the two-hour drive
from Poughkeepsie to New Haven. The guys from Yale had dressed
up as well: button-down shirts, narrow ties, and sports jackets. The
men's faces were clean-shaven, and their hair was trimmed neatly
above the ears. It was Saturday night, November 1967, and the Yale
men were ready for women.

Yale was still an all-men's college back then, and one of the only
ways to find a girlfriend was to frequent the mixers that brought in
busloads of women each weekend from elite women's colleges like
Vassar and Smith. On Saturday nights, the buses rolled into Yale at
8:00 p.m., each with their cargo of fifty girls. At midnight, the girls
returned from whence they came. In the four hours in between, the
Yale men sought to make their match. Guys who had girlfriends
already would show up at the Saturday football games with their

girls on their arms and then appear with them afterward in the dining hall or a local restaurant. But for the rest of the week, Yale undergraduates lived their days in a single-sex world.

To picture Yale as it was at the time, imagine a village of men. From Monday through Friday, students attended their men-only classes, ate meals in their men-only dining hall, took part in their men-only extracurricular pursuits, and then retired to their men-only dorms. Yale admitted scatterings of women graduate and professional students in 1967, but Yale College, the heart of the university, remained staunchly all male. The ranks of faculty and administrators who ran the school were nearly all men as well. If you were to peek through the door at any department meeting, the professors seated around the table would invariably be "white men in tweeds and casually expensive shoes," as one of Yale's rare black professors observed. Yale was an odd place, at least to a modern eye, but since its founding in 1701, Yale had always been a place for men.

Yale was the oldest men's club in the nation—older than the Kiwanis, the Elks, and the Boy Scouts; older than New York's Union Club and San Francisco's Bohemian Club; and older than Princeton and Dartmouth and the dozens of other U.S. colleges that also banned women from applying in 1967. Only two colleges in America were older than Yale: William and Mary, which went coed in 1919 for financial reasons, and Harvard, where Radcliffe women had been attending classes since 1943. Yale never had a sister school. On the weekends, though, for a brief span of hours, a fissure opened up in that men-only world. The buses from Vassar and Connecticut College, from Smith and Mount Holyoke, pulled up at the curb, and the Yale guys began vying with one another for the best of the imported women. The evening always began with such promise.

The bus doors swung apart. The women clicked open their

compacts to check their lipstick one last time and then descended one by one into the crowd of men below, wondering what the night would bring. Girl after girl stepped down off the bus, smiled, and filed past the group of college boys standing outside. They passed through the stone archway of one of Yale's twelve residential colleges and then into the wood-paneled common room where more Yale men waited. The men had been drinking already, clustered in groups around kegs of cheap beer brought in for the event, bracing themselves for the night to come.

A girlfriend was "the most prized piece of chattel in the college man's estate," explained one Yale student, but not just any girl would do. She had to come from one of the colleges thought suitable for future Yale wives, and she had to be pretty. If a guy brought a good-looking girl with him into one of Yale's dining halls, his classmates would show their approval by banging their spoons against their water glasses. Guys who arrived with a date thought unattractive would get ribbed about it later. And so the Yale men chose carefully.

A Yale sophomore appraised the women who now filled the room, picked out one of them, and approached her with his long-practiced line: "Say, aren't you from California?"

She was not, but the two chatted anyway, trading hometowns and majors. All the while, both scanned the room—was there someone better to be paired with?

In the next room over, the dining hall had been turned into a dance floor, with chairs and tables shoved over to the side, the lights turned low. A young man asked one of the newly arrived women if she wanted to dance. She smiled, and the two entered the room.

A band blared saxophone and electric bass from the front, the music so loud that conversation was impossible. There was little to do but nod and smile, pretending to hear what the other person said. A few couples over, one girl, put off by her partner's awkward dance moves, pretended she was dancing with the guy next to him. The song ended, and she retreated to the ladies' room, hoping he would be with someone else when she returned. The pairs in the room reshuffled, with men who sought a new partner excusing themselves to get a beer and women who wanted to move on explaining they needed to go find their roommates. The code in both cases was the same—*not you.*

Through the first two hours of the mixer, the cycle continued—choose, discard; choose, discard; choose, discard—a game of musical chairs where each person hoped not to be the one who turned up alone when the music stopped.

"Say, aren't you from California?"

By 10:00 p.m., the pairings became less fluid, the matches more firm. The question shifted: Would you like to see my room?

A senior with long blond hair had heard this line too many times before. "No," she answered, "I know all about your room." It had been a long night for her already. A Yale freshman had offered to give her a tour of the campus. Another guy had offered to show her his rock collection. As one Yale man observed, "Some girls that I've talked to have the idea that all we want from them is sex. Maybe they're right, but what else can you do when you don't get to know them and haven't got the time to establish a natural relationship?"

At midnight, the buses readied to leave, and the women filed back out through the stone archway, some coming from the depleted crowd at the mixer and others from the men's rooms they'd been visiting. The opening into Yale's village of men once again closed. The buses of women pulled out and began the long drive home while the men pushed the dining hall tables and chairs back into place and the band carted away its instruments. All that was left was the smell of the beer. And so the rhythm of Yale continued as it always had, with men-only weeks followed by weekends with women. Change, however, hovered just around the corner. But no one at Yale seemed to realize how fast it would come.

———

The school year passed. Another class of Yale men graduated, and a new one readied to take its place, just as the cycle had gone for decades. Yet beneath that veneer of sameness, things were shifting at Yale, and Kingman Brewster Jr., Yale's president, was the reason.

By 1968, Brewster was in his fifth year as president and had established himself as a leader who was determined to bring about change. He had tasked his admissions director with increasing the numbers of black students at Yale, and he'd supported black students' efforts to create an Afro-

Kingman Brewster Jr.
Photo © Yale University.
Images of Yale Individuals
(RU 684), Manuscripts and
Archives, Yale University
Library.

American studies major, one of the first in the nation. He increased the financial aid budget so that all admitted students could attend and halted the admissions office practice of checking on students' family income before deciding whether or not to admit them. Brewster had hired some of the most renowned academics in the nation to strengthen the faculty and raised Yale's profile in the national press. And in the process of all of this, he had attained a prominence that surpassed that of most politicians.

Brewster made the cover of *Newsweek* in 1964 and was named by President Lyndon B. Johnson to a U.S. presidential commission the following year and to a second one in 1966. In 1967, the *New York Times* published a gushing five-page profile of Brewster, and talk began in some corners of a possible cabinet position or even a U.S. presidential run. That same year, Brewster made the cover of *Time* and chaired a UN policy panel on peacekeeping missions. If Yale men, as some said, were destined for leadership, then Kingman Brewster was striding confidently down the path of his destiny.

Begin with the name: Kingman—or as old friends and colleagues sometimes called him, simply "King," his childhood nickname. For if ever there was a person who embodied the ideal of manhood at Yale, it was Brewster. He was "an imposing figure. Big," said one Yale student, and those who met him were struck by his presence. "Whatever 'it' is, he had it," remarked one Yale trustee. Brewster was handsome by most accounts, with a craggy sort of face and brown hair that was just going gray at the temples. He wore pinstripe suits and shirts handmade in Hong Kong and was descended from ancestors who had come over on the *Mayflower*—the first trip. He carried with him "the assurance that came from being a direct descendant of the Elder Brewster," explained one of his friends. "You know, 'This is my place.'" And like every Yale president since 1766 but one, Brewster had gone to college at Yale, since, as every Yale man knew, quipped the *Harvard Crimson*, "a Yale man is the best kind of man to be, and only Yale can produce one."

Yet just when it seemed one might be able to sum Brewster up in a phrase—the patrician leader, the ultimate Yale man, the nation's most well-known university president—a confounding piece of evidence arose to complicate the picture. "He was a very complex man," observed student Kurt Schmoke.

Brewster encompassed a span of seeming contradictions. He was politically conservative but open-minded on many issues. He was both a blue-blood New Englander and a man who sought to learn from others, regardless of their pedigree. He was reserved but sparkled at social gatherings, where he would amuse his friends by mimicking various political personalities or once by singing with gusto an impromptu performance from *My Fair Lady*. He was forty-nine years old, yet on some of America's hottest issues—Vietnam, race—he stood not with the men of his own generation but with the generation that challenged them.

The students loved him. For their 1968 fund-raiser, Yale's student advisory board sold T-shirts printed with the slogan "Next to myself, I like Kingman best." The following year, when Brewster entered a contentious campus-wide meeting on the future of ROTC at Yale, four thousand students rose to give him a standing ovation. On the subject of coeducation, however, Brewster and Yale students stood apart. Indeed, of all the dissonances that defined Kingman Brewster, the contrast between his progressive stances on race, religion, and class and his conservative views on gender was perhaps the most striking.

Brewster refused to frequent clubs that discriminated against blacks or Jews, and the signature change of his administration had been opening Yale's doors to more black students and students from families that could never before have afforded to send their sons to Yale. But when it came to women, Brewster was content with the world as it was. He enjoyed many a meal at clubs that banned women from the main dining room at lunchtime, and as to the idea of ending Yale's 268 years as a men's school by admitting women undergraduates…well, why would anyone want to do that?

By 1968, Yale students had been telling Brewster the answer

to that question for more than two years, ever since Lanny Davis became chairman of the *Yale Daily News* in 1966. "Coeducation should now be beyond argument," Lanny wrote in his debut editorial, which declared that the time was long overdue to end "the unrealistic, artificial, and stifling social environment of an all-male Yale." Lanny did not stop there but proceeded to publish a barrage of pro-coeducation columns and editorials, more than nineteen in all, over the next five months. "Lanny beat the drums day in and day out and, in a wonderfully positive way, harassed the hell out of us," said Brewster's top adviser, Sam Chauncey. And when the *Yale Daily News* spoke, the men who ran Yale generally listened. The *News* was one of the oldest and most powerful student organizations on campus. Past chairmen had included Supreme Court Justice Potter Stewart, *Time* magazine founder Henry Luce, and Kingman Brewster himself, who read the *Yale Daily News* and met regularly with the paper's chairman to get a read on student opinion. When it came to admitting women undergraduates, however, even the *News* could not convince Brewster that the time for change had come.

Brewster was hardly alone in his stance. America's most elite colleges had long maintained their reputation not just by the types of students they let in but by those they kept out: Jews, blacks, working-class kids—and women. Even after the wave of coeducation that followed the Civil War, upping the proportion of coed campuses from 25 percent before the war to 60 percent by 1890, the vast majority of top-tier colleges and universities in the United States stayed all male. Coeducation was solely a symptom of financial weakness, opined Harvard president Charles Eliot in 1873. The colleges that could afford to turn down women's tuitions—America's oldest and most prestigious—would continue to do so.

Nearly a century later, President Eliot's prediction held true, and in 1968, the list of U.S. colleges that still banned women undergraduates reads like an academic who's who: Amherst, Boston College, Bowdoin, Brown, Carnegie Mellon, Claremont McKenna, Colgate, Columbia, Dartmouth, Davidson, Duke, Fordham, Georgetown, Hamilton, Harvard, Haverford, Holy Cross, Johns Hopkins, Kenyon, Lafayette, Lehigh, Notre Dame, Penn, Princeton, Rutgers, Sewanee, Trinity, Tufts, Tulane, Union, UVA, Washington and Lee, Wesleyan, West Point and the other military academies, Williams, and—of course—Yale. A few, like Harvard and Brown, had created sister schools that kept the women nearby without putting them on equal terms with men, but none admitted women to the same college that the men attended. "In the minds of many," observed the *Educational Record*, "'all-male' education has become synonymous with 'prestige' education."

That status quo was just fine with Brewster, and unless he changed his position on the matter, Yale would stay just as it was. Brewster's power at Yale ran unfettered by the constraints that frustrated other campus presidents. He was not just a member of the Corporation, Yale's board of trustees, but its president, and "the faculty adored him," observed one senior professor. Brewster had raised their salaries and strengthened their reputation, and the glow from Brewster's accolades shone on all of them. Nonetheless, even Kingman Brewster could not always shape the world as he wished to.

The events of the spring of 1968 had shaken him. Martin Luther King Jr.'s assassination in April had struck particularly hard, for here was a man whose hand Brewster had clasped when, as one of the first acts of his presidency, he had awarded King an honorary degree. That same month, students at Trinity College, just forty miles up the road from Yale, had held a group of trustees hostage until Trinity acted on a long-stalled student demand for a scholarship fund for black and other disadvantaged students. A larger protest at Columbia three weeks later ended with more than two hundred students injured and seven hundred arrested.

Over the summer of 1968, Brewster retreated with his family to their waterfront home on Martha's Vineyard, where he spent his days in Bermuda shorts and sneakers, sailing and talking with friends and presiding over the grill at evening cookouts. And there, pecking out the words with two fingers on his typewriter, Brewster wrote the initial draft of his annual presidential report, his statement of Yale's accomplishments in the year just passed and the goals for the year to come. As he looked ahead to the fall of 1968, Brewster set forth two central questions: How much say should students have in university governance? What was the university's responsibility to the New Haven neighborhoods that surrounded it? Brewster typed out his answers, which in turn became his priorities for the year. His report was silent entirely, however, on the possibility of coeducation.

The summer ticked away, and as it did, the twine that held the nation together continued to unravel. In June, Bobby Kennedy was assassinated. In August, Chicago police assaulted protestors at the Democratic National Convention. And in the background was the constant drumbeat of the Vietnam War, where U.S. troop levels had surpassed half a million. The growing women's movement would unsettle the givens of Brewster's life still further, but in the summer of 1968, it was just gaining its footing. NOW, the National Organization for Women, was only two years old. Consciousness-raising groups had just started meeting in women's living rooms and kitchens. Most Americans did not yet grasp the extent of the discrimination against women in education, employment, and the law.

Aside from Betty Friedan's *The Feminine Mystique*, the major works of second-wave feminism were yet to be written.

Out on Martha's Vineyard, the days grew shorter with the coming fall; the time to pack away the Bermuda shorts drew near. Brewster finished his president's report and readied to return to campus, not yet realizing that the agenda for the year ahead would be set not by him, but by students.

———

To Yale senior Derek Shearer, the idea that women were not good enough to attend a college like Yale made no sense. He had only to look at his family for evidence to the contrary. His sister Brooke was one of the smartest kids in her high school. His mother wrote for local and national magazines, and Derek felt proud to write *journalist* instead of *housewife* on the forms at school that asked his mother's occupation. Derek had attended a coed public high school in California, and his friends there included both boys and girls. He did not like the all-male atmosphere he found at Yale, and he was determined to change it.

Yale students and their views on the desirability of coeducation had changed in the four years since Derek had arrived as a freshman. Some Yale men were still happy to attend an all-male school, with its bonds of brotherhood and freedom from the pressure (albeit self-induced) of performing for the opposite sex. But by 1968, the bulk of Yale students did not want to spend their college years trapped in a village of men. Many saw their single-sex existence as unnatural. Others just wanted girlfriends. A number, like Derek, were moved by the unfairness of a policy that gave them a chance to get into Yale while denying their sisters the opportunity to even apply. Like the growing number of Yale men who grew their hair long or wore mustaches and beards, these new views reflected the changing values of youth across the nation. And at Yale, some of that shift had been inadvertently caused by Brewster himself.

After Brewster instructed his new admissions dean, Russell Inslee "Inky" Clark, to admit the top male students in the country regardless of their race or class or religion, the prep school boys who had long formed the majority at Yale had to compete against a broader field, and their numbers declined. In their stead, Yale admitted more students from public high schools, schools that with rare exception were coed. All-male Yale, while normal for the kids from all-male Andover and all-male Exeter, was not normal to this growing group of public high school graduates, and by Derek's senior year, half of Yale's four classes had been chosen by Inky Clark.

Derek held one of the top student positions at Yale: chairman of the student advisory board. The role granted him regular meetings with Brewster, and Derek used that pulpit to push Brewster on a topic that Brewster did not wish to be pushed on. "Complete and immediate coeducation," Derek told him in February 1968, was Yale's "most pressing educational need." All that talk came to naught, however, just like the earlier student efforts to end Yale's single-sex status. Brewster simply did not want Yale to admit women undergraduates. "Kingman was *not* comfortable with the idea of coeducation," explained Sam Chauncey, whose title as Brewster's assistant gave little indication of the degree of influence he held. Chauncey had occupied the office next to Brewster's ever since Brewster became president in 1963. The two talked every day: first thing in the morning, as issues arose during the day, or by phone if Brewster was out of town. Chauncey was privy to thoughts Brewster did not share with others, and while he always supported Brewster in public, Chauncey was free to challenge Brewster privately on issues where the two men disagreed—coeducation, for example. Yet here Chauncey met the same resistance as Yale students. Brewster "believed in change," Chauncey observed, "except when it came to things that were really important to him." Keeping Yale an all-male school was one of them.

Despite his national reputation, Brewster had lived his life behind the walls of a markedly insular world. A graduate of an all-boys prep school, Brewster had attended all-male Yale, where he'd met Vassar College junior Mary Louise Phillips, the daughter of a Yale man, at a fraternity party. They'd married the following year. As Yale's president, Brewster spent his days surrounded by men, and while the elegant dinner parties he hosted began with couples seated together, after the meal the men retired to the front parlor for brandy and conversation while the wives were shunted off elsewhere. For Brewster, the notion of two parallel spheres, one for men and one for women, was so deeply embedded in the structure of his days that it was hard to imagine an alternative.

"Kingman knew girls and women as someone apart," explained Associate Dean John Wilkinson, one of Brewster's inner circle. "He wasn't accustomed to women who were his equals." That perceived difference was at the center of Brewster's opposition to coeducation.

To Brewster, admitting women students threatened the central mission of Yale: graduating America's future leaders. By 1968, Yale had produced Supreme Court justices, a U.S. president, and a small army of U.S. senators, governors, and CEOs. Along with Harvard and Princeton, Yale was "widely viewed as the training grounds for the nation's leaders," wrote historian Jerome Karabel, and Yale would confirm that reputation twenty years later, when every U.S. president between 1989 and 2009 was a Yale man.

"We are a national institution whose ambition is nothing less than to try to frame a leadership for the nation," Brewster told Yale alumni in 1966, and admitting the right students was the key to attaining that goal. The role of the admissions office, Brewster instructed his staff, was to "make the hunchy judgment as to whether or not with Yale's help the candidate is likely to be a leader in whatever he ends up doing." Since women were not leaders, Brewster reasoned, they would be taking up limited spaces that could have gone to men.

If Brewster had wanted evidence of women's potential as leaders, all he had to do was look out his office window. Two blocks up at Yale's graduate school, future Secretary of the Treasury Janet Yellen was getting her PhD in economics, while future UC Berkeley chancellor Carol Christ was getting hers in English. One block away, future secretary of state Hillary Rodham had just been accepted at Yale Law School, where future Connecticut Supreme Court chief justice Ellen Peters was on the faculty and future Children's Defense Fund founder Marian Wright Edelman had graduated six years earlier.

This blindness to women's potential as leaders was not Brewster's alone. Judging by Americans' choices at the polls, he was right in step with his era. In the fall of 1968, all 50 of the state governors were men, as were 99 of the 100 U.S. senators and all but 11 of the 435 members of the U.S. House of Representatives. Yale's brand was producing national leaders, and if examples of women leaders could not be found—despite women's exclusion to date from nearly every avenue to power—then Yale was going to waste as few admissions slots on women as possible.

Brewster was a skilled political tactician, and for the two years following Lanny Davis's editorial onslaught, he kept Yale students at bay by holding out the possibility of a sister school, a solution that would have brought women to New Haven without actually having to admit them to Yale. Brewster even tried for an entire year to convince all-women Vassar to abandon its campus in Poughkeepsie and move 120 miles east to New Haven. When that plan fell through, he was ready with another: Yale would happily build its own women's college—as soon as a donor stepped forward to pay the more than $30 million that Brewster said it would cost for the additional faculty, staff, and facilities. And there the issue sat, nicely stalled, until student adviser Derek Shearer got tired of waiting.

Derek graduated in June 1968 without making much progress with Brewster, but he wasn't done with Yale yet. While Brewster sat pecking away at his president's report in Martha's Vineyard, Derek was busy making plans of his own. Even if he would not be at Yale to carry them out himself, he knew plenty of students in the classes below him who were just as tired of Brewster's intransigence on coeducation as he was. Perhaps Derek could provide a spark to ignite student activism for change.

When Yale students returned to campus in September, they found that Derek had been there before them. On entryway bulletin boards and hallway doors, on trees and telephone poles Derek had stapled a broadside that featured a large picture of his younger sister Brooke and the question "Please, Mr. Brewster, why can't I come to Yale?" You couldn't miss it, and there was no denying the boldness of the "Operation Coeducation" idea that it proposed: Bring one thousand women students to Yale for a week. Construct geodesic domes on the Old Campus to house them. And see what Kingman Brewster said then.

Yale may have felt like an all-male island to the students who were pushing for coeducation, but the university was not totally devoid of women. Women were present at the edges, as wives and mothers and girlfriends or as secretaries and dining hall workers. A few had even found places in the roles usually reserved for men. In 1968, Yale College had 2 tenured women on its faculty—and 391 tenured men. Yale was not alone in its preference for male professors, and women faculty were equally scarce at campuses that had long been coed. Just 4 percent of the full professors at the University of Michigan were women and 2 percent at the University of California Berkeley, even though both of these campuses had been educating women students since the 1870s. Among U.S. colleges, Yale's male-dominant culture may have been an extreme, but it was no aberration.

Although Yale's graduate and professional schools were technically coed in 1968, that wasn't how it felt to the women. *Invisible* is the word they used to describe themselves. Women graduate students made up less than 10 percent of Yale's student body, and they were spread out across eleven different graduate and professional schools, from the divinity school atop Prospect Hill to the medical school two miles south on the other side of the highway.

Yale's treatment of women as somehow less capable or deserving than men did not stop at women's scant numbers. Male graduate students were given housing in a prominent building at the center of campus, while the women were assigned to an ugly 1950s structure several dark blocks past the cemetery. Yale's Health Service did not offer gynecology, and the prescriptions there were preprinted with the title "Mr.," as if women would never need medicine or somehow did not exist. Yale had one of the finest gyms in the world, but women were banned from entering it. When graduate student Carol

Christ arrived at Yale's famed Elizabethan Club with her male class-mate, he was ushered inside, while she was whisked back out to the sidewalk. Women were not allowed.

Life for women at Yale might have been easier had there been some law or court ruling to prohibit colleges and universities from treating women unfairly, but in 1968 discrimination against women at U.S. colleges and universities was perfectly legal. The Fourteenth Amendment's provision for equal protection under the law had not yet been judged to include women. The Equal Pay Act of 1963 exempted professional women, including faculty and administrators. The Title IV protections of the Civil Rights Act of 1964 applied to race but not gender; Title VII excluded colleges and universities from its ban on employment discrimination. Title IX, which would ban discrimination in any federally funded education program or activity, was not even under discussion. For the time being, those at Yale who sought to change the status of women would have to fight that battle on their own.

Had Yale's current students been the only ones pushing coeducation, Brewster might have held out a little longer. But Yale's rivalry with Harvard and Princeton for the nation's top high school students began at admissions, and that was where the woman question finally struck a nerve. In the fall of 1968, the students who shaped Yale's direction were not just those who already went there but those who kept turning Yale down.

"Speaking strictly from an admissions standpoint, a decision to educate women at Yale...is not only desirable but virtually essential," Inky Clark told Brewster in June. The numbers did not look good. By 1968, more than 40 percent of the students accepted by Yale were choosing to attend other colleges, with the majority citing Yale's single-sex status as the reason. Worse still, more than three quarters of students admitted to both Harvard and Yale picked Harvard, and again the problem was Yale's lack of women students. Yale men faced a two-hour car ride to Vassar or Smith for a date, while a Harvard guy who sought female companionship could turn to the Radcliffe girl sitting next to him in class or visit the women at nearby Simmons or Wellesley. If Yale was going to keep its standing as one of the top two or three colleges in the nation, the availability of women was an amenity it could no longer do without.

The final straw was Princeton. On September 14, while Derek Shearer was putting up his "Please, Mr. Brewster" posters at Yale, Princeton released an extensive study of coeducation that concluded that women students were "vital to Princeton's future." Princeton had not yet acted on the report; its trustees were still considering the report's recommendations. But here was a threat Brewster could not ignore. It was bad enough losing top students to Harvard. Losing them to Princeton, still a second choice to Yale for most applicants, would never do, and if Princeton went coed and Yale did not, Yale might well find itself dropping to third place among the Ivy League schools. The Princeton report whetted Yale's "sense of competitive rivalry," said Brewster, and pushed him where he might not have otherwise gone.

Two weeks after Princeton issued its report, Brewster released an eight-page memorandum in which, for the first time, he held out the possibility of admitting women directly to Yale. He listed two reasons for the change: "the loss of first-rate students" who turned down Yale to attend colleges with "coeducational attractions" and the Princeton report, which in addition to its competitive threat provided an "impressive analysis" of the financial implications of coeducation and the benefits of admitting women directly rather than opening a sister school. Missing from Brewster's rationale was any notion of admitting women for reasons of equity or fairness. Nonetheless, coeducation at Yale was finally up for discussion.

Yet still Brewster stalled. Yale could not move forward with coeducation, he said, until it received that $30 million donation. And no, he hadn't asked anyone yet. Brewster's justification for his $30 million figure was based on the idea that going coed would cause Yale to increase its enrollment by 1,500 students, the number of women undergraduates Brewster proposed in his eight-page memorandum. But in 1968, Yale had plenty of space for women students if it simply chose to reduce the number of men in each entering class, and it had a fat $575 million endowment to dip into should it want to build the facilities and hire the faculty needed to expand. Even Inky Clark, an ally of Brewster's, gave little credence to Brewster's price tag argument: "It was a bogus issue," he said. "It really was bogus." By October 1968, there was nothing stopping Yale from admitting women students except Brewster's reluctance to do so.

Derek Shearer's "Please, Mr. Brewster" posters, however, had not gone unnoticed, and as the fall semester of 1968 got under way, the clamor for coeducation from Yale students only grew louder. "So Where Are the Women?" bellowed the *Yale Daily News* in an editorial on the first Monday of classes. The following week, junior Mark Zanger, the leader of Yale's chapter of Students for a Democratic Society (SDS), joined the offensive. "Women Now. Talk Later," demanded his October 4 *Yale Daily News* column, which charged that Brewster was only "pretending" to take the coeducation issue seriously.

Perhaps Brewster simply hoped the coeducation fervor would go away, but Avi Soifer, a Yale senior, was not going to let it drop. While Operation Coeducation and its idea of bringing women students to

Yale for a week had first been proposed by Derek Shearer, Avi was the one to take the next step. Like Derek, Avi had attended a coed public high school, where the presence of girls as peers and classmates was the norm. Avi had been following the coeducation issue since his sophomore year, when he had covered Brewster's attempt to lure Vassar to New Haven for the *Yale Daily News,* and he had come to know a few women graduate students who helped him see the ways in which Yale women were assigned a parallel yet lesser existence. By September 1968, Avi was ready to act, and in September, he pulled together some friends and got to work. Kingman Brewster did not know it yet, but Operation Coeducation—or "Coeducation Week," as Avi's group came to call it—was under way.

On October 15, three weeks after Brewster released his memo noting the competitive pressure to go coed, Avi Soifer and his team went public with their plans. Coeducation Week would start on November 4 and bring 750 women college students to Yale for six days. The women would live in dorm rooms vacated by obliging Yale students, attend classes, participate in forums and panels on coeducation, and give Yale men the chance to interact with the opposite sex "under more natural conditions than the infamous mixer." Coeducation Week would prove to alumni and the public that Yale students were "serious and sincere about normal coeducational life in the near future," said Avi, and it would prod Yale to adopt coeducation now rather than in that vague distant future to which Brewster perpetually postponed it.

The day after Avi announced the Coeducation Week plans, more than fifty students signed on to help make it happen. The logistics required were staggering. Twenty-two teams were dispatched to sign up women participants from colleges throughout the Northeast. Other students went door to door in the residence halls, asking their classmates if they would move in with friends for the week so that women could stay in their rooms. The committee needed fifteen thousand dollars to pay for the women's dining hall meals. The women, they decided, would cover half by contributing ten dollars each, and the committee would pay for the rest (or at least most of it) by asking the social committees of Yale's twelve residential colleges to throw in three or four hundred each, the cost of a mixer. There was meeting after meeting of committees and subcommittees and then subgroups of subcommittees. On one night alone, Avi went to twelve different meetings.

It's not clear how seriously Brewster had taken Derek Shearer's "Please, Mr. Brewster" posters, but he was paying attention now. On October 21, Avi was summoned to meet with a roomful of administrators and Brewster himself. Brewster was not pleased. Coeducation Week was happening too soon, he argued. Avi was bringing too many women to Yale. Yale students should just be more patient.

"Well," said Avi, "we may go ahead anyway."

"I wish you wouldn't," Brewster replied. But it was already too late.

———

The rest of October filled with the buildup toward Coeducation Week, and on Monday, November 4, 750 women students arrived in New Haven ready to spend a week as "Yalies." Girls from Vassar and Smith, from Bryn Mawr and Brandeis and Connecticut College, filled out their registration forms and met the men whose rooms they would be occupying. "All over the campus there was something giddy in the air—like a giant joke that everyone was in on," observed one visiting woman. "Lots of smiling went on."

Some of the men were still hurriedly putting fresh sheets on their bunk beds as the women arrived, but on the whole, the first day went smoothly. The visiting women received meal tickets, lists of suggested classes to attend, and a calendar of the week's events. Avi's team had sent out dozens of press releases, and *Time*, *Life*, and *Newsweek* were all there, cameras flashing. "Women are people too," Avi told the *New York Times*, and the *Times* ran his statement as its quote of the week.

The week's events were somewhat eclectic. Monday featured a welcome ceremony with Yale's chaplain. Tuesday brought an Election Day rally; Republican presidential nominee Richard Nixon was polling so close to Democrat Hubert Humphrey that the outcome was anyone's guess. Wednesday included a coeducation discussion with Yale's undergraduate dean. But the event that may have raised the most questions among the young women visiting Yale was a showing of porn flicks that the Yale Law School Film Society had scheduled to coincide with Coeducation Week. The movies were shown Monday night in a classroom right on the Old Campus, and the *Yale Daily News*, which took particular delight in the event's timing, featured it on the front page. When a visiting Radcliffe student stopped by the *News* building on Monday and offered to write an article, they assigned her to cover the porn festival.

She attended one of the early showings and watched several ten-minute shorts before walking out early. "All of them consisted of ladies removing their clothing and writhing around—all by themselves—on sofas, beds, and even desk tops," she wrote in the story the *News* published on the front page the next day. Her experience of writing a review of a porn festival while in the midst of all those male *Yale Daily News* reporters was unsettling. "There I was at Yale...sitting in a strange newsroom, writing some story about some lady masturbating with a cross," she wrote a few weeks later. "It was bizarre and slightly absurd. All at once I was feeling isolated and quite lonely."

Most Coed Week visitors avoided that type of hazing, and by Wednesday, Yale students were gleeful with the success of the experiment. That evening, the Yale marching band concluded its weekly practice with an impromptu parade. With trumpets and sousaphones proclaiming their presence, the band members marched through the courtyards of half a dozen of Yale's residential colleges and on toward their final destination: President Brewster's front lawn.

All along the way, students came down from their rooms to join the band, and by the time the crowd of Yale students and visiting women arrived at Brewster's house, its numbers had swelled to the hundreds. The band played Yale football songs, and Brewster came out onto the front porch in a jocular mood, with his wife, Mary Louise, beside him. "Give us a date!" the students cried, urging Brewster to commit to coeducation. Brewster asked the bandleader if he could borrow his megaphone, and then, in a nod to the college his wife had attended, proclaimed to the crowd, "Vassar was good enough for me!" The students wanted a better answer. "Give us a date!" they repeated, and this time Brewster did: "In 1972, there will be women at Yale!" But that was not soon enough. "Next fall!" shouted the students. "1969!"

Things moved quickly from there. Coeducation Week "was just a very smart political act," observed John Trinkaus, the head of one of Yale's twelve residential colleges. "It got national publicity, and somehow brought the whole affair to a head." Meanwhile, Princeton seemed poised to act. On Thursday morning, November 7, Brewster called a meeting with a one-item agenda: admitting women undergraduates to Yale. Avi Soifer was there, as was the current chairman of the *Yale Daily News*, Sam Chauncey, and a few more of Brewster's top advisers.

Two days later, Brewster headed down to New York to meet with the Yale Corporation. Trustee Irwin Miller had been arguing for coeducation since 1967, warning that "the quality of admission at Yale...will undergo a long, slow decline unless there are women." He was not alone in his views, and the Corporation voted to accept five hundred women students for the fall of 1969. Brewster's $30 million price tag issue was set aside with barely a murmur. Yale would make do with the existing facilities and faculty: rooms designed for three students would hold four, and the few extra staff provided for the women would be covered by the women's tuitions.

Before Brewster could go public with the decision, one final step was needed. On Thursday, November 14, he presented his coeducation proposal to the Yale College faculty. The vote was 200:1 in favor, with the sole negative vote coming from history professor George Pierson, a man who had arrived at Yale as a seventeen-year-old freshman in 1922 and was still there forty-six years later.

The next morning, on elite college campuses across the country, men in presidents' suites set down their coffee cups in surprise. They looked at the front-page story in the *New York Times*: "Yale Going Coed Next September." Really? *Yale?* The last anyone outside the university had heard, Yale was still waiting for someone to write a $30 million check, and there was no mention of any donation. Yet clearly the decision was final. It said right there in the article that Yale's faculty had approved the plan the day before and that Yale's trustees had voted yes in a secret meeting in New York.

Yale had left itself just ten months to transform into a coeducational institution. "This is a crash program for next year," Yale College

Dean Georges May told the *Yale Daily News*. Within four days of Brewster's coeducation announcement, Yale received eight hundred letters of interest from female students—some still in high school, some already in college. By March, nearly four thousand women had applied. They hailed from all over the country: Chicago, Little Rock, Brooklyn, Honolulu, Tulsa, and Cleveland. Step one, then, was to read through all those applications from women that the admissions office staffing had not planned for. The housing problem quickly became pressing too, since Brewster declared that Yale would not reduce the number of incoming men just because it was adding some women. And what about student organizations? Someone had to ask each of them if they would allow Yale's new women students to join.

The list went on and on. The locks needed changing. The outdoor lighting was inadequate. Vanderbilt Hall, where the women freshmen would live, needed shades on the windows. The gym had to end its no-women rule. The Yale Health Center would have to hire a gynecologist. And then there was the worry of potential pregnancies. Could Yale do anything to avoid that?

As for the real changes that would shift an all-male institution to one in which women stood equal with men, there was no time. Such change was not, in fact, what Brewster had in mind. The goal for September, declared his hastily formed coeducation planning committee, was to admit women "with the least disruption of the current pattern" of education at Yale as possible. It would be up to Yale's first women undergraduates to do the disrupting required. But first, they would have to get in.

TWO

Superwomen

IN LITTLE FALLS, NEW JERSEY, A SUBURB OF NEWARK, in a three-bedroom ranch house on Brookhill Place, seventeen-year-old Kit McClure was working on her application to Yale. Kit was a senior at Passaic Valley Regional High, a high school like so many others in the United States that it could have come off an assembly line. Passaic Valley had a mascot (a hornet), long linoleum hallways that shone after waxing, a prom, a football team, and a marching band. At the halftime shows of the Passaic Valley football games, you could see Kit right out on the field with the band. She was the one with the bright-red hair, the only girl playing trombone.

Kit's parents, liberal on so many other matters, had forbidden it. Girls don't play trombone, they told her. Girls played flute, violin, and piano—the instrument Kit had been playing since she was seven years old. Kit was determined to play trombone, though, and she talked Passaic Valley's band director into letting her practice with one of the trombones in the band room after school. By the time Kit's parents figured out what she was up to, she had already taught herself to play. And now there was this opportunity at Yale.

Yale had one of the best music programs in the country, world-class concert halls, and the icing on the cake: building after building of science labs. After music, science was Kit's passion. The summer before, she had won a National Science Foundation scholarship and spent July and August doing research at Cornell. Yale would be an incredible college for Kit, but kids from Passaic Valley High School did not go to places like Yale. They went to Montclair State or Patterson State or became beauticians or auto mechanics. Still, it was worth a try. Maybe Kit was the type of girl Yale was looking for.

Meanwhile, 230 miles north at Simmons College, an all-women's school in Boston, Shirley Daniels was also working on her Yale application. Shirley was already a college freshman when Yale made its announcement, but in Shirley's first fall at Simmons, she'd met a guy named Sam Cooper, a black sophomore from Yale who was there one weekend on a road trip to check out the Simmons black women. Shirley and Sam started talking, and he told her about the Afro-American studies major that Yale would begin offering the next year. It would be one of the few in the country.

Shirley had lived in Roxbury, the heart of black Boston, ever since she was twelve. At Simmons, she was a member of the black students' organization. Shirley would have preferred a coed college, but she liked how Simmons encouraged its women students to get professional degrees and the way it emphasized that women should be independent thinkers. Simmons did not offer Afro-American studies, however, and as far as Shirley knew, it was not planning to. The idea that she might be able to spend her next three years of college studying black history was remarkable, and Sam said Yale was accepting transfer students as well as freshmen. "Why don't you apply?" he asked her, and so Shirley did, writing with her whole heart why she wanted to major in Afro-American studies at Yale.

From across the country, the applications poured in as girls who had grown up thinking that Yale was off-limits now went for their chance to get in. Connie Royster had grown up a few miles from Yale and so knew firsthand Yale's reputation and the incredible resources that were on offer there: a university art gallery with collections rivaling some of the best museums in the country, world-class teachers, and a thriving theater scene that included the University Theatre and the newly opened Yale Repertory Theatre. Connie's love of the arts, first cultivated by her boarding school, had grown deeper in her year as an exchange student in England and during her first semester at Wheaton, a women's college in southern Massachusetts. If colleges let you major in being a Renaissance woman, Connie would have been the first to sign up. Absent that possibility, she could not think of a better place to attend college than Yale.

For Connie, the draw of Yale was personal as well. Her family had worked in Yale's fraternities as chefs and managers since the early 1900s, and as a small child, Connie had played in the fraternity kitchens when the extended family was called in to help for a major event. Connie's family was well

Connie Royster.
Photo © Yale Banner Publications.

respected among New Haven's black community. Her grandmother had cofounded the New Haven branch of the National Association for the Advancement of Colored People (NAACP), and her Aunt Connie was well known nationally, although by a different name: U.S. district court judge Constance Baker Motley. Motley had been appointed in 1966 as America's first black woman federal judge. Before then, she worked as an attorney with the NAACP Legal Defense Fund and argued ten cases before the U.S. Supreme Court, winning nine of them (the tenth was later reversed in Motley's favor). In the early 1960s, she succeeded in overturning the long-standing ban on black students at a number of public universities in the South, including the University of Mississippi and the University of Georgia.

Connie Royster was named for her Aunt Connie, and now she had a chance to apply to Yale, something that had not been possible for women when Constance Baker Motley went to college. Connie's family took pride in their long connection with Yale, and she had always been one of the smart kids at school. Of course she would apply…but whether she would get in was anyone's guess.

———

Betty Spahn did not apply to Yale, at least not intentionally. It all started as a joke played by her roommate Caroline. Betty and Caroline were freshmen at George Washington University, and after Yale announced it was going coed, Caroline's father, a Yale alumnus, sent Caroline one of the transfer student applications. Caroline's grades weren't good enough to even bother filling it out, but Betty, thought Caroline, was perfect for Yale. Betty had just aced her first semester at George Washington, and before that, she had been an Illinois high

Betty Spahn.
Photo © Yale Banner Publications.

school debate champion. The preliminary application for transfers was no more than a form with some blanks for grades, extra-curriculars, and address—information that Caroline could easily provide about her roommate. On a lark, she and one of their other roommates filled out the form on Betty's behalf and sent it to Yale. Betty had no idea.

Betty was from Park Forest, a town an hour south of Chicago. She grew up in a neighborhood of ranch houses built right after World War II, where you could walk into any one of your neighbors' kitchens and find the exact same layout as your own. The stove was on the left as you walked in, the sink sitting under a window that overlooked the small yard out back. Betty's parents were churchgoing Republicans, suspicious of the moral bearings of Easterners. Neither was happy that Betty had decided to attend George Washington. Why couldn't she just go to the University of Illinois? It had been good enough for her mother. But Betty had spent a year as an exchange student in Germany by then. She was not interested in limiting her world to that which lay within a two-hour drive of her childhood home.

At the beginning of March, Betty opened her George Washington mailbox and was surprised to find inside a letter from the director of undergraduate admissions at Yale.

"Dear Miss Spahn," it read. "The Admissions Committee has concluded its review of preliminary candidates for transfer, and I am pleased to advise that the Committee wishes to have you submit your complete credentials." Betty was totally confused. What was this about? The letter went on: "The application for final transfer candidates and other forms and cards are enclosed... We look forward to receiving your application."

Caroline thought it was hilarious. Of course Betty had to follow through with the rest, Caroline argued after explaining what she had done, and once Betty got over her initial shock, she agreed. Yale was one of the top two schools in the country, right? Who would pass up a chance to go there? Betty wrote the essay required and sent it in with her recommendations and the other material Yale asked for. In a month, she would know whether or not she had made the next cut.

On April 13, 1969, the week before Yale's acceptance letters went out, the *New York Times'* Sunday magazine ran an eleven-page article about the young women who had applied to Yale, every one of whom, reported the *Times*, came with effusive recommendations, straight A's, and flawless board scores (or close to it). One had traveled through Bosnia with a Serbian friend, taught in the newly formed Head Start program, and choreographed the dance scenes in her high school's production of *The King and I*. Another had studied Anglo-Saxon poetry and religious art and hoped to major in medieval studies; she had tutored high school students on a Navajo reservation over the summer. Of the entire eleven-page article, however, what Yale's women undergraduates remember most is what the *New York Times* called them. They were "the female versions of Friedrich Nietzsche's *Uebermensch*." They were "superwomen."

The word stuck like a mark on the forehead of every girl admitted to Yale that year. "Oh," they'd hear, "you're one of those superwomen." It separated them from one another, as each new-comer wondered, *Why would any of these superachieving women be friends with someone like me?* For the students who harbored any inse-curities or thoughts that maybe they had been admitted by mistake, there was that *superwoman* word, feeding their doubts.

Yale sent out two types of letters that April. Most girls got the thin envelope, the one that held the sparse words of rejection. The fat envelope crammed with the acceptance letter and the accompa-nying forms was the one that you wanted.

Outside Philadelphia, in the small town of Swarthmore, a post-man wended his way through a subdivision of half-acre lots with street names that spoke to the aspirations of its residents: Columbia Avenue, Dartmouth Avenue, Harvard Avenue, North and South Princeton Avenues, Rutgers Avenue, Yale Avenue. When seven-teen-year-old Lawrie Mifflin began her senior year at Swarthmore's public high school that fall, not one of those colleges accepted women. Lawrie lived on Drew Avenue, one of the few streets in the neighborhood named for a college that was already coed. She was cocaptain of Swarthmore High School's field hockey team, and as one of the top kids in her class, Lawrie had seen for herself that boys were no smarter than girls. She deserved a shot at Yale as much as they did. Lawrie sent in her application, and then, like everyone else, she waited.

The postman turned onto Drew Avenue and walked up the short driveway to number 419. He lifted the lid of the metal mail-box on the wall beside the front door and jammed a fat envelope inside. The announcement it contained was printed at the top with Yale's coat of arms and its motto, "Lux et Veritas," light and truth. At the bottom was the signature of Yale's dean of admissions, R. Inslee Clark. In between were the words that most mattered: "Yale

University announces with pleasure the admission of Lawrie Mifflin to the Class of 1973 of Yale College and hereby extends a cordial welcome to this community of scholars." Of all the students, male and female, who applied to Yale from Swarthmore High School that year, Lawrie was the only one who got in.

The acceptances were equally slim at other schools: one girl from Lincoln High School in Kansas City, one from Susan Miller Dorsey High School in Los Angeles, and one from Passaic Valley Regional High School outside of Newark, New Jersey—a red-headed trombone player named McClure.

Kit had been excited at first when she got the letter, but then she thought about it for a moment. "Oh, no. We can't afford this," Kit said to her mother.

"Oh, no. We'll afford this," her mother replied.

For every high school girl who applied to Yale that year, one in twelve got in. It was far better to be a boy, where the odds improved to one out of seven. Yale may have gone coed, but that did not mean it wanted a school that was half girls. Even among alumni kids, that most favored group, boys were twice as likely to be accepted by Yale as girls were.

The competition for spaces in Yale's sophomore and junior classes was equally fierce. "Ever since you've been two years old, you've heard that Yale and Harvard are *the* schools," explained one Brandeis sophomore. "And suddenly now you had this chance to go." Yale offered a breadth and depth of resources and programs that none of the colleges then open to women could offer. And for many who had ended up at an all-women's college, a coed environment was just as appealing as it was to Yale men. As the letters from Yale's admissions office began arriving, the mail rooms at Smith and Wellesley, at Vassar and Mount Holyoke, filled with the shrieks of the girls who had been accepted, while others walked back to their rooms in silence. In some cases, one roommate got in while another did not. The friendships did not always survive the experience.

From Simmons College in Boston, Yale accepted two students. One was Shirley Daniels. She would get to major in Afro-American studies after all.

Shirley's father was ecstatic. "Yale! Yale! My daughter's going to Yale! She's going to Yale!" He too had once had plans for college, and while he rarely talked about himself, Shirley learned from her aunt that he had even been accepted to Harvard. But after he graduated from Boston Latin, Boston's premier public high school, World War II had broken out and Shirley's father chose to join the army instead. He served for twenty-three years and never got his college degree. But now his daughter was going to Yale. "She's going to Yale!" he said over and over.

"He could not stop talking about it," said Shirley, smiling.

In towns and cities across the United States, the envelopes from Yale arrived. Betty Spahn may have been surprised the first time she received a letter from Yale, but this time she was watching for it. Her parents were hardly enthusiastic. Both of them were proud of Betty's good grades. Her father told her she could be anything she wanted to be. But if Betty was going to transfer schools, why not come back to Illinois? She could achieve her dreams there too, and the tuition would sure be a lot cheaper. Betty had made up her mind, though. She was accepting Yale's offer of admission, and she would just have to figure out later how to earn the money she needed to go there.

New Haven native Connie Royster got the fat envelope too. Connie was thrilled, of course, but her acceptance was still bittersweet. Connie was nearing the end of her first year at Wheaton. She had made friends and a place for herself there. Wheaton had supported her love for the theater, and she had starred in a number of plays. Once the letter from Yale came, though, there was really no choice.

For Connie, going to Yale was "a kind of reclaiming or claiming." Her family had been employed at Yale since the start of the century, when her grandfather and his brother emigrated from Nevis. Connie's grandfather was no longer alive, but he would have rejoiced at the news. Connie's acceptance was not just a personal accomplishment but an accomplishment for the entire family. She would never turn that down. Besides, it was *Yale* after all, one of the top two schools in the country. "Education was the most important thing in my family, the most important," said Connie. She told her roommate first and then went to call her parents. Connie Royster was going to Yale.

The *New York Times* may have called them superwomen, but most of the women undergraduates accepted by Yale that first year were still teenagers. It's not hard to imagine each of them at kitchen tables or bedroom desks, reading through the paperwork and filling out the forms that Yale sent them in thick envelopes each month through the summer of 1969. And as they did so, all around them events unlike any they had ever seen began to reshape the world they grew up in.

In June, hundreds of gay men and women, fed up with their relentless harassment, fought back when police began arresting patrons of a gay bar in Greenwich Village called the Stonewall Inn. In July, a man walked on the moon. In August, four hundred thousand young hippies at a New York music festival made the name "Woodstock"—until then just some town in the Catskills—a permanent part of the American vocabulary. And in every part of the country, whether Spokane or Houston or Baltimore, the first women undergraduates ever admitted to Yale made ready for the next step in their education and prepared to travel to New Haven in September.

———

Less than two weeks remained before the students arrived at Yale, and Elga Wasserman, special assistant to the president for the education of women, was firing off memos.

To Lewis Beach, physical plant manager: *The ladies' restrooms are still not ready. Seven are locked. Two have broken toilets. You can barely find sixteen of them.*

To Kingman Brewster, president of Yale: *We need a woman in the admissions office; I'll come up with some names.*

Elga Wasserman.
Photo © Yale Banner
Publications.

We need a write-up of our coeducation plans to give potential donors; I'll work on it. And yes, with some luck, I think the housing for the girls will be ready by the time they arrive.

That a woman at Yale would be signing her name to such memos was startling. *Power* was not a word one associated with women on college campuses in 1969—not at Yale, not anywhere. Deans of women, who had once held sway at the big state schools like the University of Kansas, had been losing their jobs for two decades to the new deans of students, invariably men. Ninety-five percent of coed colleges had men as presidents, and even some of the top women's colleges had male presidents too. "The higher, the fewer" was the rule that applied to women in college administration, and so just like the women undergraduates who would soon be arriving at Yale, Elga Wasserman was breaking new ground.

Wasserman was the most visible woman administrator at Yale, the only one reporting directly to Brewster. The job of overseeing coeducation was not hers alone, though—at least, not at first. The day after the Yale Corporation voted to move forward on coeducation, Brewster turned to his adviser Sam Chauncey and said, "You son of a bitch, you pushed me into this thing. You've gotta make it happen."

Chauncey agreed to take a temporary leave from his role in the president's office and help Yale prepare for coeducation, but Brewster wanted a woman to lead the coeducation effort—it wouldn't look right to have it led by a man—and he wanted a woman from inside of Yale. Yale was special. No outsider could understand what made it that way, and Brewster almost always hired administrators who, like him, had gone to college at Yale. No woman could yet lay claim to that credential, but at least a woman who worked at Yale would have a feel for the place. Yet Brewster's choices were slim. Like other colleges, Yale had not made it a practice to hire women administrators.

In the fall of 1968, when Brewster began his search for a Yale woman to lead coeducation, fifty-three of Yale's top fifty-four administrators were men. The one woman was the associate librarian for technical services—not exactly a position of influence. Widening the pool from Yale's central administrative ranks to its graduate and professional schools expanded the list of women candidates by four: two nursing school deans and two assistant deans at the graduate school. And Assistant Dean Elga Wasserman wanted the job.

Wasserman was forty-four years old, with a string of accomplishments unusual for a woman of her era. But when the *Yale Alumni Magazine* introduced her to the broader Yale community in a December 1968 article, it described Wasserman as "a housewife, mother of two, skating and skiing enthusiast, sometime interior decorator, chemist, teacher, and former assistant dean of the Graduate School," burying at the end of the sentence the achievements that most qualified her for the job. Wasserman was in fact a chemist with a PhD from Harvard, a college chemistry professor, and an administrator with six years' experience at Yale Graduate School. And she had three children, not two.

By the time Brewster chose her to lead coeducation at Yale, Wasserman had lived in New Haven for twenty years, ever since Yale's chemistry department hired her husband, Harry, in 1948. Wasserman's two decades at Yale had not left her bitter; her personality did not tend that way. But like any woman with aspirations, Elga Wasserman bore a few scars.

She had graduated summa cum laude from Smith College, and when she and Harry first moved to New Haven, they came with the identical degree: a PhD in chemistry from Harvard. Harry stepped right onto the track leading to a tenured position on Yale's faculty, but for Wasserman, that PhD was a path to nowhere. Yale did not hire women chemists. Instead, the university routed them into positions as research assistants, a job where women could tread water and watch men with the same qualifications move swiftly by. This was the job that Wasserman got when she first came to Yale.

Women with degrees in history or English didn't do much better. There was not yet a single tenured woman on the Yale College faculty when Wasserman first got there. Neither Princeton nor Harvard had a tenured woman professor either. But at least in Boston a woman with a PhD might teach at Wellesley or Simmons. For those who sought to work at a top-ranked college, New Haven was a one-company town, and if you were the woman in a two-PhD couple, as Wasserman was, you were out of luck. "Women were sort of the ornaments to the men, which was not my style," said Wasserman. "I was very unhappy."

But Wasserman was resilient. She had learned that trait as a young girl. She was German by birth, and until she was twelve, her family had lived a comfortable middle-class life in Berlin. Hitler's rise did not bode well for Jewish families like hers, though, and in 1936 the family fled, eventually settling in Great Neck, New York. There, Wasserman mastered a new language, made new friends, learned the routines of a new school, and excelled. That early practice at negotiating change served her well.

Wasserman had her first child a year after she and Harry moved to New Haven, and over the next thirteen years, she crafted a life from the options available. She pulled together a series of part-time jobs, working as a lab assistant and teaching a few courses at the local state college. She raised her three children and made some friends. Then, in 1962, Elga Wasserman got a break. Yale Graduate School dean John Perry Miller, who lived down the street, called and asked if she would be interested in working as assistant dean. It was an unusual move. Outside the nursing school, Yale had no female deans at that point, and the job that Miller offered Wasserman was not just assistant dean but assistant dean in charge of sciences, the land of men. When Miller agreed to let her work part time so she could be home when her kids got out of school, Wasserman accepted his offer and became assistant dean at the Yale Graduate School, the spot from which, six years later, Kingman Brewster hired her to lead the transition to coeducation at Yale.

Those, then, are the outlines of Wasserman's life up to age forty-four, when Brewster tapped her to work on coeducation with Sam Chauncey. Over the next four years, she had both fans and critics. But of all the things said about Elga Wasserman, the sentence perhaps most worth noting is one she uttered herself, a comment on Brewster's decision to hire her: "I don't think he knew who he was getting, really."

———

The first women undergraduates arrived at Yale on September 12, a Friday. Shirley Daniels came by bus, making her way from her home in Boston's Roxbury neighborhood to the Trailways station downtown and then settling into her seat for the three-hour trip to New Haven. The bus let her off across from her residential college at Yale, Timothy Dwight, and Shirley carried her bags through the college's arched entryway and into the courtyard beyond. She could hardly believe it. Less than a year ago, she had not even realized it was possible to major in Afro-American studies, and now here she was, ready to begin. Shirley found her room, unpacked her belongings, and then went out to walk around Yale.

It was quite a sight. The college rose up from the city around it like some Gothic mirage, as if the campus had been airlifted out of fifteenth-century England and deposited neatly in downtown New Haven. The school's stone buildings, with their towers and turrets, pressed up tight to the sidewalks. Gargoyles stared down from the rooflines. Yale's campus included museums, concert halls, courtyards, sculptures, and one building older than the nation itself. The gym was the largest in the world, the library as majestic as a European cathedral. Yale was a place where one walked with head craned upward, trying to take it all in.

It was quiet the day that Shirley arrived, with a misty rain cloaking the city, but by Saturday, the tempo picked up. The streets of New Haven clogged with cars bearing out-of-state plates and cruising for parking spots. Students arrived from all over the country. Some came by airplane, others by train or by bus. But mostly, Yale's first women undergraduates came by car, arriving in Pontiacs and Chevrolets from Pennsylvania and New Jersey and the outskirts of Syracuse.

"It was an hour and twenty-five minutes via the Throgs Neck Bridge," said a woman sophomore who drove up from Queens, her father behind the wheel of the family's light-blue Chevy Chevelle. "And it was exciting, I tell you."

Yale enrolled 575 women undergraduates that year: 230 freshmen, 151 sophomores, and 194 juniors. The senior class remained all men, since Yale did not award undergraduate degrees to students who had not been there at least two years. For the most part, the new female students mirrored the racial and ethnic diversity of their male classmates, which was to say, they were not that diverse. Ninety percent of the women were white. There were forty black women students in all: twenty-five freshmen, eight sophomores, and seven juniors. The numbers of Asian American women were smaller still: thirteen across all three classes. As for Latina students, there were three: one Chicana freshman and a sophomore and junior of Puerto Rican heritage. Native American women, if there were any, went uncounted.

Over the weekend, the students streamed onto campus, with cars parked every which way along Chapel Street. The sidewalks crowded with parents and kids carting boxes and suitcases up to their rooms while reporters and film crews who had traveled to New Haven to chronicle the arrival of coeducation trailed after them. "Oh, you're a *Yale* woman!" they called out to the girls. "Tell us what it's like to be a Yale woman." The *New York Times* was

Reporter approaches freshman girl right after she has enrolled at Yale, September 1969.
Photo © Yale University. Yale Events and Activities Photographs (RU 690), Manuscripts and Archives, Yale University Library.

there, along with the *International Herald Tribune*, *Time* magazine, and *Women's Daily*. Everyone wanted to hear what the superwomen would say. But there were bags to unpack and roommates to meet, and so the young women went about the task of moving in, dodging the press as they did so.

Connie Royster and her parents drove to Yale from their home

in Bethany, Connecticut, on Saturday. The family had moved from
New Haven when Connie was in junior high school, but on Sundays,
they still worshipped at St. Luke's Episcopal Church, a few blocks
up Whalley Avenue from Yale, and work and family were in New
Haven as well. They made the half-hour drive in all the time. Yet this
trip was special. Connie's family had put in lifetimes at the fraternities at Yale, and now Connie was enrolling as a student there. She
had been assigned to Berkeley, one of Yale's residential colleges, and
given three roommates: two juniors and one who was a sophomore
like Connie, a girl from Illinois named Elizabeth Spahn. Connie
had been close with her roommate at Wheaton. With any luck, this
Elizabeth Spahn might become a friend too.

As the Royster family approached New Haven, Betty Spahn
stood alone in the Berkeley dorm room that she and Connie had
been assigned. Betty's parents had not been able to take her to Yale.
It was a long way from Park Forest, and they had her three younger
brothers to take care of. Besides, it was not as if this was Betty's
first time leaving home. She had already been at George Washington
University for a year by then and in Germany for the year before
that. Betty caught a ride east with her high school boyfriend and his
father, who were headed to Harvard and agreed to drop her off at
Yale on the way. Betty had never been to Yale before. She knew it
was famous. But until she asked to look at the map at the start of the
trip, Betty had thought Yale was in Boston.

The drive took more than fourteen hours, mile after mile
through Illinois, Indiana, Ohio, Pennsylvania, New Jersey, and New
York. It was an uncomfortable journey. Betty and her boyfriend had
continued dating through her first year at George Washington, and
she had traveled to see him at West Point, the college he attended
for his first two years. But over the summer, they had drifted apart,

and Betty was taken by surprise when he told her that he was transferring to Harvard. His family, however, blamed Betty for his decision because she was the one who had started to question why the United States was in Vietnam.

They had Betty wrong, though. True, Vietnam made less and less sense to her, but even President Richard Nixon was promising an end to the war. Betty was no radical—they didn't grow them out there in Park Forest—and she wasn't a feminist either, at least not yet. Few of Yale's first women undergraduates would have described themselves that way. They all were aware of their pioneer status. How could they not be? But Kingman Brewster wasn't the only one who hadn't yet read Betty Friedan's *The Feminine Mystique*. "Most people didn't experience 'the sixties' until the seventies," wrote novelist Julian Barnes. So too with the women's movement.

The car pulled up in front of the arched stone entryway of Yale's Berkeley College. Betty Spahn unfolded herself from the backseat and stretched her cramped legs. Her high school boyfriend and his father were quick with goodbyes, and Betty watched as their car pulled back onto Elm Street and drove off. Betty was nine hundred miles from home, alone in a place where she did not know a soul. She got the key to her room, carried her suitcase up the stone stairway, and slowly opened the door. The room was entirely empty. No roommates. No furniture. Yale provided a bunk bed, a desk, and a bureau, but the rest of the furniture was up to you. No one had told that to Betty, and she had assumed Yale would be like George Washington, where her room came fully furnished. *They must do things differently at Yale*, she thought. At least they had sent her a postcard with the names of her three roommates. Two were juniors, but the other, like her, was a sophomore: Constance Royster from Connecticut. Maybe Constance would be the friend that Betty Spahn needed.

———

Over in the Coeducation Office on Grove Street, Elga Wasserman was pleased with how smoothly the move in was going. She and Sam Chauncey had worked well together in the lead-up to September. Chauncey managed the renovations made to the freshmen women's dorm in Vanderbilt Hall, and Wasserman handled pretty much everything else with the brisk, get-it-done efficiency for which she'd been known at Yale Graduate School. Gynecology service set up in the Yale Health Center? Check. Women students assigned roommates? Check. Women's locker room added to Payne Whitney Gym? Check. Academic advisers assigned to each incoming woman? Check. Speakers organized for the women students' orientation meeting? Check. Yet not everything had not gone as Wasserman wanted in the initial months of her new job.

Transforming Yale into a college where women felt as welcome as men was already a formidable goal. Institutions do not slough off their history so easily. But before the women had even arrived, Kingman Brewster put in place two ground rules that made Wasserman's task even harder.

Rule number one was that the addition of women would not reduce the ranks of Yale men, and so the women were outnumbered seven to one, a ratio whose costs would soon become clear. The second ground rule was that the women would be divided evenly among Yale's twelve residential colleges, thus diluting their small numbers still further. These colleges were far more than just dormitories with fancy names. They were enclosed communities within the larger campus, complete with their own academic deans, fellowship of faculty members, and masters (the heads of the colleges). Yale had no student center where undergraduates could gather. Instead, there were the twelve colleges, each turned inward to a central courtyard accessible only through the college gate. Students ate in their college, formed their closest friendships in their college, attended the social events of their college, took part in the student government of their college, and from sophomore year on, they lived in their college.

Some stereotypes arose about the college personalities—Calhoun was supposedly for the beer-drinking jocks; Ezra Stiles was full of eccentrics—but such characterizations did not hold up to much scrutiny. Yale sought to make each college a microcosm of the university as a whole, and so they chose students' colleges for them in the summer before their freshman year. Transferring to a different college required all sorts of permissions and paperwork, so students generally stayed where Yale put them. For the white male undergraduates whom Yale had long served, the system worked to create a smaller, more intimate environment. For groups that were in the minority—students of color, women—dividing a small number still further only made things worse.

The freshmen girls would seem to have avoided this splintering up since—save for the dozen assigned to Timothy Dwight College—they all lived together in their own dorm on the Old Campus, Vanderbilt Hall. Yet even here, the residential college divisions separated the women from one another. If you were in Trumbull College, then your roommates were too and so were the women across the hall. These were the same women whom you would see at meals and the social events of your college. There may have been 230 freshmen women at Yale, but each of them would graduate having never met most of the women in their class. The women sophomores and juniors had it harder still, for Yale parceled them out in groups of thirty to each college, where they lived in the same buildings, although not on the same floors, as the 250 men who lived there.

Brewster himself had argued at first against splitting the women up. Women students should not be housed as "a small isolated minority" in each college, he told the residential college masters right after the coeducation decision went through. The solution was straightforward: some colleges would have women students in the first year of coeducation, but others would have to wait until women's numbers increased. Yale's male students, or at least the ones Brewster listened to, saw it differently and pushed hard for assigning women to all twelve colleges. By February 1969, Brewster gave in. Every college would have its own small group of girls. As a *Yale Daily News* columnist explained, Yale had to divide the women up "to prevent a spring riot by giving every undergrad a slice of—or at least a look at—the pie." And if the cost was creating an environment that was harder for the women, well, so be it.

Elga Wasserman fought the decision to split up the women long after Brewster stopped listening to her, and she assured incoming women students in an August letter that Yale would soon have a plan in place to expand women's enrollment from the initial 575 to "at least 1,500," the number Brewster had initially promised. That target would still leave women students outnumbered four to one by the men, but at least it was a start. Achieving even that meager goal, though, would prove far more difficult than Wasserman ever anticipated.

By the time the women students arrived, Wasserman was overseeing coeducation on her own, and Chauncey had moved back to his office next to Brewster's. Wasserman was ready to lead, and she had the intelligence and charisma required. "There was something hard-edged, but hard-edged like a finely cut diamond, when she walked into a room," said a student intern in Wasserman's

Coeducation Office. "She glowed…and not because she was flamboyant. It was her intelligence and her personal energy." But the traits that worked well for men in positions of power did not always work so well for women.

Wasserman had been in her new role at Yale for seven months by September and was beginning to see the walls of the box she had been placed in. When she first got the job, a male colleague described her as "a really brilliant gal who doesn't push it." That wasn't just a description of Wasserman, though. It was a job requirement. Push too hard as a woman, and you would get labeled as "strident" or "aggressive" or "difficult." Fail to push and nothing changed. For a woman leader at Yale, the space in between was only a few inches wide. And so Wasserman learned to stay in the "safe middle ground," as she put it,   but that did not mean she was happy about it. She had come to her new role at Yale with such a strong vision of what she wanted to accomplish.

Yale could be a leader in the education of women. It could show the nation how to build an institution where women with talent got the same chance as men.   The work was not just about students, thought Wasserman. Faculty, staff, graduate women, and careers after college—Yale needed to move forward on all of them. Up until September, the logistical crises created by Yale's hasty coeducation decision had required all Wasserman's attention, but now that most of those problems were behind her, there was time to consider real change. And that is where things had started to get murky. Did Brewster intend to give her the power she needed, or was she just the one brought in to tidy up details after the decision makers had left the room? Wasserman knew the role that she wanted. But she had been at Yale long enough to recognize the signs that she might in the end be just the gal with the broom.

Maybe the title was a small thing, but she still burned every time she had to put it at the bottom of a letter: Special Assistant to the President on the Education of Women. It was "an insane title," said Wasserman, a mouthful of words no one ever got right. "Associate Dean of Yale College" was the title she wanted. The associate dean was a recognizable role at Yale, one held by men. It was the logical next step from Wasserman's assistant dean position at the graduate school. But Brewster said no. Some of the male deans in Yale College objected, he told her, explaining that they felt it would be demeaning to them for a woman to hold that title. So Wasserman became a "special assistant," a position well off to the side of the hierarchy at Yale.

The slight, like many Wasserman bore, was invisible to the students. But each time Wasserman's standing at Yale was diminished, so too was her power to advocate for the young women who were unpacking their bags at Yale.

———

Across Yale's campus, the women students continued to arrive. For the Yale men who hoped to gain a girlfriend, move-in day offered a chance to meet the new women before the prettiest ones were all taken, and Yale men were quick to introduce themselves to the thirty women sophomores and juniors assigned to their college. The 230 freshmen women in Vanderbilt Hall were a particular draw. There were more to choose from, for one thing, and a sense perhaps that the freshmen girls might be more impressed than the female sophomores and juniors by all the charms of Yale men.

Out in the Vanderbilt courtyard, the men waited, surveying each new arrival. When a girl caught their eye, they leapt up with a smile

Arrival of freshmen women to Vanderbilt Hall on move-in day, September 1969.
Photo © Yale University. Yale Events and Activities Photographs (RU 690), Manuscripts and Archives, Yale University Library.

and offered to carry her luggage. Some men skipped this step and just knocked on the doors of the women who had already moved in. "Oh! I lived here when I was a freshman!" they told the girls, who invited the visitors in so they could see what had changed. The boys surveyed the room and stayed to talk for a while afterward.

Eventually they left, smiling their goodbyes. "Oh, how nice," the women said to one another. And then, a few floors down, the men knocked on a new door and exclaimed to the young women who answered: "Oh! I lived here when I was a freshman!"

By Sunday, the weather grew hot, and the women students who arrived that day—some dressed in bell-bottomed blue jeans, others in short skirts or dresses—gratefully accepted the men's offers to carry their suitcases up Vanderbilt's long flights of stairs. Among those ferrying belongings from their car to their rooms, it was hard to miss Kit McClure. Her red hair fell in waves down to her shoulders, and out of her car came the trombone. For a girl in 1960s America, it was like some bright piece of contraband. A few other freshmen arrived with possessions that puzzled the Yale men as well. The hairdryers, the typewriters, the posters and desk lamps—those were expected, but from one station wagon came a girl with a stick that was polished and sturdy and curved at the end. Lawrie Mifflin had driven up from Swarthmore with her parents and was carrying her field hockey stick up to her room with the rest of her things. It would be exciting to play field hockey for Yale. Hopefully she was good enough to make the team.

Back and forth went the shuttles from car to dorm room until eventually some of the parents began saying their goodbyes, the mothers trying not to cry, the fathers long practiced at avoiding such emotion. The moment weighed hard on Yale's first women freshmen as well. Most were leaving home for the first time.

The 575 women undergraduates who arrived at Yale in 1969 came from the West Coast and East Coast and most states in between. They came from big cities and suburbs and places so small the address was a rural free delivery number. They differed in race and ethnicity and in whether they worried about their family's ability to pay the

$3,600 it cost for Yale's room, board, and tuition that year—the same amount of money it cost then to buy two Volkswagen Beetle cars. In many ways, Yale's first women undergraduates were as different as a group of 575 can be, but they did hold a few things in common.

These girls were smart—smarter than the boys, as the first term grades would show. And they were tough. Or at least, that's how they had appeared on their applications.

Sam Chauncey and Elga Wasserman had made the final decisions about which women got in that year. The admissions office had already started reading the applications of male students by the time Yale decided to admit women, and so a compromise was struck. The admissions staff would manage the initial processing of the women's applications—ensuring they were complete, sorting them into folders, arranging the folders into stack upon stack of file boxes—and Wasserman and Chauncey would take it from there. Over the winter, the two spent hour after hour reading through the applications of each of the nearly five thousand women who had applied.

Typically, Yale employed a two-part ranking system that emphasized applicants' leadership potential as much as their intelligence, a reflection both of Yale's perceived mission and, before Brewster became president, its long-standing anti-Semitism. Yale had stopped admitting students based solely on academics in the 1920s, when too many Jews began passing its entrance exams. By the 1940s, the *Yale Alumni Magazine* defined Yale's mission as educating "fine citizens" who would be "rather unscholarly" but demonstrate "character, personality, leadership in school affairs, and the like." And so it continued through the years. By the late 1960s, Yale economics professor Ed Lindblom, who served on the admissions committee, was appalled to find that Yale's admissions staff saw scholarly excellence as "a source of personality disorder or sickness or queerness."

Despite the inherent subjectivity of measures like character, Yale's admissions process had at least the appearance of objectivity. Each folder had two readers. Each reader ranked the application from one to nine on two different scales: academic promise and personal promise, the leadership piece. Thirty-six was the perfect score, a nine on both scales from both readers. These scores were then condensed into one of four numbers: one for the strongest applicants, two for those who were reasonably strong, three for applicants who were shakier, and four for the weakest group. The admissions staff did this initial ranking, and then from the beginning of March through early April, an admissions committee of faculty members and Yale College deans worked with the staff to decide which applicants to admit. The ones almost always got in; the fours never did, and most of the deliberation focused on the twos and threes: which to admit, which to reject, and which to wait-list.

That was the process used for the male students who entered Yale in 1969, but there was no time for that for the women, and besides, Chauncey and Wasserman were looking for a quality in that first group of women that was not as necessary for the men. After screening for academics, they chose the women for grit.

Girls who had four brothers, who had attended a huge high school, who had worked for a year, who had lived abroad, who had played sports, who had endured a traumatic event—those were the ones that Chauncey and Wasserman wanted. Yale's first women undergraduates may not have yet understood the challenges that awaited them, but Chauncey and Wasserman did. "There was no point in taking a timid woman and putting her in this environment," said Chauncey, "because it could crush you."

THREE

A Thousand Male Leaders

LAWRIE MIFFLIN WAS READY TO PLAY FIELD HOCKEY.
She had played every autumn since she was eleven—many of the
girls in her high school had played too. The streets of Swarthmore
may have been named for colleges that only men could attend, but
the playing fields were filled each fall with girls wielding hockey
sticks, smacking the ball down the field as hard as they could.
"Being a member of a team gives you confidence and power," said
Constance Applebee, who introduced field hockey to the United
States in 1901. Lawrie had brought her shin guards and a bag of
balls to Yale along with her hockey stick. She just needed to figure
out how to sign up for the team.

Yale's orientation week schedule listed introductory meetings
for a half-dozen men's sports but made no mention of field hockey,
so after saying goodbye to her parents, Lawrie set off for the other
side of campus, where the athletic office was. "Where do I sign up
for field hockey?" she asked the man behind the desk. He looked
confused. There were no sign-ups, he told her. There was no team.
There was also no women's soccer team, no women's basketball, and

no women's tennis or swim team or crew. Yale was not offering any competitive sports for women.

Athletic girls did have a few options to choose from. Lawrie could take classes in modern dance, ballet, and something called "women's exercise," a watered-down version of the fitness training offered to men. She could learn synchronized swimming from a part-time instructor from Southern Connecticut College. She could help exercise the polo ponies, although girls could not join the team, and she could be a cheerleader, sort of. Yale's cheerleading squad announced that it would include four girls on the team that year, a limit that kept the nine men in the majority. And no "girl-style" cheerleading. "We don't want rah-rah cheerleaders here at Yale," the team captain warned any woman who considered trying out. Cheerleading at Yale was manly, full of muscle beach tricks like headstands, pyramids, and forward rolls. While the guys performed in long pants, the girls would be baring their legs in culottes.

Lawrie Mifflin was not interested in cheerleading or any of the other choices Yale was offering to women. No field hockey? It was hard to believe.

Lawrie would miss all that she loved about playing on a team: the adrenaline of competition, the bonds built with teammates, the structure of daily practices, and the joy of the game. What was more fun than a day in September with the smell of fall leaves and the sun on your skin and a shot flicked just beyond the goalie's fingers after a perfect pass from your friend? Yale's failure to provide women's sports teams also robbed women students of the visibility and prestige that came from representing Yale on the sports field. Just like at any other college, Yale's athletes were campus stars. But you could only be one if you were a guy.

It wasn't much better with the other student groups. The *Yale*

Daily News said it welcomed women, but if you looked at the bylines, you could barely tell that Yale was coed. Other groups banned women outright. "It would make an inferior sound to have girls singing," explained a member of the Yale Whiffenpoofs, the most prestigious singing group at Yale. The Whiffenpoofs toured internationally and produced a record album each year, but they saw no reason that they should allow women to join. To make sure that Yale's new women would not complain about being excluded, the Whiffs went on offense and helped found an all-women's singing group, the New Blue. If the women had their own group, the reasoning went, they would not ask to audition for the Whiffenpoofs.

Not all student organizations treated women this way. Connie Royster found a home right away at the Yale Dramatic Association—"the Dramat," as everyone called it. Many of the less prestigious student groups—the Outing Club, the literary magazine, the Mathematics Club—welcomed women in. But girls were still barred from great swaths of extracurricular life at Yale: all competitive sports, five of Yale's six a cappella singing groups, the marching band, and Yale's most elite senior societies, the secret brotherhoods whose members included some of Yale's most prominent student leaders.

Kit McClure did not know yet that Yale's marching band would not accept women members. She planned to play her trombone in the band, just like she had in high school. But back in January, before Yale had even sent out its acceptance letters to women undergraduates, band director Keith Wilson called Sam Chauncey to explain that the marching band would be staying all male. Women could play in the concert band if they were good enough, said Wilson, but the guys in the marching band had told him they did not want any girls marching with them. Besides, no Ivy League marching band allowed women musicians, nor for that matter did most of the Big Ten. Wilson saw no reason for Yale to be different.

Chauncey sent Elga Wasserman a memo about the phone call. "Sounds OK," she wrote back in reply. She could not take on every injustice at Yale, at least not at once, and perhaps Wasserman, who had always made her mark in the classroom, underestimated how central extracurriculars were to life at Yale. A month later, her coeducation planning committee made that indifference to women's exclusion from Yale student groups official. "Pressure should not be put on [student] activities if they were not eager to admit women to their number," the minutes read. Yale may have given its young women students a room to sleep in and the ability to enroll in classes, but the roles as athletes and marching band members and other prestigious student positions were still reserved for men.

Lawrie Mifflin was having none of it. *Damn it*, she thought, *I'm not going to let them stop me.* Lawrie had met another student who played field hockey, and the two girls began talking. A few days later, handwritten fliers appeared on the entryway doors of Vanderbilt Hall: "Anybody want to play field hockey? Contact Jane Curtis in Vanderbilt Room 23 or Lawrie Mifflin, Vanderbilt 53." Lawrie did not see herself as some feminist crusader. She never thought, *I must do this to strike a blow for women.* She just wanted to play hockey, even if Yale thought "women's exercise" was good enough. "Doing what you're told doesn't amount to much," U.S. field hockey founder Constance Applebee taught her players. It was a lesson Lawrie Mifflin already understood.

As for Kit McClure, well, she had never been too good at following the rules either, and this was not the first time she'd been told she couldn't play in a band because she was a girl. In high school, a guy who had heard Kit play trombone asked if she wanted to join his rock band, but when she showed up for practice, the other band members all had the same reaction: no girls allowed.

The guy who had brought Kit to the practice made a deal. The band would audition every high school trombone player from the surrounding three counties over the course of three months, and if they found a guy who could play trombone better than Kit, they would take him. None of the other band members had needed to pass that type of test, but three months later, the spot was Kit's. As for the Yale marching band, Chauncey and Wasserman may have backed down, but Kit was not going to. Director Keith Wilson gave in—but there would be no girls apart from Kit. One was enough.

—————

Up in their dorm rooms, lounging on secondhand sofas, or sitting outside in the warm autumn sun, Yale men studied their *Old Campus*, the Yale freshman face book. It was small enough to carry around with you, a paperback just about a half-inch thick. Inside it was page after page of photos of each of the first-year students, both male and female, along with their high school, nickname, and Yale dorm and room number. The *Old Campus* face book had been published for years, but with the advent of coeducation, the 1969 edition provided Yale men with an invaluable resource: for $3.95, they could have a catalog of every freshman girl on campus. "I think every man at Yale memorized the info in that book," observed one freshman boy.

The men made good use of their *Old Campus* booklets, selecting the photo of a woman they deemed attractive and then phoning her up to ask her out on a date. The enterprising student editors of the *Old Campus* knew a market opportunity when they saw one, and

along with the class of 1973 edition, they published *Old Campus* sup-
plements for the classes of '71 and '72 with photos and information
on the women sophomores and juniors. They didn't even bother
with photos of the men transfer students. It was the women whom
everyone was interested in. With seven men for every woman, guys
who wanted a shot at dating a Yale girl had to move quickly.

Some men studied the books intently enough that they could
identify Yale women whom they had never met in person. Junior
Jessie Sayre was stopped by a Yale student one day on her way back
from the gym. "Pardon me—is your name Sayre?" He had recognized her from her photo. And lest any Yale woman wonder
about the desires of the men who sought their attention the *Yale
Daily News* spelled it out in its lead story that Monday: "The Yale
University campus awoke from its annual summer siesta this week
to discover that its 268 years of celibacy had come to an end." For
some Yale men, it wasn't just women who arrived at Yale in 1969. It
was sex.

The advent of undergraduate coeducation at Yale coincided
almost exactly with another major change that was reshaping U.S.
college campuses. The sexual revolution was in full swing—at least,
that's what the headlines all said—and the rules through which colleges had long sought to curtail student sex were being swept away
in its wake. Administrators should not be meddling in matters that
were none of their business, students argued, and after pausing a
moment to consider, college administrators had tended to agree. The
girls at Yale "will have to obey the same rules as the boys—which
is virtually no rules at all," tut-tutted the *New York Times*. "Many
alumni, and some students as well, are concerned about the moral
level-to-be."

Some remnants of Yale's old rules regulating student sex

remained, at least on paper. Technically, girls were not allowed in the boys' rooms nor boys in the girls' rooms after midnight, and Yale's undergraduate regulations ranked the violation of these visiting hours ninth of the ten offenses that were "of particular concern to the University": not as serious as cheating, riots, drugs, and improper use of fire extinguishers but ahead of unauthorized possession of master keys.   No one enforced Yale's rules about dorm room visitors, though, and even the guard at the entrance of the freshmen women's dorm in Vanderbilt Hall did little to hinder the male students who sought to enter.   A Yale ID got men past the guard any time before midnight, and after that, they easily met the challenge by hoisting themselves up and through the first-floor bathroom windows that the girls left open for the purpose.

Male students' easy access to Yale women did not bother Elga Wasserman. Like many, she saw the shift in sexual norms as a sign of progress, an end to the days when colleges took it on themselves to patrol the virtue of their female students. "Yale is a contemporary urban university, and it would be unrealistic for us to establish regulations which are not appropriate today," she wrote to the parents of incoming women students that summer. "Your daughter will therefore be called upon to make many of her own decisions."   If Yale men were free to choose to have sex, then Yale women should be free to do so as well. One problem, however, stood in the way of that goal: the risk of pregnancy.

The answer, of course, was birth control, and by 1969 the Pill had been available for almost a decade—if you were married. In Connecticut, as in many states, the use and prescription of birth control for unmarried women was illegal and would remain so until 1972, when the U.S. Supreme Court ruled that such prohibitions were unconstitutional.

But Yale could get around that problem if it chose to. The university benefited from a sort of gentlemen's pact with local authorities: Yale oversaw its students' behavior as it saw fit, and for the most part, the police looked the other way. The legal drinking age in Connecticut was twenty-one, for example, but you would never know that from the surfeit of sherry parties Yale college masters hosted for freshmen or the kegs of beer consumed at Yale-sponsored mixers. If Yale wanted to make birth control available to its undergraduates, then it would just go ahead and do so.

The men who ran the Yale Health Service resisted the idea and feared that access to birth control would encourage promiscuity, but Wasserman had little patience with such views. They weren't backed by data from colleges that did offer contraceptives, and they reflected the outdated image of "woman as princess, and protected, pure," she argued.   Early in her tenure as the chair of the coeducation planning committee, Wasserman discussed the matter with Robert Arnstein, the psychiatrist in chief at Yale Medical School and a member of her planning group. Both agreed that Yale should open a gynecology service for its women undergraduates, but it needed the right person to run it. Bob Arnstein had a suggestion.

Philip Sarrel was a Yale-trained gynecologist whom Arnstein had met through the sex education course that Sarrel designed for Yale medical students.   Sarrel served on a national scientists' committee with all the big names in U.S. sex research, including Paul Gephardt from the Kinsey Institute and William Masters of Masters and Johnson. His wife, Lorna, was a pediatric social worker at Yale–New Haven Hospital, and the couple was young enough—just in their low thirties—that Yale students would not see them as old or out of touch. Wasserman agreed that Sarrel was the right choice, and Arnstein picked up the phone.

The job of starting a gynecological service for Yale's new women undergraduates was a perfect fit for Phil Sarrel, but when Arnstein made the offer, Sarrel replied with three conditions. First, "I don't come alone," he said. "Lorna comes with me. We're going to be a team like Masters and Johnson." Second, the couple would teach a human sexuality course open to every undergraduate. And third, the Sarrels did not want to just hand out condoms and diaphragms and prescriptions for the Pill. They wanted to do so within the context of a confidential sex counseling service where students could come to get answers to their questions about sex and be prompted to think through their sexual decisions in the context of their own goals and values.

Phil Sarrel's proposal went well beyond what Arnstein and Wasserman had initially envisioned. The idea that Sarrel and his wife would work as a professional team was unusual enough for Yale at that time, but teaching a human sexuality course and running a sex counseling service? Open to the whole student body? No other college in the nation had anything like it. Wasserman was delighted. This was just the type of leadership role she had envisioned for Yale.

Had Wasserman been the only supporter of the Sarrels' approach to sexuality education, the idea might have died there. But Arnstein, a close friend of Brewster's, was widely respected, and Arnstein supported the idea too. If Bob Arnstein vouched for Phil Sarrel, then Sarrel must be okay. Moreover, a powerful motivator was at work that spring, one that made Yale's male administrators far more open to bringing in a guy as progressive as Phil Sarrel than they might have been otherwise.

"There was a whole anxious thing around the sexual aspect of coeducation," explained Lorna Sarrel. "The male administrators

thought all these women [were] going to get pregnant; they definitely feared pregnancy. And that inclined them to think, 'We need
to do something.'"

The worry was not just about the consequences for the pregnant women students. The administrators wondered too: "What's
going to happen to these guys that impregnate them?" Wasserman
put the matter on the coeducation planning committee's agenda
in February. Phil Sarrel's proposal may have been a stretch for Yale,
but it was better than pregnant coeds wandering the campus. The
committee voted to approve. The Yale Sex Counseling Service
would open at the start of October, a few weeks after the new
school year began.

On September 17, the third day of the semester, Wasserman held
an orientation meeting for all of the new women students. "You are
urged to attend," said the memo announcing the meeting, and most
women did. It was the only time that most of the 575 women
undergraduates who arrived that year were ever in the same room
together. Wasserman had a broad agenda for the night—the "present
and future plans for coeducation at Yale"—but that's not the part
that students remembered.

It was "very scary," said a freshman girl from a small town on
Cape Cod. "Elga Wasserman sat us all down in one of the lecture
halls and said, 'By Christmas, six percent of you are going to be
pregnant.'"

The statistics came from similar populations of young women.
There was no reason to think Yale, absent intervention, would be
different. Yet whatever the press said about the unleashed libidos of
the sexual revolution, few of the young women gathered in Yale's
Strathcona Auditorium that night were sexually experienced; 75
percent of the freshmen girls were virgins, as was half of the total

undergraduate population. Some Yale women welcomed the new equity in relations between the sexes. "To me it was the dawn of a new era," explained a woman sophomore. "I mean, that's the essence of women's lib. If you just sit there and go, 'Oh, God, he's looking at me,' you might feel set upon and scrutinized. But in my case, *I'm* looking at *him*." For many women students, however, this new era was coming far faster than they were ready for.

At the meeting in Strathcona Auditorium that night, Wasserman introduced Phil Sarrel. He told the girls about the Sex Counseling Service that would open in a few weeks and gave them the phone number to call for an appointment if they needed contraceptives, got pregnant, or simply wanted to talk about the relationship they were in.

"I was being very cool," said a freshman girl from Chicago, "but inside I was thinking, 'My God! Do they think this is all going to happen to me?'"

By 9:00 p.m., Wasserman's orientation meeting was over, and the girls filed out of Strathcona Auditorium, some with eyes wide about what they had heard. It would not be the last time, though, that they were confronted with the issue of sex. Over the next year or two, it would sometimes seem that they couldn't get away from it.

———

The days set aside for registration and move in passed in a rush of activity as the women set up their rooms, purchased their books, and met some of the whirlwind of new people: faculty advisers, freshman advisers, college deans, college masters, and men—so many men. But on Thursday, September 18, classes began.

Darial Sneed, a freshman from Manhattan, was the only woman

in her economics class. "Hello, lady and gentlemen," the professor announced as he entered the room, a small joke to start the day. Every guy in the class turned to stare at Darial.

Yale may have called itself coed, but 87 percent of its undergraduates that year were men, and by the end of the first week of "coeducation," the new women students began to understand how that skewed ratio would shape their experience at Yale. "The worst part was being constantly conspicuous, which is something you don't think about until it happens to you," said one freshman girl. As one professor observed, Yale's women students were denied "the most precious right any of us ever achieves…the privilege simply to be able to disappear." Instead, the young women lived their days dogged by the knowledge that they were always being watched.

"Everybody knew your business at Yale, as a woman. Everybody knew who you were dating," explained a woman sophomore in Saybrook College. "You moved in there, and you were one of just a handful of women, and all the men knew what you did every minute." The dining hall was the worst. Each woman felt it from the moment she entered: forty pairs of male eyes watching as she walked up the long center aisle to where the food was served, forty pairs of eyes as she carried her tray to a dining hall table, forty pairs of eyes any time she got up to get a glass of milk or a cup of coffee. The self-consciousness from having all those men watching was so acute that two freshmen girls made a pact. If one of them went up for coffee, they both would go up for coffee. Somehow, that made it not quite so awful.

Underlying the day-to-day difficulties caused by Yale's gender quota was the symbolic sting that came with it: a woman who wondered how Yale valued her worth need only be reminded that Yale gave admissions preference to men. Before coeducation even began, that bias had been condensed to a tagline: "a thousand male leaders." Yale had a responsibility to the nation to graduate a thousand leaders a year, the argument went, and since men were leaders and women were not, men should get preference in admissions. Kingman Brewster denied he ever said it, but every woman at Yale, including his wife, assumed that he did.   It was the same rationale that had stalled coeducation in the first place and the same one now used to justify Yale's admissions quotas, which limited women to 230 in each entering class while holding 1,025 places for men—the thousand leaders plus a cushion of 25 extra in case the admissions office made some mistakes.

By September 1969, the phrase "a thousand male leaders" was widely known at Yale and widely repeated. "I remember that 'a thousand male leaders' line," recalled a freshman woman in Yale's Silliman College. "I remember being pissed off at that."

The phrase rankled, and some women liked to extend it: "one thousand male leaders and two hundred concubines," they would say to each other, underscoring what the tagline implied for their own status.   The male undergraduates were the given, the nonnegotiable, the heart of Yale's mission. The women were add-ons. Within just a few months, the fight to end Yale's gender quotas would begin. But in those first few weeks of coeducation, just being a woman at Yale was challenge enough.

The days veered crazily between two extremes. To be a young woman at Yale was to be simultaneously invisible yet unable to blend in. Sometimes, the women would scan the classroom and find that they were the only one there.   Usually there were at least a few others. Either way, each girl felt the weight of proving not just her own merit but that of the entire gender.   "Not bad for a woman," a professor wrote across the assignment of one student.   In some classes, boys would stare when girls spoke, as if the furniture itself had offered an opinion. If the women stayed silent, professors sometimes closed the discussion by asking, "Now what is the woman's point of view on this subject?"

Before coming to Yale, most of the women had thought that being surrounded by men would be great, a perk of their first-at-Yale status. Their friends and family had teased them about how many boyfriends they would have, and that didn't sound half bad for those who had suffered through high school with the social handicap of being

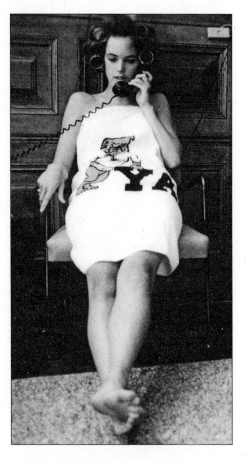

Photo of Yale freshman girl from *Look* **magazine feature on coeducation at Yale.**
Photo © Jill Freedman (photographer). Library of Congress, Jill Freedman, LOOK-Job 69-5318.

labeled "the smart girl." But none had ever imagined it would be like this.

The experience was confusing. All those men. All that attention. This was exactly what every girl wanted, right? Yet sometimes it seemed as if responding to all the attention from men left little room for anything else. "Without fail, every time I sit down to write a paper or do some reading, the phone rings," wrote a freshman from a suburb of Hartford. One guy would ask her to dinner, the next to a movie, and a third would suggest playing Frisbee. It wasn't just the interruptions, though. There was an unpleasant edge to the attention as well, "an uncomfortable sense of being observed, judged, and if one was not strikingly beautiful, perhaps found wanting," explained one woman sophomore.

Many of the men liked what they saw. As a Morse College senior observed, "We do have the best girls, I think, and we are known for it." Others were less pleased. A group of seniors had been watching one of the women in their residential college with concern. One day at lunch, they all walked over and sat down with her. She had never met any of them before, never talked to them, but they had some advice. She walked across the college courtyard "too quickly, too purposively," they told her. She sat in the dining hall "too far in the corner, too hunched over, too often with a book." She held her head "tilted too far up towards the sky or too far down towards the ground." No need for despair, though, they assured her. With some effort, she could improve.

———

As hard as most women found those opening weeks at Yale, there was one at least who was thriving. Connie Royster had been sad to leave behind her friends at Wheaton College, but she loved being at Yale. In many ways, she was home. Connie still had some older cousins who worked in the York Street fraternities, and some days she'd ride by on her bicycle to say hello. They were so proud of her. "How are you doing?" Connie's cousins would call out. "Great!"

she would answer. Connie thought of her cousins as her guardian angels, looking out for her at Yale, and they weren't the only people she knew when she got there.

Connie had gone to junior high in New Haven and grown close to the small group of kids in the top track who took all their classes together. Connie's junior high friends had continued on in New Haven public schools when Connie went off to boarding school, but she had remained friends with two in particular, the two who had gone to Yale. Both were among the first people she called when she learned she had been admitted. Connie knew those friendships would be waiting for her when she got to New Haven. What she had not expected was getting a roommate with whom she would become fast friends so quickly.

The girl had looked so forlorn when Connie first saw her on move-in day. Connie and her parents had swung open the door to her room in Yale's Berkeley College, and there was her roommate, standing alone in the empty dorm room with her one little suitcase beside her. The space echoed. Neither of the other two roommates was there yet, and this one looked so confused. She said her name was Betty Spahn.

Betty was a white girl, about five foot two, with long, dark hair down to her shoulders. She had driven to Yale from Illinois, she said; a friend and his dad had given her a ride on their way to Harvard. Connie was long practiced in making friends from all races and backgrounds, but there was something about Betty she connected with right away. Betty felt the same way. "It was like we had always been friends," said Betty.

Connie's father offered to drive the two girls to the Salvation Army to see if they could find a couch for their room, and by the time Connie and Betty returned with a suitably shabby acquisition, they were laughing and joking together and had made the first steps toward the friendship that would sustain them through Yale and for many years later. Over the following weeks, their days pulled them different directions—Connie to her art classes and theater rehearsals, Betty to her history and politics classes—but the two still managed to find time at the end of the day to touch base.

Betty would have loved to get involved in an extracurricular activity like Connie, maybe the Yale Political Union, but she had little time for extracurriculars. Betty needed to earn money to help pay for her tuition, and Yale had given her what was known as a bursary job as part of her financial aid package. Some of the women students on financial aid worked in offices of administrators or faculty, filing or making copies on the mimeograph machine. But many worked in the dining halls serving the students whose families did not need help paying Yale's tuition. Yale assigned you to a college that wasn't your own, so at least you weren't serving your roommates. Betty worked the dinner shift in Silliman College, where she stood behind the steam tables, ladling out food to the students who came down the serving line with their trays.

Male bursary students worked at Silliman too, but their job was bussing the tables. Apart from Betty, the women serving the food were all townies. Betty didn't mind her dining hall job, and she enjoyed the women she worked with. They were kind to her, and once Betty had her uniform on, she blended right in. A few days after she started her new job, though, something strange happened, something that she had trouble figuring out.

It was right at the start of Betty's shift, before the Silliman students came in for dinner. The dining hall manager came over to Betty and tapped her on the shoulder. "I want to see you in my office," he said. Betty knew who he was, but up until then it had always been Mary, the black woman in charge of the steam tables, who told her what to do. Betty turned to follow him anyway. Mary saw right away what was happening. "No, you can't! She's a Yale student," Mary shouted, and she put her body between Betty's and the manager's. "Go back to your station," she told Betty sternly. Betty did as she was told. The manager went back to his office. And then it was over. Still, it was all very odd.

A week later, the dining hall manager beckoned again, but this time the target was not Betty but a young black woman, a townie who was also new to the job. When the manager asked her back to his office, the woman left her station at the steam table to follow. While she was gone, the Yale students entered for dinner and Betty's coworkers covered the woman's station. Eventually, the young woman returned to the dining hall, disheveled and crying. Mary, the senior steam table worker who had protected Betty from the manager before, hugged the young woman tightly and took her off to the ladies' room. Betty was puzzled and asked the women in the serving line beside her what was going on. "Shush, honey, you don't need to know about this," was the answer she got. "She's going to be fine."

Betty did not know what had gone on in that manager's office, but she knew her coworker was crying. She kept listening as the other women talked. "Her husband doesn't need to know," they said. "It would just rile him up." Such things were so far beyond Betty's experience that she barely had words to describe them. She did not understand the details of what happened, but she did know one thing for certain: where she came from, it was *not* okay to make women cry by forcing yourself on them. Before the students came in for dinner one night, Betty approached Mary about what happened.

Mary's response was swift: "Now, don't you make any trouble, because it'll just come down on her head." The young woman was still in her probationary period, Mary explained. "This is a good job. It's got benefits," she continued, making clear that Betty was not to put that in peril. The woman had a young baby. If she wanted the job, she needed to wait out the months that remained in the probationary period. After that, the union could protect her. "Don't you make any trouble for her," said Mary. "She's got enough trouble." Mary had worked there a while. She knew how the system worked. She looked at Betty: "This is just the way the world is."

———

A week after the start of fall semester classes, Kingman Brewster donned his tuxedo and walked the three blocks from Yale's president's mansion to Sprague Hall, where he was scheduled to deliver a speech to the Yale Political Union. Four hundred people had gathered to hear him, for this was Brewster's first major address of the year, and he had prepared his thoughts with a national audience in mind. In colleges throughout the country, students were demanding more involvement in university decisions, and that night Brewster countered their call for "participatory democracy" by suggesting minor adjustments instead: performance reviews of university presidents, more attention paid to student petitions, and more transparency. Brewster was not interested in sharing more power with students, and he suspected many other presidents agreed with him. The next day, the *New York Times* ran the speech on its front page, exactly as Brewster had hoped.

And now on to the next issue: Vietnam. The Moratorium to End the War in Vietnam, with its call for college students across the nation to boycott their classes and hold antiwar rallies instead, was just a few weeks away. Yale took no official stand on the matter, but Brewster did not hide his own views. The war needed to end, and Yale students who attended the October 15 antiwar demonstration on the New Haven Green would find Brewster there too, as one of the rally's lead speakers.

As for coeducation, the woman issue was done as far as Brewster was concerned. The goal was achieved. Acceptance rates were up: 64 percent of the men offered places at Yale had said yes that year, compared with 56 percent the year before coeducation began. True, Brewster still needed to find someone to donate the money for more housing—he had promised 1,500 women after all. But that aside, Yale's foray into coeducation could be declared a success, and the woman issue moved off the agenda.

Had he spoken with any of Yale's women students, Brewster might have altered his assessment. It could be so very lonely to be a woman at Yale. "I could walk for blocks at night without seeing another woman's face," said a freshman girl from Rochester, and other women also struggled to make female friends. "It is virtually impossible to meet other girls," another freshman observed. "I am lost in a sea of men." Even the architecture at Yale kept women apart. The dorms had no long hallways onto which multiple rooms opened. Instead, the colleges were designed with entryways that had just two or three rooms to a floor. "The structure is such that it's like living in a hotel," the distressed master of Davenport College wrote to Wasserman once he realized how few of the women there had even met each other.

Yale women were not instant friends. Within the small group of women in their residential college, many had little in common save their gender. Field hockey player Lawrie Mifflin found some women friends in her college, Saybrook, but other girls were not as lucky. "If you didn't find a really close simpatico friend in your college, that was hard," said Lawrie. "You really felt alone then." There was something else too, a feeling at Yale that friendships between women were not all that important. A freshman from all-girls boarding school Concord Academy called it Yale's "antiwoman conditioning."   Her Concord Academy classmate, also at Yale, saw it too: "Yale men see nothing wrong with their all-male gangs and activities, but groups of girls are regarded as pathetic and queer." And so Yale's women were divided—by decisions made before they had even arrived, by buildings that kept them apart, and by a culture that said their friendships did not matter.

"How is your daughter doing?" one of the ubiquitous inter-viewers asked a father after the initial weeks had passed. "Well, I think she is like most freshmen," he answered. "She is very lonely, and it's a lonely time." The interviewer kept pushing. "Has she met many people here?" The father paused and then, not hiding the pain he felt for his daughter, replied, "I don't think so."

———

Like their white women classmates, the black women were separated out across the twelve residential colleges. Ezra Stiles had three black women; Branford, Calhoun, and Pierson each had four. No college had more than eight. Four colleges—Jonathan Edwards, Silliman, Saybrook, and Trumbull—had no black women at all, a situation about which the black men complained.

"There are no black women in Silliman," one of the Silliman men scrawled at the bottom of the fall housing survey. "This is one faux pas that cannot and will not be overlooked. Due to this situation, I have strongly considered transferring out of this college."

Shirley Daniels lived in Timothy Dwight, where she was one of five black women students. From her first days at Yale, though, Shirley spent a lot of her time at "the House," the nickname the black students gave to the black student center that Yale had just opened on Chapel Street. The build-ing really was a house, with a front porch and a kitchen. "It was a homey atmosphere," said Shirley's friend Vera Wells, another of Timothy Dwight's five black women. "You could study there and just have conversations."

Shirley Daniels.
Photo © Yale Banner Publications.

The House was the place where black students could let down the guard that came with being outnumbered and different. "It was a place where blacks could go where they didn't have to worry about what they said, what they did, what they believed, because of being in mixed company," said Shirley. Shirley never experienced any overt racism from students at Yale. But that did not mean it was comfortable to be one of the few black women in what was still a school of white men.

Black students had been attending Yale in sparse numbers well before there were undergraduate women. The first black student graduated from Yale in 1857, although for the next cen-tury Yale rarely admitted more than one black student per class. In 1962, Yale enrolled six black freshmen men. In 1964, there were eighteen. And now in 1969, there were ninety-six black freshmen at Yale, including twenty-five women. The class of 1973 was "the blackest class in the history of that ivy-draped institution," wrote student Henry Louis "Skip" Gates, who arrived at Yale in 1969. That did not feel very black at all, however, when 90 percent of the freshman class was white.

Many black women, Connie Royster and Shirley Daniels among them, were used to attending schools where they were part of a small minority. Connie had been the only black student in her entire high school, and before moving to Roxbury, Shirley attended army base elementary schools that never had more than a few black kids. For some of the black women students, though, Yale was their first immersion in a place full of white people. One freshman girl walked back to her dorm room after every class the first week and climbed into bed. "I wouldn't sleep. I was just hiding. I was out of my mind frightened. It wasn't so much Yale as coming to a white college."

Classroom interactions could be difficult. "They would sometimes look at me like I'm 'the black opinion'; I'm 'the female opinion,'" said Vera Wells, the junior who was in Timothy Dwight with Shirley. "It's not that they meant to be cruel. It's like I was a curiosity factor." That didn't make it any easier to be the one who was singled out. "I can't speak for all black people or all women," Vera explained to them. *I'm not your experiment*, she thought to herself.

Many of the white students cared deeply about ending the racial injustice they saw all around them. "We were searching, trying to do a better job navigating race than our parents' generation had done," explained one white woman freshman. Theirs was the generation that grew up with the civil rights movement. Rosa Parks had refused to give up her seat when they were in kindergarten. In middle school, Martin Luther King had told a crowd of 250,000 that he had a dream, and by the time they packed for Yale, both he and Malcolm X were dead. Yet supporting civil rights was one thing; figuring out how to negotiate an interracial friendship was another.

Close friendships between white and black students were not unheard of at Yale. The drama group with whom Connie Royster spent most of her time was mixed, and of course she and Betty were close. Lawrie Mifflin became friends with her black classmate Skip Gates after they suffered together through "Bio for Poets," the science class that humanities majors took to check off their distribution requirements.   But overall, Yale was not the integrated utopia that many white students hoped for. There were not enough black students to make that possible, and even so, many white students found it hard to reach across the divide of race. They had gone to white schools and lived in white neighborhoods, and that racial isolation had left many uncertain about how to approach a friendship with someone who wasn't white. "Interactions," said one white woman student, "were awkward."

A white sophomore from Queens felt it too. "We didn't want to offend; we weren't quite sure," she explained. "We gave a certain space to the black students."   Sometimes when Shirley Daniels entered a room full of white students, she could feel a ripple of discomfort.

There was no denying that Shirley stood out, whatever the racial makeup of the crowd. "Shirley had a lot of leadership presence about her," said Carol Storey, a black premed student from Los Angeles. Shirley was articulate and insightful and not shy about sharing her views, but she had a big laugh too, the kind that made you smile along with her. She wore her hair in a tight Afro and had wire-rimmed glasses. When she walked in a room, an aura of certainty swept in along with her. "She was very bright," said Sam Chauncey, who knew Shirley through his work as Brewster's point man on increasing black student admissions. Shirley did not have white friends at Yale, but that was through her own choice. She was oriented instead toward the black students at Yale and the black community of New Haven that surrounded it.

Coeducation arrived at Yale right when black students nationally were embracing Black Power's vision of "racial solidarity, cultural pride, and self-determination," and Yale was in step with the times. "We knew we had dreamed white dreams long enough," wrote student Skip Gates, who may have been friends with Lawrie Mifflin but also wanted to spend time among fellow black students. "To understand, to preserve ourselves as black people...we turned inward individually and collectively."

Black students sought one another out at mealtimes, and nearly every black student joined the Black Student Alliance at Yale (BSAY), which was in its third year in 1969. And while most black students did not major in Yale's Afro-American studies program, many took at least one Afro-American studies class. The distance between white and black students at Yale came from both sides, albeit for different reasons.

On weekends, most of Yale divided by race. The white social committee chairmen almost always hired white rock-and-roll bands for their mixers, but the black students liked to listen to soul music, and so the BSAY hosted its own Saturday night parties. When smaller groups gathered in someone's dorm room, they were white or black but not often both. When black students got together, "we might be playing music, or watching a movie, ordering some pizza, or playing some cards," said Carol Storey. "We played Bid Whist. That was the African American game."

Some white students resented black students' desire to spend time with one another. "If black students won't be friendly and eat with me at dinner," wrote junior Jeff Gordon, "then let them fight their own battles." Connie Royster could have explained to him why black students ate together: "There is a comfort in being with your own," she said, "especially if you're feeling like an outsider." That was an answer that white women at Yale were beginning to understand.

Connie did not spend much time at the House herself—she was always in one play rehearsal or another—but Shirley was there more often than not. Some of the black students Shirley met at the House were unlike any she had ever known. Shirley's father was a career serviceman in the army, her mother a schoolteacher-turned-home-maker. Shirley had never before met anybody whose parents were millionaires, but she met them at Yale, and the wealthy students she met there were black. Far more of the black women students, how-ever, came from families that knew what it was like to come to the end of the week without much money left over.

There were poor white students at Yale, to be sure. One soph-omore woman had a male friend from deep Appalachia with an accent so thick that at first she could barely understand him. He had never watched a television before coming to Yale. But only 4 percent of the white women students were classed by Yale's finan-cial aid office as "economically disadvantaged" compared with more than half of the black women students. Shirley Daniels was thus an outsider on three counts at Yale: she was black, she was a woman, and she was working class.

Shirley marveled at the wealth of Yale: the thick oriental car-pets, the gilt-framed portraits, and the wood paneling on the walls of her room in Timothy Dwight. Yale's buildings were "extra-ordinarily beautiful," said Shirley. "And the meals were out of sight." The black students found out about a black cook who knew how to make the food they had grown up with: collard greens, sweet potatoes, cornbread, fried chicken, and black-eyed peas and rice. Shirley nicknamed him "Candy." Yale rotated its cooks from one residential dining hall to another, and up at the House, they all knew Candy's schedule. "Wherever Candy was, all the black students went there for dinner," said Shirley. "I don't care what college it was; we were there." Like the House, Candy's food was a refuge. "We would just look forward to it," said Shirley. "For all of us, it brought back home."

FOUR

Consciousness

YALE'S FOOTBALL SEASON BEGAN ON THE LAST Saturday in September, with trepidation the mood in the stands. Legendary running back Calvin Hill and quarterback Brian Dowling had graduated the previous June, and the Yale Bulldogs now ranked just fifth in the Ivies, which in truth made them fourth from the bottom. But if the afternoon was filled with fumbles or failed plays, at least the new women cheerleaders were worth watching. The *Yale Daily News* kept the fans well informed with football columns and articles every Monday. Yale lost its opener to UConn that afternoon, and the *News* was there with the reason. Quarterback Joe Massey, the paper explained, "had trouble putting the snap on the kicking tee."

Although the football team did not appear bound for glory that year, the autumn brought other pleasures. The leaves on the campus's ancient maples and oaks blazed scarlet and gold, and temperatures hovered near seventy. Out on the Old Campus, Frisbees sailed through the air, and the students leapt up high to retrieve them. Some afternoons, Lawrie Mifflin was out there too. It was time to play field hockey, whether Yale said so or not.

Lawrie strapped on her black shin guards, grabbed her hockey stick and some balls, and headed outside. A dozen girls had gotten in touch after she and Jane Curtis put up the "Want to Play Field Hockey?" notices on the doors in Vanderbilt Hall, and they had begun holding informal practices together. The women hit the ball back and forth for an hour or so in one of the open spaces that lay between the Old Campus's oak trees and its crisscrossing paths. It wasn't really field hockey. They had no goal cages, no coach, no proper field, no locker room, and no fans or opponents. But the makeshift practice at least reminded Lawrie of what it had felt like to play on a team.

Some of the male students had never seen field hockey before, and a few laughed when they saw the girls playing. In the dining hall, when conversation turned to athletics, Lawrie could predict the question they would ask her: "You play what?" Lawrie was five feet tall and slender, with glossy brown hair parted on the side—not how men pictured women athletes. Girls who played sports were supposed to be big and clunky, unfeminine. Yet here was petite Lawrie Mifflin with her field hockey stick, as passionate about her sport as they were about football. "You play what?" She would try to explain. The game came from England. It was sort of like soccer except the ball was much smaller. You hit it with your stick, or sometimes you flicked it or dribbled or push-passed—whatever it took to get the ball into the goal. The men nodded along, but few understood why playing field hockey would matter. "Why do you want to start a field hockey team?" some would ask after listening to Lawrie. "Don't you have more important things to do?"

———

September passed into October, and as promised, the Yale Sex Counseling Service opened its doors. Wary of another scolding from the *New York Times* for not standing firm against premarital sex, Yale kept the news of the opening quiet, but students were informed that Phil and Lorna Sarrel were available, and all of the thirty-minute appointments that first day were filled, as they would be for the rest of the year. The Sarrels saw four student couples and eleven solo women on opening day, and while the visits concluded with the standard physical exam, they began with an extensive discussion.

"Have you had intercourse?" the Sarrels would ask. "Do you have questions or worries about sex response or specific sexual experiences? How do you feel about your sexual experiences—Happy? Sad? Perplexed? Conflicted? Ecstatic?" The Sarrels would ask students about their past relationships and how those had gone and about the relationship they were currently in: "Are there any major problems?" The conversation concluded with questions about the sex education the student either did or did not receive at home and her family's attitudes about sex. This last topic "usually raises moral issues," observed the Sarrels, but it was one that women students seemed to welcome.

In the half-hour appointments at the Sex Counseling Service, students too asked plenty of questions. Phil and Lorna Sarrel "pierced the fog surrounding the subject of sexuality," said a freshman girl from Manhattan. "And they were wonderful people."

The Sarrels' openness to talking with students about sex did not mean that either of them thought every student should be sexually active. And by early October, they both were concerned about what they were seeing at Yale. "[I hope] that a coeducational system can exist in this institution without girls paying a high price," Phil Sarrel told the *Yale Daily News* in an interview that month. He was "very worried about a lot of girls getting involved in a relationship they don't really want, and are not really ready for, but are getting involved in because of social pressure here." Lorna Sarrel agreed. "This pressure is going to be a real problem."

It already was. The seniors were the worst, many women observed. "The freshman guys were as befuddled as we were," said Patty Mintz, a white freshman from Massachusetts. Not so with the older Yale students. "There was so much pressure from the upper class guys to bed down with the women," said Patty. Some of the seniors Patty knew would take the student directories and systematically cross out any girl they'd had sex with. "So it was kind of feeling like you were being the opposite of predator...prey." Not all Yale men were like that. "There were many lovely, smart, kind, funny, wonderful guys," said Patty, and Los Angeles premed student Carol Storey, one of the twenty-five black women freshmen, felt the same. Before coming to Yale, Carol had asked her mother whether any of the male students at Yale were black. Her mother didn't know the answer, but Carol was pleased to find out that some were. The guys in Carol's Los Angeles high school had been too intimidated by her intelligence to go out with her, but at Yale, the black men were different. Carol found guys who were "absolutely entertaining, and future leaders, and people of high integrity." Some were even smarter than she was.

Like Patty and Carol, many Yale women found male friends and boyfriends who saw them as peers and equals. But there were enough men who did not see women that way—who saw them instead as sexual targets—to shape what it felt like to be a young woman at Yale. One freshman girl was solicited so many times by Yale men that she talked to one of Yale's ministers about it. She wished there was a residential college at Yale that operated like a convent or a monastery, she told him. That way you would not have to "deal constantly with questions about your sexual availability."

By early October, Shirley Daniels had grown concerned about Yale's sexual climate too. Shirley felt the pressure herself, but she was a sophomore. She had a year's worth of experience with college men. It was the twenty-five black women freshmen that Shirley and some of the other black women sophomores and juniors worried about. Shirley talked about her concerns with her friend Vera Wells, and the two of them and a few of the other black women upperclassmen decided to call a meeting of all forty black women undergraduates at Yale so that they could talk together about relationships. The freshman girls should understand that when the question of sex arose, they were allowed to say no.

The black women met once or twice, but after that the freshmen girls stopped coming. When Shirley ran into them at the Afro-Am House and asked why, the answer was always the same: "My boyfriend doesn't want me coming to a woman's thing." Shirley never imagined she would meet this kind of resistance, but the act of getting the women students together turned out to be far more radical than she had realized.

"In those days, women didn't meet. They didn't talk. They didn't support each other," said Shirley. The meetings stopped. The pressure from men continued. And the black women students went back to managing the overtures on their own.

————

Over in the coeducation office on Grove Street, Elga Wasserman was still writing memos. She had been at Yale long enough to know that this was not how things got done there. A staff, budget, title, and position that others recognized—those were the tools that male administrators had at their disposal. Yet Wasserman had only a threadbare budget, no staff beyond her secretary and a nineteen-year-old intern, and that ridiculous title. Her position reporting directly to Brewster could have provided her with some of the strength that she lacked, but Brewster did not attach the same degree of urgency as Wasserman did to the issues that confronted Yale women. It was frustrating. If Wasserman wanted power at Yale, she was going to have to create it herself, and the memos were one place to start. At least it was harder for others to ignore the challenges that Yale women faced once Wasserman put those problems down on paper.

In the fall of 1969, Wasserman was increasingly concerned about one problem in particular: the safety of women students. Yale's campus was so dark at night that girls were afraid to walk back to their room from the library. The lighting improvements Wasserman had requested in February had not been done, and the provost's office would not run the new evening shuttle bus until well after it got dark. Nothing terrible had happened so far, but Wasserman worried. And so she wrote Brewster a memo. Security, she advised him, was "not what it should be."

The women students knew nothing of Wasserman's concerns. Four weeks into the semester, they were all finally settling in. They had each figured out where Yale's rare ladies' rooms were, and most were not finding their coursework as difficult as they'd feared. Attention from the boys had not let up, but at least the girls knew to expect it. And on Saturdays, pretty much all of them joined their male classmates at the Yale Bowl or the stadium of that weekend's rival to cheer the Yale football team on to victory.

October 11 marked the Bulldog's third game: away versus Brown. The previous Saturday had brought Yale's first win, and while few would argue that Yale's roster was as legendary as in years past, perhaps there was still hope for the season. On Saturday morning, thousands of students and alumni made the trip up to Providence to see Yale take on Brown. If the football team did not dazzle, the halftime show by the Yale Precision Marching Band was always sure to entertain.

The marching band's name was a joke. The Yale Precision Marching Band did not even bother marching out onto the field at halftime. Instead, it ran out there en masse in a pell-mell display that smacked more of chaos than order. The band's reputation came not from precision but from its no-rules halftime shows, which featured unusual formations, accompanied by music selected to match and off-color text read out over the public address system by the band's announcer. Sometimes the shows were political. At one game, the band showed its opposition to the Vietnam War by arranging itself in an enormous peace sign. But coeducation offered a unique opportunity for humor, and the band's halftime shows were also known for their crudeness. In one show, seeking to mock an opponent that was not yet coed, the band played "Yes! We Have No Bananas" and marched into a penis formation. In another, the band's announcer hid the joke in a double entendre. "Yale coeds make our fans' root harder," he announced over the loudspeaker.

Kit McClure had not realized that Yale's marching band took pride in being so raunchy, but no way was she going to quit and give band director Keith Wilson a reason to say that girls weren't up to being marching band members. The band had issued Kit a uniform so large that the jacket reached halfway down to her knees and the sleeves covered her fingers, but as a five-foot-tall girl with wavy red hair tumbling down to her shoulders, Kit stuck out from the rest of the band members even with her marching band uniform on. At the football game in Providence against Brown, Brown's mascot, Bruno, a big guy in a furry brown bear suit, had no trouble spotting her.

The Yale band was playing "The Star Spangled Banner" when Bruno ran out onto the field, picked Kit up, and kept running. The Brown fans roared their approval, but Kit was scared. Some big guy had just grabbed her and would not put her down. What was he going to do with her? Nothing beyond the initial gag, it turned out, but Kit was not interested in being the punch line of someone else's joke. The Yale marching band was important to Kit—it gave her a way to meet other musicians and get better at playing trombone—but she had come to Yale with a far bigger dream than being a marching band member.

All you had to do was run your finger down the Top 40 list to see the problem that Kit was determined to solve: The Beatles, the Band, Led Zeppelin, the Who, the Rolling Stones, Three Dog Night, and Creedence Clearwater Revival. None of the top rock and jazz bands had a single woman musician. Four guys, five guys, or seven with Three Dog Night—the formula was always the same. You could find women singers at the top of the charts: Aretha Franklin, Diana Ross, Joan Baez, and Janis Joplin. But to play in a professional rock band, the rule up until then was that you had to be male.

Kit was going to change that. The goal looked pretty distant from where Kit was now, tucked under the arm of Bruno the Bear as he raced around Brown's football field. But Kit was tough—at least that's what Wasserman and Chauncey had thought when they moved her application to the "admit" pile. Hopefully, they would be right.

———

On Wednesday, October 15, classrooms across the nation sat empty as students on three hundred campuses staged a boycott to protest the Vietnam War. Antiwar sentiment had hit a new peak, with six out of ten Americans believing the United States should never have been involved in Vietnam in the first place, and citizens of all ages joined the students in protest. The Vietnam Moratorium was the first of two major demonstrations planned for that fall. A month later, a march on Washington would follow.

For many, opposition to the war was not just philosophical but personal. The body count was rising. Every morning, the *New York Times* listed the previous day's war dead from the New York City area: "Bronx G.I. Killed in Vietnam." "Jerseyan Killed in Vietnam." "Suffolk G.I. Killed in Vietnam." On the day of the Moratorium, the *Yale Daily News* filled its front page with the yearbook photos of twenty-five Yale students, each of whom had been killed in the war. Yale men who had not yet been called to fight worried that they soon might be.

The war was ever present. Every U.S. man was eligible to be drafted from the time he turned eighteen and a half to the time he turned twenty-six. An exemption existed for college students, but the war was waiting for them once they graduated. In the meantime, every male student at Yale filled out a Selective Service Card each fall with the number and address of his local draft board and his own four-digit Selective Service number, the information used in turn by the Yale registrar's office to secure his draft exemption for the year. Yale women were affected less directly, but few did not know at least one person who had been drafted or volunteered to fight, and some knew men who had died—all for a war that Congress had never declared and whose goals remained unconvincing to most students. As one Yale woman observed, "It really seemed like killing young men for no practical purpose."

On October 15, the day of the moratorium, Yale students grabbed a quick breakfast and walked down together to the rally on the New Haven Green. By noon, when the first speaker took the podium, the crowd on the Green had reached fifty thousand. "Enough," said the giant banner that was hung up as a backdrop. The speakers in New Haven included "old-style politicians and reformers, white and black, leaders of business and labor," reported the *New York Times*. And among them was one very prominent university leader, Yale president Kingman Brewster.

Brewster spoke slowly, pausing between phrases. "Our ability to keep the peace—requires above all—that America—once again become a symbol—of decency and hope—fully deserving—the trust and respect—of all mankind." Students responded by making the two-finger peace sign and then holding their arms up high above their heads. They looked around them at the fifty thousand people gathered on the New Haven Green. There was power in numbers.

Antiwar fervor so dominated the fall that little room remained for other issues. Discrimination against women was rarely mentioned at Yale. Compared with Vietnam, said one woman student, the issue of gender seemed "puny." The problem of racism had been pushed to the background as well, but the Black Student Alliance at Yale (BSAY) moderator Glenn DeChabert was unwilling to let the war become an excuse for inaction on discrimination. DeChabert was not scheduled to speak at the October 15 rally, but he stepped up to the microphone anyway. Blacks in New Haven, he explained, had been plagued by police brutality. "With all due respect to the Moratorium," DeChabert told the crowd, "I say we also have had enough."

Shirley Daniels had joined the BSAY back in September. She knew Glenn DeChabert. Through him and BSAY member Ralph

Dawson, Shirley learned how Yale's black students had accomplished so much in recent years: the opening of the House, the Afro-American studies major, and the rise in black student enrollment. The key was to provide a solution along with the problem. You couldn't just go into a meeting with Yale's administration and demand things. You needed to present a plan that the university could live with.

The BSAY had tried that approach with the police harassment issue but so far had made little progress. Glenn DeChabert had met with Brewster and shared the BSAY's ideas: set up a civilian police review board, start racial sensitivity training for campus and New Haven police, hire more black policemen, and have Yale Law School conduct a national study of racism and policing. But Brewster had not yet responded.

By October 20, the BSAY was tired of waiting. "Stop the Cops!" went the chant. "Stop the Cops!" Seventy-five black students, Shirley Daniels among them, walked into Yale Law School, split into three groups, and entered three different classrooms. They handed out copies of their proposal for change and positioned themselves along the walls of the classrooms. "Stop the Cops! Right on! Stop the Cops!" Professors and students looked on in shock. "It just brought the entire law school to a standstill," said Darial Sneed, who was there.

Darial was one of the twenty-five black women freshmen. When all eyes had turned to look at her in economics class at the start of the school year, the men had stared because Darial was the sole woman. But in the month that she had been at Yale, Darial had also grown more conscious of being black. Her roommate Mamie had been prodding her to pay more attention. The two had grown up just ten blocks from each other in New York City but saw the world differently. Darial had always thought of herself not as a black person but as just one of the crowd.

She was not "political enough," Mamie told her. "[You're not] paying enough attention to the black plight in America." No one had ever said that to Darial before. By the time the BSAY launched its protest against police harassment, Darial was ready to join in.

"Stop the Cops! Right On! Stop the Cops!" From the law school, the students marched down Wall Street to Beinecke Plaza and continued chanting for another ten minutes. The law school dean was furious. "We will not tolerate this!" he shouted from atop the roof of a car parked on Wall Street. But Darial believed in what she was doing. Shirley Daniels did too. The police behavior needed to change, and the BSAY strategy made sense to Shirley. The whole protest was over in less than a half hour. It was not "We're going to shut down the school" or "We're going to have a riot," Shirley emphasized. It was a message to Brewster, a man whom the black students saw as an ally: We want to talk to you. We need to talk to you. There are some issues here that are pressing. And perhaps most importantly, we've now got the numbers for you to listen to us.

———

The football team was winning. They had beaten Brown 27 to 13, defeated Columbia the following week, and thrashed Cornell the week after. The fans could not quite believe it. Glass-half-empty types pointed to the upcoming game against unbeaten Dartmouth, almost certain to give the Elis a thumping, but for now, it was still possible to dream of victory. Underdogs could sometimes surprise you.

The autumn had settled into its decades-old rhythm, with the football game as the punctuation to the end of each week. Other traditions continued as well. On the weekends, buses from Vassar and

Smith pulled up at the curb with their cargoes of women, there to attend mixers hosted by Yale men. The Yale women bristled. Had coeducation changed nothing? The "weekend women," as the Yale women called them, arrived wearing bright-colored dresses and makeup. Traditions die hard, but Yale's gender ratio was partly to blame. There were so few Yale women that most men who wanted girlfriends had to look elsewhere. Still, it confused things come Saturday. Once the buses arrived, there were not two genders at Yale but three: men, weekend women, and coeds—the ones in T-shirts and jeans. Junior Dori Zaleznik watched as a male classmate, arm-in-arm with his out-of-town date, approached. "Hey," he said to Dori and a few other girls. "Hey, I'd like you to meet Sue. Sue, these are our coeds!"

The Yale women chose the natural foe: the girls who came in on the weekend. "The weekly invasion force strikes again," muttered Dori. But eventually the weekend women climbed back into their buses and left. By Monday mornings, Yale returned to normal. "What's your name?" asked the guy in the dining hall line, smiling at the woman behind him. And then came the inevitable follow-up: "What are you doing tomorrow night? Would you like to get together?" Sometimes the Yale social scene just seemed impossible. And it was not the only thing troubling Yale women that fall.

As Wasserman had feared, Yale was still not a safe place for its new women students. The campus lighting had not been fixed. The girls' entryways and bathrooms had no locks. In Yale's Pierson College, a stranger had walked right in off the street and into a bathroom, where a woman was standing naked in the shower. Women in other colleges were having problems too. Girls walking home to Berkeley College were harassed on Chapel Street by drunks. A woman in Timothy Dwight had been chased. Some in Jonathan

Edwards got obscene phone calls. In Vanderbilt Hall, a freshman girl had looked up from her shower to the trapdoor in the ceiling above and seen neighborhood boys looking back at her. It was hard to stay focused on your coursework with all that going on.

At least Elga Wasserman was no longer the only one worrying about Yale's lax security. Sam Chauncey was concerned. The Council of Masters was concerned. Pulitzer Prize–winning author John Hersey was concerned. Hersey was the master of Pierson College, where there had been more than one incident. At one point, an older man had hidden in one of the bathrooms and exposed himself when some of the women students walked in.

Memos had been pinging back and forth on the problem all fall, with James Thorburn, the head of Yale's housekeeping division, often on the receiving end. Some of the memos came from Wasserman and some from Assistant Dean Elisabeth Thomas, who had been hired in September as the first woman to work in the Yale College Dean's Office who wasn't a secretary. At the end of October, Thorburn sent Elisabeth Thomas what he called a "summary of action and nonaction" in response to her various queries, and his list was heavy on the nonaction. The locks on the women's entryway doors were "ongoing," Thorburn wrote. Locks on the bathrooms were not needed. "The collective decision is 'no,'" he explained, "pending further indication of necessity."

Wasserman followed up with another memo to Brewster: "As you know, I have been concerned about security since last spring." Responsibility for student safety was divided among multiple offices, she explained. Thus nothing could get done quickly. This time, Wasserman had Brewster's attention, or perhaps it was Sam Chauncey who pushed the issue. In any case, Brewster responded within a week and set up an oversight committee, just as Wasserman suggested. She was not a member—no woman was—but at least Brewster had named Chauncey to the group. Yet even with this new structure in place, Wasserman was not seeing enough progress. She met with Jim Thorburn again and then followed up with a memo. Her language was gracious and polite. "Many thanks for taking the time yesterday to discuss renovations in the residential colleges." But Wasserman was not going to let the issue drop, and she repeated her request that Thorburn install the locks she had asked for.

Jim Thorburn wasn't used to receiving memos like that, at least not from a woman, and in 1969, there were plenty of midlevel male administrators at Yale who "just didn't like having a woman telling them what to do," said Chauncey. Whether Thorburn was one of those men is unclear, but this much was certain: save for the new committee, progress on security for women at Yale seemed to have stalled.

———

Few people at Yale worked harder than Elga Wasserman to ensure the safety of Yale women, but Wasserman had a blind spot on this issue. All of her efforts had centered on outsiders. Neither she nor other Yale administrators seemed to consider that men Yale employed might also pose a threat to Yale women. Had they spent any time with the Silliman College dining hall workers, they might have shifted that perspective.

Betty Spahn had not been able to let the predations of the Silliman dining hall manager go. She knew it was not her place to do anything that would threaten her coworker's job. She had listened to what Mary, her supervisor, had said. But a man shouldn't be able to get away with forcing himself on a younger woman, particularly one who worked for him, thought Betty. Maybe she could do something about the larger issue.

Betty's boyfriend told her that Yale's branch of Students for a Democratic Society (SDS), with which he had long been involved, was active in supporting workers' rights, and in October, Betty went to her first SDS meeting. That night, the group discussed the treatment of a different black dining hall worker, a single mother of four named Colia Williams, who had been fired after arguing with the Yale student who supervised her. Like the woman in Silliman, Colia Williams was newly hired and thus not yet protected by the union. The SDS students were outraged at her treatment: her children depended on her income, and she'd been dismissed without even a hearing. When the group decided to stage a protest outside the Yale business manager's office in Wright Hall, Betty said that she'd join them. The date was set for November 3.   Everything unraveled from there.

The protest began at 2:00 p.m. with 175 students, but after two and a half hours and no progress to speak of, only 80 students remained. Betty wasn't leaving, though. All that would do was prove that the white men who ran Yale's dining halls could get away with whatever they wanted. Betty listened as the SDS student leaders, all of them men, decided on a new strategy. They would not allow the business manager and two of his subordinates to leave Wright Hall until the men agreed to hear Colia Williams's side of the story.

Yale had never had a sit-in before, and the administration did not look kindly on students holding three Yale employees hostage. Brewster was in Washington, DC, attending a black-tie dinner at the White House, but at 5:15 p.m., Provost Charles Taylor arrived at Wright Hall, accompanied by all twelve of Yale's residential college deans. Any student who did not leave at once, Taylor warned, would be immediately suspended. Another man, maybe midforties and wearing jeans and cowboy boots, strode into the crowded room and climbed on top of a table so that all the students could see him. Betty didn't know who he was, but the others told her that he was Yale's chaplain, William Sloane Coffin, a man widely admired by students for his civil rights and antiwar activism. The students should leave at once, Coffin urged. Otherwise, the consequences could be severe. Coffin would see to it that any injustice in Yale's dining halls was addressed. He gave the students his word.

A minister's promise was good enough for Betty. "We should leave," she said to the others. "Let's let the chaplain have a stab at this." Some students, concerned by Coffin's warning, did leave Wright Hall, but the SDS men kept on talking. "We should leave," Betty repeated. "Come on, guys, let's go." But no one was listening to Betty. At 5:50 p.m., nearly three hours after the protest began, Provost Charles Taylor picked up a megaphone and made good on his threat. Every student protester still in Wright Hall was suspended, he told them, and banned from their dorm room, the dining halls, the library, their classes, and their bursary job if they had one. At this point, the students began filing out of the building, but as they did so, the deans from each of their residential colleges identified them. Yale suspended forty-seven students, including three women. Betty Spahn had nowhere to go.

"Come home," her parents told her when she called them, but Betty was not leaving. Too much was at stake. Her boyfriend's parents, who lived just north of campus, offered to have her stay with them, and Betty gratefully accepted. Still, she was scared. All she had done was go to a protest, and now her entire college education was at risk. The next day, Betty received a formal notification from Yale confirming her suspension and requesting that she appear before the faculty executive committee, which would decide whether to revoke her suspension, extend it, or expel her altogether.

The rest of the week passed in a blur of meetings and protests and nights without sleep. Hundreds of Yale students, galvanized by the punishment of their classmates, organized mass meetings demanding amnesty for the Wright Hall protesters. The BSAY got involved. While the protest had arisen over the firing of a black woman worker, it was Colia Williams's race, not her gender, that the SDS emphasized, and now several BSAY members accused SDS of using Williams's plight to advance their own standing as a force to be reckoned with at Yale. The whole thing was a mess.

Betty attended her hearing before the faculty executive committee and shared her account of what happened. The other suspended students did the same, and one week after the sit-in, the committee issued its verdict. Yale would readmit the suspended students, but each of their transcripts would carry the stain of the brief suspension—a red flag that Betty would be forced to explain to the law schools she applied to and to future employers and others who wondered what the suspension said about her character. No, she hadn't cheated or broken the law, she would tell them. She had just gone to a protest.

The action itself was successful. Yale rehired Colia Williams and ensured that she lost no back pay. Williams's sister wrote the students to thank them for what they had done. And so Betty took away two lessons from her Wright Hall suspension. First, if enough people take a stand, change happens. Second, SDS was not the right place for her. In that crowd of men, Betty's voice had been lost. If you were a woman at Yale, there had to be a better way to be heard.

———

Vietnam. Vietnam. Vietnam. In mid-November, scores of Yale students piled into cars and buses and headed south to Washington, DC, where they joined a half million other protesters committed to bringing an end to the war. It was the largest antiwar demonstration in U.S. history. "We were being the conscience of the country," said one freshman girl. "We were telling truth to power."

The Yale students who joined the March on Washington included at least a few football fans who skipped the big game against Princeton that weekend in order to take part in the protest. On Monday, when they were back in New Haven, some turned to the back page of the *Yale Daily News* to learn how the Bulldogs had fared. Sophomore wingback Bob Milligan "ran a post pattern and caught the ball running over the middle from right to left," explained the reporter, describing the key play of the game. To Yale's shock, their football team had beaten Princeton.

In Ezra Stiles College, sophomore Lydia Temoshok was working on a different article for the *News*, a review of a Haydn opera performed at Ezra Stiles Sunday night, complete with a twenty-one-piece orchestra. Two weeks had passed since Yale head of housekeeping Jim Thorburn had declared he would not install locks on the women's bathrooms until he saw "further indication of necessity." It was two in the afternoon on a Monday. No one else was around. Lydia was having trouble getting her article started, so she decided to go take a shower. As she stood under the hot water, the curtain was wrenched aside, and two young men stepped into the shower with her.

"Be quiet now, hear, or I'll cut you," one of them said as he showed her his knife. "Gimme a kiss... I'm crazy, hear, just be quiet... It'll be over soon."

Lydia tried to think quickly. If she just started screaming, they might panic and stab her. So she told them she was going to count to ten—and then she would start screaming. "One. Two. Three. Four." When she got to five, Lydia began to shout—"Leave me alone! Leave me alone!"—and the assailants fled.

Afterward, she returned to her room, shaken. Lydia did not want to go running to authorities at Yale about what happened—at least, not right away. She "wanted to show that the women they had admitted were tough, not delicate flowers." If Lydia told someone official, she worried that they might overreact and "protect" Yale women by restricting their actions. Lydia had transferred to Yale from Smith in part to escape Smith's curfews and overvigilant housemothers. She hated how Smith had treated her as vulnerable, like some child who needed to be taken care of. *They're going to start doing the Smith thing on me again*, she thought. *No, it's not going to happen.* And so, for the moment, Lydia kept quiet about the incident.

She finished her opera review for the *News* and handed it in. She had dinner with three friends in Stiles. She went to hear drug guru Timothy Leary speak at the Yale Political Union. She finished reading *Othello* for class. But that night, Lydia began to worry that if she didn't report what had happened, some other woman student might get hurt. On Tuesday, she walked over to the office of Ezra Stiles College Dean Ernest Thompson to tell him about the assault.

"Look, I'm okay," Lydia began, before saying a word about what had happened. Thompson listened closely as Lydia went on. "You know, we do need to act on this," he said when she was done speaking. Lydia agreed to call the campus police. When she left, Thompson took action as well. "The physical security of the girls," he told the *Yale Daily News* a few weeks later, was his "major problem at the moment."

The rest of November passed quickly. Yale's football team won its game against Harvard and closed the season tied for first in the Ivies. Brewster acted on some of the black students' proposals on police harassment, and the campus police hired four black policemen. Jim Thorburn instructed his men to install locks on the women's bathrooms in Ezra Stiles. The November weather turned cold and wet; the days grew dark too quickly. But if you listened closely, you could hear the faint tap-tappings of change.

Up until November, the national press had not yet published a major article on the rise of feminism, but just before Thanksgiving, *Time* magazine ran a three-page feature on the women's movement. The word *sexism* was so new that *Time* put it in quotation marks. "Many of the new feminists are surprisingly violent in mood, and seem to be trying, in fact, to repel other women," *Time* reported, a characterization that many feminists were interested to learn about themselves. Feminists were "furious…militant…radical," *Time* continued. In one place, it called them "the angries."

Yet even if *Time* had little positive to say about feminists themselves, its article included a few pertinent facts. Only 2 percent of the members of Congress were women, as were just 3 percent of U.S. lawyers and 7 percent of U.S. doctors, and the gap between what women and men were paid was getting worse. Women who worked full time earned 58 cents for every dollar earned by men, down from 64 cents ten years earlier. Women across the country looked up from their own lives in surprise at such patterns and began to see the broader landscape around them.

A few things were improving. Airline stewardesses could no longer be fired the day they turned thirty-two. The National Organization for Women had three thousand members. And those "militant women" that *Time* warned about were meeting all over the country. There were twenty-five women's groups in Boston, thirty in Chicago, thirty-five in the San Francisco Bay Area, fifty in New York, and even one in Gainesville, Florida. Change does not always come accompanied by rallies and posters. The women's movement "promises to grow much louder in months to come," predicted *Time* publisher Henry Luce III, Yale class of 1945.   And the dissidents were even closer to Luce's alma mater than he realized.

FIVE

Sex-Blind

CONNIE ROYSTER HAD NEVER EXPECTED TO HAVE A roommate who got herself suspended in her first semester at Yale, but once the ruckus was over and Betty was able to move back into their Berkeley College room and start attending classes again, Connie began to tease her about it. Connie was good for Betty that way. It never helped to take yourself too seriously.

"Betty the Red" was the new nickname that Connie gave to her roommate. The name came in part from the red T-shirt Betty never seemed to take off—there were only so many shirts you could fit into the small suitcase that Betty brought with her to Yale, and she had no extra funds to buy more. But red was also the color associated with communism, and thus captured the new hue of Betty's politics. Betty might not have liked the macho aspect of Students for a Democratic Society (SDS), but what it said about workers' rights made sense to her, and now Betty had joined one of the most left-wing student groups at Yale—the Collective, whose forty student members met Monday nights with the goal of building a radical student movement at Yale. Phrases like "bourgeois ideology" now peppered Betty's conversation. Connie would listen to a point. "No, I haven't read *Das Kapital*, and no, I don't want to read it right now!" she would finally say, laughing. Connie was too busy with other things, anyway.

On most days, you could see her riding her bike from one activity to the next: over to York Street, where her cousins worked in the fraternities and the Yale Dramat was located, down to Haitian dancer Emerante dePradines's studio in Wooster Square, or out Prospect Street to the house of one of her Yale classmates. Connie was everywhere. She had a knack for being comfortable in a wide range of places, for moving easily from one circle to the next.

Connie went to Yale, but she was of New Haven. She went to the Black Student Alliance at Yale (BSAY) meetings but did not hang out at the Afro-Am House like Shirley and Shirley's friend Vera Wells. She was deep into drama and arts, but she also volunteered in the community—tutoring elementary school children at Dixwell Congregational Church and helping teach the dance classes that dePradines, who had danced with the legendary Katherine Dunham, offered to disadvantaged children. Connie was black and hailed from a family long active in civil rights, but Betty and many of her other close friends were white.

If there was one thing that rose above Connie's wide-ranging activities at Yale, it was her love of drama. Connie had been acting since high school. In a family with such a strong emphasis on academics, with an aunt whose career as a lawyer and judge was so prominent, theater gave Connie a path that felt new and untrodden: "It was my way of being me."

The Dramat, where Connie spent so much of her time, was an unusual island at Yale where the presence of women had long been normal. There were not many plays with roles solely for men.

Through the 1800s, Yale solved this challenge by having men play the women, but at the turn of the century, anxiety about homosexuality produced a new rule: a man could not play women's roles for more than two years in a row. People might talk. By the time Connie arrived, the Dramat had been casting women graduate students and faculty wives for decades, and the undergraduate women fit right in. Women could act at the Dramat. "They could be directors," said Connie. "Nobody there said that you couldn't."

Other Yale women heard different messages, of course. No, you can't play field hockey. No, you can't be a member of the marching band. No, you can't sing in the Whiffenpoofs or be an editor at the *Yale Daily News*. No, you can't be the one with the microphone at the front of the room when one protest or another is afoot. Yale women were learning to ignore such messages, although you still would not have labeled them feminists—well, except for one or two of them. And to understand why Kit McClure arrived at Yale already a committed feminist, it helps to go back to her freshman year in high school.

From the outside, Kit McClure's life before Yale looked a lot like that of many of the other girls in the freshman class. She grew up in a suburb thirty minutes from Newark, in a town of modest homes and neatly mowed lawns where all of the families were white except one. If you walked through the front door of Kit's house, though, the differences were readily apparent. Kit's family was the only one in Little Falls, New Jersey, she was sure, that subscribed to both *Ebony* and *Jet*. James Baldwin's *The Fire Next Time* was out on the coffee table. And sitting together at the dinner table each night throughout Kit's years in high school were four people: Kit, her parents, and one of her two black sisters: Emily Smoot and Mary Jane Western.

Kit's mother was active in the civil rights movement, and as part of that commitment to racial justice, she decided that their family should offer to have a black high school student from the south come live with them for two years and attend the local high school. Passaic Valley Regional High was not the fanciest school in New Jersey, but it was better funded than many of the schools that black students attended. The arrangement would also benefit Kit. It wasn't good for white kids to grow up in neighborhoods and schools where all the other kids were white too.

The family of Emily Smoot from Natchez, Mississippi, took Kit's mom up on her offer, and when Kit was fourteen, Emily came to live with her family. The two girls soon thought of each other as sisters. Kit was starting ninth grade at Passaic Valley that year, and she and Emily, a junior, attended together. Other than a kid who played in the marching band with Kit, Emily was the only black student in the entire high school. Emily had a loving family of her own, and Kit traveled down to Natchez to stay with them for a while. As Kit's mother had hoped, the education of both girls benefited from the arrangement.

When Emily graduated in 1967 as the top student in Passaic Valley's senior class, Mary Jane Western of Cookeville, Tennessee, came to Little Falls for two years and became part of Kit's family too. Both Kit and Mary Jane were juniors that fall. When one of Kit's neighbors saw Mary Jane arrive, she took Kit aside and asked with concern, "Is her whole family moving here?"

Mary Jane was quite the athlete, and Kit's mom would drive the two girls to Newark to play in a girls' basketball league, where Kit was the only white girl on the team and Mary Jane, for a few hours at least, could drop the burden of being the sole black girl in the room, as she was every day in high school. Like Emily, Mary Jane was not what Kit thought of as politically radical, but seeing the world through Emily's and Mary Jane's eyes changed what Kit saw as she looked out at a world where both pasts and futures were shaped by your race.

Kit wanted to learn more about race in America. The ideas of the black liberation movement felt urgent to her. She read *The Autobiography of Malcolm X* and then read it again. From there grew questions about discrimination against a different group: women. As a girl who played trombone, Kit had tasted some of that bile herself. She read Betty Friedan's *The Feminine Mystique*, and then, in the summer after her junior year of high school, Kit took the next step in her feminist education. The first consciousness-raising groups had just begun meeting in hotbeds of women's activism like New York and Chicago. Kit was curious. She was spending that summer at Cornell doing science research, and maybe the students there could tell her more. At Cornell, Kit hung out with some of the SDS students—they were the ones who convinced her to take a bus to Chicago that summer for the protests at the 1968 Democratic National Convention—and she kept asking the SDS students she met the same question: "How do you find the women's movement in New York?" Eventually, she found one who knew the answer.

Kit followed the lead she'd been given, and in the fall of 1968, as Yale was making its decision to go coed, she took the train from Little Falls to Manhattan in search of the apartment where the consciousness-raising group she had learned about was being held. When she found it, Kit knocked on the door and asked if she could come in. Some of the women took one look at Kit and thought, *Why are you here?* All of the other women in the room were adults. The group had never had a member who was still in high school. "Well, she's got to learn some time, and she wants to be here," one woman said, and the others agreed that Kit could join them.

All through her last year of high school, Kit took the train from New Jersey to the women's group she'd found in Manhattan. She practiced her trombone and imagined the day when women musicians would have the same respect as men. By the time Kit got to Yale, she had decided that the women's movement was something she wanted to stay involved in. But where was the women's movement in New Haven? At the start of December 1969, Kit was still looking. It would not take her much longer to find out.

———

Yale's two-week Christmas vacation gave women students their first major break from the challenges they had faced since September. They returned to campus on January 5 for the final three weeks of the semester. The tumult over the Vietnam War had subsided by then, at least temporarily. U.S. troop levels were down, and the cold winter weather brought an end to prime protest season. December's changes to the draft law had calmed things as well. Barring national emergency, men were now eligible to be drafted for only one year rather than seven, from the day they turned nineteen to the day they turned twenty. Nineteen-year-olds who were in college received a temporary pass. They could finish their degree without fear of being drafted but then became eligible the year after they graduated, whatever their age at that time.

The second change in the draft law was to institute a lottery, thus reducing the injustices of the previous system, which sent a disproportionate number of black and working-class youth to Vietnam. The lottery was held in December, with every day of the year drawn from a fishbowl. Yale students whose birthdays were drawn first were the ones who would be drafted once they graduated. April 11 was number 14, certain to be called up, while April 12 was number 346—a student born then was not going to Vietnam unless he volunteered. Male students at Yale now knew where they stood, for better or worse. As one draft counselor explained, "They either had a lucky number or an unlucky number, and from there they could start to make choices."

With the urgency over Vietnam abated, other issues had room to emerge. On January 21, the outgoing board of the *Yale Daily News* used its final editorial to argue that Yale should abandon its thousand-man quota and admit more women students. Women, it observed, seemed quite capable of being leaders too. The editorial stopped short of advocating sex-blind admissions. Admit 800 men and 450 women to the class of 1974, the editors urged, still giving preference to men. But the thousand-man policy had been publicly challenged—and by a group that no one at Yale would call radical.

While the *News* was tossing its editorial barbs at Brewster, women at Yale were organizing. By January 1970, Yale had two different women's groups dedicated to improving the lot of women at Yale. The Graduate Women's Alliance had been meeting together on Tuesday nights since September. One block down Wall Street, the new Yale Law Women Association met Tuesdays as well, and on Sunday nights, some of the women in both groups walked down together to Orange Street, where New Haven Women's Liberation met above the Buster Brown shoe store. Sophomores Shirley Daniels, Connie Royster, and Betty Spahn were not members of any of these groups, nor were freshmen Lawrie Mifflin and Kit McClure. Yale undergraduates would not have their own women's group until later that spring. But the actions of the graduate school women and the New Haven feminists started to slowly change the climate at Yale, even for women who did not know they existed.

The goals of the new women's groups were still emerging. At the time, the idea of getting together as a group of women was radical enough. New Haven Women's Liberation, a year older than the other two groups, had opened a day care center—there were almost none in New Haven before then. The Graduate Women's Alliance began to document for the first time the numbers of women faculty members in each of Yale's academic departments, a project that included interviews with department chairs about hiring practices, graduate student admissions, and assumptions about women graduate students. "There is something about the biology of a woman," one department chairman told them, "that makes her apt to be less ambitious than a man."

In January, the Alliance began to make its presence felt among undergraduates when one of its members convinced the university bookstore to add a women's book section to its offerings. Students could now pick up a copy of Simone de Beauvoir's *The Second Sex* or Betty Friedan's *The Feminine Mystique* along with the required reading for chemistry and political science. It had taken five separate appeals to accomplish this feat, but in the end, the bookstore manager relented, although not without a final snide remark at the woman who had asked for the new book section. "Let me assure you," he asserted, "there is nothing less sexy than the approach of a feminist."

The women students at Yale Law School were busy as well, and one Thursday in January, eighteen of them walked over to Mory's, the club where Yale's male administrators and faculty liked to eat lunch, and sat down at a few of the restaurant's polished oak tables. The men who were already eating at Mory's turned to stare as the women entered. The maître d' was incensed. It was 1970, and women were not allowed in Mory's at lunchtime.

The practice of barring women from clubs where powerful

men dined was not uncommon. At New York's Russian Tea Room, the Oak Room at the Plaza, Stouffer's in Pittsburgh, Schroeder's in San Francisco, and top restaurants in Atlanta, Beverly Hills, Chicago, Dayton, Detroit, Miami, Minneapolis, Syracuse, and Washington, women who tried to enter during the midday "executive hours" were all turned away.   Even Connie Royster's aunt, U.S. district court judge Constance Baker Motley, had faced exclusion from the discussions of her fellow judges, who met at one of New York City's all-male clubs. In the end, an asterisk in the club's rules that allowed the men's secretaries to join them saved Motley from being left standing outside. As the youngest member of the court, she was technically its secretary.

In New Haven, Mory's was the place to meet: the venue for Yale department meetings, law firm recruiting parties, lunches with outside guests, and regular concerts by the Whiffenpoofs, the Yale singing group that Cole Porter had been in.   Professors lunched with students at Mory's, department chairs hosted candidates for job openings, and formal meetings elsewhere would end with a drink or a meal at Mory's. And why not? Mory's was a cozy, clubby place with lots of dark wood, walls filled with photos of Yale's sports teams, and a see-and-be-seen main dining room where one might bump into President Brewster having lunch with a key staff member or a group of Yale's trustees relaxing after their meeting in Woodbridge Hall. Decisions were made at Mory's; information was shared there, relationships and networks built. The place fairly throbbed with power.

Yale's use of the club for its meetings worked beautifully for all of the men. The women, however, were excluded, allowed in the main dining room only after 5:00 p.m.—and only then if a man brought them. No women were permitted to be members. The rules at Mory's were perfectly clear, the maître d' told the women law school students who had dared to enter on that January afternoon. If they stayed any longer, he would have them arrested for trespassing. The women rose from their seats and walked back out the front door. The fight to end Mory's no-woman rule had begun.

Yet one more initiative was still in the works: the Free Women Conference, a joint effort by the Graduate Women's Alliance, the Yale Law Women, and New Haven Women's Liberation. The conference would be held at Yale Law School over four days in February and would bring feminist speakers and activists to Yale from as far as Chicago. Workshops were scheduled on topics including women and the law, abortion, and coeducation at Yale. Radical feminists Naomi Weisstein and Kate Millett had both agreed to be speakers. The gathering would give Yale students a way to learn more about the burgeoning women's liberation movement and, perhaps most importantly, provide like-minded women and men a chance to meet one another and plan together what might come next. What could they do, for example, to enable women to have safe, legal abortions rather than the back-alley procedures to which many resorted? How might they use the law to end some of the rampant discrimination against women in academia? How could they push Yale to drop its quota on women undergraduates?

To advertise the event, the women printed fliers and hung them all over campus and in downtown New Haven. Most of the posters were ripped down within hours. Others were defaced with obscene graffiti, and so the conference organizers took to standing on New Haven street corners and handing out the leaflets to people who walked by. That's how Kit McClure first heard about the Free Women Conference. She was walking across the New Haven Green one afternoon, and a woman approached her with the fliers. Would she be interested in going to the conference? Kit took a flier and began talking with the woman who had given it to her. She told her that she wanted to start an all-women rock band and was still looking for musicians to join her. "Great," said the woman with the fliers. "Come to the conference, and we'll make an announcement."

She would be there, Kit said. She had been looking for the women's movement in New Haven ever since she got to Yale, and now she'd found it.

———

On January 22, the day after the *Yale Daily News* challenged Brewster's thousand-man quota, Elga Wasserman met with seven members of her Women's Advisory Council. She had set up the group back in September as a way to give women students a voice in how Yale approached coeducation, and every week she had lunch with half of the members: sophomores and juniors one week, freshmen the next. Each residential college had at least one representative, which gave Wasserman a good feel for what was going on around campus, and this week she did not like what she heard. "The problem of security in the bathrooms is pressing," the students told her. Ezra Stiles College, where the knife incident had happened, now had locks on the girls' bathrooms, but ten of the other eleven colleges did not. It was infuriating. Wasserman could not simply order change to happen, however. She did not have that type of power.

Wasserman chaired two committees at Yale related to coeducation. One was this Women's Advisory Council, which served in an advisory capacity to Wasserman and was made up of students. The other was the University Committee on Coeducation, which served in an advisory capacity to Brewster and was mostly made up of faculty and administrators. Both groups that year were concerned about security, but in both cases, discussions never went beyond the threat to women students posed by outsiders. The term *sexual harassment* had not yet been invented, but that did not mean it wasn't happening.

"There were many inappropriate approaches to women on campus, by professors, by mentors, very, very upsetting, all ages, all marital situations, sometimes advisers, sometimes people whose courses one took over and over again," explained one sophomore. When one freshman girl went to a professor's office hours seeking academic help, he tried to kiss her. She never went back there again.

Graduate students were also preyed on by some of their professors. For one of them, the incident happened before she had even enrolled at Yale. During the admissions process, she had presented her portfolio of artwork, and when she'd finished discussing the final picture, the professor had grabbed her by the shoulders and asked, "Now don't you have something else to show me?" Another student was invited by her faculty adviser to meet in his office, where "he demanded that I perform perversions with him." She subsequently dropped out of Yale. A third was harassed by her adviser as well. "He doesn't seem to learn that I don't like to be touched while discussing data," she said. "We have had numerous exasperating discussions about this."

For a fourth graduate student, the trouble came from her department's director of graduate studies, who was supposed to help her plan her coursework but instead spent their meetings patting her thighs and pinching her rear. A fifth female student went to see a professor to learn more about a class he was teaching, only to have him ask her to sleep with him. A sixth was propositioned by two different professors. The first overture came from a man who was prominent nationally, the second from one on whom she depended for her job recommendations. It was the second one that particularly bothered her. She knew the man's wife, and here he was, suggesting an affair. As she had with the first professor, she turned him down. After she did so, "he seemed kind of ashamed," she said. Neither he nor the other professor made further advances. No retribution followed her refusals. She had been lucky on that point at least.

By January, the undergraduates had barely been at Yale a full semester, but a few professors had started right in on their targets. Freshman Kate Field had been flattered when her poetry professor asked her to join the weekly literary lunches he held with a small group of upperclassmen and graduate students. Kate had grown up in a house in the midst of woods and marshland on the far western edge of Massachusetts. The Housatonic River ran nearby. Her parents had sent her to a girls' boarding school that had been founded to prepare young women to meet the requirements for admission at Wellesley College, one of the prestigious "seven sisters" colleges, and by the time Kate got to Yale, she was already a published poet. Kate assumed the professor had invited her to the literary lunches because he thought she had talent.

Kate attended the weekly lunches for about a month, and then the professor invited her to go on a walk through Yale's Grove Street Cemetery, known for its landscaping and famous gravesites. Kate was seventeen years old, about as young as you could be and still go to Yale. When the professor lunged at her, she quickly backed off. He had her all wrong, Kate told him. She was not interested in that kind of relationship. Kate was not scared of the professor, but she was disappointed and angry—so much for being identified by one of Yale's faculty members as a young woman writer with promise.

Denise Maillet, a sophomore, had transferred to Yale from

Wellesley. She did not fit any of the standard categories of ethnicity or class into which students at Yale could be sorted. Denise was born in New York, where her mother was from, but grew up in Venezuela and Puerto Rico, where her father was stationed by his company. Denise was not Latina, but she spoke fluent Spanish. She had traveled to Europe, but her father was nearing retirement, so at Yale, Denise got a job as a waitress. Denise was intellectual. Every week all through high school, she and her father would read a book together—one week in French, the next week in Spanish, the third week in English—and then they would talk about the literature for hours. Denise was also glamorous. She had been modeling since she was fourteen, and all her clothing, which her mother made for her, came from *Vogue* patterns.

Denise's first semester at Yale had gone well. She was already dating a Yale senior when she arrived, one of the famous Yale Whiffenpoofs. They had met over Christmas break her freshman year at Wellesley, when his singing group performed in Puerto Rico and her family attended the concert. Denise would have applied to Yale regardless of whether she was dating him or not, but his presence helped her fit in quickly there. Weekends were filled with Whiffenpoof concerts, parties, and going to football games with her boyfriend. Like most other women students, Denise had few female friends, but her status as "already taken" saved her from the barrage of male attention faced by many Yale women and made it easy to have comfortable friendships with guys. Denise and her boyfriend broke up in November, but by then she was well settled at Yale. The trouble began in February.

One of her professors started calling her at night. Denise had a rare single room at Yale. Caller ID and answering machines had not yet been invented. And so when the phone rang, thinking it might be her parents or friends or the new guy she was dating, Denise picked it up. "The professor would call me at night and want me to describe what nightgown I was wearing, and how soft it felt, and was it tight, and things like this," she recounted. In class, the professor gave Denise different assignments and tests than the men, and hers were filled with sexual references. Denise felt compelled to drop the course, but by then it was too late in the semester to enroll in another. She fell behind in her credits.

Denise was serving on a campus committee that spring, chaired by a Yale administrator. One day, he asked her to meet him in his office about the work the committee was doing. When she got there, he tried to rape her. On the wall were photos of his wife and children. Denise managed to escape, but afterward she continued to feel vulnerable. For the rest of the semester, she spent a lot of time at home in Puerto Rico with her family.

Like other Yale women who experienced assault and harassment, Denise did not report the incidents. Why would she? She risked being thought a liar or being tainted by the assumption that whatever happened must have been her fault: the clothes she was wearing, the signals she sent. "Nice girls did not tell what happened to them," observed a woman professor. If you told, then you must not be a very nice girl at all. And even if a woman was willing to risk such costs, there were no procedures for filing a complaint, no consequences for the perpetrators, and no language to even describe what had happened. A Yale assistant professor, a married woman who had been propositioned by a senior professor, kept the incident to herself for years. "It was very clear when something like that happened, there was nobody you could go to officially. Nobody. Officially, unofficially," she explained. The problem was not confined to Yale. Stanford's dean of women resigned in 1965 over the university's failure to do anything about faculty harassers other than request that they stop.

At Yale, when harassment occurred, "mostly you just changed advisers, changed classes, avoided professors, for whom there was no punishment if they pressured a female student," explained one woman undergraduate.   And so, for the time being, the cost of harassment by men was borne by the women they targeted.

———

Final exams for the first semester that year ended January 24, and the spring term began two days later. To some, it seemed that at least a few of the strains of being a woman student at Yale had eased. Aside from the photo shoot of Yale coeds in the January *Mademoiselle*, the media had moved on to other stories.   Word was out on which professors had made clear their dislike for coeducation, so women students knew not to sign up for their classes.   Some women had overcome the many barriers to female friendships and now had a friend or two who were women. Roommates Connie Royster and Betty Spahn were close. Shirley Daniels was grateful to have junior Vera Wells as her mentor. Lawrie Mifflin grew tight with some of the other girls who played field hockey. Kit McClure's roommate Candace went out of her way to be kind to Kit.

But at the end of January, when Elga Wasserman asked the freshmen girls on her Women's Advisory Council what was hardest about being a woman student at Yale, their answer had not changed since the fall: their "feeling of isolation from each other." Given the lopsided gender ratio, they said, their friends at Yale were almost all men. The solution seemed obvious. "Admit more women!" the girls told Wasserman. One freshman had already

Freshman girl walks alone across Yale's Old Campus, September 1969.
Photo © Yale University. Yale Events and Activities Photographs (RU 690), Manuscripts and Archives, Yale University Library.

started a petition calling on Yale to drop its thousand-man quota, but she was disheartened by her progress. Even some of Yale's women students had told her they would not sign it.

Wasserman felt just as strongly about increasing the numbers of women at Yale as the girls seated around the table, and she liked their petition idea—Brewster had said he would take student petitions seriously in his big speech on governance in September. But Wasserman warned the girls to drop any mention of reducing the number of men. Alumni whose sons were turned down as a result of fewer male spaces were "likely to blame women," she told them, and that would be "quite damaging to alumni support." And so the petition idea was set aside. Or at least that is what Wasserman thought.

After her meeting with the Women's Advisory Council, Wasserman returned to her office on Grove Street. She had a Coeducation Committee meeting the next day to prepare for. Just because she discouraged the students from challenging Brewster's thousand-man quota did not mean she was abandoning the fight to improve the lot of Yale women. She could not set herself up as Brewster's adversary, though. That would be foolish—Brewster was the most powerful man at Yale. Yet there were ways to advance the cause of Yale women that did not require publicly crossing Kingman Brewster, and Wasserman had begun to make use of them.

She went to a lot of meetings at Yale, for example, even ones she wasn't required to attend: the Master's Council, the Admissions Committee, and the Housing Committee. The main point of attending these gatherings was rarely the decisions that were made there. Wasserman had been at Yale long enough to know that the big decisions were usually made elsewhere, in discussions held quietly over dinner or lunch. No, the value of committees at Yale was the contact they provided with the other committee members. If you weren't allowed to eat lunch in the main dining room of Mory's, you needed another way to get to know the people who mattered at Yale, and the conversations that took place around the dull drip of committees' actual agendas was one way to do it. Wasserman learned things at those committee meetings as well, information that others had not bothered to tell her, and she had made sure to stock her Coeducation Committee with some of the top insiders at Yale.

The Coeducation Committee was a roster of the powerful at Yale. It included Pulitzer Prize–winning author John Hersey, Yale College Dean Georges May, Associate Provost George Langdon, student leader Kurt Schmoke, law professor Ellen Peters, and Chief of Psychiatry Bob Arnstein, who was a personal friend of Brewster's. Wasserman's position may not have carried weight at Yale, but those of her committee members did. And so she prepared for her meeting.

Wasserman's knowledge of the workings of power at Yale paid off in other ways too. Without it, she never would have succeeded in gaining approval for a women's studies course. Yale's male-focused curriculum ignored women's experiences and accomplishments, but getting a new course approved by Yale's conservative academic departments was almost impossible, especially if you weren't on the faculty. Wasserman spied an opportunity in a new program at Yale: residential college seminars. These seminars awarded regular course credit, but they bypassed the regular course approval process. Instead, they only needed the consent of a college seminar committee that was nearly half students and the blessing of a faculty committee that seemed to approve every proposal it saw. Wasserman had no trouble spotting this loophole, and in January, Yale offered its first women's studies course, Women in a Male Society, at a time when women's studies was so cutting edge that Yale was one of just ten U.S. colleges that offered it.

Wasserman also managed that spring to increase the meager budget she had been given. Money gave you the ability to be innovative and independent—but not when you barely had enough funds for an office and a secretary. So Wasserman asked Radcliffe trustee Susan Hilles, a woman with money, for a grant, and Hilles was glad to provide it. Yale's fund-raising staff was furious. "You had no right to get money from her," the men in the development office told Wasserman. "She's got to give it to us."

Sue Hilles did not see it that way. Wasserman used the grant to increase the bare-bones staff Yale had given her, launch a career advisory program for women, create a directory of women's resources at Yale, and hire five women students over the summer to advance the projects she never seemed to find time for.

And so, through the first year of coeducation, Wasserman used the toehold she had been given at Yale to build power in other ways. Outwardly, she was careful to be seen as a team player, one who publicly supported Brewster's views on women. "I would not like to see the limited number of places now available for men reduced substantially," she wrote in an article on coeducation at Yale that spring. Had she received in turn the support she sought from Brewster, she might have continued to play nicely. But Wasserman was destined to be seen in the end as "difficult," even if that was the last thing she wanted.

———

December's temperatures had loitered at a tolerable midforties, and the freshmen from California, warned by their families about

New England's harsh weather, had thought to themselves, *Is this it?* But since the students' return from Christmas break, the days had barely broke freezing, and in late January, an arctic front dropped the temperature to the single digits. It was too cold even to snow. The weather did nothing, however, to slow the long line of students who sought to meet with Phil and Lorna Sarrel at the Yale Sex Counseling Service. Every appointment with the couple had been filled since October.

Yale men, of course, had been hopeful about the possibility of having a Yale girlfriend since before the women had even arrived. That was why some of them had supported coeducation in the first place. Yet the interest in the opposite sex at Yale went both ways. Even if Yale's women students were some of the smartest undergraduates in the country, that did not mean they wanted to spend their Saturday nights in the library.

"We wanted a boyfriend," said Shirley Daniels. "It was nice to have a boyfriend." Shirley and her boyfriend, a fellow BSAY member, had been a couple almost from the start. Kit McClure met her boyfriend in the band. Betty Spahn's boyfriend was a junior high classmate of Connie Royster. Other girls began dating guys they met in their residential colleges or even one of the ones who came knocking on their door after spotting their *Old Campus* photo. It was nice to have a boyfriend, and being part of a couple brought a side benefit too. "If you had a boyfriend, then guys weren't moving in on you all the time," explained one freshman girl. Having a boyfriend brought its own challenge, though: deciding what to do about sex.

Just because reliable birth control was available did not mean that every seventeen- and eighteen-year-old girl at Yale wanted to lose her virginity. Most had grown up in families where sex before marriage was taboo. Less than 10 percent of Yale students believed that the world beyond Yale's walls saw premarital sex as acceptable, and at Yale, the double standard for sexually active students persisted: boys were studs, and girls were sluts.

A transfer from Wellesley saw what happened to the girls who were seen as promiscuous: "I heard a lot of the talk about them, and it was such trash talk, you know." In addition to concerns about reputation, some of the women had been hurt by relationships where their boyfriend had not seen sex as any kind of a commitment or where he even had another girlfriend on the side. All knew the fear of pregnancy.

There was no *Roe v. Wade* yet. Abortion was illegal in every U.S. state, and Connecticut had one of the harshest antiabortion laws in the nation. It was a felony there for a woman to seek an abortion, to allow one to be performed on her, or to try to perform one on herself. The law was enforced, with penalties of up to two years in prison. In May 1969, four months before Yale's first women undergraduates arrived, the Connecticut state legislature had voted down a bill that would have allowed abortion in cases of incest or rape.

As with birth control, Yale opted to make abortions available to undergraduates that year. But two medical professionals had to first declare that the pregnancy put the mental or physical health of the student so much at risk that her life was endangered, and the student had to know in the first place that the health service even offered abortions. Many students, apparently, did not. As one sophomore woman explained, "If you made a mistake, if you got pregnant, there were very few options."

The answer to the question of sex was an easy *no* then, except for the fact that it seemed an obvious *yes*. "There was this feeling that you should lose your virginity, and it was the sexual revolution and all that," said a freshman girl from New Jersey. In the midst of all that confusion, however, at least the Sarrels were there for Yale students to talk to.

Being able to talk to the Sarrels was "remarkable," said a freshman girl from Washington, DC. "You were nineteen years old and trying to understand your sexuality and there were these two people who were willing to talk to you about it."

The Sex Counseling Service gave students a place to ask questions about forbidden topics like orgasms and being gay. Students could learn about men's and women's anatomy and other basics no one had taught them. But the discussion went beyond just the facts. "We are trying to help [students] think through the meaning of their sexuality and sexual behavior for themselves and their partners," Phil Sarrel told the *Yale Daily News*. "We don't preach."

In an era when many still thought of sex as something men did to women, the respect that Phil and Lorna Sarrel showed for the values and desires of each student they met with was revolutionary. They were trying to shift the rules of sex itself and ensure that it was based on a foundation of good communication and trust. Yet the numbers of students the Sarrels could see were limited—the Sex Counseling Service was only open one day a week—and the demand for good information and open discussion about sex was pressing. In February came a solution. For the first time, the Sarrels offered the class that Phil Sarrel had bargained for when Bob Arnstein first called him about coming to Yale: Topics in Human Sexuality.

The course carried no credit. It did not show up on students' transcripts. The only committee whose approval it needed was Wasserman's. But after the notice on the course went out, 1,200 students signed up for it—one quarter of the undergraduate student body. Topics in Human Sexuality was the largest course that had ever been taught at Yale College. "It was the hot ticket on campus," said one freshman woman. "It seemed like everybody was taking the course."

As with their sex counseling service, the Sarrels took an unorthodox approach to the class. Back in October, they had formed a student committee to work with them as partners in creating and running the course. Such a collegial relationship between adults and undergraduates was unusual at Yale. As one of the sophomore women who joined the committee explained, "You were more accustomed to [being] in a class and a professor who has been there for many years, often male, often white, is lecturing. And he's the expert. And you are taking your notes, and writing your papers, and giving in your exams."

The Human Sexuality Committee, as the Sarrels' student group came to be called, was different.   It included fifteen undergraduates, half of them women, and six graduate students. The committee met at the Sarrels' home, a beautiful house in the woods six miles west of New Haven. The Sarrels involved the students so deeply in the course planning that when the initial announcement about the course went out to Yale undergraduates announcing that Topics in Human Sexuality would be taught in the spring, it was signed not by the Sarrels but by the students on the Human Sexuality Committee.

The class combined lectures, films, and small-group discussions, and it covered birth control, abortion and its alternatives, interpersonal relationships, orgasms, sexual response, pregnancy, birth, venereal disease, and homosexuality. For some students, the scope may have been more than they bargained for. Not every student at Yale was ready to see a film of a couple giving birth to a baby or listen to a discussion about masturbation. A *Yale Daily News* spoof issue the following year announced that Phil Sarrel was writing a memoir titled, *Everything You Don't Want to Know About Sex…But I'll Tell You Anyway.*

To enroll in the class, students had to fill out an anonymous questionnaire and pay five dollars, which created a fund for the Human Sexuality Committee's future projects. Scholarships were available for those who couldn't afford the five-dollar fee, but the rule on completing the questionnaire was unbending. At the first class, students who had not finished filling theirs out stood outside the door, hurriedly scribbling their answers. "True or False?" asked the questionnaire, and one hundred statements followed.

#26.   There was as much premarital coitus a generation ago as there is today.

#45.   A man's sexual performance is related to the size of his penis.

#91.   In general, women retain their sex drive longer than men.

Even to consider the questions challenged the truths with which students arrived. "Rate the following views from strongly agree to strongly disagree," the questionnaire said, and sixty-four questions were listed.

#6.   Masturbation is generally unhealthy.

#51.   Mouth-genital contact should be regarded as an acceptable form of erotic play.

#52.   Abortion is murder.

#60.   Abortion should be permitted whenever desired by the mother.

Among the most challenging questions were those related to gay men and women:

#4.   Strong legal measures should be taken against
        homosexual acts.

#53.   Homosexual behavior in private between consenting
        adults should not be punished by the law.

The sexual revolution may have loosened attitudes about sex
between young men and women, but in 1970, gay sex was still
a felony in every state but Illinois.   The American Psychiatric
Association classed homosexuality as a mental disorder,   and the
bestselling *Everything You Ever Wanted to Know About Sex* informed
readers that gay men and women were a "sexual aberration."
Author David Reuben, a doctor who featured his "MD" promi-
nently on the book's cover, devoted an entire twenty-two-page
chapter to gay men. "Homosexuals," Dr. Reuben informed his readers, "thrive on danger"   and were prone to inserting "pens, pencils,
lipsticks, combs, pop bottles, and ladies electric shavers" up their
anuses.   "Female homosexuality" was dealt with in three pages as
part of the chapter on prostitution. "The majority of prostitutes are
female homosexuals," Dr. Reuben explained.

At Yale, the topic of gay men and women "was all very hush-
hush," said one undergraduate woman. In some corners, it was safe
for gay students to come out to straight ones. There was no stigma
in the arts community. "We all knew who was and who wasn't," said
Connie Royster. "It was one big family... We were very, very tight.
Very tight."   But elsewhere at Yale, it wasn't so easy.

There was a "marked *fear* of homosexuality at Yale," observed
two women graduate students.   Being gay at Yale is "painful and
difficult," said one gay man, and few women students could even
think of a classmate they knew who was a lesbian. As Kit McClure
said, "To find a gay woman at Yale, it would be harder than finding

the black women." The gay women were there, of course, but the climate made sure most kept that identity hidden. Many aspects of sex at Yale went unseen in 1970. The presence of gay students was just one of them.

SIX

Margaret Asks for the Mic

THE STAFF OF THE YALE ALUMNI OFFICE WAS QUITE pleased with itself. The annual midwinter Alumni Day would take place on Saturday, February 21, and this year's event looked to be the most successful one yet. More than one thousand alumni and wives were coming, the largest turnout ever. The group would be fêted at a white-tablecloth lunch in the imposing University Dining Hall. Kingman Brewster would speak. Awards would be given. And then the gathering would move next door to Woolsey Hall for the grand finale: the dedication of the new Becton Engineering and Applied Science Center, during which Brewster would be handed the keys to the building by the man who had donated the money for it.

Henry P. Becton was the perfect alumnus: loyal to Yale, remarkably generous, and very, very rich. In 1947, ten years after graduating from Yale, Becton and his partner, Fairleigh Dickinson, took over the medical instruments company that their fathers had founded. By 1970, Becton Dickinson had reached the Fortune 500. Annual revenues topped $200 million, with profits of more than $16 million a year. Becton's loyalty to Yale ran deep. He had sung in the Whiffenpoofs and had even written the words to "Sons of Eli"—not one of the more well-known odes to Yale men but in the official Yale songbook nonetheless. And Henry Becton had two children at Yale: Jeffery, a senior, and Cynthia, one of the 230 women freshmen. The men in the Yale Alumni Office would have been wise to ask Cynthia Becton about how things were going at Yale. But in all of their planning, this was one step they forgot.

On Friday, the day before the alumni event, Cynthia and her roommate Margaret Coon sat down over lunch with a group of their friends. The topic of Yale's limit on women undergraduates arose and, with it, the challenges caused by the resulting seven-to-one ratio. Margaret had attended a coed public high school, where being a girl was certainly a part of who you were but not the only thing others saw when you walked in a room. Yale's version of coeducation was nothing like that. Margaret resented being asked for "the woman's opinion" in class and disliked how Yale had continued to bring in busloads of girls from other colleges every weekend. Other women at the table added their stories. The men sitting with them didn't much like the skewed ratio at Yale either, but so far, no one had come up with a good way to change it.

Yale had come a long way already from the village of men it had once been. The first women undergraduates had brought change just by the fact of their being there: raising their hands to ask questions at the end of lectures, titrating solutions in the chemistry lab, racing after field hockey balls hit across the Old Campus. Since 1701, Yale had banned women from such spaces, and now here they were, pushing aside the barriers that had long defined women at Yale as somehow less than men. Not every barrier, however, melted away just through the presence of women. Sometimes more direct action was needed.

One of the students sitting at the lunch table with Margaret and Cynthia threw out an idea. What about the big alumni lunch at Yale the following day? What if the students did something there? Excitement coursed around the table. Most students at Yale assumed that the alumni were the main opponents to admitting more women. If only the alumni would drop their insistence on the thousand-man quota, the students reasoned, then Brewster and the Yale Corporation would be free to increase the pace of coeducation. The alumni lunch was the perfect opportunity to present the case for change. By the end of the day, Margaret and Cynthia had sketched out a plan for their protest, assembled a team to carry it out, and chosen a name for their group: Women and Men for a Better Yale. While the group was coed, only the women would take part in the protest. That way the alumni could see for themselves some of the coeds they had been hearing so much about.

At 1:00 p.m. the next day, a throng of business-suited alumni, their wives in cocktail dresses beside them, entered the University Dining Hall and took their seats for the alumni lunch. The guests began eating and chatting among themselves. None of them noticed when one of the bursary students who had served them their lunch opened a locked door behind the podium and let the girls in. Forty girls, all freshmen like Margaret and Cynthia, entered the dining hall. Some of them were carrying signs: "End Women's Oppression" and "Women Up from Under." While most of them wore jeans, Margaret had put on a dress and pulled her long hair back neatly with a bow. She ascended the podium where Kingman Brewster and some other dignitaries were seated and, using the calmest voice she could muster, asked Brewster a question: "Mr. Brewster, I'd like to address the alumni for a few minutes. Would that be OK?"

Brewster was surprised. Alumni lunches were typically dull and predictable affairs, not the site of impromptu protests, but Brewster was an innately gracious man, and he was open to hearing student views. He gestured Margaret over to the microphone, and she stepped up and looked out at the crowd. Although she had acted in high school and been the valedictorian for her class of sixty-seven students, she had never spoken before to an audience this large or one so potentially hostile. Margaret grasped the long stem of the microphone with her right hand, glanced down at her notes in her left, and began to speak.

"There are not enough of us," Margaret told the alumni. "We are scattered in tiny groups." As Margaret spoke, the other freshmen girls circulated silently among the rectangular banquet tables where the alumni and their wives were seated, handing out leaflets about the challenges caused by their small numbers. Kit McClure was among the protesters. The night before, when word spread through Vanderbilt Hall about the action planned by Women and Men for a Better Yale, Kit did not hesitate to say she would be there. At the rate Yale was going, women students would still be vastly outnumbered by the time she graduated, and no one was even talking about enacting sex-blind admissions. Planning the protest was one thing, however. Actually doing it, Kit found, was scary. It was intimidating walking through that huge room filled with important men, knowing you weren't supposed to be there.

Margaret spoke for three minutes. "To accept 1,000 'male leaders' while accepting only 250 women is not only sexual discrimination but bad education," she said, and then she presented the group's solution: "Limit the class of 1974 to 1,000 people…700 men and 300 women." Margaret asked that Yale agree to the group's proposal by the end of the week, eliciting scattered laughter from the crowd and a chuckle from Brewster. That was not how things worked at Yale.

Margaret stepped down from the podium, and the student protesters left the University Dining Hall as quickly as they had entered.

Kit had hoped that Brewster would make the case to alumni for equal opportunity for women, but that was not his intention. Before commencing his prepared remarks on the economics of running Yale, Brewster responded to Margaret Coon's comments. He started by seeking the audience's sympathy, noting that he had suffered "harassment" of late not only from students but also from alumni. Brewster had been stung in particular by a recent book, *The Rape of Yale*, authored by a Yale alumnus who charged that Brewster was a radical leftist. "After having been wedded to Yale for seven years," Brewster told the crowd, "it's a little hard to be accused of rape by your father-in-law."

Brewster was right to be concerned about the alumni. Some, like the author of *The Rape of Yale*, thought Brewster should keep his views on civil rights and Vietnam to himself. Many alumni were angry that their children were no longer getting into Yale as easily as they once had, now that Brewster and Inky Clark had reduced the alumni child preference in admissions. But while many Yale students assumed otherwise, there had been no grand bargain between Brewster and alumni that gave him coeducation in return for holding firm on the number of undergraduate men. The final decision had been so hastily made that the alumni were barely consulted. Some may have worried that alumni who became angry over the admission of women would stop donating to Yale, but in the first year of coeducation, alumni donations topped $4.6 million, a record high. Brewster's problem with alumni over coeducation, if there was one at all, was entirely of his own making.

The week after Yale announced it was going coed, Brewster promised a Yale Alumni Fund audience that Yale's coeducation decision would not impact the number of men admitted to Yale. Two months later, he repeated that promise to a different Alumni Fund audience. And at the alumni luncheon where Margaret Coon had just spoken, Brewster added a new reason Yale could not go below its thousand male leaders: "accountability to alumni." The promise may have been made unnecessarily, but it was not one Brewster was prepared to renege on. Brewster then repeated his standard line on Yale's mission. Coeducation has been "a terrific success," he observed, but Yale had an "educational responsibility to the nation." It could not consider any step that would "increase the number of women at Yale at the expense of the number of men."

As for the protesters themselves, Brewster dismissed the girls as a "much too small band of women undergraduates." But those who had read the January editorial of the *Yale Daily News*—and many alumni subscribed to the publication—knew that it was not only women who were calling for change. The name and membership of Women and Men for a Better Yale made that clear too. Yet Brewster also dismissed the Yale men who supported a more equal ratio: "We can't give them women as a new gesture every year." His comments on coeducation complete, Brewster returned to his speech on Yale's finances. When he concluded his remarks, the alumni and wives rose in a standing ovation, and then the room stood together and sang Yale's anthem, "Bright College Years," pulling out their handkerchiefs and, as traditional, waving them overhead for the closing words: "For God, for country, and for Yale."

———

Shirley Daniels was not at the protest. None of the sophomore or junior women were—the freshmen had organized it. But even had she known about it, it was unlikely Shirley would have been there. The lines of race that often divided Yale students' social lives ran through much of Yale's student activism as well. At the start of the alumni lunch protest, a few black women freshmen had entered the University Dining Hall with their white classmates, but they didn't like what Margaret Coon said and left early. "We listened to the speaker, but it sounded more like an anti-male than a pro-female kind of thing, so we left," one of them explained later. Any rifts over matters of gender threatened the unity of Yale's two hundred black undergraduates, almost all of whom were members of the Black Student Alliance at Yale (BSAY). And besides, black women at Yale did not see their male classmates as the problem.

"Women felt respected in the BSAY," said Los Angeles premed student Carol Storey. The group "felt unified by ethnicity more than gender-divided." White women students did not often experience that same respect in the male-led white activist groups that they joined. There, women "weren't given a speaking role," said junior Judy Berkan, who was involved in Students for a Democratic Society (SDS) and a number of leftist ad hoc initiatives. "We were the ones who licked the envelopes." Betty Spahn felt the same way about her experience in the Wright Hall sit-in. No one liked to feel like they were invisible.

At Afro-Am House, black women did not experience that type of silencing. During the BSAY strategy sessions, the men listened to Shirley and the other black women. Sometimes discussions grew heated. Shirley did not shy from speaking her mind. And unlike in many of the white-led student organizations, women in the BSAY quickly rose to positions of power. At the end of the first semester, Shirley and her classmate Sheila Jackson were elected to two of the BSAY's top leadership positions: Sheila became the BSAY treasurer, and Shirley became chair of the BSAY's largest committee, the Recruitment, Tutorial, and Counseling Committee, which ran the group's massive effort to recruit black students to Yale and ensure they graduated once they got there. During Christmas and spring breaks, Yale's black undergraduates traveled to black high schools in a dozen different cities, from Los Angeles to Detroit, Little Rock, and Philadelphia. Yale paid the costs of the airfare, food, and local transportation; students stayed with family or friends. In addition to coordinating all those student visits, Shirley managed an annual budget of $10,000 and met regularly with Associate Director of Admissions W. C. Robinson, one of Yale's few black administrators, and with Sam Chauncey, whom Brewster had charged with increasing Yale's enrollment of black students. Shirley also managed the BSAY's financial aid initiatives and its counseling and tutoring program for incoming students. It was exactly the job she had wanted when it came time that winter for the BSAY elections.

Yet the BSAY's priorities did not encompass many of the issues that affected black women. On those, the black women students needed to act on their own. The attempt to have the forty black women meet regularly as a group had not lasted much more than a month, but at the Afro-Am House, the women sophomores and juniors had kept talking. How did they fit in American society? What did it mean to be a black woman? The discussion was important, Shirley observed, "because a lot of times, black women don't think about who they are and what they are, and what they need to do. We basically serve everybody else in the world."

Shirley began looking into women's issues on her own, and one thing stood out from her research: "There was a kind of totem pole situation, and black women were always at the bottom of it." U.S. wage statistics put numbers to Shirley's statement. The median annual salary of white men was $7,900 in 1970. That fell to $5,300 for black men, $4,600 for white women, and $3,500 for black women—less than half that of the white men.

Some of the men in the BSAY argued that black women were getting jobs for which black men weren't hired. "Look," said Shirley. "I've looked at the statistics and that's not true. We are still earning less than you are. We are still not able to get the jobs that you are able to get as a black man." *Time* magazine did not disagree. "Black women are the lowest-paid members of the work force," it reported. "A black man with an eighth-grade education has a higher median income than a black woman with some college education." As Shirley observed, "That wasn't a conversation men liked to hear."

Shirley's friend Vera Wells joined those discussions, but she was more focused on a different problem at Yale, the absence of black women faculty. Her first two years in college had been far different. Before transferring to Yale, Vera had attended Howard University, a historically black college in Washington, DC. But the summer after her sophomore year, Vera married a Howard Law School graduate and moved with him to New Haven before getting her bachelor's degree. Vera's mother, a Pittsburgh beautician, was so disappointed. Vera was the first in her family to ever attend college, and now she was not going to graduate. A few months after Vera and her new husband moved to New Haven, however, Yale announced it was going coed and Vera got her second chance. The following September, she became one of the seven black women in the junior class.

At Yale, Vera was shocked by how white the faculty was. "It just seemed so strange to me," said Vera. Of the hundreds of faculty members and administrators at Yale, only five were black women—two at the nursing school, two at the Yale Child Study Center, and one at the drama school—and none of them taught undergraduates. Black women were also missing from Yale's curriculum. The syllabus for the new women's studies course did not mention black women, and the classes offered by Yale's Afro-American studies program focused almost exclusively on men. And so Vera wondered: Why couldn't they have a course at Yale that focused on black women and hire a black woman professor to teach it?

When Vera told the Afro-American studies program director about her idea, he said he had no room in his budget for a course on black women but suggested she try getting the course approved as a residential college seminar, the same path Wasserman had used to slip Women in a Male Society into the curriculum. Vera talked to her classmate Cecelia McDaniel about what she had learned about starting a class on black women. "This is something we should do," the two students agreed. Over the spring, Vera and Cecelia put together a proposal for a class that would study black women leaders from Nzinga and Nefertiti through Sojourner Truth and Rosa Parks. Sylvia Boone, one of Cecelia's former professors at Hunter College in New York, would teach it—there was no one at Yale who knew the material. When the class was approved, Vera was thrilled. The Black Woman: Yesterday and Today would be offered the following fall.

———

News of the alumni lunch protest organized by Women and Men for a Better Yale spread rapidly through the campus. "It was a very 'un-Yale' thing to do," observed two graduate school women, and thus it was a story all the more amazing in the telling. *Did you hear?* went the word through the dining halls. *Did you hear what a group of freshman girls just did?*

Elga Wasserman was horrified when she first heard what had happened. Increasing the numbers of women students at Yale was critical. Wasserman had known that for months. But this type of action—interrupting the winter alumni gathering of all things—risked creating a backlash. You had to be careful when trying to change a place as set in its ways as Yale, thought Wasserman. You couldn't push too hard. She had made just that point the previous month when she warned the petition enthusiasts on her Women's Advisory Council against suggesting that Yale reduce the number of male students. And now this. Even those sympathetic to the girls' cause could be turned away by their methods. "They should have taken this matter up quietly with the president, rather than making a fuss in here," one alumnus complained. *Exactly*, thought Wasserman. If change became associated with "radical elements," as Wasserman called them, even the incremental progress she hoped for would be threatened.

To describe Jenkintown High School valedictorian Margaret Coon, in her dress and neatly bowed ponytail, as a "radical element" would seem a far stretch indeed. A three-minute interruption of an alumni event may have created some discomfort for Brewster, but he had always been quick on his feet, and the girls had left quietly. "We were not bomb throwers," explained one male member of Women and Men for a Better Yale. "All of us were trying to work within the system rather than blow it up." Most people, however, had learned about the protest from accounts in the press, and the *New York Times* had done the students no favors in the way it portrayed the event.

The *Times* ran the protest right on the front page of its Sunday edition. "About 40 of Yale University's new coeds invaded a quiet Alumni Day luncheon…and, with clenched fists and placards, protested the ratio of women to men," the article began. "One coed strode to the dais, seized a microphone and lectured the 1,000 stunned guests." Margaret Coon barely recognized herself in the description.

Other papers picked up the story, including the news service of the *Los Angeles Times*. The *New York Post* sent a photographer, who posed Cynthia Becton and Margaret in front of the door to their Vanderbilt entryway. By the time the story ran in Spokane the following week, Margaret was being described as both a "militant" and a "pretty freshman." Margaret's father saved the *New York Times* article and showed it to friends. He was proud of her actions. But for Margaret, the experience of being splashed across the front page of the *Times* at age eighteen was a bit overwhelming.

The alumni seemed far less upset about the student protesters than the *New York Times* was. "Their demands are reasonable," observed one Yale graduate who had been at the lunch, and at the end of Margaret's remarks, the alumni had applauded. Many saw the new women students as part of the Yale family—both figuratively and literally. Henry Becton was not the only one with a daughter at Yale. Becton himself had not been bothered in the least by the protest, and he stopped by Cynthia and Margaret's room in Vanderbilt Hall afterward. "He was a very nice man," Margaret said. "He seemed amused by the whole thing."

Yet Wasserman's concerns about the alumni reaction were not totally unfounded. "I think it was a bit presumptuous of them," said a member of the class of 1926. "You invite them here, and now they want to take over the place." One of the men said something awful to Kit McClure, who, of course, was still just a teenager: "No wonder you're feminists—you're so ugly." But more shocking than the alumnus's response were the remarks of a few of the girls' male classmates: "Women's liberation? What you need is a good lay." Kit wrote down the comments in careful cursive in her diary. And then she added at the end, "The reactions disturbed and surprised me."

———

One week after the alumni lunch protest, a graduate student dressed as the Statue of Liberty entered the Berkeley College dining hall at lunchtime, accompanied by six other graduate school women and Kit McClure. The Free Women Conference would be held at Yale Law School the following weekend, and conference organizers wanted to make sure that every Yale undergraduate knew about it. Kit played a musical fanfare on her trombone as the group entered the dining hall, and then, with all eyes now on them, the women performed a short skit. "Take her torch and give her a mop!" they shouted, pretending to be male chauvinists harassing Ms. Liberty. "Take her crown and give her some curlers!" Some of the Berkeley College students applauded. Others heckled. Kit and the other women handed out leaflets with details on the Free Women Conference, and then they moved along to the lunch crowd at the next residential college to repeat their performance.

Two days later, the conference began. Thursday night featured a showing of feminist films, but it was Friday night's two keynote speakers who drew the biggest crowd—about five hundred women and a noticeable contingent of men. Radical feminists Kate Millett and Naomi Weisstein were scheduled to give speeches, and everyone wanted to hear them. Millett went first. She was a few weeks away from defending her Columbia University dissertation, which would be published later that year

Yale's Free Women Conference, February 1970.
From left to right: Kit McClure, Naomi Weisstein, Kate Millett, and Risa Tobis, the woman who first handed Kit the flyer about the conference. "Up from Under" is written on the chalkboard behind them.
Photo © Virginia Blaisdell.

as *Sexual Politics* and, with its application of Marxist theory to gender politics, would become a seminal work of second-wave feminism. A current of excitement ran through the law school auditorium as Kate Millett stepped up to the stage, and she delivered a message far bolder than that which Betty Friedan had given in a speech at Yale earlier that month. Women needed to go further than just amending a few laws, Millett told the crowd before her. Attitudes, assumptions, systems, and power structures all needed to change. But there was hope. "We have 53 percent— the most powerful political force in the nation!" she declared. "Right on!" came the shouts from the crowd.

Once the applause for Kate Millett died down, Naomi Weisstein took her turn at the podium. Weisstein lived in Chicago and was less well known than New York–based Millett, but the personal story she shared that night resonated with many of the women in the audience, particularly the graduate school students. Weisstein was twenty-nine years old with a PhD in psychology from Harvard and a faculty position at Loyola University in Chicago. That night in New Haven, she told the audience about her goal of an academic career and the gender discrimination that had stalled her: a Harvard library that banned women from entering lest they distract the men; a Harvard professor who prohibited her from using the research equipment she needed because, being a woman, she might break it; nepotism rules at the University of Chicago that kept her off the faculty since her husband taught history there. Weisstein had thought she could get where she wanted by working harder, being smarter. But individual credentials, no matter how impeccable, she argued, were not enough for a woman. Weisstein's message was clear, wrote a woman graduate student afterward: "Changes in social structures require a social movement." You couldn't do it alone.

Few women at Yale would have agreed with her. Individual accomplishment had worked well for each of them so far. They were at Yale, weren't they? "To me, what you do is you go to classes, you participate, you do well, you impress people with how great it is to have women around and women as equals. That's what you do," said one sophomore woman.

Field hockey player Lawrie Mifflin saw no need to get involved in a women's group either. True, the absence of any Yale sports teams for women had surprised her, but she was already working to change that. *Just make your way*, Lawrie thought. *Just make your way and make your mark in your subject area, in your sports, in the* Yale

Daily News. *Whatever is your thing, do your thing and show that you're good at it.*

The idea of challenging the rules with which Yale began coeducation did not even occur to most women. They simply felt lucky to be there. Being accepted at Yale "felt like a generosity," said Los Angeles premed student Carol Storey. "The first year…women felt so grateful," observed Elga Wasserman. "They felt like guests invited to be in a fancy home, and weren't we great to have them here." Some girls were just hunkered down in survival mode. *Let me just get through this in one piece and get my degree*, one freshman girl would say to herself on the days that were particularly hard.

Yale women were all so different anyway. It was hard to imagine how they might join together to bring about change. They had grown up in different places. They studied different subjects. They lived in different residential colleges and would graduate in different years. They came from families with different incomes, different religions, and different politics. "We were all as different as any other group of heterogeneous people," said a freshman who had grown up in Kansas. Her father was a mailman who hadn't finished high school, her mother a homemaker. What did she have in common with the boarding school girls from the Northeast? All that bound them together was their experience of being women at Yale. For a few students, however, that shared experience of being a Yale woman was enough.

The Free Women Conference sold out all its women's lib buttons and literature and had to send away as far as Baltimore for new supplies. It introduced like-minded women to each other and exposed Yale students to the ideas and goals of feminism. It produced a two-page document, "Unofficial Proposals for Equality," that listed priorities for action:

WHY NOT DEMAND a 50–50 undergraduate admissions policy beginning with the Class of 1974?

WHY NOT DEMAND a department of women's studies, designed, administered and taught by women?

WHY NOT DEMAND that Yale stop separate job categories for men and women and inequities between men's and women's wages?

WHY NOT DEMAND that Yale and Yale New Haven Hospital openly demand an end to Connecticut's anti-abortion law?

WHY NOT DEMAND that the percentage of full-time women faculty be increased until it at least equals the percentage of women students at Yale?

For Kit McClure, the Free Women Conference could not have gone any better. Kit met other feminist activists, who gave her their phone numbers so that she could get in touch later, and at the Saturday session, the conference organizers pointed Kit out to the crowd and announced that she wanted to start an all-women's rock band. Afterward, three women came up to Kit. Did she want to join their band? They'd had one practice already, and they even had a name for the group: the New Haven Women's Liberation Rock Band. Virginia Blaisdell played French horn, Jennifer Abod sang and played tambourine, and Judy Miller, whose idea it all was in the first place, had bought a used drum set and was taking lessons on how to play from Virginia's husband. A trombone player would be terrific. Kit answered yes to their offer, of course. The New Haven Women's Liberation Rock Band had gained one very dedicated musician, and Kit McClure was that much closer to achieving the goal she had brought with her to Yale.

———

For those who attended the Free Women Conference, the weekend brought a rush of hope and excitement. Yet the postconference euphoria was tempered somewhat by an event that occurred on the conference's last day, an early reminder that change would not be won quickly or easily. The schedule called for a final gathering on Sunday afternoon in which women and men could "come and hash things out together." When participants arrived at the law school for their final session, they found six hundred people, mostly students, waiting in line for a different event. The Yale Law School Film Society was hosting another porn festival, and it had scheduled this year's affair to overlap with the Free Women Conference. The Russ Meyer Film Festival featured six movies by the national leading producer of low-budget sex films. "Russ Meyer is coming: Hold onto your popcorn," read the advertising posters papered all over New Haven.

The Film Society's decision to hold the porn fest at the same time as the Free Women Conference, just like the timing of its previous porn fest on the first day of Coeducation Week, was intended as a hilarious joke. *Women's lib conference? We'll show them.* The showing of Russ Meyer skin flicks was granted a small measure of respectability by questions being debated nationally at the time: Was pornogra-phy art, or was it just smut? Should it be celebrated as an aspect of free speech or banned for its obscenity? Such philosophical debates, however, had little to do with why six hundred guys, and a few women as well, were waiting in line at the law school that Sunday.

Russ Meyer flew in from Hollywood for the festival along with two of his starlets, "beautiful, bosomy broads," according to one Yale student writer. Being the focus of a film festival at Yale lent cred-ibility to Meyer's pornography, and he walked Yale's campus trailed by a bevy of East Coast reporters and a young *Chicago Sun Times* film critic, Roger Ebert. The crowd that filled the law school auditorium that Sunday was treated to a Russ Meyer double feature: *Cherry, Harry, and Raquel* and *Faster Pussy Cat, Kill! Kill!*, the latter of which starred "three go-go Watusi dancers [who] embark on a whirlwind tour of violence and seduction." Russ Meyer was "the last great undiscovered talent" in American cinema, Roger Ebert proclaimed in his introductory remarks to the audience.

A few days later, Russ Meyer and his "bosomy broads" were back home in Hollywood, his talents, for the moment, forgotten. Conversation at Yale instead revolved around the feminist activ-ism that the campus had witnessed over the previous weeks. For the first time since the start of coeducation, Yale's discrimination against women nudged aside Vietnam and race as the topic of the moment. In less than a month, Yale had witnessed the freshmen women's alumni lunch protest, the efforts of Women and Men for a Better Yale, and now the Free Women Conference.

Its interest sparked by all this activity, the *Yale Daily News* ran a long, front-page story that explained the U.S. women's movement to those who had not yet been following it. A photo of Kate Millett ran alongside the article, a rare instance of a woman on the *News*' front page. Admissions Dean Inky Clark, who by then had announced he was leaving Yale to become headmaster of a New York prep school, went public with his own views on how coeducation was going at Yale. Yale's quota limiting women was "not healthy," Clark told the *Yale Alumni Magazine*; it should be abolished. And in every Yale College dining hall, Women and Men for a Better Yale circulated a petition that called on Yale to adopt sex-blind admissions.

The issue came to a head at the Yale Corporation meeting on March 7, 1970. Women and Men for a Better Yale presented its petition, which had been signed by 1,900 students, more than a third of the student body. Corporation members met with a delegation from the group and declared themselves impressed with the students' arguments. And then the fifteen Yale trustees, each one a white man, voted to leave Yale's gender quotas unchanged.

"I had thought that an issue like admitting men and women to Yale College on an equal basis would not be considered extremely threatening to Yale," Kit McClure wrote in her diary. "I was mistaken."

SEVEN

The Sisterhood

AFTER THE MARCH 7 VOTE OF THE YALE CORPORATION to leave Yale's admissions quotas in place, Women and Men for a Better Yale disbanded. Yale activist groups in those years were often short-lived, forming around one event or another—such as the March on Washington or a political campaign—and then dissolving right afterward. New groups emerged and then folded within a matter of weeks. The Graduate Women's Alliance and the Yale Law Women, however, had not succumbed to this pattern and were both meeting regularly to discuss the discrimination they saw against women at Yale and what they might do to stop it. Halfway through the second semester, no similar group yet existed for undergraduate women, but one week after the Corporation vote, Kit McClure and Betty Spahn decided to change that. "Meeting for Yale Women," read their fliers. "Vanderbilt Lounge. Monday evening. 7:30." Betty got out her staple gun, and by the end of the day, the notices were posted all over campus.

It was unusual at Yale for a freshman and a sophomore woman to be friends, particularly when, like Kit and Betty, they were in different residential colleges and had not gone to the same high school or even grown up in the same part of the country. But Betty and Kit had one thing in common: their dismay at how women were treated at Yale. Before the alumni lunch protest, Kit had assumed that Kingman Brewster would be an ally of Yale's women students, but now she knew otherwise. If change was going to happen, Kit decided, undergraduate women had to organize and push for it themselves. Some of the New Haven feminists whom Kit had met at the Free Women Conference urged her to start a women's group for Yale undergraduates. "We'll walk you through it," they promised, but they couldn't do it for her.

Betty had not gone to the Free Women Conference, and she was not involved with New Haven Women's Liberation like Kit was. But Betty was tired of going unheard at the men's political meetings she went to and she missed being with other women. It was exhausting being with just men all the time. She and Kit met through the left-wing circles at Yale that both frequented, and the two began talking about the problems they saw. Betty liked Kit's style. Kit was "just tough as nails," said Betty, "and outspoken," and Betty loved this idea of starting a women's group. And so she pulled out her staple gun. Neither Betty nor Kit was certain that anyone else would show up to their meeting, but "What did they have to lose?" asked Betty. If no one else came, Betty and Kit would be no worse off than they already were.

On Monday night at 7:30 p.m., Betty and Kit met in the lounge in Vanderbilt Hall. Other women soon joined them: a freshman who had been missing the company of other girls, another who had collected signatures for the petition on sex-blind admissions, and Judy Berkan, the junior who was as fed up as Betty with the way she was treated in Yale's white radical groups. Judy had attended the Free

Women Conference in February. It gave her "this incredible lift," Judy said. "It was the first time since I had been at Yale that I had really spoken to girls." Maybe this group of women in Vanderbilt Hall could provide the same feeling.

By the time the meeting began, nearly twenty students had gathered in the Vanderbilt lounge. They sat together on the sofas and armchairs; some took a seat on the carpet. Almost none of them had met before. Betty and Kit began by having each girl introduce herself and say why she had come to the meeting. Freshman Marie Rudden was there because she was tired of dealing on her own with the challenge of being a Yale woman. "There was such a feeling of being curiosities, of feeling like you weren't really part of the college," she explained. "It seemed like it would be really helpful to be able to talk about that." Others voiced similar reasons.

The girls in the Vanderbilt lounge included freshmen, sophomores, and juniors. They came from a range of Yale colleges: Berkeley, Calhoun, Morse, Pierson, Silliman, and Trumbull. Having twenty women in a room together, crossing so many of the divisions that had separated them so far, was remarkable, yet the twenty in the room that night were just a tiny slice of Yale's 575 women students. From the freshman class, Kit McClure was present but not Lawrie Mifflin; of the sophomores, Betty Spahn came but not Connie Royster or Shirley Daniels.

No black women had come to the meeting. None would for another three years. All of the students in the Vanderbilt lounge were white save for Anna Tsing Lowenhaupt, whose mother was Chinese and father was white. The group's whiteness was predictable, at least at 1970s Yale. Statistically, a gathering this size would have included 1.5 black women if it had reflected Yale's racial makeup, but even so, "I'm not sure we had anything to offer black women," said Betty.

Shirley Daniels and her friend Vera Wells were committed to pressing the concerns of women too, but this activism took place on their own terms, not as part of a group that white women had founded.

After the introductions were over, the students began talking about what to do next. Few of them knew much about the women's liberation movement. Kit may have joined a women's group when she was in high school, but the word *feminism* was new to Betty, as it was to almost all of the others. There was one freshman at the meeting, though, a dark-haired girl from Manhattan, who was in touch with a radical feminist group in New York, the Redstockings. She had learned from them a process that she thought the Yale women should try. It was called "consciousness-raising."

New Haven Women's Liberation had been holding consciousness-raising sessions for a few months by then, and the women's group that Kit attended in high school had used consciousness-raising too. Women sat together in groups of a dozen or so and shared stories of experiences like being in high school, and "the importance of having boobs, and what it was like to be smart, and…whether you could major in math or science." From their individual stories, patterns emerged as women realized that what they had thought was a personal problem was in fact something that other women had experienced too. The title of UC Berkeley's feminist news-letter summed it up: *It Ain't Me, Babe.* Being in a consciousness-raising group changed how women saw the world. One day, a woman in the New Haven group looked at the front page of the newspaper and realized that it did not contain a single woman's name. "I had been reading the newspaper all my life," she said, "and I had never noticed that."

The women students in the Vanderbilt lounge agreed to try consciousness-raising and to meet the following week. "We need a name," said one student. Another suggested "The Sisterhood." Everyone in the room was enthusiastic. And so it was decided. The Yale Sisterhood had begun.

———

Ever since January, Yale's limit on the number of women under-graduates had been under fire—from the *Yale Daily News*, from Wasserman's Student Advisory Council, from the Free Women Conference, from Women and Men for a Better Yale, and from the 1,900 Yale students who had signed the petition calling for an end to Yale's gender quotas. Yet throughout this rising debate, one significant group had remained silent: the faculty. Didn't Yale's admissions quotas concern them too? Apparently not, at least if the views expressed in a 1962 faculty report still held true. If Yale admit-ted women students, the report had declared, "there should be no reduction in the number of men," a position that preceded Kingman Brewster's first public statement on this topic by six years.

Whether the faculty had changed its stance since then, no one knew, since the dean had never placed the question on the faculty meeting agenda again, and no Yale professor had spoken out against the practice individually. On March 26, that status quo changed when Assistant Professor Keith Thomson sent a letter to Brewster that put at least one faculty member on record as opposing Yale's policy.

Thomson was one of the ten faculty members on Yale's Admissions Committee, the group that decided which students got into Yale and which did not. In 1969, the committee had stayed focused on male applicants while Elga Wasserman and Sam Chauncey had handled the admission of women, but in 1970, women applicants for the class of 1974 were brought into the regular

admissions process, with the same two-reader system and final rank-
ings as men: one for the strongest applicants, two for those who
were reasonably strong, three for applicants who were shakier, and
four for the weakest group. The admissions office staff did this initial
ranking, while the final decisions were made by the full Admissions
Committee: fifteen staff members, ten faculty members, four deans,
and Elga Wasserman. Only five of the committee's thirty members
were women: Wasserman, Assistant Dean Elisabeth Thomas, instructor Paula Johnson, and two junior members of the admissions office
staff, whose senior members were all men.

The admissions process began in the fall, with recruitment and
interviews and the processing of applications, but March was the
month when decisions were made. The work of the Admissions
Committee kicked off with a February 27 meeting with Brewster,
who liked to instruct the committee members in person at a special gathering in Woodbridge Hall. They had each already received a
copy of his 1967 "hunchy judgment" letter to the admissions office
staff, and Brewster reiterated the central point he had made in the
letter: the Admissions Committee's job was to admit the candidates
who seemed most likely to be leaders.

On Tuesday, March 2, the work began in earnest. The committee convened that morning in the second-floor conference room of
the admissions office on Prospect Street, a room they would soon
grow weary of. The schedule was grueling: 9:15 a.m. to 9:30 p.m.
on Monday through Friday, with two-hour breaks for lunch and
dinner, and then another seven hours on Saturday and three more
on Sunday afternoons. Admissions Dean Inky Clark hoped to have
the work completed by early April. If a faculty member had a class
or an administrator had a meeting, they just missed that particular
session. Decisions were made by a majority vote of those present.

By March 26, the committee had been at this schedule for more than three grueling weeks: Admit. Reject. Reject. Reject. Reject. Reject. Reject. Admit. Reject. Reject. Reject. Reject. Reject. Reject. For the women applicants, the "rejects" came twice as frequently, an outcome forced by the gender quota. After three weeks of witnessing the impact of Yale's policy on women's chances of admission, Assistant Professor Keith Thomson sent a letter to Brewster.

"Dear President Brewster," he began, "I am not naturally a petition signer or a writer of hectoring letters, but this is a matter that has affected me considerably in the last few days." The problem, Thomson explained, was that Yale's admissions policy was causing the committee to reject 400 women candidates "who have <u>every</u> qualification for acceptance" and to wait-list another 250 with "qualifications that many of our male candidates would envy." Thomson proposed a modest solution: free up one hundred slots in the class of 1974 that were now reserved for men and make them available to women. Otherwise, the Admissions Committee would be forced to "reject exceptionally well-qualified women in large numbers and at the same time accept some 10 percent of men who are…<u>relatively</u> less impressive."

Although Thomson was anguished at the task he'd been given, Yale was not alone in its bias against women applicants. A 1970 American Council on Education study found that male high school students in the top fifth of their class had a 92 percent chance of being accepted by a selective U.S. college, while the odds dropped to 62 percent for the top-ranked high school girls. A similar gap occurred at every level. Even among the weakest male candidates, those in the bottom three-fifths of their class, 36 percent of those who applied to selective colleges were accepted, compared with 4 percent of the women. With many of these colleges, one had to wade through statistics to see the pattern of discrimination. Yale put its policy right out there: the class of 1974 would have 230 women and 1,025 men, with the twenty-five-student bonus ensuring the eventual graduation of 1,000 male leaders.

The day after Thomson sent his letter to Brewster, English instructor Paula Johnson, another Admissions Committee member, wrote Brewster too. She began by emphasizing her "gratitude and commitment to Yale," as if dissent called that into question, and then reiterated Thomson's point about the injustices caused by the limit on the numbers of women. Yale's policy, she wrote, "results in a crueler double standard than the simple exclusion of women ever did." Like Keith Thomson's letter the previous day, Paula Johnson's was an act of courage. Neither Johnson nor Thomson was protected by tenure, and when it came time for Yale to decide whether they would remain on the faculty, such a public challenge might not be overlooked.

A week later, Brewster received a third letter on the problem, this one from Elga Wasserman. "You have received two very thoughtful letters from Keith Thomsen and Paula Johnson which pinpoint the serious problems encountered in the selection of the women," she wrote. And then, banging home the point, she added, "The problem would obviously be less if we could increase the number of women admitted." Wasserman still did not challenge Brewster publicly on this issue. She confined her concerns to her letter. But Brewster certainly now knew how she felt.

―――――

At the start of April, the *Yale Daily News* published a front-page story on the academic outcomes of the first semester of coeducation.

Despite all the challenges the women students had faced, they had outperformed their male classmates.

"Of course we're smarter," one sophomore teased her boyfriend when the article came out. "Why do you think we're here?" Women sophomores and juniors received Honors, Yale's highest grade, in 31 percent of their classes, compared with 23 percent of the men. Freshmen women got 22 percent Honors, on par with freshmen men, but outflanked men 49 percent to 41 percent in High Pass, the second-highest mark. If academics had been the bar that Yale women needed to leap, they did so with room to spare. But at Yale, the emphasis on "character" over intellect did not end at admissions, and doing well academically was not an accomplishment most students wanted their classmates to know about. As author Mary McCarthy observed, the "wrong sort of seriousness in study" was considered "barbaric" at Yale. Student leaders were known by their achievements outside the classroom, not within it.

So where did that leave the Yale women? Yale may not have valued their academic success, but had they faltered, it would have been noted. And for many Yale women, their coursework was not just a test to prove that women deserved to be students at Yale but a source of personal joy.

"We were all very much involved in our study. Just cared about it, worked on it," said a woman junior from Maine. "I loved studying," said freshman Patty Mintz of Massachusetts. "I'd go up to the stacks, or I'd find a little desk and a comfy chair and just read." Patty's classmate, Los Angeles premed student Carol Storey, found the same spark in the lab. "Science…was an area of intense curiosity and interest for me."

But while academics mattered to Yale women, they did not matter all that much to Yale. As economics professor Ed Lindblom explained, "The official tradition here at Yale is that we are not producing intellectuals, we are producing leaders." The worth of Yale women was thus measured not by the academics at which they excelled but by the extracurricular activities from which they were largely excluded. President George W. Bush, Yale class of 1968 and a Delta Kappa Epsilon fraternity brother, captured this indifference to academic achievement in his remarks to graduates at a Yale commencement many years later: "To those of you who received honors, awards, and distinctions, I say well done. And to the C students I say, you too can be president of the United States."

Kit McClure had no presidential ambitions, which was a good thing since her grades at Yale were much better than George W. Bush's. She was earning Honors in American Social History, receiving High Passes in Revolutionary Thought and Communism, and acing American Jazz. But by the second semester, what occupied the center of Kit's days even more than her coursework was "music, music, music." Kit was teaching herself the saxophone and earning money as the trombone player in a professional brass quintet. And the New Haven Women's Liberation Rock Band was thriving. "We had so much fun," said freshman Kate Field, who played guitar in the band that spring. Kate lived in the same Vanderbilt entryway that Kit did, and the two had gotten to know each other through the Sisterhood. Kate had never told Kit about the incident with the poetry professor who had tried to seduce her. For that matter, she hardly told anyone. But Kate went to the Sisterhood meetings, and now she was in the Women's Liberation Rock Band.

There were six women in the band that spring: the three women who had first come up to Kit at the Free Women Conference in February and three freshmen from Yale: Kit McClure, Kate Field, and Anna Tsing Lowenhaupt. The band members' skills as musicians varied widely. A few of them "barely knew how to play their

Kit McClure.
Photo © Virginia Blaisdell.

instruments," while Kit and French horn–player Virginia Blaisdell were both accomplished musicians. Anna also had formal musical training, but she played the cello, not your typical rock band instrument. "Well, close enough," said Kit when Anna showed her the cello. "I can teach you to play the bass."

The band had a rehearsal space in a loft on State Street, a few blocks down past the New Haven Green, and Blaisdell would often give them a ride in her Panama Beige Volkswagen Beetle convertible. Kit and the other women spent hours in that loft, practicing covers and writing feminist lyrics to Rolling Stones songs. Sometimes other women musicians would be in town, and they would all get together for jam sessions. The New Haven Women's Liberation Rock Band was not nearly good enough yet to perform in public, but with enough practice, Kit knew they would get there. On Monday evenings, however, practice was off. The Yale Sisterhood met then, and all three of the band's freshmen were members.

By April, about a dozen women students were regularly attending the Sisterhood meetings in the Vanderbilt lounge. Consciousness-raising formed the heart of the evening. The students shared stories about their experiences at Yale. They talked about what happened sometimes when they spoke up in class and had their comments ignored by their professors and male classmates. Ten minutes later, the women would watch as a different student, a man, made the exact point and the class reacted with a gush of admiration, as if Benjamin Franklin had wandered in and offered an insight. It had happened to Betty Spahn more than once. "I thought I just wasn't articulate enough, and Judy Berkan, who's very articulate, thought she wasn't articulate enough, and Dahlia Rudavsky thought she wasn't articulate enough," said Betty. "It turned out it wasn't us, was it? It was them."

The incessant attention the women received from the men came up also. It never felt "normal to be a woman student" at Yale, said freshman Marie Rudden. "It was hard to have it just like normal." Over time, some of the women shared stories about dates with Yale men who had forced them into sex that they hadn't agreed to or wanted. Many struggled afterward with guilt and shame, as if somehow they were at fault. The stories shocked Betty Spahn. "I had no idea this was going on. None. No idea. And the other women, to whom it happened, had no idea it was so widespread."

At the Yale Sex Counseling Service, Lorna Sarrel had begun to hear stories as well. "Sexual assault and rape were not front and center of our awareness or awareness on the campus," she said. "It really was still hush-hush, like pretending it never happens." Sometimes in her discussions with students, however, Sarrel would hear, "Oh, I didn't have a very good experience the first time." As they spoke further, "it would turn out that it was a sexual assault. The women did not want to recognize that themselves...In some instances, the word *rape* may have applied, and to see yourself as victimized in that way is not easy. So there was a lot of denial. And of course at the professional level there was also a kind of denial."

Women students who found a safe place like the Sisterhood or the Sarrels' office to talk about what happened to them were more fortunate than those who did not, but nothing stopped the male students who assaulted Yale women from continuing. There was not yet even the language to name the experience. The term *date rape* would not be invented for seventeen years.

At their meetings, the Sisterhood members paid close attention not just to what each girl said but to the way in which the group held conversations. "Things like everyone getting a turn to speak, things like no one interrupting anyone else, things like no one attacking anyone else"—the Sisterhood paid attention to that, explained one of its members. Each woman picked up a handful of poker chips at the start of the meeting, and every time she spoke, she tossed in a chip. When she ran out, she couldn't talk any more at that session. That way, the Sisterhood made sure that everyone's voice would be heard.

Like much of what the Sisterhood did, the choice about how conversations were held did not fit the mold of what some students thought of as protest. There were no angry speakers shaking their fists in the Vanderbilt lounge, no marchers carrying banners. Yet the Sisterhood challenged Yale's culture too, just as surely as more standard strategies. Yale was a place where male students spent hours in "bull sessions" that gave center stage to those with quickness and wit, yet the Sisterhood rejected that model of competitive talking. Women students at Yale were expected to be constantly on call as "mother, lover, sister, confidante" to men, yet at the Sisterhood meetings, no men were present. At Yale, women did not go out on the weekends unless they had a date, but women in the Sisterhood did. "They would get up the nerve to go to the theater together. In other words, they didn't wait for a date. They would go in groups with women," explained one shocked freshman woman.

The Sisterhood was not for everyone. Some students "kind of stumbled in thinking that we were going to sit around and discuss fashion and their boyfriends," said Betty. Those women rarely returned. But for others, the Monday night Sisterhood meetings became the anchor that made the rest of the week possible. "I just really liked being with the other women," said Betty. The Sisterhood "was my safe haven. It was my place to go. And I think a lot of us felt that way." Over that first spring, the Sisterhood did not speak out publicly about any of the issues then roiling Yale. The group really was just getting started. Yet even without the Sisterhood's voice, the volume of the conversation about the status of women at Yale grew louder. Some days, it seemed as if that was the only thing anyone was talking about.

On April 6, stacks of *Yale Break*, Yale's new feminist newspaper, appeared in Yale dining halls, offices, and libraries. There were three thousand free copies for the taking. The publication was written by women students, secretaries, and faculty wives. "Divided We Fall," read its headline. That same day, the *Yale Daily News* ran Yale's admissions discrimination as its lead story, and a fourth Admissions Committee member voiced his dismay. If Yale had selected the class of 1974 without regard to gender, Associate Professor John Ostrom told the paper, three hundred acceptance letters that were just mailed to men would have been sent instead to women.

The *Yale Alumni Magazine* jumped into the fray and devoted its entire April issue to coeducation. For the first time, the voices of women students filled the magazine's pages. "We desperately need more girls," said freshman Sarah Pillsbury, the daughter of a prominent alumnus. A second alumnus's daughter made the same point. Her father was a Connecticut state senator.

The *New York Times* picked up the story and got a quote from

Admissions Dean Inky Clark. The Admissions Committee "was frustrated over turning away many highly qualified women," Clark said. "Only one of every 14 women applicants…could be accepted, compared with one out of 7.5 men." The *Times* article went beyond Yale admissions and chronicled women's activism as well. "A general campaign for women's rights has been mounted," the paper reported. The law school women's sit-in at Mory's, the alumni lunch protest, the Free Women Conference, and the student peti-tion—it was all in the *New York Times* article. Yale dining halls buzzed with talk of coeducation and the actions by women at Yale.

"At long last," observed one male junior, "women were begin-ning to be viewed as a factor to be reckoned with." The momen-tum that had been building since January seemed on the verge of bringing change for Yale women. But then a high-profile trial being held two blocks from Yale's campus and the massive protest that accompanied it diverted Yale's attention. It could not have been otherwise. Both matters were urgent. But once again, the needs of Yale women were forgotten.

———

The trial that began in New Haven that spring centered on the 1969 murder of a member of the Black Panther Party named Alex Rackley. The case had drawn national attention because of the prominence of the defendants: nine Black Panther Party members, five men and four women, including national chairman Bobby Seale and New Haven Black Panther leader Ericka Huggins. Many on the left suspected that Seale and Huggins were being framed as a part of the larger government campaign to destroy the Black Panthers, and Panther supporters had planned a protest rally on the New

Haven Green, right across College Street from Yale's campus, for the weekend of May 1. But up until April 14, Yale had not paid much attention to either the upcoming protest rally or the trial itself.

That morning, the presiding judge in the case shocked onlookers when he sentenced two Black Panthers who were merely talking in the courtroom visitors' section to six months in jail for contempt of court. News of the incident spread quickly through campus, where the severity of the judge's penalty for such a minor infraction raised fears that a larger miscarriage of justice might occur, with Seale, Huggins, and the other Panthers being convicted for a murder they did not commit. That worry in turn tapped into the deep well of concern that most Yale students felt about racial injustice and that had led many to volunteer in the black communities that surrounded Yale.

Yale students, both women and men, served as tutors in New Haven public schools. They founded a day care center for the children of Yale's predominantly black dining hall workers. They worked in a local nonprofit that was creating low-income housing. They woke up early to work in a free breakfast program for school-children that was run by the Black Panthers, who had a network of community help programs in New Haven. "There was a particular spirit in the air," said Yale freshman Darial Sneed. "It seemed like the whole youth mentality was that we're going to do better than our parents, we're going to make this a better world."

Students at Yale had also watched as their peers on other Ivy League campuses—Columbia, Penn, and Harvard—staged strikes and sit-ins in an effort to halt university expansion that was harming black neighborhoods. And so on April 14, when news spread of the judge's harsh penalty at the Black Panther trial, Yale students were ready to listen. Many believed that Yale had a responsibility to ensure that the Black Panther defendants were treated fairly, and within days, the trial and what students should do about it was all that anyone at Yale was talking about.

A series of mass meetings pulled increasing numbers of students into the conversation: 400 in Harkness Hall on April 15; 1,500 in Battell Chapel on April 19; and 4,500 in Ingalls Ice Rink, the largest venue at Yale, on April 21. From these meetings emerged the idea that a student strike could pressure Brewster and the Yale Corporation to demand a fair trial for the Panthers and, equally important, increase Yale's efforts to end the ravages of racial discrimination in the two black communities that it bordered. By April 22, the strike was on, and three quarters of Yale students stopped attending classes. The May 1 protest in support of the Panthers—"May Day," as the students called it—would show the nation that Yale students would not stand idly by as injustice took place on their doorstep.

Yet another concern had surfaced by then, one that would dominate Yale as much as the goal of racial justice. On April 15, a four-hour riot at Harvard had left 241 people hospitalized and caused $100,000 in property damage after a crowd of angry protesters from Boston converged on the university. "When Harvard was trashed…we understood for the first time that something dangerous could happen [at Yale]," said Associate Dean John Wilkinson. Abbie Hoffman, cofounder of the radical-left Yippies and the ringleader of the Harvard riot, stoked fears of violence still further when he proclaimed on a New York radio station that the Harvard riot was just the prelude to even greater mayhem at Yale, which some saw as a symbol of "the establishment" that was behind the Vietnam War and the nation's racial and class injustice. The May Day protest at Yale, said Hoffman, would be "the biggest riot in history."

Up until then, campuses such as Columbia and Harvard had reacted to major protests by calling in armed police to restore order, a response that had failed to prevent violence and, some thought, only made matters worse. Yale faced a challenge greater than any campus to date. Thirty thousand protesters, a group seven times the size of Yale's undergraduate student body, were expected to flood into New Haven for the May Day rally, with many intent on doing Yale harm. After consulting with experts, Kingman Brewster decided on a new approach to mass protest. Yale would welcome the May Day protesters in, providing free meals and a place to spend the night, and the university would thus become an ally rather than a foe of those who sought justice. No one was sure, however, whether Brewster's unorthodox strategy would prove to be a stroke of genius or the cause of unprecedented damage and injury.

As May Day approached, the threat of violence pervaded the campus. The *New York Times* ran front-page stories for days about the anticipated destruction. Store owners on the streets surrounding Yale locked their doors and boarded up windows. Yale and New Haven prepared for May Day "like it was an approaching hurricane," said a member of Yale's football team, and adding to the anxiety were the hordes of reporters and camera crews, more than six hundred in all, who began flooding into New Haven so as to have front-row seats for the violence predicted.

In the midst of this rising tension, Kingman Brewster uttered a statement that could have cost him his job. Hundreds of Yale faculty members had convened in Sprague Hall to discuss the Panther trial and student strike, and in the midst of the meeting, Brewster offered his opinion, "I am skeptical of the ability of black revolutionaries to achieve a fair trial anywhere in the United States." Two days later, the quote was on the front page of the *New York Times*, and conservatives nationwide were outraged that Yale's president would question the fairness of America's justice system. The following week, U.S. vice president Spiro T. Agnew stated that Yale's trustees should replace Brewster with "a more mature and responsible" president. Students admired Brewster for his statement and saw it as brave, but while the Corporation stood by him, Brewster had permanently damaged his image with Yale's more conservative alumni.

Meanwhile, parents who learned about the upcoming protest grew increasingly concerned, and some asked their sons and daughters to come home. Many students worried about safety as well, and dining hall conversations turned to a new question: Are you going, or are you staying? Carol Storey decided to leave and start her summer job early. "There was word spreading that it might not be such a good idea to be around over May Day," said Carol, and with the strike ongoing, there were no longer any classes to attend. Another freshman girl left after several heartfelt conversations with her parents. "You could stay, and everything could be fine," her mother told her, "but if something happens and you want to leave, you might not be able to do so." Yet another left Yale because her roommate planned to let some of the demonstrators come sleep on their floor. "I felt personally threatened by that possibility, people that I didn't know," she said. As the eve of May Day approached, only two-thirds of Yale students remained.

————

Connie Royster did not leave. New Haven was Connie's city; she was not going to abandon it when violence threatened. Lawrie Mifflin did not leave either. For Lawrie, the May Day protest was a time to stand and be counted among those who opposed the

Vietnam War and the injustice of racism. "Our generation was going to be different," said Lawrie. "We weren't going to stand for this." Kit McClure wasn't going anywhere either. She had been spending more and more time with the feminists in New Haven Women's Liberation, who had been protesting the treatment of the imprisoned Black Panther women as far back as November.   Shirley Daniels and Betty Spahn were staying for May Day too. Both were focused on the goal of keeping the weekend nonviolent, although each took a different path to that end.

Shirley was worried about the safety of black New Haven high school students. A few of the Boston Black Panthers had come down to New Haven and were riling up the high school kids and encouraging them to walk out of school and cause trouble. If police overreacted, the reasoning went, the headlines that followed might force action to remedy long-standing discrimination. Shirley tutored students at Hillhouse High School, and she was there when the Panthers showed up. She tried to talk the students into returning to class, but not many listened. "The kids didn't know what they were getting into," said Shirley, but the BSAY did. The BSAY had been concerned about the New Haven police since well before the "Stop the Cops" rally in November.   The last thing black teenagers should be doing was provoking police into a confrontation.

The issue erupted when a Boston Black Panther attended one of the BSAY meetings. Shirley knew the man from her involvement with the Simmons College black student group before she came to Yale, and she did not like how he operated. "You can't be doing this to the kids," she told him. "Someone's going to get hurt!"

Shirley got so angry that other BSAY members escorted her from the room, but they too worried about the younger students, and a few days later, the BSAY came out publicly against any action that would harm New Haven's black community. If the Panthers sought to stir up black teenagers, the BSAY would not support them.

Betty Spahn was concerned about the possibility of violence too but was more focused on the dangerous mix of thousands of protesters, some bent on violence, and the four hundred young and inexperienced National Guard troops whom Connecticut's governor had ordered to New Haven for the weekend. Betty and a large group of Sisterhood members volunteered to be trained in how to de-escalate conflict and serve as peace marshals over the May Day weekend. During the demonstrations, the marshals would station themselves among the crowds on the New Haven Green. If tensions arose, the marshals would step in quickly to calm things, with small groups of women going in first, since women were seen as less likely than men to inflame any conflict. They should try to soothe the angry protester, Betty and the Sisterhood members were coached: "Kiss him on the cheek if he'll let you. Be very feminine." It helped Betty to know that other Sisterhood members would be with her on May Day. That made the peace marshal role less scary.

The peace marshal initiative was massive, with hundreds of undergraduates, graduate students, and New Haven residents volunteering to serve. Sisterhood member Kate Field was in charge of coordinating the effort as part of her role on the Student Strike Steering Committee, where she was the only woman member. Kate was just a freshman, but she was dynamic and knew how to organize, said Yale minister Phil Zaeder, who worked out of the same building where the Strike Steering Committee was headquartered. Kate was a "very accomplished, formidable, wonderful person," said Zaeder, and Betty Spahn was also impressed by Kate's unyielding insistence on nonviolence. Betty attended some of the Strike Steering Committee meetings, and when Boston Black Panthers advocated the use of weapons, Betty and Kate stood up to them. "No guns," said the Sisterhood women. Betty was proud of how they stuck together on that issue. "The women, we hung together. We hung firm on that," said Betty.

Meanwhile, Connie Royster joined a different effort to prevent violence. The Strike Steering Committee had quickly focused on entertainment as part of their strategy—bored protesters got into mischief. The committee lined up bands for the May Day rally, and Connie joined black theater students from Yale Drama School to present an original performance, "Black Celebration," on the main stage of the university theater. The show would donate its proceeds to the John Huggins Free Health Clinic on Dixwell Avenue, which was run by the New Haven Black Panthers. While many Americans connected the Panthers with violence and some party members fit right into that stereotype, the Black Panther Party as a whole had set aside its earlier militancy in 1968 and begun establishing programs to help urban black communities. The John Huggins Health Clinic, to which "Black Celebration" would contribute its earnings, was one such effort.

Connie's connection to May Day ran deeper than her role in "Black Celebration." What few Yale students besides Betty Spahn knew was that Black Panther John Huggins, for whom the health clinic was named, had been Connie's cousin. Like Connie, John Huggins had grown up in New Haven. After graduating from Hillhouse High School, he'd joined the navy and fought in the Vietnam War. When he returned to the U.S., he'd made his way to Los Angeles, where he had led the local Black Panther chapter until January 1969, when he was killed by members of a rival organization.

Connie's family was devastated by John Huggins's death. He was the son of Connie's great uncle, one of the family patriarchs, and John and his wife, Ericka, another Black Panther, had a three-month-old daughter. After the funeral, Ericka moved to New Haven with the baby to be closer to John's family, and she soon became a leader in the local Black Panther Party. When the police arrested local Black Panthers for Alex Rackley's murder, Ericka Huggins was sent to the state women's prison in Niantic and separated from her daughter. The baby's grandmother, Connie's aunt, took care of the child, and Connie's father helped drive the baby and grandmother the hour to Niantic for regular visits so that Ericka Huggins could spend time with her baby.

Connie's decision to stay in New Haven over May Day did not stem from her family ties to John and Ericka Huggins. She would have been there regardless. Doing her part to prevent violence that weekend "was the right thing to do," said Connie. Yet the May Day events wove through Connie's life very differently than they did for other Yale students. Her family was close. They still felt the pain from what had happened to John Huggins and his young family. Not many at Yale, however, knew that a fellow student was connected so deeply to May Day.

———

As May Day drew near, a sense of impending crisis filled the entire state of Connecticut. Governor John Dempsey deployed the National Guard and then, fearing it could not contain the violence on its own, sent a telegram to U.S. attorney general John Mitchell asking for backup from federal troops. On April 30, two thousand army paratroopers and two thousand marines were flown up from North Carolina and stationed at air bases near New Haven. That same night, President Nixon increased tension still further when he

Woman student approaches National Guard soldier in front of boarded-up stores surrounding Yale, May Day 1970.
Photo © Virginia Blaisdell.

announced that the United States had invaded Cambodia, sparking outrage across a nation that had thought the war was nearing its end. The following morning, May 1, chartered buses filled with demonstrators began arriving in New Haven for the protest. The tinder for a conflagration at Yale was set.

Thirty thousand protesters poured into New Haven that day. Guardsmen with guns and tear gas masks lined up shoulder-to-shoulder along the streets, while National Guard tanks stood at the ready on York Street right next to Yale's Saybrook and Davenport Colleges.

Yale stuck with Brewster's plan, however, and opened its doors to the protesters. Hundreds of Yale students, both women and men, volunteered for the work details required to carry out the strategy. Some pulled on clear plastic gloves and served up rations of brown rice and salad by the handful. Others cared for protesters' children at a day care center set up in Davenport College or volunteered as peace marshals and medics, while still other students worked shifts on their college's security patrol.

The protest began on the afternoon of May 1, and students and outsiders packed the New Haven Green while Brewster and Sam Chauncey stationed themselves in a secret command post nearby. But the day was sunny, the bands at the rally were good, and the hundreds of daffodils that Yale had planted that fall to beautify the campus for the new women students were blooming. The long line of speakers at the rally tended to ramble rather than rouse the crowd to violence, the peace marshals prevented the most radical protestors from causing harm, and BSAY members walked the New Haven streets to keep the high school kids out of trouble.

By dinnertime, none of the chaos predicted had happened, and the protesters dispersed to Yale's twelve residential colleges. But at nine thirty that night, word spread quickly that police had arrested several black men on the New Haven Green, a rumor that was untrue but nonetheless inflamed latent anger among some who had come to New Haven. A crowd one thousand strong returned to the Green, chanting, "Fuck Brewster! Fuck Yale! Get the Panthers out of Jail!" The mob threw rocks and a stink bomb, but New Haven's police chief kept the young National Guard troops from letting their inexperience get the best of them. The police launched volley after volley of tear gas, and the New Haven Panthers, despite earlier calls for violence by some members, worked to calm angry protesters. As tear gas exploded around them, the Panthers circled the New Haven Green in their sound truck, urging the crowd to disperse. Violence would only bring harm to the neighboring black communities. Kate Field had sent the peace marshals back to the Green as soon as she got word of the trouble there, and even though she was hit in the head with a tear gas canister and knocked out, the marshals' training proved effective. The protesters settled and returned to Yale's residential colleges with no one seriously hurt and no significant damage.

The following day, the crowds were half the size of those on May 1. Once again, the scheduled rally went smoothly, but that night, as students were still leaving the Green, a group of two hundred white radicals began throwing rocks and bottles at police. Lawrie Mifflin was walking back with the crowds to her dorm room when the National Guard began firing tear gas. She could hear the ominous thump as each canister was launched in the air. Seconds later, clouds of caustic white smoke exploded on the sidewalk, and students' eyes burned from the chemical fumes. When they tried to take a breath, it felt like swallowing fire. *Why are they doing that?* thought Lawrie. *We're not doing anything. We're not being destructive.*

Like most students, Lawrie didn't know the cause of the trouble. It was dark, and all was confusion. The tear gas billowed up Elm Street and down College, and Lawrie began to run with her friends to the Old Campus. Tear gas canisters exploded around them, and soon there was nowhere to escape. Kit McClure had retreated to Vanderbilt also, but tear gas was filling the hallways. "What do we do?" asked Kit's roommate Dixie. "I can't breathe." Kit showed her how to put a wet washcloth over her face and duck down to stay beneath the chemical smoke. Kit had been through this before, when the SDS students at Cornell convinced her to go to Chicago for the 1968 Democratic National Convention. The tear gas didn't burn any less the second time.

The gas spread to Yale's residential colleges. "The entire campus was saturated," said one Berkeley senior, who spent the next few hours dabbing his eyes with a wet towel.   Betty Spahn was back in Berkeley by then too. The May Day events were done as far as she knew, and then all of a sudden, tear gas was coming in under the doorway. Betty couldn't understand it. "Why are we getting tear gassed?"   But once again, the crowd on the Green dispersed.

By Sunday, May 3, the thirty thousand demonstrators who had come to New Haven for the weekend had left. "Shock, like when wild rock suddenly ceases," wrote sophomore Lydia Temoshok in her diary. "No one is here."   The weekend had passed without a single serious injury, and the marines and paratroopers went back to North Carolina having never set foot in New Haven. Despite all predictions otherwise, Yale and its students had succeeded in keeping the weekend peaceful. Those who had hoped to free the Black Panthers were disappointed, however. The trial continued, and Ericka Huggins remained in prison in Niantic while her daughter, who had turned one year old by then, was raised by others.

Another three weeks of the spring semester remained, but classes never really resumed. On May 4, four unarmed students at Ohio's Kent State University were shot and killed on their campus by National Guard soldiers during an antiwar protest. Eleven days later, it happened again, when the Mississippi State Highway Patrol and local police fired into a student dorm at Jackson State University after a protest. Two students died. By then, 448 campuses across the nation were on strike, with student demands tied to democracy and the war: pull the United States out of Vietnam and Cambodia; end repression of political minorities; stop military research at U.S. universities. Now no one at Yale was going to classes. Students could take incompletes and finish their work over the summer. Exams that year were optional. "It was all a complete shambles," said one Yale professor.   Instead of coming to a clean close, the first year of coeducation simply disbanded.

Elga Wasserman thought May Day had been good for the women students. The crisis created an "us" at Yale that for the first time did not exclude women. Yet Sisterhood member Judy Berkan, who had volunteered as a peace marshal and had long been involved in antiwar activism, saw May Day differently. "May Day sucked the oxygen out of a lot of what we were doing," said Judy. Compared with May Day and the Vietnam War, "there was a sense among male activists, and I think we bought into it ourselves, that our struggles as women were kind of trivial. And so it sucked the oxygen out."

EIGHT

Breaking the Rules

ELGA WASSERMAN HAD BEEN AS ENGAGED IN THE
May Day crisis as most people at Yale. She attended the multiple
meetings that preceded the protest and read with growing concern
the predictions of mayhem and rioting. Yet she had not let May Day
distract her. Yale was still not doing right by its women students, and
while the rest of the campus lost focus on that problem over May
Day, Wasserman and her Coeducation Committee did not.

On April 21, the committee gathered for its regular biweekly
meeting. By that point, Yale was in a frenzy over the threat of
impending violence, but all except two of Wasserman's committee
members attended. In the packet sent out in advance, Wasserman
included some calculations she'd done on the students Yale had just
admitted to the class of 1974. High school girls needed to rank
in the top 5 percent of their class to be accepted by Yale that year,
while high school boys in the top 30 percent got in. The committee was shocked. Yale's gender quotas were "intellectually indefensible," said some at the meeting. "Irrational," said history professor
Edmund Morgan.

Two weeks later, Wasserman put Yale's gender quotas on the committee's agenda again. By that point, the flood of May Day protesters had come and gone, and the semester was pretty much over. Only three committee members missed the meeting, and those who were there included some of the weightiest names on Wasserman's roster: Chief of Psychiatry Bob Arnstein, Pulitzer Prize–winner John Hersey, Yale College Dean Georges May, history professor Edmund Morgan, law professor Ellen Peters, and Assistant Dean Elisabeth Thomas.

Wasserman was preparing to issue a year-end coeducation report that would be widely distributed and serve as a public report card on the first year of coeducation at Yale. She did not want her name to be the only one on this report, however. She wanted her committee members' names right on the cover, and hence it was critical to have their support of whatever recommendations she made. Had Wasserman planned to declare coeducation a success, those names would not have been necessary. But that was not her intention.

Up until that point, Elga Wasserman had behaved. Whatever her private thoughts, she had kept from publicly challenging Brewster. She played by the rules, which at Yale called for patience, acknowledging the multiple priorities of a university president, and never, ever pushing too hard. A lot of good it had done her. Women students remained a small minority, scattered across all twelve of Yale's colleges. The numbers of women faculty and administrators were almost too small to speak of. And Wasserman's own position was still off to the side of Yale's administrative structure, as if to make sure she could not cause any trouble. Women at Yale would never get what they needed if they kept playing by rules that were made by Yale men. In May 1970, for the very first time, Elga Wasserman began breaking the rules.

At their meeting on May 5, the Coeducation Committee discussed some possible recommendations to include in the report and quickly focused on one issue: the token numbers of women. For coeducation to be successful, Yale needed to rapidly increase the numbers of women students, and the committee saw only one way to do so: abandon the thousand-man quota.

None in the room could have misunderstood the weight of what they were considering—a public challenge to Kingman Brewster by some of the most prominent professors and administrators at Yale—but by the end of the meeting, the Coeducation Committee decided on its recommendation: for the class of 1975, Yale must end its thousand-man quota and instead accept eight hundred men and four hundred women, a two-to-one ratio. Rather than vote then and there, the committee decided to pause and make sure there were no objections from the three members who were absent or second thoughts by those who were there. They would meet again on May 26 and vote on their recommendation then.

In the meantime, a second issue burned in Wasserman's chest: her own position and title. Back in March, when the topic of women's careers arose at her Women's Advisory Council, she told the sophomores and juniors seated around the table that "often, women simply are not considered for promotions, despite seniority, skill, and other qualifications they may have." Wasserman knew well the sting of that experience herself, and by May, she had put up with her "special assistant" title and the minor role it implied for a year. It was time to send a memo to Brewster.

"Confidential," Wasserman wrote at the top. "RE: Administrative Structures Related to Coeducation." Wasserman's timing was terrible. On the day she sent her memo, Brewster was in Washington, DC, with fifteen busloads of Yale students, lobbying Congress to end the Vietnam War. The adrenaline from May Day still lingered as well, and Brewster was basking in widespread praise for the way he had handled the protest. Elga Wasserman was about the last thing on his mind.

Wasserman continued writing: "As Special Assistant to the President, I was able to carry out initial planning for coeducation effectively." But now that the initial administrative tasks were done, she observed that "it will be increasingly difficult to respond to [women's] special needs without being directly, rather than periph-erally, involved in some aspect of the university." Wasserman knew exactly the position she wanted: associate provost, a role held by women at Wesleyan and Brown. Yale would simply be following its peers by placing a woman in a senior administrative role. "I believe that a position in the Provost's Office would provide the best oppor-tunity for influencing future policy," she wrote. "An appointment in this office could also establish a significant precedent for the partic-ipation of women in policy making at Yale."

Wasserman copied the memo to Sam Chauncey and then sent it off to Brewster. She had a meeting scheduled with Brewster two days later and hoped that when she walked out of Woodbridge Hall afterward, she would do so with a new position and title. Once again, however, Brewster denied Wasserman's request. She would spend the second year of coeducation just like the first, as Brewster's special assistant.

Two weeks later, the Coeducation Committee convened to vote on its year-end recommendation for the coeducation report. Wasserman began by sharing some news she had just learned at a meet-ing of the Council of Masters. Corporation member Jock Whitney had donated $15 million to build two new residential colleges for Yale, enough to house another six hundred students. Would that change the committee's recommendation? The men and women seated around the table, however, were unmoved. Even in the best scenario, Yale's current students would graduate long before the new housing was built. Correcting Yale's unbalanced gender ratio was "urgent," they agreed, and the recommendation stood: for the class of 1975, Yale should decrease the number of male freshmen to eight hundred in order to make room for more women. The vote was unanimous.

Two days later, Wasserman forwarded the committee's recommendation to Brewster. She was now openly opposing him and his first ground rule of coeducation—that Yale would not reduce the number of men just because it was accepting some women. The next move was Brewster's. Wasserman, who had broken enough rules already, would wait to release the recommendation and the full report until Brewster responded. In the meantime, the Coeducation Committee's rejection of his thousand male leaders sat like a time bomb on Brewster's desk in Woodbridge Hall, awaiting the moment when it would go public.

———

Over the summer, the women students scattered. One taught swimming at a summer camp in New Hampshire to help pay her tuition. Another took a "mind-numbing" clerical position in suburban New York after she got turned down for a job scooping ice cream at Baskin-Robbins—girls just weren't strong enough, the store manager told her. Betty Spahn had a secretarial job too, typing up bills in an office in Illinois. She hated it, but her parents had insisted she come home for the summer. That year at Yale—with the predatory dining hall manager and then Betty's suspension and finally May Day—had just been too much for them.

Sisterhood member Kate Field was in Maine with a job as an electrician for a summer musical theater. She had thought that she might stay in New Haven, playing guitar in Kit McClure's rock band and doing political work, but she quickly realized that she needed a break. May Day "had just been so crazy," said Kate: the intensity of the crowds, the night she'd been knocked out by the tear gas canister, the morning she had been woken at five because the National Guard tanks rolling by on the street outside were causing her house to shake.   Kate had worked theater tech at the Yale Dramat. That skill gave her a ticket to elsewhere.

Few of the women students were in touch with one another that summer. There was no social media, no email. Long-distance phone calls were expensive enough that one felt the cost mounting with every hurried minute. Whatever thinking the women students did about their first year at Yale, they did on their own. But many still reached the same conclusion. "Something had been missing," said a freshman girl from Columbus, Ohio. "I missed having women friends."

Roommates Patty Mintz and Betsy Hartmann had been two of the lucky few who had ended their first year at Yale with a close female friendship. Yet like other Yale women, they spent their summer apart. Patty was in South Dakota, teaching summer school on a Lakota Sioux reservation. Betsy had a job in Seattle. Over the summer, as both girls tried to sort through the confusing experiences of that first year at Yale, the two weren't in contact. But each realized that Yale had to change if it was going to be as good a college for women as it was for men. "Something needed to shift, something was wrong," Patty decided.   Out in Seattle, Betsy was thinking the same thing.

Back in May, the two had gone to a Sisterhood meeting

together. Betsy had never really thought about the women's movement until then, but over May Day weekend, a high school friend
who was at Yale for the protest told her that she should look into it.
"Betsy, you need to become a feminist," he said. "My sister is really
getting into this."

So Betsy had asked Patty to go to a Sisterhood meeting with her.
The group met right in Vanderbilt Hall, where the two girls lived.
At the meeting, Betsy found it powerful to be with other women
students who, like her, were beginning to question the givens of Yale
and "starting to feel ever more pissed off" at the way that women
were treated. Betsy's older sister had also become somewhat of a
feminist, and that summer in Seattle, Betsy began reading Simone de
Beauvoir's *The Second Sex*. It "was like lights going off in my head,"
Betsy said. Suddenly all that she had experienced in her first year at
Yale began to make sense.

While most Yale students left New Haven for the summer, there
were some who stayed. Kit McClure was there, practicing with the
rock band and attending the meetings of New Haven Women's
Liberation, whose discussions often included the ongoing Black
Panther trial and the conditions faced by Connecticut's women
prisoners. Students on Phil and Lorna Sarrel's Human Sexuality
Committee were also in New Haven that summer, working on a
new project for the fall. Up until then, the group had focused its
efforts on the human sexuality course—collecting the anonymous
questionnaires needed to enroll, taking care of the myriad details
required for a class of 1,200 students, evaluating the class afterward, and making suggestions on how to improve it. The course's
enrollment was unprecedented at Yale, but the Human Sexuality
Committee still asked: How can we reach more students?

At one of the meetings around the Sarrels' dining room table, a new idea emerged: What if they wrote a book on human sexuality for Yale students? The need, students felt, was enormous. Students came to Yale with so much misinformation, yet there was no good book they could turn to. *Everything You Always Wanted to Know about Sex* had barely been in the bookstores a year, and some of the "facts" it contained just weren't true. *Our Bodies Ourselves*, the groundbreaking women's health book, was still a stapled-together newsprint pamphlet that few students had even heard of. Making the content of the human sexuality course available to every Yale student would fill a real need. The Human Sexuality Committee had its summer project: it would write a booklet on sex to distribute to all Yale undergraduates. Just like the human sexuality course and the sex counseling service, no other college had anything like it.

Over the summer, the students worked on their book, researching and writing up drafts. The project was ambitious, but the committee had the funds to pay for it. The proceeds from the human sexuality course—1,200 students multiplied by the $5 fee—had brought in $6,000. In the fall, when students registered for classes, every Yale undergraduate would be able to get a free copy of their new booklet: *Sex and the Yale Student*.

Phil Sarrel was the book's medical consultant, but the editors were three students. The full team included Lorna Sarrel, six more students, and Associate Minister Phil Zaeder. The project "gave us a very good sense of purpose, and there was an element of pride in that," said Debbie Bernick, one of the students on the team. "This information was new, and a little scary and experimental. It affected our feelings. It affected our relationships. It wasn't just book learning."

By the time the first draft of *Sex and the Yale Student* was finished, the booklet was sixty-four pages long. It covered anatomy, birth control, pregnancy, and venereal disease. "It was solid information," said Debbie.

Phil Sarrel had always been careful about keeping Yale's top administrators fully informed about his work with Yale students. College administrations don't like to be surprised, particularly with a topic as potentially volatile as sex education. Chief of Psychiatry Bob Arnstein saw the draft of the booklet first, and once it passed muster with him, three more administrators got copies: Elga Wasserman, Assistant Dean Elisabeth Thomas, and Dean of Undergraduates John Wilkinson.

Wasserman had been a supporter of the project from the start, and she kept her comments to minor edits: On page 7, "alot" should be replaced with "a lot." On page 8, "irregardless" should be "regardless." On page 10, "public" should be "pubic." Elisabeth Thomas's comments were more substantive. Next to a section on birth control, she wrote in the margin: "Seems to be addressed only to women." But it was John Wilkinson who really pulled out the red pen.

Wilkinson was known as an ally of Yale women, but *Sex and the Yale Student* pushed him right to the edge. "What a word!!" he scribbled in his large, looping script after circling *preorgasmic*. "Is this necessary?" he scrawled in huge letters next to "All males at some time or another compare their penis size with other males." By the time Wilkinson got to page 33—"Almost fifty cases of condom failure were treated last year"—all he could do was write, "Stop!!" But Wilkinson let the book through, as did Brewster, who also was initially shocked. Students needed good information on birth control and sex, and Yale had long stayed away from censorship. When students returned to Yale in September, *Sex and the Yale Student* would be waiting for them.

As the students on the Human Sexuality Committee worked away on their booklet, Elga Wasserman was busy as well, and she had not backed off her new strategy of breaking rules. Handing Kingman Brewster a unanimous Coeducation Committee recommendation to reject his thousand male leaders was her first open challenge to the status quo. Before the summer was out, Wasserman threw down two more.

The Coeducation Committee had given Wasserman the go-ahead to raise the issue of women faculty in her report, but the way in which she decided to do so made no pretense at subtlety. The report's appendix E consisted of only two charts, both displayed on the same page, and there was no getting around the story they told: the persistence over time of Yale's preference for hiring men rather than women. Students and faculty may have sensed how few women professors Yale hired, but appendix E of Wasserman's report displayed that problem for all to see. Over the last eight years, Yale had increased the total number of tenured professors from 223 to 430, yet in the same period, the number of tenured women had grown from 0 to 2.

Coeducation Committee Report, 1970, appendix E

Total Members of the Yale College Faculty, 1963–1970

	1963	1964	1965	1966	1967	1968	1969	1970
All Faculty	562	588	606	620	668	817	869	839
Tenured Faculty	223	243	252	269	285	393	407	430

Women Members of the Yale College Faculty, 1963-1970

	1963	1964	1965	1966	1967	1968	1969	1970
All Faculty	24	25	26	32	32	48	52	43
Tenured Faculty	0	1	2	2	2	2	3	2

The chart was not yet public. It was sitting on Brewster's desk along with the recommendation on Yale's admissions quotas. But like that recommendation, Wasserman's chart violated the norm of keeping quiet about problems that Yale did not wish to address.

Wasserman took aim at one final target before the summer was out: Mory's. The women law school students' January sit-in had drawn attention to Yale's habit of holding meetings at a facility that barred women from entering, but nothing had changed as a result. Not only did Yale departments continue to hold meetings at Mory's, but Yale continued to pay the Mory's bills afterward. When pushed on the issue, Brewster refused to take action. "Yale cannot legislate where members of the University community may eat, even when the cost of the meal may be properly charged to a University account," he and the other university officers declared back in February. Wasserman's Coeducation Committee discussed the problem at five separate meetings that spring and reached a unanimous conclusion: Yale was supporting discrimination against women.

At first, Wasserman tried to address the matter discreetly. In March, she and Sam Chauncey met with Mory's president Stanley Trotman to urge that Mory's change its no-woman rule. In May, Chauncey sent a letter to Yale department chairmen and deans listing various lunch venues that allowed women to enter. Neither strategy worked. Yale men kept holding meetings at Mory's, and at the end of May, Trotman advised Wasserman that the rules of the club were not changing. By June, Wasserman had had enough.

"Dear Faculty member," she wrote. "It seems to me inappropriate to conduct university business in a facility from which some members of the university community are arbitrarily excluded." Wasserman's letter went on to discuss the impact on women of meetings at Mory's and the fact that other Yale venues existed. And then Wasserman asked her assistant to send out her letter to every single faculty member at Yale.

Over the summer, she received a few letters back in support, but the reply she got from Professor George Pierson, the sole faculty member to have voted against coeducation, was almost too hot to touch. "I wonder whether it is altogether 'appropriate' for you to adopt some of the language of the more aggressive women of the Liberation persuasion," scolded Pierson, who copied his letter to Sam Chauncey. "It will hardly, in any case, make for good feeling."

Wasserman may have been tempted to just crumple Pierson's letter into a ball and toss it in the trash, but "Pierson" was an important name at Yale, chiseled along the top of Woodbridge Hall in large letters along with the names of other revered Yale men. Abraham Pierson was Yale's first president, and George Pierson was his direct descendent. Wasserman wrote back to apologize: "If my tone seemed hasty or aggressive to you, I am sorry. I did not intend it to be either." Yet Elga Wasserman did not back down. "I really do believe that it is inappropriate for the university to conduct its business in an all-male facility," she told Pierson. The solution seemed obvious. If Yale men simply stopped patronizing Mory's over their discriminatory policy, then Mory's would have to treat women fairly or go bankrupt. But Yale men liked going to Mory's, and while some of them boycotted, most didn't. Yale's famous Whiffenpoofs continued to sing at Mory's every Monday. The sports team captains agreed to have their photos hung on the wall. Yale continued to pay the Mory's bills. If women wanted to end their exclusion from Mory's, they would need to find a different solution than relying on the help of Yale men.

———

By the end of July, Kit McClure had been playing trombone in the New Haven Women's Liberation Rock Band for five months, and the band, if not exactly good yet, was definitely enthusiastic. It even had a sister band: the Chicago Women's Liberation Rock Band. Naomi Weisstein, one of the speakers at February's Free Women Conference, had started the Chicago band that spring, and there was overlap between the two groups. Virginia Blaisdell in the New Haven band was one of Weisstein's best friends. Susan Abod in the Chicago band was the sister of New Haven band member Jennifer Abod.

The mix of instruments in each band was eclectic to be sure. The roster included slide whistle, tambourine, French horn, drums, and trombone. When the Chicago group first started, it had eleven vocalists, only three of whom could carry a tune. Weisstein compared it to "a hippy version of the Mormon Tabernacle choir." But no matter. With enough practice, they would soon sound as good as Janis Joplin, and in the meantime, they were all having fun.

At the end of July, however, the carefree nature of the New Haven band's early practices was supplanted by something much closer to panic. The band had scheduled their first public performance, and the date was approaching rapidly. August marked the fifty-year anniversary of U.S. women winning the right to vote, and on August 26, women across the country would take part in demonstrations and marches to celebrate that anniversary and to protest ongoing discrimination. The New Haven Women's Liberation Rock Band would perform in New Haven as one of the day's events.

The Women's Strike for Equality, as the August 26 protest was called, was part of a surge of attention to women's rights. The House of Representatives had just begun debate on the Equal Rights Amendment, which proposed banning discrimination on the basis of gender. Congresswoman Shirley Chisholm was running for president as the first woman to seek the Democratic Party's nomination and the first black candidate for president in either major party. And in Congress, Edith Green was doing her best to advance equal opportunity for women.

Green was one of ten women in the 435-member U.S. House of Representatives. She had represented Oregon's third congressional district, Portland, for the past fifteen years, and she chaired the House Special Subcommittee on Education. The chairmanship gave Green the power to sponsor legislation and hold hearings, and on July 31, Green concluded seven days of hearings on discrimination against women in America's schools and colleges. "Let us not deceive ourselves," she told those in the hearing room. "Our educational institutions have proven to be no bastions of democracy."

By the late 1960s, U.S. colleges and universities were receiving millions in federal dollars for research, financial aid, tuition grants for veterans, and support services for low-income students. Yet at the same time, they continued discriminating against women, who had lower pay scales than men, fewer job opportunities, worse odds of being admitted as students, and smaller financial aid awards. "Coeducational institutions that receive federal funds are no more justified in discriminating against women than against minority groups," Green declared, and her hearings that summer were the first step to ending that injustice.   By the time they concluded, Green's hearings had produced 1,261 pages of testimony on the inequity faced by women in U.S. colleges and universities.   Nothing like it had ever before been assembled. With this evidence in hand, Green and her colleague Patsy Mink began to draft legislation that would deny federal dollars to colleges and universities that discriminated against women.

Women in the know were following Green's progress, but for the most part, her work stayed fairly quiet. No good would come from drumming up opposition unnecessarily, Green warned her supporters. There was no missing the August 26 Women's Strike for Equality, however.   It was the largest women's protest since the suffrage movement. Women in forty-two states marched and demonstrated and made their voices heard. In New York City, ten thousand women, both black and white, marched arm-in-arm down Fifth Avenue. "At last, we have a movement," Kate Millett told the Bryant Park crowd in the rally that followed.

In New Haven, events included workshops and films and rap sessions on the New Haven Green, but the day's most exciting event, at least for Kit McClure, was the debut of the New Haven Women's Liberation Rock Band. For their performance that night, the band had rented space at Yale's Delta Kappa Epsilon (DKE) house, the fraternity where George W. Bush had once been president. Bush would not have been allowed into DKE house that night, though. The concert's audience was restricted to women. While Kit may have been nervous about the band's first performance, the crowd loved what they heard. At the end of the first set, the audience stood and applauded, and a few people held up a ten-foot long banner: "A Standing Ovulation for Our Sisters."

Five days later, the weekly issue of *Time* magazine devoted its cover story to the women's movement. There on the front cover was a portrait of Kate Millett, who glowered out from the newsstands with her sleeves rolled up. "Who's come a long way, baby?" *Time* asked, mimicking a Virginia Slims cigarette commercial.   And with that question, the second year of coeducation at Yale began.

NINE

The Opposition

SEPTEMBER BEGAN, AND NEW HAVEN ONCE MORE was overtaken by the annual onrush of students. The numbers of Yale women were somewhat higher this year now that Yale's last all-male class had graduated. With the arrival of the 230 women freshmen in the class of 1974, Yale now had 800 women undergraduates in all. But given the 4,000 men, it was still a five-to-one ratio.

Over in the Coeducation Office, Elga Wasserman was drumming her fingers. Kingman Brewster had still not responded to her May 26 letter conveying the news that the Coeducation Committee had voted against his thousand-man quota. He had made no comment on the final coeducation report she sent afterward. Wasserman had stepped well over the line with that report, but she was not prepared to go one step further and take it public before Brewster responded. As a result, few at Yale knew of the committee's stance on Yale's gender quotas, and no one had seen the damning data in appendix E on the near absence of women faculty at Yale. All was on hold until Brewster acted.

At least the final steps of publishing *Sex and the Yale Student* had gone well. The initial run was ten thousand copies: five thousand for Yale's undergraduates and five thousand for Yale faculty, administrators, and graduate students. The students on the Human Sexuality Committee had needed a place to store the booklets once the Yale University Press finished printing them, and so now the boxes of *Sex and the Yale Student* were stacked in Wasserman's office. She was happy to help. The booklets were not there for long, however. The committee began distributing them on September 10, and within two weeks, they ran out and Yale had none left to send the fifty different campuses that sought copies for their own students. "Your interest in Yale's new sex booklet is shared by so many others that we are currently out of copies," Wasserman wrote the dean of admissions at Skidmore College. A second printing was ordered.

Classes that fall started September 17, but a different beginning caught some students' attention. Fliers advertising the Sisterhood's first meeting of the year were papered all over campus: "Vanderbilt Lounge, September 21, 7:30 p.m." By the time the meeting started, seventy women students filled the room—freshmen, sophomores, juniors, and seniors—nearly five times as many as at the meetings last spring. It was "a huge number" of women, said Patty Mintz of Massachusetts, who was now a sophomore. It felt like "a quarter to a third of the women in the school."

The meeting began with an introduction by one of the Sisterhood veterans, and then the students went around the room, each saying why she had come and what she hoped the Sisterhood might accomplish. The older girls talked about how isolated they had felt in their first year at Yale, how hard it had been to meet other women. The freshmen in the class of 1974 had only been there a week, but they were already realizing the challenge. It was one thing to read about the ratio before coming and quite another to experience it firsthand. The Old Campus quadrangle that held all the freshmen was as long as two city blocks. The women were at the end of the quadrangle in Vanderbilt Hall, but every other dorm on the Old Campus was filled with the freshmen men.

Patty Mintz listened carefully as each student at the Sisterhood meeting spoke. She was struck by how so many had the same goals. After a year at Yale, she knew how many differences divided Yale women, yet that night "there was so much coherence and unity even though we were very different people." Forty years later, Patty would look back on that meeting and say, "It was really one of the five most powerful experiences in my life."

The group was enthusiastic about continuing the Sisterhood's consciousness-raising sessions, but the girls were also impatient for change. Most Yale men believed that "coeducation is something that happens to women," one sophomore woman observed later that year. It was long overdue for coeducation to happen to Yale. Students brought up the need for more women's studies courses. Some observed how they had spent a whole year at Yale without being taught by a single woman professor. Others mentioned the lack of decent career guidance for women, the long waits to get an appointment with the Sarrels at the Yale Sex Counseling Service, the need for more than one self-defense class. Subcommittees were formed to take action.

Of all the issues raised by the girls in Vanderbilt Hall that night, the one they ranked highest was this one: Yale's gender quotas in admissions. Until that changed, women students would remain a small minority at Yale and thus robbed of a voice in every other issue that mattered. The Sisterhood formed a subgroup to act. The class of 1974, it declared, would be the last where Yale decided who got in based on their gender.

The arrival of autumn marked the start of the field hockey season, and Lawrie Mifflin was ready to play. Yale may not have known yet that it had a women's field hockey team, but Lawrie and her classmate Jane Curtis certainly did, and so did the half-dozen colleges the two girls had written to over the summer to ask if they would scrimmage against Yale's newest team. Since Yale showed no signs of providing a team for its women, Lawrie and Jane had decided to do it themselves. The games would be nothing official, just a practice session really, but four nearby colleges and one local high school said yes, and after that, Lawrie had what she needed to talk to the Yale Athletic Department. "Look, we can do this," she said to the administrator who'd been assigned to deal with Yale girls. "There are schools who will play us. Would you just give us a field and some equipment?"

The strategy worked—sort of. Yale assigned the women's field hockey team to Parking Lot A, which was used for football game tailgating. When the girls came out on Mondays after a home game, their field would be covered with charcoal briquettes and beer cans and other debris from football fans' picnics, and they would have to begin practice by picking up garbage. Even then, the field was no good. The ball would careen off in unexpected directions when it hit one of the ruts left by the tires of the cars that had parked there. Yale also gave the field hockey players a coach—sort of. Yale's varsity football team had eight coaches that year. For the women field hockey players, Yale paid for a local high school phys ed teacher to come over two afternoons a week after her day job was done. She "was really a nice person," said Lawrie, but she did not know much about coaching field hockey.

The women's field hockey team did not have uniforms, and it played with an odd assortment of sticks, some that the girls brought from home and others that Lawrie convinced Yale to buy them. The team showed up at away games in a motley array of cars they had begged and borrowed from friends—Yale did not provide transportation. Officially, the team had twenty-five players, more than enough to field the eleven required, but it was hard getting everyone together, and one time they had to borrow a few players from the other team in order to not call off the game. It was "ragtag," said Lawrie. But still, Yale women played field hockey that year, and on fall afternoons, you could find them dodging the ruts in Parking Lot A as they sprinted down the field toward the goal.

A few of the other extracurriculars were beginning to make room for women, some more graciously than others. The Political Union, the largest student group at Yale, had elected a woman sophomore as treasurer, but when the *Yale Daily News* announced its new group of editors, seventeen out of seventeen were men. The Yale Dramat continued as a leader and elected women to two of its six board member positions. One of them was Connie Royster. Connie had continued to find a home at Yale among the theater students. With each new production, they were swept up together in the excitement of rehearsing, building sets, designing costumes, and figuring out the lighting and sound in the lead-up to opening night.

The theater undergraduates worked together as a team, and one of the drama school teachers, actress Norma Brustein, had taken them under her wing. They all took classes with Brustein, and she invited them to come to her home. When Connie contracted a case of meningitis bad enough to send her to the hospital, Norma Brustein showed up with a big pot of chicken soup. "Norma was no cook at all. She was a complete diva," said Connie, but she came

with her soup to help Connie get better and brought Connie's theater classmates to the hospital with her. "Everybody came," said
Connie. "It was just very special."

Connie and Betty Spahn both lived off campus now—Connie
in an apartment on her own and Betty a few blocks away with
a sophomore she had met in the Sisterhood. Like almost all Yale
women, Connie spent most of her time with her male friends. She
and two of them were almost inseparable. But whenever Connie
and Betty were together, their friendship clicked right back into
place. For Betty, knowing that Connie was there was like having
close family nearby. Betty could be totally herself with Connie, and
Connie relied on Betty as well. If either of the two friends had a
problem, they would create a space in their day to meet. Connie
might want advice on her boyfriend; Betty might need Connie to
help her settle down when she got too overheated about one injustice or another. Sometimes Betty was just not feeling at home at Yale,
a place where Connie was always so comfortable.

One time, Connie suggested they go to a restaurant that had
recently opened, a Chinese place called Blessings. Betty had never
eaten Chinese food before. She had no idea how to use chopsticks.
"Okay, so I know how to use chopsticks, and you don't," said Connie.
"I'll teach you. That's fine. No problem."

The two women also counted on each other to fill the gaps
that neither had time for. Connie knew about the arts. Betty stayed
up on politics, and together, their knowledge spanned both. Betty
would call at the end of a long week and tell Connie, "I need to go
out to the theater tonight. What's good?" Connie might wonder
what was going on with one political ruckus or another. Betty
always had the answer.

In between their phone calls and Chinese food dinners, both

women were busy at Yale: Connie with her theater and community work and Betty with the Sisterhood and the two jobs she was working to pay her tuition and living costs. Betty's parents had paid for her first year at George Washington and most of her first year at Yale. But those two years had already cost more than four years at the University of Illinois, and Betty's parents could not keep paying for Yale and still help Betty's three younger brothers with college. For her second year at Yale, Betty was paying all her college and living expenses herself. Yale's financial aid calculations, however, assumed that her parents were helping, and Betty had to cover the gap. It was a huge financial burden for a college student to take on, even with Betty's weekend job as a guard at Yale's Peabody Museum.

Help had come in a letter from Illinois Republican senator Chuck Percy. Percy was proud to have an Illinois girl in that first group of Yale women, and he asked if there was anything his office could do to help Betty out. She replied right away. "Could you get me a job in the post office or something?" All through her second year at Yale, Betty worked the night shift at the New Haven post office, sorting mail by zip code from midnight to 8:00 a.m. The guy who worked next to her, Eric, had been premed at Yale, but when his girlfriend got pregnant, he married her and then had to drop out of Yale to support his young family. Chatting with Eric as she sorted mail, hour after mind-numbing hour, convinced Betty that however hard it was to earn the money required, getting an education was worth it.

When her post office shift ended, Betty took the bus back to her apartment and then showered and went to classes. After that, she slept for a while. In the evening, before heading back to the post office, she did her coursework. Betty was a quick study and could read as fast as most people turned pages, but it was still an exhausting schedule. Nonetheless, she always made time for the Sisterhood.

The Sisterhood meetings were different that year, and it was not just because more women were coming. The students did consciousness-raising on some nights just like before, but on others they talked about feminist theory and what they were reading. The world had exploded with a wave of feminist books: Kate Millett's *Sexual Politics*, Toni Cade Bambara's *The Black Woman*, Germaine Greer's *The Female Eunuch*, Robin Morgan's *Sisterhood Is Powerful*, and Shulamith Firestone's *The Dialectic of Sex*. Major publishing houses were now coming out with books on women's liberation—some so powerful that women would never forget where they were the first time they read them. Sisterhood member Dahlia Rudavsky was sitting under a tree in the courtyard of Branford College when she first read *Sexual Politics*. "That book just blew my mind," said Dahlia.

The Sisterhood was also far more outspoken that year, and its subgroups on women's studies and ending Yale's gender quota were particularly active, with frequent meetings and strategy sessions. Other Sisterhood members grew bolder about challenging the ways they were treated at Yale. Fed up with yet another prank by men students, one sophomore linked hands with other girls and walked across the Old Campus shouting, "Fuck off, you male chauvinist pigs!" Yet ambivalence underlay the excitement of taking a stand. "Underneath it all," she said later, "I really wanted these same m.c.p.'s [male chauvinist pigs] to like me and respect me and date me." If you were a woman student at Yale, feminist activism was complicated.

By mid–October, the fall semester was well under way, and women students were outshining the men academically, as they had in their first year at Yale.   Los Angeles premed student Carol Storey, now a sophomore, was engrossed in her science classes, while other women discovered the joys of one academic discipline or another: Afro-American studies, medieval history, or calculus of multiple variables. The classroom conditions were not much different than they had been the previous year. The women still were greatly outnumbered, and there was always the chance you would end up with one of the professors who should never have been in a class-room in the first place: the music teacher who put porn pictures on the music stands,   the faculty member who announced that he would never award a girl a high grade and held true to his promise, and the chemistry teaching assistant who provided a handout detailing the properties of an unusual element: "Wo"—Women. "Accepted Weight," it read, "120 +/− 10; Occurrences: frequently appear when you wish they wouldn't; Properties: half-life about 35 years." Yet Yale's faculty also included professors who went out of their way to support and nurture Yale women.

Trombone player Kit McClure met Professor Boell that fall through her interest in cell fusion. Kit thought there might be a way to enable two women to have children without any need for a man or his sperm. *What happens when you fuse two egg cells together?* she wondered. *Can you get differentiation?* The idea "sounded totally whacky to everyone else," said Kit, but when she presented it to Boell, he took her seriously.

Boell was an expert in experimental embryology and a senior professor at Yale, and up near the top of Yale's Science Hill, on one of the floors of Kline Biology Tower, was a lab with a large group of South African toads that Yale biologists used for experiments.

"It was easy to get their eggs, poor things," explained Kit. Boell gave Kit access to the Kline bio lab and the toads that she needed for her research. He checked in on her there and provided guidance for her work. When Kit's early results showed promise, he arranged for her to meet with an advanced cell fusion specialist at Rockefeller University in New York—a woman. "That was a nice touch on his part," said Kit, "to send me to a woman professor."

Boell was not the only faculty member who mentored women students at Yale. Shirley Daniels met Visiting Professor Sylvia Boone that fall, and after that Shirley spent as much time with Boone as possible. "She was just an extraordinary woman, an absolutely extraordinary woman," said Shirley.

Boone was the Hunter College professor whom Shirley's friend Vera Wells had recruited to teach The Black Woman seminar, and Shirley had signed up for that class as soon as she heard about it. Boone had studied at the University of Ghana in the early 1960s and become part of Ghana's black expatriate community of intellectuals, authors, and artists, which included Maya Angelou and W. E. B. Du Bois. She was also a friend of Malcolm X, whom she first met in Ghana when he stopped there on his return to the United States from his pilgrimage to Mecca. Boone's own experiences were remarkable, but what drew students to her was the interest she took in their lives. She was "always focused on you, always focused on your needs," said Vera. You didn't always get that at Yale.

Sylvia Boone talked to Shirley about financial independence and how important that independence was to women. Shirley had been dating her Yale boyfriend for more than a year by then, but Boone told her to make sure she had a marketable skill. That way, she would always know that she could take care of herself if need be. In an era when marriage was still seen by many as women's best path to

security, it was unusual advice. Boone also expanded Shirley's sense
of what was possible. Yes, Shirley would need a job to support herself
and her family, but "you could have a career in something that you
love," Boone told her. No one had ever said that to Shirley before.

While students in The Black Woman seminar were grateful
for the support they felt from Sylvia Boone, Betty Spahn's interactions with Yale faculty about adding more women's studies
courses weren't going so well. Yale had just two courses that fall that
addressed the experience of women: Sylvia Boone's class and a new
course, Sociological Perspectives on Women.   Demand for both
was high. Boone had to offer her seminar in two different residential colleges when the original seminar filled up, and sixty-four students—forty-one women and twenty-three men—signed up for the
sociology class. The papers they wrote there spanned a wide range of
topics: "Role Conflict among Women with Careers and Families,"
"The American Housewife on the Sacrificial Altar," "Women in
Collective Living Situations," "Women in Labor Unions," "The
Development of Sex Differences," and "The Amazons." Betty and
eight other Sisterhood members took that class. For the first time at
Yale, they had a woman professor, readings authored by women, and
the experience of not being one of just a few women in a classroom
of men. It was like a door opening up to an incredible room they
had not even known was there.

Betty was determined to open more of those doors. She spent
hours waiting outside the offices of Yale department chairs in the
hopes of persuading them to offer a women's studies course in their
field: psychology, economics, history, English, or any of the other
subjects at Yale whose curricula seemed to imply that the world
contained nothing but men. The Sisterhood members usually went
in pairs to those meetings, and after a while, the department chairs

would eventually usher them in. For Betty, the meetings merged together into a "blur of these old white men sitting behind their desks." The girls often had to go back several times, and they were almost never successful. Most women's studies courses still had to come in through the back door of the residential college seminars.

Of all the professors Betty met with in her efforts to expand Yale's curriculum, one of the worst was George Pierson, the same person who had given Elga Wasserman such a hard time about her Mory's letter. Pierson was the director of Yale's humanities division, and one afternoon Betty and Dahlia Rudavsky approached him about offering a women's history course. The idea was "absurd," Pierson responded. What was there to teach about women's influence in history? "Why not a history of children?" he asked. But the two women students "were not to be put off," Pierson complained later to another faculty member. He eventually approached one of the most junior members of his department, a woman lecturer, and asked if she would be willing to teach women's history. He could hardly ask a man to do so.

Elga Wasserman had avoided any further tangles with Pierson, but even so, her second year as special assistant was not going much better than the first. She had been excited about her coeducation report, but Kingman Brewster still had not given her the go-ahead to release it, and after nearly five months on his desk, the report had grown stale. On October 15, Brewster finally met with the Coeducation Committee about Yale's cap on the numbers of women students. The discussion was brief. Reducing the number of men students was not negotiable, said Brewster, and then he set forth yet a new roadblock to change: before altering its male-female ratio, Yale needed to reexamine the basic assumptions underlying its entire approach to undergraduate education. Brewster's list of necessary topics included the optimum size of Yale College, the size of the university as a whole, and whether undergraduates should be awarded a bachelor's degree after three years rather than four. Nothing could be decided about women until these other matters were settled.

Brewster's new position on coeducation was stunning. With his refusal to reduce the number of Yale men, increasing the number of women was already on hold until the two new residential colleges were finished. This new obstacle threatened to keep women undergraduates to less than 20 percent indefinitely.

In his 1968 Report of the President, Brewster had devoted a few pages to discussing the levers of power afforded to the president of Yale.   He noted his role as the head of the Yale Corporation and his power to set the budget. He remarked on the extra weight accorded his views because of his position as president. But one power that Brewster did not mention was perhaps the most important of all: the power to do nothing. As Kit McClure wrote in her diary after the Corporation's March 1970 vote to leave Yale's gender quota unchanged, "The campaign for full coeducation has been stopped by the Yale Corporation's decision to ignore it."   If the goal is protecting the status quo, the best move by those in power is no move at all.

———

All through the first year of coeducation and even before the women students arrived, Elga Wasserman had raised concerns about safety. The word *rape*, however, had not made it into her memos or the pages of the *Yale Daily News*. At the start of December, that changed. Two other assaults on Yale women served as prelude. On Thanksgiving, a student was walking to the New Haven train station in the evening when she was grabbed by a man with a knife. Fortunately, three other pedestrians approached, and he fled before causing her harm. On December 3, another Yale woman was attacked at night near the housing annexes of Yale's Pierson and Ezra Stiles Colleges. She screamed, and the assailant hit her, but he was frightened away by two approaching groups of people. In both cases, the chance arrival of passersby enabled the women to escape. On December 9, Yale sophomore Christa Hansen was not so lucky.

Christa had come to Yale the year before from a small coed school in Spokane. She was pretty, with a wide smile and long, light-brown hair parted just off to the side. Christa was thinking of majoring in psychology. She was walking back to her dorm room in Morse College after spending the evening studying at Yale's Sterling Library. It was late, and there were not many people around. A car pulled up next to Christa, and one of the men inside jumped out and grabbed her. He told her to get in the car. What she felt pressing into her back through her coat was a knife, he said. Get in the car, said the man. Christa got in, and the group of men drove off with her. She was gang raped in the car.

Afterward, Christa was "utterly distraught," said a woman student who tried to help her. Christa's father was beside himself and let Kingman Brewster know it. "How could you have let this happen to my daughter?" The following day, the *Yale Daily News* ran a front-page article about Christa's rape and the two rape attempts that had preceded it.

The Yale police responded to the assaults by advising Yale women to take "safety precautions." Even Elga Wasserman, who had fought to prevent such a terrible thing from happening, put the blame on the women. Women needed to recognize that "we

do live in a city and it isn't all that safe," she scolded, saying nothing about Yale's responsibility to keep its women students safe.
The following month, Wasserman repeated the same point at the
regular monthly meeting of the masters of Yale's twelve residential
colleges. "Many women students at Yale seem reluctant…to accept
the seriousness of the risks involved in walking alone outdoors
after dark," she told them.

Over the course of the second year of coeducation, the Yale
campus police documented four rapes, including that of a sixty-
year-old secretary who was attacked in the third-floor ladies' room
of Sheffield-Sterling-Strathcona, the same building where Elga
Wasserman worked. These police numbers are almost certainly
low. As with sexual harassment, the costs of reporting a rape out-
weighed any benefits for women, and so most went unreported. In
1970, rape survivors could expect callous treatment from police and
hospital workers. If a woman chose to press charges, her own sexual
history became fair game for courtroom discussion, and she had to
show that she had resisted her assailant. In some states, women had to
provide a witness to prove they weren't lying. Most people believed
that a raped woman had "asked for it."

Whatever the actual number of student rapes at Yale, even those
that the administration knew about were not often known by Yale
women. The *Yale Daily News* published no more stories on rapes that
year. The residential college deans—the administrators most directly
responsible for the welfare of Yale students—only learned about a
rape if it happened to a student in their own college. "Yale wasn't
going out it of its way to say, 'Girls can be raped,'" said one freshman woman. "It was more like they were quietly putting it in the
closet… But it was going on. It was very much there."

As for Christa Hansen, graduate student Margie Ferguson tried to offer some support afterward. Before coeducation started, Elga Wasserman had set up a new system of women graduate assistants to serve as advisers and role models for the undergraduates, and Margie was the graduate assistant in Morse, Christa's residential college. Christa came to Margie's office several times to talk about what happened to her, but Margie was just a well-meaning graduate student with no training as a counselor. "I don't think I did any more than give a sympathetic ear to a terrible story," she said.   Like most colleges, Yale had nothing in place to support students who were raped, no one with the training to counsel them.   Christa dropped out of Yale and went back home to Spokane.

———

Meanwhile, over in Woodbridge Hall, Kingman Brewster was focused on other issues. The conversation about Yale women, at least as far as he was concerned, was over. Advocates for more women students would just need to wait until the two new colleges were built and Yale had sorted out all those policy questions that needed to be resolved before the gender ratio could be reconsidered. Yet Wasserman would not let the issue drop. Two weeks after Brewster's October meeting with the Coeducation Committee, she wrote Brewster about her coeducation report, which was still stalled on his desk. He had told her earlier that he wanted to include a reply when the report went public. "Could you let me have such a letter stating your position?" Wasserman asked.   A week passed with no reply from Brewster. Another. Still more.

On December 4, Wasserman wrote Brewster again. "There is widespread sentiment among many students and faculty that the male-female ratio should be improved as rapidly as possible," she observed. "As far as I am aware, we still have no specific plans for attaining the ratio announced as a goal in 1968, 4,000 men and 1,500 to 2,000 women." Wasserman kept pressing: "Are we planning an expansion to 5,500 or 6,000 students in the near future? If not, how will a 2:1 or 3:1 ratio be obtained?" Such persistence did not endear Elga Wasserman to Brewster.

"She grated on him," said Sam Chauncey. "She would get her teeth into a particular idea about something and she couldn't let it go…I think that was her way of saying, 'Look, we're not going to let any of these issues slide under the table.' So it was a good thing, but it was annoying." Women saw Wasserman's tenacity differently. "Elga was very good at making sure that the women's question was on the front burner," said Jackie Mintz, who joined the Yale administration the following year. "She was an advocate," said Margaret Coon, who had led the alumni lunch protest. "She went to bat for us over and over again, and we just really loved her," said Sisterhood member Kate Field. Yet it was Brewster who was Elga Wasserman's boss, not the women who admired her.

In early December, however, Brewster gave Wasserman an opening, or at least the appearance of one. The Yale Corporation was convening in New Haven on the weekend of December 12, and Wasserman would be allowed to present the Coeducation Committee report at its meeting. It would be the first time that Yale's admissions policy had made the Corporation agenda since its vote the previous March to leave the gender quotas unchanged, and it was just the moment the Yale Sisterhood had been waiting for.

Yale's trustees were still all men in 1970, although the Corporation now had its first black member, U.S. district court judge Leon Higginbotham. The fifteen men gathered for their meetings in a special room in Woodbridge Hall, with an enormous polished wood table lit from above by fine chandeliers. As Yale's trustees seated themselves in their large leather chairs that December, they could hear the sounds of a boisterous rally being held right outside in Beinecke Plaza. "No more thousand male leaders!" shouted the Sisterhood members and their supporters.   One hundred students had gathered. The women held signs and listened as student after student stepped up to the mic and called for Yale to adopt sex-blind admissions. And then they chanted some more: "No more thousand male leaders!"

Inside, Wasserman presented the coeducation report to the Corporation, and with it the recommendation that Yale admit eight hundred men and four hundred women for the class of 1975. The proposal, with its two-to-one male-female ratio, was hardly revolutionary. Prestigious private colleges such as Duke, Middlebury, Oberlin, Swarthmore, and the University of Chicago all seemed to be surviving with two-to-one ratios or even higher percentages of women.   The March 1970 student petition had gone a step further and called for sex-blind admissions, as did the new petition that Sisterhood members were busily circulating through Yale dining halls. But even the Coeducation Committee's more moderate suggestion never stood a chance after Brewster shared his own views on the issue.

Brewster began graciously, acknowledging the hard work of "Mrs. Wasserman's Committee on Coeducation."   Yet even this introduction was an opening jab, since the group's actual name—the University Committee on Coeducation—held far more weight than the "Mrs. Wasserman's Committee" that Brewster chose to call it, and the group in fact reported directly to him, not to Wasserman. Brewster continued with a step-by-step dismantling of the committee's recommendation. First was Yale's mission of graduating men.

Brewster would never have recommended that Yale admit women undergraduates, he explained, "if I had not been able to assure anyone who asked that we did not intend to reduce the number of men in Yale College." And besides, he went on, presenting his new reason for inaction, Yale had to rethink its entire approach to undergraduate education before it could reconsider the numbers of women. Last was the problem of alumni, said Brewster, thus fueling the false notion that coeducation was the main cause of alumni discontent, when the real problem was that Yale was no longer giving alumni children the preference in admissions they had once enjoyed.

All these reasons provided a rational packaging of Brewster's support for Yale's thousand male leaders, but he probably could have swayed the trustees' vote simply by saying he opposed the Coeducation Committee's recommendation. As one Yale trustee once told Brewster when he tried to pin an unpopular decision on the Corporation, "Kingman, come off it. You know perfectly well that the Corporation will do anything you tell them."

———

On Saturday, December 12, the Corporation met again. The Sisterhood had worked hard on its petition for sex-blind admissions and had 1,930 signatures in all, even more than the petition that Women and Men for a Better Yale had organized the previous spring. Unlike this earlier group, though, the Sisterhood was not invited to meet with the Corporation. Undeterred, they walked right in to Woodbridge Hall: fifty women students, some in jeans, some dressed up in skirts and blouses. "We stormed the Yale Corporation," said Patty Mintz of Massachusetts. "We went in and disrupted this Corporation meeting to demand that they do something about this horrible ratio, and how bad it was making people's lives," said Betsy Hartmann, her roommate. Given the holiday season, the students had wrapped the stack of signed petitions in Christmas paper as "a present to the Corporation," and Dahlia Rudavsky proudly presented this gift once the girls had ascended the stairs to the room where the Corporation met. Yale's trustees would vote later that day on whether to alter their admissions policy or keep the current gender quotas in place.

As the Corporation deliberated in Woodbridge Hall, Vera Wells was busily completing the final tasks for a different event that weekend: an academic conference on the experience and history of the black woman, the first ever held in the United States. Sylvia Boone's Black Woman seminar had been so successful that Boone and Vera had wondered together if they might go one step further and have Yale host such a conference. Boone could use her connections to bring in some of the leading voices in the field while Vera would work to find resources at Yale to pay for the event. The two obtained funding from Yale's prestigious Chubb Fellowship, which had never gone to a woman in its twenty-one-year history, and on the evening of December 12, the Conference on the Black Woman opened with its first speaker, Maya Angelou. *I Know Why the Caged Bird Sings* was so new that Vera had not even had a chance to read it yet.

Angelou stood before a rapt audience of two hundred students, educators, and New Haven residents. She was tall—"Statuesque," said Vera—and dressed in a patterned African dress with her hair wrapped tight in a head cloth. The question of the role of black women in the Black Power movement arose. Should black men be the ones to take the lead there? "No good. That's out. That's out to lunch," Angelou thundered back. "We were also packed, spoon-fashion, on the slave ships, we shared the auction blocks, we shared the lash and the cotton fields—now we cannot share the same sidewalk?"

The following day brought three more black luminaries to speak to the audience at Yale: author Shirley Graham Du Bois, who was the widow of black civil rights activist W. E. B. Du Bois; black cultural historian John Henrik Clarke; and Pulitzer Prize–winning poet Gwendolyn Brooks, the poet laureate of Illinois. The *New York Times* was listening, and the next day, it published a full-page story on the remarkable conference at Yale.

The *Yale Daily News* led with a different story that day: the results of the Yale Corporation meeting. Perhaps the verdict was predictable, but it was disheartening nonetheless. There would be no change to Yale's gender quota. Two days later, Wasserman finally released the Coeducation Committee report, nearly seven months after she had first sent the group's recommendation to Brewster. "Committee Urges More Coeducation," read the *Yale Daily News* headline, but no one was paying attention. Christmas vacation was two days away, and besides, everyone already knew what had happened. It would be two more years before the Corporation considered the matter of Yale's discrimination against women again.

TEN

Reinforcements

AS THE YALE CORPORATION MET IN NEW HAVEN
that December and decided once again to leave Yale's gender quotas
unchanged, a fundamental shift was occurring in Washington,
DC. For the first time, the federal government halted payment on
a university contract because of sex discrimination. Unless the
University of Michigan stopped blocking women from applying for
jobs reserved for men, stopped underpaying their women employees,
and stopped the discrimination that kept women to just 4 percent of
its full professors, Michigan would lose $4 million in federal funding.

The day after the Michigan news hit the press, Yale assistant professor Charlotte Morse bumped into her colleague Bart Giamatti in
a New Haven coffee shop. "What the hell difference would it make
to Yale if the feds cut off our funding?" she asked. Giamatti looked
at her with a raised eyebrow. "About 33 percent of the annual oper-
ating budget."

No laws yet barred colleges and universities from discriminating
against women. Instead, an executive order signed by former president Lyndon Johnson had blocked Michigan's money. Executive

Order 11246 had been on the books since 1965, but its use to fight gender discrimination was new. The order had initially barred discrimination by federal contractors on the basis of race, color, religion, or national origin—but not gender. Johnson amended it in 1967 to add women, but even then the order sat unused for that purpose until Bernice Sandler read about it in 1969.

Sandler held a PhD from the University of Maryland and had been told a few months earlier that she was unsuited for any of the seven open positions in her department because she "came on too strong for a woman." After two more job rejections—the first because the interviewer said he never hired women, the second because Sandler was "not really a professional" but "just a housewife"—Sandler began researching to see what the law had to say about how she was treated. Not much, it turned out, but one afternoon, while reading about the efforts of black Americans to end public school segregation, Sandler came across Executive Order 11246 in a footnote and shrieked out loud at the discovery. Here was the tool that women could use to gain equity in U.S. colleges.

By December 1970, when the University of Michigan penalty was announced, Sandler had used Executive Order 11246 to help women file sex discrimination complaints at more than two hundred U.S. campuses. Yale was not yet on the list, but that was about to change. On January 29, 1971, U.S. secretary of labor James Hodgson received two letters from Yale, one from women clerical workers and the other from women faculty and administrators. Both letters alleged rampant gender discrimination and requested an immediate federal investigation. Two days later, Hodgson was copied on a third complaint against Yale, this one from Sandler herself.

Kingman Brewster may have delayed Wasserman's coeducation report long enough the previous year that its challenge to

Yale's thousand-man quota was ignored, but the report also contained a dozen pages of data on the status of women at Yale, and Bernice Sandler had a copy. Sandler knew Elga Wasserman. They both were part of a group that worked behind the scenes with Congresswoman Edith Green to bring change on college campuses for women, and Wasserman's report contained exactly what Sandler needed to back the sex discrimination complaint filed by Yale women: data. Sandler's letter took its statistics right from Wasserman's appendix E: Yale women faculty. "Out of a faculty of 839, only TWO women have tenure," Sandler wrote. It was a fact that tended to get people's attention.

Sandler's charges against Yale did not stop with faculty hiring. Yale discriminated against women in admissions decisions, in awarding financial aid, and in faculty salaries and promotions, Sandler wrote. And then she sent her letter to more than fifty Washington officials, including the secretary of the Department of Health, Education, and Welfare (HEW) Elliot Richardson. HEW has since been disbanded, its functions divided between two new federal agencies, but at the time, few college presidents did not know those initials. HEW was the agency that enforced Executive Order 11246.

Filing the discrimination complaint was "exciting," said Yale graduate student Margie Ferguson, whose research helped bolster the findings. "There was a sense that the federal government was going to be a really important partner." Even Brewster's top legal adviser observed that "a prod from Uncle Sam" might move Yale toward change. Sandler's letter and the two from Yale women had all made the same request: put any new federal contracts with Yale on hold until all discrimination against women was corrected. That should get Brewster's attention.

Meanwhile, up in New Haven, the freshmen in the class of

1974 had settled in to their lives as Yale students. And once they did, these new reinforcements were asking the same question that Yale students had posed for over a year now: Is this what Yale thinks coeducation looks like? Many of the freshmen girls had felt the same shock on arrival as did the first women undergraduates the year before. Linden Havemeyer had come to Yale from all-girls Concord Academy. She grew up in a family of six girls. "Everything about entering Yale was overwhelming," said Linden. "Suddenly, I was not only at a coed institution, but I was outnumbered four or five to one." Yet despite students' dismay at Yale's gender ratio, progress toward increasing the numbers of women was stalled right where it had been the previous year.

No ground had yet been broken on Yale's new student housing. Brewster had not even named a committee to consider all the issues that he'd placed in line ahead of Yale women, and the groups that had pushed him to increase women's numbers were not quite as strong as they had been. The Coeducation Committee had retreated after the Corporation's December rejection of its recommendation, while Wasserman seemed unable to make progress on Yale's gender quotas whether she acted as a team player or provocateur. The Sisterhood was increasingly focused on other issues, from abortion rights to women's studies to the HEW sex discrimination complaint against Yale. A new group, and new energy, was needed if Yale was to adopt sex-blind admissions any time in the foreseeable future.

Alec Haverstick, one of the freshmen in the class of 1974, might have seemed an unlikely candidate for that role. The status quo had worked pretty well for him so far. Alec grew up on Manhattan's exclusive Upper East Side and attended St. Paul's, one of the nation's most elite boys' boarding schools. He looked just like the preppy guy he was. Yes, his dark hair almost reached down to his shoulders, but Alec still wore Levi's and Topsiders and cleaned up well in his sport jacket and khakis. His smile displayed perfect teeth. Yet there were things about Alec that did not show up in the St. Paul's School yearbook.

His mother, a single parent, was "pretty much…a women's libber," said Alec, and she was one of the trustees at Barnard College, where she was working on her doctorate. Women faculty from Barnard would come down to the Haversticks' East 70th Street apartment to talk. Alec was there once when Kate Millett, who taught at Barnard, walked in, and his education in how women saw the world continued at Yale.

A few weeks after Alec arrived there, he had dinner with a group of women students who had all gone to Concord Academy, the girls' boarding school that Linden Havemeyer had attended. The Yale sophomores from the academy invited Linden and the other Concord Academy freshmen to join them for dinner in Yale's Freshman Commons, and Alec came along too. Alec knew the Concord Academy girls from the three weeks he had lived there as a high school exchange student. When the sophomores at the dinner began explaining to the others what that first year at Yale had been like, their report was not what Alec expected.

"The bitterness oozing out of this conversation…was extraordinary," he said. "It was anger personified. It was just coming out and out." Alec was hurt to hear the women's assumption that men were all chauvinists who saw women as inferiors. "I don't feel that way," said Alec. But if that was how things were at Yale, he asked, then what was the solution? "Numbers," said the women. "Numbers?" asked Alec. The sophomore women responded. "Until there are more of us, we're always going to be treated like fourth-class citizens."

The antiwar movement had been dormant for months, but in February, it reemerged with vigor following news of the U.S. invasion of Laos. Protests erupted at campuses all over the country: Kansas State, Notre Dame, and the University of Alabama, of Nebraska, of Oklahoma. On February 22, Yale's Woolsey Hall filled with 2,500 students who had come for an antiwar rally. The speeches that night lasted nearly four hours, but the one that drew the most applause was that of a twenty-seven-year-old Yale graduate who had fought in the war and was back now, a guy named John Kerry. Vietnam Veterans against the War was planning a massive protest in April, Kerry told the students before him. He hoped Yale students would support the veterans' efforts.

As before, Yale women were involved in the antiwar activism, but their protest against sex discrimination did not stop. A year had now passed since the maître d' of Mory's had told the women law school students to leave, and the ranks of those who sought to change the club's men-only policy had grown larger. In October, a dozen members of New Haven Women's Liberation had picketed in front of Mory's for a week. In November, the newly appointed dean of Yale Law School, Abe Goldstein, informed Mory's that any account Mory's was carrying in the name of the law school should be discontinued immediately. Until women were admitted to Mory's on the same basis as men, Yale Law School was no longer a customer.

Yale economics PhD student Heidi Hartmann had been part of the weeklong picketing of Mory's in October. Every time a Yale professor or faculty member crossed the picket line to enter Mory's, a woman protester would walk up and ask him, "Are you a racist and a sexist or just a sexist?" Like Kingman Brewster, many of the men who frequented Mory's boycotted clubs that discriminated against blacks. It angered the women that these men would not find discrimination against women equally objectionable. As Heidi was standing in the picket line at Mory's, she spotted one of her professors, James Tobin, pacing back and forth across the street. Tobin was watching the protesters and clearly holding an internal debate over whether to stand up the men he was supposed to be meeting at Mory's or walk through the picket line to join them. He decided on the latter, and as he did so, Heidi walked up and asked him the same question the women were asking every man who passed by them: "Are you a racist and a sexist or just a sexist?"

Tobin, troubled, entered Mory's. Tobin was one of the most distinguished economics professors at Yale and would go on to win the Nobel Prize, but he was also well known for his integrity and commitment to racial justice. "He was a highly ethical person," said graduate student Janet Yellen, who was Tobin's advisee and a hotshot economics student, well known by the younger students like Heidi for her reputation for brilliance. A few weeks later, Heidi received a long, heartfelt letter from James Tobin, explaining why he was neither a sexist nor a racist.

In February, however, women doctoral students in the economics department learned that some of their professors were still meeting at Mory's, and they responded by sending a letter to the entire economics faculty. "We cannot accept the exclusion of women from the channels of communication and power which such a club represents," the women wrote, detailing the impact on women of men's continued patronage of Mory's. It took courage to sign your name to that letter. The men who received it would soon be deciding which students to recommend for faculty positions. But at the bottom were the signatures of every female doctoral student in the economics department, thirteen in all, including twenty-four-year-old Janet Yellen.

A few days later, Mory's received word that the Yale Economics Department would no longer be conducting business there either.

———

Yale was offering four different women's studies courses that semester, double the number of the previous spring: Women in the U.S. Economy, Images of Women in Literature, Psychological Perspectives on Women, and Women and the Law. The first three were residential college seminars, but the last course was taught at the law school to 147 students: 126 men and 21 women. Betty Spahn and a group of Sisterhood women were there every week, and Connie Royster signed up for it too.

Connie loved that class. She found the two law students who taught it, Gail Falk and Ann Hill, inspiring, and she liked that the class supported the thinking she had been doing about law and feminism without being on the "raising flags and marching" side of activism. Instead, Women and the Law was the "academically rigorous, thoughtful yet passionate and compassionate side of the women's struggle," said Connie. Betty might be comfortable out marching, but for Connie, the law school students' approach to change was where she best fit. The paper Connie wrote for the class explored legal strategies to force fair representation for women in the media. It received Honors, the highest mark at Yale.

When they weren't teaching Yale undergraduates or finishing their coursework at Yale Law School, Gail Falk and Ann Hill were involved in another feminist initiative: *Women v. Connecticut*, which sought to overturn Connecticut's antiabortion law. Many women at Yale had seen the cost of that law when a classmate made a mistake and got pregnant. In Betty and Connie's first year, a woman in their dorm started hemorrhaging one night after going through an illegal abortion. The girl's roommate had pounded on their door. "Call the police! Call the police! She's bleeding to death!" An ambulance arrived, and the student was saved, but she was never able to bear her own children afterward.

Some students were able to obtain safe abortions performed by a doctor. In the first three years of coeducation, about twenty under-graduates did so through the Yale Health Center, and after New York State passed its abortion law in April 1970, pregnant women could make the trip there. Sometimes, however, Yale women who got pregnant just dropped out. "It was like women, whether in high school or college, just faded away once they became pregnant," said a Yale sophomore who learned only later why one of her classmates had left.

The effort to make safe and legal abortions possible in Connecticut had begun the previous year, and the goal of the dozen New Haven women behind *Women v. Connecticut* reached even further than changing state law. Up until that point, the conver-sations about abortion law in Connecticut had all been conversa-tions among men. The judges were men. The legislators, lawyers, and expert witnesses were men. *Women v. Connecticut* set out to change that. Women "were the experts about the effects of the abortion laws," they believed, and women would be the plaintiffs, witnesses, and lawyers. At a time when only 4 percent of U.S. lawyers and 1 percent of judges were women, the women's presence in the court-room alone counted as rebellion.

The strategy was to have not just a few women plaintiffs but dozens and dozens of women. That organizing effort could bring women together, and for each woman plaintiff, the mere act of signing her name to the plaintiff card was powerful. That's where the Sisterhood got involved. To qualify as a plaintiff, women needed only to live in Connecticut, be of childbearing age, and state that they did not wish to bear a child at that time. Sisterhood members signed on as plaintiffs and then recruited other women to join them. Some stood out in their residential college courtyards with a pile of *Women v. Connecticut*'s bright-yellow pamphlets and spoke with women who passed by about the lawsuit.

Others did speaking engagements arranged by the Yale Law School women. Judy Berkan and Anna Tsing Lowenhaupt drove down to Stamford and met in a church there with twenty white suburban women who had agreed to come hear them speak. Betty Spahn did radio and TV interviews. She played well in the Connecticut media—a nice Midwestern girl, one of the first coeds at Yale, and well-spoken.

The efforts of the Sisterhood and others succeeded. Plaintiffs signed on. Momentum built. On March 2, Yale Law School graduate Katie Roraback, the lawyer who was defending Ericka Huggins in the ongoing Black Panther trial, filed suit against the state of Connecticut in U.S. district court, charging that the state's antiabortion law was unconstitutional. By the time Roraback filed *Abele v. Markle*, as the *Women v. Connecticut* suit became formally called, the case had 858 women plaintiffs.

The Sisterhood was involved in other efforts as well, and its presence at Yale that spring was made all the more prominent by the new Women's Center that had opened in Durfee Hall, one door down from the student mailroom. The Women's Center was a space where women students "could just drop in and talk to each

other, and leave some reading material, and not have to be with the
men all the time," said Betty.   Yale had not provided the Durfee Hall
space to the women without a tussle. A few of the Sisterhood members had laid claim to it over May Day, and Yale had not taken kindly
to their appropriation of the two unused rooms. Elga Wasserman
and Undergraduate Dean John Wilkinson, however, spoke up for the
girls, and Yale backed off its talk of eviction.

The Yale Women's Center was nothing fancy. "Scruffy" was a
little more like it.   But it was a comfortable space, with some beat-up
old chairs and colorful paint. There were coffee and doughnuts and
feminist magazines spread on the table. "We hope that everyone
will see it as a place they can be comfortable with other women,"
Sisterhood member Barbara Deinhardt told the *Yale Daily News*. The
center welcomed all Yale women, she said, no matter their politics.

In March, the Women's Center hosted a special visitor. Kate
Millett was back in New Haven. "Ask yourselves the question," she
told the room full of women. "Are you in this for solace, or are you
in this for change?"   Consciousness-raising could only go so far. For
many in the room, Millett's question felt like a turning point. The
answer was obvious. They were in it for change.

———

Kit McClure was not involved with the Sisterhood's efforts to get
plaintiffs for the abortion lawsuit or with its work to set up the Yale
Women's Center. By the second year of coeducation, Kit was not
involved in the Sisterhood at all. She and Betty Spahn never talked
about it. Kit just "sort of disappeared," said Betty.   But if the two had
spoken, Kit could have explained in just a few words: "I had other
things to do."   Kit was working on her cell fusion experiments in

Kline Biology Tower and loading her schedule with music courses. She was an active member of New Haven Women's Liberation. And buoyed by the rock band's August performance, she was spending more time than ever practicing her trombone and doing musical arrangements for the band.

By the second year of coeducation, Kit barely resembled the freshman girl with bright-red, shoulder-length hair who had arrived at Yale carrying a trombone. She had cut all her hair off, for one thing, and now kept it cropped short above her ears. She wore dangly hoop earrings and wire-rim glasses, and she had long ago broken up with her freshman-year boyfriend. Kit was dating women now. Some of the radical lesbians at the Free Women Conference had made an impact on Kit, and she was finding it more and more contradictory to put all her energy into the women's movement "and then relate to a man." Before freshman year was out, Kit made a conscious decision to change her sexuality. "It was hard at first," she said, "but I tried it, and I liked it."

Kit's days were filled with her political work and Yale academics, but at the center was the New Haven Women's Liberation Rock Band, now almost one year old. Practice and concert, concert and practice—there was always something going on. Mostly the band played at events around Yale and for dance parties held by New Haven Women's Liberation. They played at other colleges too, and one afternoon, they loaded up their instruments into band member Virginia Blaisdell's Volkswagen Beetle convertible and drove an hour east to Niantic. The warden at the state women's prison had agreed to let them perform.

Kit and the band were taken to a large room where two hundred women prisoners, including the four women Black Panthers still on trial, were seated in rows on folding chairs. Ericka Huggins's

The New Haven Women's Liberation Rock Band, summer 1972.
From left to right, outside car: Harriet Cohen, Kit McClure,
Rika Alper, Jennifer Abod, Pat Ouellette. *From left to right,
inside car:* Leah Margulies, Virginia Blaisdell, Judy Miller.
Photo © Virginia Blaisdell.

daughter was two years old by then. The women prisoners were not
allowed to dance, but the New Haven Women's Liberation Rock
Band performed with its usual exuberance and mix of instruments:
bass, drums, flute, sax, trombone, tambourine, French horn, and
guitar. The band played every song it knew, and since it did not
know very many, it supplemented the performance with feminist
raps the band members had composed for the occasion. When it
came time for the last song, though, the band just kept on playing,
improvising and tossing the melody back and forth from one musician to another in one long, glorious jam session.

A few of the women prisoners leapt out into the aisle by their folding chairs and started dancing. The guards rushed over to tell them to sit down, but women jumped up and started dancing on the other side of the room. "Soon there were more dancers than guards," said Virginia Blaisdell, and as the band continued to play, the numbers kept growing.   Finally, the prison matron rushed up to the makeshift stage. "You *must* stop now," she said to the band, and with the end of the music, the room calmed.   Afterward, the band received a letter of thanks from Ericka Huggins. She was grateful, she told them, to have had the experience of looking across at her fellow women prisoners and "watching faces smile, really smile for the first time in months."

Kate Field was not part of the Niantic Women's Prison concert. She wished it were otherwise, but when Kate returned to Yale for her sophomore year, she found that the band had been practicing all summer while she was in Maine, and another woman guitar player had taken her place. Kate was still in the Sisterhood, though, and like many Sisterhood members, she was now living off campus. Kate and one of her freshman-year roommates had moved into a three-story house in New Haven with several philosophy professors and grad-uate students whom Kate had met when she coordinated the peace marshals over May Day. Kate had a room on the ground floor.

Kate's second year at Yale had been going well. No more poetry professors had asked her to go for a walk in the Grove Street Cemetery and then made a pass at her. The frenzied work leading up to May Day was behind her. She liked her housemates and living off campus. Late one night, however, when Kate was asleep in her bed, a man with a knife broke into the house and entered her room. He was wearing a ski mask. If she screamed, he said, he would kill her. He raped her in her bed.

After the rapist was gone, in the terrible hubbub that followed, someone called the master of Kate's residential college at Yale, and he arrived at the house with some whiskey. "He was just so kind," said Kate. Everyone was "amazingly kind." Yet that could not erase what had happened.

Kate was taken off to the hospital, where they refused to examine her without parental consent. Kate was damned if she was going to wake her parents up at four thirty in the morning and tell them she had just been raped. "Yale Health Service has permission to treat me," she told the friends who had come with her, and so Kate was put back in the car without having been seen by a doctor and driven to the Yale Health Service.

Kate reported the crime to New Haven police, who came to the house and saw signs of the break-in. Stereos and other goods had been stolen. They believed Kate about the rape once they saw the other evidence, but they did not want to believe that her assailant was white. "How do you know?" they asked, since she had told them about the ski mask. "He had a New Haven accent," Kate answered. White men from New Haven had a certain way of speaking, black men another way entirely. "It was a white man," said Kate. But the police "were put out. They were offended." It was simpler to believe that the rapist was black.

Kate's rape would have been hard enough if it had ended that night, but it didn't. She got pregnant. She had to go to New York to get an abortion, since abortion was still illegal in Connecticut. Kate had arrived at Yale as a freshman proud of the poetry prize she had won and with dreams of becoming a writer. Now "nobody knew what to do with me," she said. "I didn't know what to do with me." And so, like Christa Hansen, she dropped out of Yale.

On April 16, two federal investigators arrived in New Haven to
meet with Yale women about their sex discrimination complaint
against Yale. The Sisterhood was there. Over the previous two days,
Sisterhood members had stood outside residential college dining halls
at mealtime, collecting signatures for a petition that called on Yale to
"form a strong affirmative action program for the total elimination
of all discriminatory practices in education and employment." By
the time the girls presented the petition to HEW, 1,973 students
had signed it. The Sisterhood left a copy in Woodbridge Hall for
Kingman Brewster, although few still believed Brewster's September
1969 pledge that he would take student petitions seriously.

The HEW investigators met with representatives from five
women's groups at Yale: the Sisterhood, the Graduate Alliance, Yale
Law Women, the Yale Faculty and Professional Women's Forum,
and the Yale Non-Faculty Action Committee. The agenda covered
multiple types of sex discrimination at Yale, including the gender
quotas in admissions and a topic that had never come up before in
an HEW investigation: sexual harassment. It was "a new idea" to the
HEW team, who said it had never heard the term *sexual harassment*
before. The team promised to look into it when it got back to
Washington.

Meanwhile, over in Saybrook College, Denise Maillet had found
her own path to recovery from the sexual harassment and assault
she experienced in her first year at Yale. After being harassed by the
professor who phoned her at night to ask how tight her nightgown
was and the attempted rape by the administrator in his office deco-
rated with photos of his wife and children, Denise began attending
a woman's therapy group. Most of the other women there were

Yale graduate students. Like Denise, none had reported what had happened to them. They all "had the feeling that nobody would do anything." But within the group's weekly sessions, they shared their experiences of being assaulted. Those other women gave Denise a safe space to talk about what had happened to her, and their accounts "sort of normalized the experience," she said.

Denise spent the summer after her first year at Yale home in Puerto Rico, and then she returned to New Haven. She kept her job as a waitress at the various event banquets Yale hosted. She liked the financial independence the job gave her, and she liked the women she worked with, mostly townies from New Haven. Denise felt comfortable with these women workers. Yale was "somehow a little more foreign" to her than they were. Once Denise turned twenty-one, she also began bartending at Yale events. The job was easier than waitressing—no heavy trays of food to carry up and down stairs—and it paid a lot better. Yale normally reserved the bartending jobs for men, but the woman who screened the applications had read Denise's too quickly and thought that her name was "Dennis." When Denise showed up for work, the woman was appalled, but the standard excuse to turn away women did not work with Denise. You could hardly say she lacked the strength for the job since she had done all that waitressing and was taller than most of the men.

Other aspects of Denise's life were going better as well. She never had another professor sexually harass her. She got off the committee with the administrator. And during the fall seminar, she met a guy named Elliott. By spring, they were dating. Once Denise and Elliott started getting serious, Denise made an appointment with Phil and Lorna Sarrel.

By the spring of 1971, the Sarrels had been running Yale's Sex Counseling Service for nearly two years, and six hundred of Yale's eight hundred women undergraduates, 75 percent, had been to see them. The Sarrels "were wonderful," said sophomore Becky Newman. "They were like house parents." Becky would climb the stairs to the Sarrels' third-floor office at the Yale Health Service, and the Sarrels would check in on both her and the women in her circle of friends. "How's Abby doing? How's Joan?" When one of Becky's friends told the Sarrels that her boyfriend wanted to get married, they told her, "You know, marriage is a wonderful thing—at the right time. Why don't you go away and think about it and then come back and talk to us in a couple days?" Becky's friend credited the Sarrels with saving her from a terrible early marriage. Once she thought about her boyfriend's proposal, she realized she did not want to marry him at all.

When students sought birth control, the Sarrels hoped to see the couple together, but Yale men were far more reluctant to visit than Yale women, and only 150, less than 4 percent, had met with the Sarrels so far. Denise did not realize that most women at Yale went solo to the sex counseling service, and she did as suggested and brought Elliott with her. The visit went well. Denise and Elliott both felt comfortable with Phil and Lorna Sarrel. Afterward, Denise continued to visit, and her letters home to Puerto Rico would often say, "Oh, I went to see Dr. Sarrel again." Like other students, she found the adult support and mentorship she needed in Phil and Lorna Sarrel, and she and Elliott eventually became discussion group leaders in the Sarrels' Human Sexuality course.

The Sarrels had another new couple come see them that year, freshman Alec Haverstick and his girlfriend, Linden Havemeyer. Like Denise, Linden felt grateful for the Sarrels' presence at Yale, and she continued to go see them on her own. Alec also kept up his connection with Phil and Lorna Sarrel. They "were so together and so interesting and so nonjudgmental," said Alec. "They were real outside-the-box thinkers." Phil Sarrel was equally impressed with Alec, and that winter, he phoned Alec with a request: "Will you join the Human Sexuality Committee?" Sarrel asked Linden to join too. She was happy to do so, since the Sarrels had been so helpful to her.

By spring, Alec and Linden were a part of the dozen students who formed the core of the Human Sexuality Committee. The group worked on running and improving the human sexuality class, which was offered again that year, and it was revising *Sex and the Yale Student* for distribution the following fall. The work gave them a front-row seat to some of the problems caused by Yale's gender imbalance, although the Human Sexuality Committee had not yet been involved in any of the activism to end Yale's gender quotas. By the following fall, that would change.

———

Through the spring of 1971, Yale had been engaged in increasingly contentious negotiations with Local 35, the union that represented its blue-collar workers. The union asked for higher wages and better fringe benefits. Yale refused, and when the contract expired on May 1, Yale's 1,100 dining hall and maintenance workers went on strike. Students boycotted their classes in support of the strikers; Denise Maillet stood beside her waitressing coworkers in the picket line. The dining halls closed. There was no hot water in the showers. Trash pickup stopped, and bags of garbage piled up on the sidewalks. Yale issued a daily $3.35 rebate for food, and students bought groceries and cooked on hot plates in their rooms or lived off of tuna grinders from Yorkside Pizza.

In the midst of it all, the Black Panther trials finally ended. The charges against Bobby Seale and Ericka Huggins were dropped. Seale's jury was stuck at 11 to 1 for acquittal, Huggins's at 10 to 2, and when neither jury could reach a verdict, the judge declared a mistrial and then dismissed the charges entirely, stating that it would be impossible to find new jurors who were impartial. By that point, however, many students had already left Yale, given the chaos from the strike. Like the previous year, the campus scattered early.

Shirley Daniels went home to Boston for the summer. Her father, who had been so proud when she got into Yale, was sick with lung cancer. But other women students stayed on in New Haven. Elga Wasserman hired five of them—Judy Berkan, Barbara Deinhardt, Connie Royster, Betty Spahn, and one more Sisterhood member—using some of the Sue Hilles grant money and some funding thrown in by Sam Chauncey. For the first time, she had something that resembled a staff, even if it was only five undergraduates on summer stipends.

The second year of coeducation had been rough on Wasserman. All year, she would learn about meetings that had been held about policy affecting Yale women, meetings to which Wasserman was never invited. Frustrated, she met with Brewster in March and then followed up with a letter. "Without participation at the policymaking level, I cannot be effective in improving coeducation at Yale," she wrote. "If, as you indicate, you want me to continue to share responsibility for women at Yale, I will need your active backing."

Little changed. In May, Wasserman wrote Brewster again. "I continue to feel a lack of day-to-day contact with individuals involved in policy making and implementation as well as a need for more clear-cut agreement concerning my specific responsibilities. Can we discuss these issues soon?" The discussion that followed was predictable. Wasserman would spend the third year of coeducation the way she had spent the first two, as Brewster's special assistant.

The summer, at least, went well. Students and faculty had been pressing to end the Yale Corporation's insularity since the spring of 1969, and Yale's top rivals were changing with the times. Harvard had appointed the first woman to its Board of Overseers in 1970, and in the spring of 1971, Princeton was poised to appoint its first two women trustees. When four slots became open on the Corporation in June, Yale could no longer dodge the calls for diversity, and the university appointed its first women trustees: civil rights lawyer Marian Wright Edelman and University of Chicago professor Hanna Gray. The third slot went to a twenty-nine-year-old Harvard Law School assistant professor with shaggy brown hair and long sideburns named Lance Liebman. For the fourth, the Corporation chose a man who seemed more in the mold of Yale's traditional appointments: William Beinecke, class of 1936, whose father and two uncles had donated the money for the Beinecke Rare Book Library. Yet even Beinecke brought a new perspective. His daughter Frances had just graduated as a member of the class of 1971. The next time the matter of Yale's gender quotas came before the Corporation, at least four of the trustees might see things differently from those who had now voted twice to support the status quo at Yale.

In addition to the appointment of women trustees, Wasserman was pleased by the progress that the five women students she had hired were making. They created *SHE*, a resource booklet provided to every Yale woman, and held a fund-raiser for the Women's Center. They worked with faculty member Cynthia Russett to create Yale's first course on women's history and contributed bibliographies from Yale's women's studies courses to the National

Women's Studies Clearinghouse. They produced a critique of the ways that Yale's male-focused recruiting materials discouraged women from even applying. They wrote a welcome letter to entering freshmen women, the class of 1975, and organized three fall gatherings of female freshmen and upperclassmen to help ease the new students' transition.

As one of the members of Wasserman's team, Betty Spahn focused her efforts on the women's history course. It was hard to find any history material on women, and Betty spent hours doing research. One evening in Sterling Library, she discovered the writings of suffragist Elizabeth Cady Stanton, one of the leaders of the women's rights movement in the late 1800s. It "was like she was speaking to me across the ages," said Betty. "No longer was I just weird. I was part of a tradition." After that, Betty read everything she could find that Stanton had written as well as works written by Lucretia Mott and Frederick Douglass. Betty's hours in Sterling that summer were an "unearthing of all this history that had always been there, just waiting to be reclaimed and brought into the sunlight again. It was wonderful. It was transformative. It was liberating."

Betty was working three jobs that summer to earn enough money to pay for her Yale senior year: her midnight to 8:00 a.m. shift at the post office, a day job at the New Haven Head Start program, and her evening and weekend position as one of Wasserman's five summer interns, for which Wasserman paid a stipend. Connie Royster was working hard too. She was trying to earn enough money to finance a trip to Ghana and Nigeria at the end of the summer so she could conduct research for her Yale senior thesis on African art. Connie had obtained a partial fellowship for the trip, but it was not enough money, and so she patched it together with the stipend from Wasserman, money she made working at Yale alumni reunions, and a small grant from Undergraduate Dean John Wilkinson. In August, Connie boarded a plane for Ghana.

Meanwhile, Elga Wasserman was still in New Haven. She closed the summer by issuing her annual coeducation report. Anger leaked out at the edges. The report protested the small percentage of women students and railed against the continued lack of women faculty. "Many students never meet a woman faculty member during their time at Yale," Wasserman wrote, and in an interview later, she was even more pointed: "How could you have an education if the message out there is, 'You're going to be taught by men because women aren't capable of being professors'? What kind of education is that?"

Mory's made Wasserman's coeducation report also. There had been progress that summer. In July, Kathryn Emmett of the Yale Law class of 1970 filed a petition with the Connecticut State Liquor Commission, challenging the renewal of Mory's liquor license. It was a brilliant move. Mory's brought in $10,000 a month from alcohol sales; losing that income would cripple it. Emmett argued that state law required agencies to consider discrimination when issuing licenses. And as Emmett worked to disable Yale's practice of holding meetings in men-only facilities, Wasserman used her coeducation report to lambast Yale's continued patronage of men-only Mory's one more time. Mory's, she wrote, "symboliz[es] Yale's pervasive maleness and its lack of concern for women members of the Yale community." And with that verdict, the second year of coeducation ended.

ELEVEN

Tanks versus BB Guns

WHEN YALE OPENED FOR THE THIRD YEAR OF COEDU-cation in September 1971, the ratio among undergraduates was still one woman to five men, women made up one percent of Yale's tenured faculty, and Elga Wasserman was still Brewster's special assistant. There was one difference, however. Kingman Brewster was in London, and he was not coming back until January. Following a glowing performance review from the Yale Corporation, Brewster had been granted a six-month sabbatical. In July, he and his wife, Mary Louise, boarded an ocean liner bound for England. Within a few hours, the shoreline was just a speck in the distance, as were the problems Brewster had left behind him. However, despite what it said in that performance review, all was not well in New Haven.

The Department of Health, Education, and Welfare (HEW) investigators had started their work—asking for documents and rummaging through Yale's file drawers because of the discrimination complaint from Yale women. Meanwhile, construction on Brewster's two new residential colleges was on hold, grounded because of long-standing friction with New Haven. Yale was rich.

New Haven was poor, and the city resented, among other things, Yale's 350 tax-exempt acres. The Board of Aldermen had just passed a law requiring its approval for any construction that removed land from the tax rolls, which was exactly what Yale planned in order to build those new colleges. For once, the city had the upper hand. Yale was "going to have to realize that we are not peasants and they are not the manor on the hill," said New Haven Democratic Party chairman Arthur Barbieri.

Negotiations over the new housing went nowhere, and Brewster had asked for help from Corporation member Cyrus Vance, Yale class of 1939, who had played a lead role in the 1968 Paris peace talks with North Vietnam. Vance agreed to meet with New Haven mayor Bart Guida, who was no fan of Yale. The discussions were high stakes for Brewster. If that housing failed to move forward, he would acquire one very public failure and lose the only real solution he had offered to solve the skewed gender ratio among Yale's undergraduates.

Yet one more problem beset Brewster that fall: the financial mess Yale was in after five years in a row of deficits. "Where has all the money gone?" asked a student reporter, a question that troubled the Corporation as well. News of Yale's financial worries had broken a year earlier when Brewster announced a hiring freeze. Columbia and Princeton were running deficits too. U.S. colleges as a whole were "in a state of financial shock," said the *New York Times*, with a double punch of increasing expenses from inflation and shrinking income from the stock market slump and the decline in government and foundation grants.

But Yale had brought on some of its money problems itself. Brewster had lived large in his first years as president and spent generously to accomplish his goal of acquiring a better faculty than

Harvard. In the five years before Yale women arrived, Brewster had doubled the number of full professors, the most expensive kind, and increased faculty salaries to a level that history professor John Blum called "splendid." Brewster and his provost "set out to make the Yale faculty the best in the country and to pay whatever cost was entailed in so doing," said Blum, and the previous spring, the *New York Times* had declared Yale the victor, noting that Yale's faculty, not Harvard's, was the one "aglitter with famous names." Even the student editors of the *Harvard Crimson* agreed. "Suddenly, things are different," they observed. "Yale wears the bell bottoms in the Ivy League family." The price tag for that victory, however, was high.

At least no one could point a finger at coeducation as the source of Yale's money problem. Without the tuitions of women students, the $4.4 million that Yale rang up in deficits between 1969 and 1971 would have been 50 percent higher. Yale netted $2.1 million from the first two years of coeducation. The path to that windfall was straightforward: the college took in hundreds of thousands in tuition payments from women students without expanding its faculty, administration, or housing. Save for the cost of the Coeducation Office, a meager athletic budget, and women's financial aid, it was all profit. Yet even this was not enough to turn Yale's bottom line from red to black. A few weeks before he set sail for England, Brewster sent a memo to every administrator and department chair at Yale. Yale's financial situation had worsened, he wrote, with a deficit for the upcoming year projected at $6.5 million. With nowhere to squeeze for more income, further cuts were the only solution.

As the stress levels boiled over in the budget office that fall, out on the playing fields came victory. Lawrie Mifflin finally had a field hockey team—sort of. Yale had granted club status that year to three women's teams: field hockey, tennis, and squash. The hockey players had a real field now—no more picking up empty beer cans from Parking Lot A—and Yale gave them goal cages and equipment. There was no money for uniforms, though, and their coach was the same one as last year, a kind woman but no expert on field hockey. Yale paid Dottie O'Connor $5,000 that year to coach all three women's sports, less than half of what it spent on the pregame steak breakfasts it served to the men on Yale's varsity teams.

It was so easy to play sports at Yale if you were a guy. The men could just show up in September and choose from a menu of seventeen varsity teams: baseball, basketball, crew (both lightweight and heavyweight), cross-country, fencing, football, golf, ice hockey, lacrosse, skiing, soccer, squash, swimming, tennis, track, and wrestling. To get even one women's varsity team in some as-yet-unspecified future, women would need "to prove they were serious," said Yale. So Lawrie and her teammate Jane Curtis set a goal for themselves. By next year, field hockey would have varsity status.

Yale had set out a list of hurdles they needed to leap to get there, but at least the athletic department no longer seemed confused by the idea that women could be athletes. Lawrie and Jane had to show that the interest in field hockey would continue after they graduated, that they had players from all different classes, and that they could compete against other colleges and universities. And they had to pass all those tests without adequate funding or other support. But if those were the tasks required to be a varsity team, Lawrie and Jane would do them. The two friends recruited more players, and thirty women played field hockey that season. Lawrie and Jane set an ambitious schedule: Wesleyan, Trinity, Connecticut College, Southern Connecticut, and Radcliffe. The big game of the season would be against Princeton in New Jersey on November 13.

One afternoon, Lawrie walked over to the *Yale Daily News*, which filled one or two pages each day with sports stories. "You should be covering our games," she told them. "We've got a big field hockey team." That just was not possible, said the sports editors. The *News* couldn't cover everything, and field hockey was not a varsity sport. Besides, none of the guys knew anything about girls' hockey. Lawrie was not having it. "We're going to be a varsity sport," she answered, "and then you're going to cover us."

———

Brewster may have relocated to London that fall, but the men who reported to him stayed busy. Yale's treasurer was consumed by the deficit crisis, the provost by HEW. Brewster adviser Al Fitt had his own special problem—two of them, actually: Congresswomen Edith Green and Patsy Mink, both of whom were determined to end gender discrimination in U.S. colleges.   Mink, who represented Hawaii, was the first woman of color and first Asian American to serve in the House of Representatives. Green was called "the most powerful woman ever to serve in the Congress" by her Republican colleague from Oregon, U.S. senator Mark Hatfield.   Together, both women were formidable adversaries, even for an institution as powerful as Yale.

As for Al Fitt, he was Brewster's adviser on governmental affairs. The two men had met in 1968, when Fitt, Yale class of 1946, handled Ivy League ROTC issues for the army. Brewster had taken to him at once. At the end of their first conversation, he had turned to Fitt and said, "Maybe you ought to come up to Yale, and we can figure out something for you to do there."   Fitt arrived in New Haven eighteen months later to an office right next to Brewster's. When asked once who Al Fitt was, faculty member Hester Eisenstein answered, "One of Kingman's lackeys."

Fitt's main annoyance at the moment was a bill voted out of the House Education and Labor Committee at the end of September. The proposed legislation would ban federal funding to any college whose admissions policies discriminated against women. A law passed by Congress was a far more permanent solution to U.S. colleges' bias against women applicants than an executive order, which could be rescinded by any new U.S. president or more quietly undermined through lack of enforcement. That is why Patsy Mink and Edith Green had worked together to include the antidiscrimination language in the House legislation and why Al Fitt was now so concerned.

The bill classed schools into three groups. Those that were single sex, like Dartmouth and Smith, could stay that way without losing federal dollars. Those that were newly coeducational, like Yale and Princeton, had seven years to remove quotas on women students. Finally, schools that had long been coed, like Stanford and Michigan, had to eliminate such quotas at once. Yale could not afford to walk away from its federal funding, which topped $30 million in 1971. If Green and Mink's sex discrimination language held firm, Yale would have to end its thousand-man quota.

Al Fitt sent off a letter to Edith Green in protest, and on October 14, she wrote back. Yale was perfectly free to keep giving preference to male applicants, she explained, but the federal government had no business subsidizing discrimination. Yale was not the type of place that backed down quietly, however. By October 21, Al Fitt was publicly framing the issue as a matter of governmental intrusion. The action "offended" him, he told the *Yale Daily News*. "It's a question of the wisdom of the University versus the wisdom of Congress, and I would rather trust Yale."

Yale had used its muscle before to prevent the government from curtailing its discrimination against certain categories of applicants. Through the 1940s and 1950s, Connecticut civil rights groups had sought to pass legislation that would stop Yale from turning down qualified blacks and Jews. In 1949, a state-wide commission documented a widespread pattern of admissions discrimination in Connecticut's private colleges. Nonsense, said Yale. Connecticut's private colleges had no record of prejudice. The facts, however, spoke otherwise. In the twenty years between 1924 and 1945, only seven black students graduated from Yale. When Jewish students rose above 10 percent in the early 1920s, Yale began denying them financial aid. When that didn't work, Yale changed its admissions policy from one based on academic merit to one that considered qualities of "personality and char-acter"—qualities best demonstrated, in Yale's view, by white Protestant men. Between 1949 and 1957, Connecticut legislators tried four separate times to pass laws stopping Yale's discrimina-tion, and each time Yale prevailed. By 1959, the legislature finally gave up, leaving Yale to continue its prejudice.

Yale's numbers of Jewish and black students stayed low for the following five years, but when Kingman Brewster became presi-dent, Yale changed. Brewster found discrimination against blacks and Jews repugnant, and the percentages of black and Jewish freshmen admitted by Yale increased. Discrimination against women students, however, was something different entirely, at least to Brewster and Yale. The legislation that Edith Green and Patsy Mink had proposed would need to be changed, and Al Fitt began making phone calls. The freedom to turn down qualified women was a cause Yale was willing to fight for.

On October 27, as the House of Representatives began debate

on the bill, Republican representative John Erlenborn of Illinois announced his intention to offer an amendment that would exempt undergraduate admissions policies from the ban on sex discrimination. Using the same reasoning as Al Fitt, Erlenborn argued that such intrusion "would create a serious threat to the autonomy of our institutions of higher education." Over the next week, five colleges—Dartmouth, Harvard, Princeton, Smith, and Yale—sent letters to Congress. Every one of them repeated the same talking point: unless the bill was amended, it would compromise U.S. colleges' autonomy. Smith may seem a curious ally to this cause given that the law would not affect its all-women status, but Smith president Thomas Mendenhall argued that the bill would hurt Smith's enrollment by giving women students more choices in where to attend college. A letter of protest came in as well from the Association of American Universities (AAU), of which Harvard, Princeton, and Yale were members. The forty-four AAU presidents, all of them men, were united in their opposition to the idea of barring federal funding for colleges whose admissions policies discriminated against women. Such a ban would "establish an undesirable degree and kind of Federal influence over the ability of institutions to select students," explained the AAU executive president.

Al Fitt had been equally outraged in the letter he sent to Congress from Yale. Unless the bill were amended to allow colleges to give preference to male applicants, Fitt wrote, the proposed law would keep Yale "from exercising its own judgment" in undergraduate admissions. And as Fitt had told the *Yale Daily News* a week earlier, he would rather trust Yale on such matters than Congress.

———

The eleven students on the Human Sexuality Committee began the third year of coeducation with an ambitious agenda. By September, they had already distributed the revised edition of *Sex and the Yale Student* to all the new freshmen. On November 4, they would host the first of three freshman orientation sessions. The human sexuality class, with student pairs leading discussions after lectures by Phil and Lorna Sarrel, would start in February. And on top of all this, the Human Sexuality Committee—six women, five men—was launching a brand-new initiative that year: a student-to-student counseling service. It was a lot to take on for such a small group, but the students were committed to what they were doing, and the Sarrels "were really very gifted in finding students of passion and intelligence," observed Associate Chaplain Phil Zaeder, who helped advise the committee. Half of the students on the committee were juniors or seniors. Half were in the class of 1974, including Linden Havemeyer and Alec Haverstick, who were both now sophomores.

Alec had been appointed in September to another committee at Yale, the Coeducation Committee, but he was unimpressed with what he saw there. Alec felt the urgency of increasing the numbers of women students at Yale, and the Coeducation Committee seemed to be the group that should be pushing for such change. Yet instead, the committee "would meet and discuss—nothing," said Alec. "It wasn't a brave committee. It was an 'OK, can we do something better in the dining halls?' kind of committee."

Elga Wasserman was well aware of the Coeducation Committee's more subdued stance compared with the boldness it had shown in May of 1970, when it had dared for the first time to reject Brewster's thousand-man quota. The sound defeat the committee had suffered had led to the current timidity. It was a rational response to what had happened. Yet that reality only made Wasserman angry, as did the myriad other ways that Yale continued to fall short of what she had once hoped it could be: a model to other colleges and universities of an institution where women stood equal to men. All that fall, Wasserman would storm into the Coeducation Office "just furious" about some meeting she'd had with one group of male administrators or another, said her assistant. "Elga had a hell of a time," said one of her friends. "She was miserable from the time she took the position."

Like the women undergraduates whom she and Sam Chauncey first admitted to Yale, Wasserman was tough. No one disputed that fact. She had spent most of her life as an outsider: the German immigrant girl in middle school, the woman PhD student in a chemistry department filled with men, the woman dean in the Yale Graduate School, and the one woman administrator in the Yale president's office. Up until that last role, Wasserman had always managed through intelligence and hard work to succeed. But in the end, if you weren't the boss and the guy who was did not agree with your ideas about what was important, you weren't going to get what you wanted. Some days, said Alec Haverstick, Elga Wasserman just seemed "beaten," and once, she even broke down at a Coeducation Committee meeting, saying, "This is too hard. I can't win."

"They were tears of frustration," said Alec. "Not 'woe is me' and not self-directed, but very much, 'I'm up against a tank and I've got a BB gun.' And it just all seemed so useless and hopeless."

The Coeducation Committee may have retreated, but others were impatient with Yale's halfway version of coeducation. Over on the Yale Admissions Committee, there were a few members who at least possessed slingshots. That November, they decided to use them and see what Goliath would do. Nearly two years had passed since committee members Keith Thomson and Paula

Johnson had written Brewster, decrying the unfairness caused by his thousand-man quota. On November 3, they tried again, and this time, three other committee members joined them: the dean of Davenport College, an associate professor of German, and Assistant Dean Elisabeth Thomas. "We felt brave," said Thomas, but being part of a group made it easier for her to speak up. "It wasn't just the woman dean making a noise."

The group addressed their letter to Acting President Charles Taylor. "We write to you as veteran members of the Undergraduate Admissions Committee," they began, a fact that gave strength to their slingshots. Having five names at the bottom of the letter helped too—no one could dismiss them as lone outliers—and one name of the five in particular bore notice. Residential college deans were junior appointments; the faculty spanned multiple views. Elisabeth Thomas, however, held one of the top six jobs in the Yale College Dean's Office. Her title had weight, and men found her easier to work with than Wasserman. Thomas fought hard for Yale's women students just like Wasserman did, yet she tended to work more quietly at that task than Wasserman. That changed with the November 3 letter.

It was a scathing denunciation of Yale's policy on women. The group of five Admissions Committee members called Yale's gender quotas "deeply disturbing," "demoralizing," "painful," "injurious," and "anguishing." Yale's insistence on quotas, they charged, undermined the university's "commitment to coeducation and to quality." Still, Thomas was unsure. "How assertive can you be without losing credibility?" she wondered. It was a question she struggled with often.

If the five committee members had hoped for a positive reply, they were soon disappointed by Taylor. Yale could not possibly take up the question of the quota on women, Taylor wrote back, before first considering "the maximum desirable enrollment on campus at any one time, the length of the course of study, and other issues." And that work could hardly begin for five or six months, when the committee charged with investigating these questions issued a report on the matter. The five protesting Admissions Committee members would just need to be patient.

———

By November 13, the field hockey team's record—three losses, two ties—was not quite what Lawrie Mifflin had wished for, but given that it was their official first season and they barely had coaching, it was still a respectable record.   The Princeton game would be their chance to show what the women's field hockey team was made of. The women now even had uniforms! Sort of. Up until then, the girls had worn cutoff jean shorts and Yale T-shirts they bought at the co-op, while their opponents arrived at games wearing the standard field hockey uniform of kilts, white blouses, and knee-high socks. But a few weeks before the Princeton game, Lawrie saw a copy of the *Princeton Alumni Magazine*, which featured right on the cover a large color photo of Princeton's field hockey team holding fancy new sticks and wearing black-and-orange-striped socks, black kilts with orange in the pleats, and white blouses with Peter Pan collars. Lawrie marched over to the Yale Athletic Office with the magazine. "See this? You're sending us down to Princeton to play girls who look like this in our cutoff jeans?"

Joni Barnett, initially hired by Yale to teach women's swimming, had just been promoted to director of women's activities, which meant it was her job to deal with any complaints from Yale's women athletes despite being given no money. Barnett had worked at Southern Connecticut College, whose colors, like Yale's, were blue and white. Southern Conn's colors weren't Yale blue, more of a gray-blue, but it would be close enough. Barnett called someone she knew there: "Can we borrow your kilts?" Those were the uniforms the Yale women's team wore against Princeton: hand-me-downs from the local state school. Lawrie had to roll her kilt up at the waistband four times to get it to fit right, but at least it was a step up from cutoffs.

The night before the game, the men's football team stayed in a Princeton hotel so they would be well rested, but Yale did not give the field hockey team any money for accommodations. Some of the women slept on the floors or couches of Princeton players who offered to put them up for the night. Yet even with that generosity, six of the girls had no place to stay, so Barnett arranged for them to sleep in the top-floor guest quarters of Cap and Gown Eating Club. Not being an Ivy League person herself, she did not realize that "eating club" was Princeton-speak for frat house.

It was late by the time the field hockey team got to Princeton; the players were given no money for meals, so they had stayed to eat dinner at Yale. Lawrie and five of her teammates climbed the stairs to the top floor of Cap and Gown, got settled for the night, and turned out the lights. Tomorrow was the day they had all worked for, and they needed a solid night's sleep. Several floors down, in the raucous party Cap and Gown was hosting for the big Yale football game weekend, a rumor began circulating: there were six Yale girls, field hockey players, sleeping up in those beds on the top floor! Half a dozen guys decided to go meet them.

The women woke up startled when the Princeton men walked in and flipped on the lights. "It was not scary," said Lawrie, but "it was deeply frustrating." The six Cap and Gown guys, who were drunk, sat down at the end of the women's beds to chat. Lawrie and the other field hockey players needed to sleep. "We didn't want to get annihilated, beaten six nothing by Princeton."

The women told the Princeton guys it was nice to meet them but the men really had to go now. The men asked to see their field hockey sticks. There was no phone up in that attic space and no one to call if there had been. And the men wouldn't leave. It was 4:00 a.m. when they finally tired of their amusement and went back down the stairs. The next morning, the six field hockey players arrived exhausted for the start of their 10:00 a.m. game. The first half did not go well. The women who had stayed in Cap and Gown included cocaptain Sandy Morse, who led the defense; cocaptain Lawrie Mifflin, who led the offense; and four other forwards, whose job, like Lawrie's, was to make goals. By the time the whistle blew for the half, Yale was down 0 to 3.

Yale started the second half headed right toward that 0-to-6 humiliation Lawrie had feared when, all of a sudden, the entire Yale Precision Marching Band, there early to get ready for the afternoon football game, marched over. The band had changed in the two years since Kit McClure had joined as its only woman member. The drum major who led the group onto the field, Larry Tucker, was black, and ten women musicians were among the seventy-three band members who marched in behind him. The band lined up behind Princeton's goal with their drums and tubas and trumpets and began belting out Yale's decades-old fight song: "Boola Boola." "We didn't expect that," said Lawrie. Yale scored twice in four minutes and then kept Princeton scoreless for the whole second half, ending the game at 2 to 3. They had lost by one goal. Yet the Princeton game felt like a victory.

Back in New Haven, the possibility of change seemed less hopeful. If there was a low point in the fight for women at Yale, the fall of 1971 was that moment. The previous victories now all seemed fragile. It was hard to keep fighting when the status quo kept winning. Yale was "like the Vietnam War," one undergraduate woman told a reporter that weekend. "There's not going to be any change." Even Sisterhood cofounder Betty Spahn was tired of trying to reform Yale. "It just seemed like too daunting a task."

Yale's gender quotas in admissions had not made the Corporation agenda for nearly a year now, and although the Connecticut Liquor Control Commission was discussing whether to revoke Mory's license, it was infuriating that Yale men continued to patronize a place that openly discriminated against women. *Abele v. Markle*, the formal name of the *Women v. Connecticut* abortion lawsuit that had been filed with such excitement in March, was on hold pending appeals after a U.S. district court judge ruled that the 858 women plaintiffs, the Sisterhood members included, had no standing. Even the Sisterhood itself seemed less sturdy. The group held a meeting in October, but all the energy that Wasserman's five women students had generated the previous summer now seemed to be gone.

Judy Berkan had graduated, as had a number of other Sisterhood members who started at Yale as juniors, and many of the Sisterhood students who were a year or two younger went different directions as well. Cookie Polan was studying in England, Joan Ausubel in France. Betsy Hartmann was working in India, and her roommate Patty Mintz was deep into her psychology major and her work at Yale's Child Study Center. Kit McClure had not attended a Sisterhood meeting for months. Dahlia Rudavsky had skipped a year and was a senior now, living off campus with her boyfriend and feeling "pretty alienated" from Yale.   Barbara Fried had dropped out, as had peace marshal coordinator Kate Field. Marie Rudden was back, but she had not rejoined the Sisterhood. Christa Hansen was also back after dropping out, working hard to finish her psychology degree and trying to put the memory of her gang rape behind her.

Of those who had been active in the Sisterhood's first two years, Barbara Deinhardt, now a junior, was one of the few who were left, and she served as the group's lead organizer. Barbara had been one of the five women students hired by Elga Wasserman the previous summer to work on projects like the *SHE* booklet and the women's history course, and Wasserman had appointed Barbara to the Coeducation Committee. Wasserman liked this feisty young student and the way that she stood up for women at Yale.

Barbara "is a very bright and able girl and trying hard to take a stand on behalf of women in this male stronghold," Wasserman had written Radcliffe trustee Sue Hilles the previous spring, after arranging for Hilles to meet Barbara.   Yet Barbara Deinhardt found it no easier taking on Yale than anyone else did. "We felt hostility from the administration toward our work with the HEW investigation," said Barbara. "We felt hostility from faculty members in our attempts to set up women's courses; and we felt hostility from the men we might have been involved with who demanded all our time."   Barbara stayed involved in feminist activism at Yale but felt the isolation that hemmed in so many Yale women. It was exhausting to keep taking on tanks.

Perhaps all those who were discouraged by the slow pace of progress at Yale would have felt more hope had they been at the New Haven Women's Liberation Rock Band performance on

November 13. The band was playing at Yale Law School as a part of the "Developing a Feminist Economics" conference being hosted by women graduate students in Yale's economics department and by the law school women's group. Academics had come from all along the East Coast to be there, and in the evening when the sessions were over, the New Haven Women's Liberation Rock Band played.

"Oh, wow, they were great," said Yale sophomore Tricia Tunstall, who heard the band for the first time that night.   Kit and her bandmates played both original songs and covers, and that night the number that got the crowd on its feet was Dusty Springfield's 1964 hit single, "I Only Want to Be with You." Tricia was dancing along with the rest of them. "I was so excited to hear this group of feisty, smiling, energetic women play music together so infectiously, so happily," she said. She had never heard anything like them.

Kit spent almost all of her time practicing those days. She was doing what she loved best. As for her classes at Yale, those were getting harder and harder to manage. She had carried more than a full course load for her first two years there—five classes every semester—but in September, she dropped down to three, the minimum to stay registered as a student. Kit was a junior now, halfway through her degree, but Yale seemed more and more distant from what she most cared about.

Kit was living in a women's collective on Alden Avenue, three miles west of Yale's Science Hill, where she took her chemistry and physics classes. The women in the collective pooled their resources and paid together for their rent and food. One of them helped write the Black Panther newsletter, which paid almost nothing, so the others covered her rent share. Some of the women played in the rock band with Kit. Some were gay. Some were straight. But Kit was the only Yale student in the Alden Avenue house. "What does she do?" a visitor might ask. "She goes to Yale," would be the reply. "Really?" would be the surprised response.

The weekend after the law school concert, Kit and the rest of the New Haven Women's Liberation Rock Band piled into Virginia Blaisdell's Volkswagen Beetle convertible and one other car and headed south to Washington, DC. They had a gig there the next day, their biggest one yet. The Women's National Abortion Action Coalition, formed in New York that July, was holding a protest against laws that limited women's access to safe and legal abortions, and they wanted the band to perform there. Hundreds of women would march down Pennsylvania Avenue and then stop in front of the U.S. Capitol for a rally. When they got there, the New Haven Women's Liberation Rock Band would be waiting for them.

The day of the protest broke cold, barely above the high forties, which made it tough for Kit's fingers to be nimble on the saxophone keys. But that didn't matter. It was thrilling to be up on that stage as a part of this moment, one of the first national protests ever held in support of women's access to safe abortions. Kit and her band-mates watched as the throngs of protesters marched toward them and began to gather in front of the stage. "Power to the Women!" came the shout from the crowd. "Sisterhood is Powerful!" called out others. As the New Haven Women's Liberation Rock Band played, the 2,500 women in front of them danced and clapped to their music, while behind them rose the white-columned dome of the U.S. Capitol, with the Statue of Freedom—a twenty-foot-tall helmeted woman dressed in classical robes—gazing down from the top of it. Her right hand rested on the hilt of a sheathed sword, but in her left, she held the shield of the United States and a laurel wreath for victory.

News of the abortion rights protest in Washington spread

through the loose network of women's centers that were opening in cities nationwide. In Cambridge, Massachusetts, the women's center was seven months old, and Marian Leighton Levy could often be found there.   More likely than not, that's where she first heard about the New Haven Women's Liberation Rock Band.

Levy had been living in Cambridge for just over a year by then, ever since graduating from Clark University in Worcester with a bachelor's degree in history. She was twenty-three years old with long, dark hair parted in the middle and had come to Cambridge in pursuit of a dream. Levy had no music industry experience. She was not even a musician. But "there was a void in the record bins," she said, where music like bluegrass, blues, Cajun, Celtic, country, and folk should have been.   Levy was close with two guys from Tufts, Ken Irwin and Bill Nowlin, who were just as passionate about American roots music as she was. And so the summer after Levy graduated from Clark, the three friends decided they would start a music company together. That year, they founded Rounder Records.

By the fall of 1971, when the New Haven Women's Liberation Rock Band performed at the protest in Washington, Rounder had issued its first two albums, one by a New England string band, the Spark Gap Wonder Boys, and the other by a seventy-six-year-old banjo player from North Carolina. But Rounder was a political collective as well as a record company, and Levy and her two partners were looking to issue the first album in what they had decided would be a political protest series.

Of the three people who then made up Rounder Records, Marian Leighton Levy was most involved with the radical women's movement, but Irwin and Nowlin were as excited about the idea of recording a feminist rock band as she was. In 1971, there weren't any albums of women's liberation rock bands. "For that matter, there

were barely any women's liberation rock bands," said Levy. The
Rounder trio wanted to help get this music out to a broader audience so that feminists could listen to it and be inspired. Maybe other
women would form their own bands. Levy decided to go down
to New Haven to hear the New Haven Women's Liberation Rock
Band for herself.

On December 10, the band was playing at a dance for gay men
hosted by Yale's Gay Alliance. The Alliance had formed a year earlier when the Homosexuality Discussion Group changed its name
and expanded its mission to include social events. Most weeks, its
Friday night dances at the graduate center discotheque drew more
than one hundred people. Marian Leighton Levy listened to the
New Haven Women's Liberation Rock Band perform and then
went up to Kit afterward. Kit had never met Levy before. She had
never heard of Rounder Records. But Kit could barely believe what
Levy said after she told Kit the story of the young record company:
"We'd like to record you." Kit's bandmate Virginia Blaisdell was
equally stunned. "The idea was preposterous and terrifying," she said.
"We weren't good enough. Maybe we could get good enough. What
would we play?" The band had less than four months to figure that
out. In March, the New Haven Women's Liberation Rock Band
would record its first album.

———

While Kit McClure's band was performing its way to its first record
contract, the Human Sexuality Committee had been busy checking
off the items on its to-do list. Its November orientation sessions
for freshmen had gone well, but the group was surprised by what
it had heard there. The students began each session by showing a

short film—*What Do You Think about Sexuality?*—and then Phil
and Lorna Sarrel led a discussion with the freshmen. But instead of
asking questions about the film they had just seen or the upcoming human sexuality class, Yale's newest students wanted to talk
about something else: the lopsided gender ratio. Human Sexuality
Committee member Carolyn Grillo typed up the minutes: "A great
deal of talk centered on the [male-female] ratio as a cause and scape-
goat for social adjustment problems on campus. We heard a lot of
unequivocal feeling that a more equal ratio is urgently required to
'normalize' life at Yale."

Carolyn, Alec Haverstick, Linden Havemeyer, and the other
students on the committee talked over what they had heard. The
freshmen's arguments against Yale's gender quotas had all been made
by other students before, but it was surprising how strongly the new
students felt after less than two months at Yale. In fact, the committee members realized, none of them knew any Yale student, from
freshmen to seniors, who supported Yale's discrimination against
women applicants. The Human Sexuality Committee was not battle
weary like others at Yale, and the odds in favor of an effort to end
Yale's gender quotas seemed at least even. In November 1971, the
group added one new goal to its list: advocacy for sex-blind admissions. When they sorted out tasks for the year, Carolyn Grillo and
one of the juniors took the lead on starting the student-to-student
counseling initiative. Linden Havemeyer took responsibility with
another student for organizing the human sexuality class. And Alec
Haverstick stepped up to organize the campaign to end Yale's gender
quotas in admissions.

Alec was perfect for the job, said Carolyn. "Alec belonged.
He had the lineage. He had the history. He had St. Paul's." It did
not hurt either that he was a guy. An insider like Alec might be

just the right person to lead an effort that depended on the Yale Corporation to succeed in the end. Without its vote to change Yale's admissions policy, the gender quotas would stay just as they were. Those credentials would have meant little, however, if Alec had not cared so deeply about the cause.

"I was a preppy," said Alec, "but I had something I believed in." The lesson from those Concord Academy women had stuck, as had the ones Alec had learned from his feminist mother. Yale's discrimination against women applicants was just wrong, he felt, and it was long past time to end it. Alec quickly assembled a team of male and female students, largely a replica of the Human Sexuality Committee, and it soon began shaping a strategy that was focused on Brewster. In February, once Brewster returned from London, the committee would present him with statements supporting sex-blind admissions from every constituency at Yale. The Ad Hoc Committee on Coeducation, as the members called the group, was not asking Brewster to lead, said Alec. "People were just asking him to get out of the way."

The Ad Hoc Committee was small, just nine students, but it was well networked at Yale. The members spanned most of the residential colleges and included a *Yale Daily News* reporter, athletes, and a contact on the Yale College Council. The adults who advised the Human Sexuality Committee—Phil and Lorna Sarrel and Associate Chaplain Phil Zaeder—were connected as well and were close to Yale chaplain William Sloane Coffin. Coffin could be helpful with this effort, they thought, and in mid-November, Alec Haverstick arrived in Coffin's office for a meeting.

Two men at Yale had national prominence in that era: Kingman Brewster and William Sloane Coffin. Coffin had been making headlines for years for his antiwar and civil rights activism. At Yale, students were drawn to his passion and courage. Every Sunday, they filled the eight hundred seats in Battell Chapel to hear Coffin's impassioned sermons. "It was always full," said Carolyn Grillo. "You went to church every Sunday even if you weren't a churchgoer just to hear [Coffin]. He was the conscience of the university." Coffin's outsized stature made the prospect of a one-on-one meeting intimidating to Alec. "It was like meeting a member of the New York Yankees." But Coffin allayed Alec's apprehension right at the start, saying, "I've been told I should take you seriously."

Coffin had spent the past fifteen years fighting for social justice, but the inequity experienced by Yale women had never been one of his causes. In November 1971, that changed. Alec gave his pitch on sex-blind admissions, and from there, the conversation moved right to strategy. "If you want a radical result," said Coffin, "do not let the process be publicly radical." It seemed a strange message coming from Coffin, whom Alec had thought of as "a Chicago Eight kind of guy," given Coffin's arrest for antiwar activism. But Coffin was a Yale insider too. Just like Brewster, he came from Pilgrim stock, and Coffin's uncle had served on the Yale Corporation for twenty-three years. His cousin was married to trustee Cyrus Vance, and as a student, Coffin had been in Yale's most elite secret society, Skull and Bones. Just because Coffin opposed the Vietnam War did not mean he had cut ties with the powerful. All those connections were part of the strategy. At least he could get people to listen to him.

Coffin himself had been doing some listening by the time Alec Haverstick met with him. Coffin's wife, Harriet, was "a very strong feminist, a very strong person," said Associate Chaplain Phil Zaeder. Before marrying Bill Coffin, she had worked as a United Press Service reporter in Japan, and after that, she founded the Department of Health Education at Children's Hospital in Boston.

For the previous two years, Coffin had also often heard about the situation of Yale women from Sarah Pillsbury, a Battell Chapel deacon. Sarah was one of the Concord Academy sophomores with whom Alec had dinner when he was a freshman, and she had been quoted in the *Yale Alumni Magazine* about the problems caused by Yale's limit on women. Sarah was outspoken on the issue of Yale's gender ratio and was "the kind of person who had some very sparking discussions with Bill Coffin. She was the kind of person who did that," said Zaeder.

Yale's discrimination against women applicants was thus not a new issue to Coffin when Alec came to meet with him, but on Sunday, November 21, Coffin spoke out about it for the first time. "The morality of justice," he bellowed from the Battell Chapel pulpit, required that Yale adopt "a fifty-fifty ratio between men and women... It is time to give visible faculty and student support to those five people on the admissions committee who recently objected to the quota system." The battle once more was on, although this time it was less clear who had the tanks and who had the BB guns.

TWELVE

Mountain Moving Day

KINGMAN BREWSTER RETURNED FROM HIS SABBATICAL in London on January 10, 1972. The transatlantic crossing on the *SS France* that week was stormy, perhaps foretelling the challenges that faced him on his return. Yale's deficit had not fixed itself. Cyrus Vance had failed to get New Haven's permission to build the new residential colleges, thus sinking Brewster's favored solution to the demand for more women. And beyond Yale, the world had not held still in Brewster's absence. Yale feminists may have felt discouraged that fall, but the status quo was now playing defense. Carnegie Corporation president Alan Pifer had laid out the problem in a speech in November. The question of discrimination against women, he warned, was not going to go away, no matter how much some men might wish that it would.

Pifer came from the same circles as Brewster. He had gone to boarding school at Groton, college at Harvard, and he used the word *militant* to describe the women students and faculty who had filed sex discrimination complaints against America's colleges. Many men, said Pifer, "find themselves rather offended at standing accused

of an injustice they do not feel they have committed." This obser-
vation made sense to men like Brewster. It was Pifer's conclusion
that rattled him. "It seems to me this issue comes down basically to
a matter of human justice... Until we have righted the wrong done
to women in our society, the promise of American democracy will
remain unfulfilled." If a man like Alan Pifer could make such a claim,
there was no telling what lay in store back at Yale for Brewster. He
had only to pick up a copy of the January *Yale Alumni Magazine* to
find out.

The editor had reprinted the letter that the five Admissions
Committee members had written back in November chastising Yale
for its discrimination against women. Their charges were right there
on page 31 for Yale's ninety thousand alumni to read, along with
the terrible adjectives they used to describe Yale's admissions policy:
"deeply disturbing," "painful," and "injurious." The outcry now
went well beyond those five committee members and those who'd
been pushing for change from the start. Bill Coffin was calling for
sex-blind admissions from the Battell Chapel pulpit, and a new student group was pushing to overturn Yale's gender quotas. This Ad
Hoc Committee for Coeducation that Brewster was hearing about
had not been there when he set sail for England.

All through December, while Brewster was enjoying the view
from his London townhouse or taking his Jaguar out for one last spin
through the byways of Surrey, Alec Haverstick and the other eight
members of the Ad Hoc Committee on Coeducation were working. "We weren't going to stop the Vietnam War," said Alec, "but we
could get more women at Yale." There was no disagreement on the
goal. It was sex-blind admissions, none of this incremental stuff that
Yale had been playing with up until then. The only question before
the group was strategy.

"How do we get this done?" the members asked each other, and people took their roles. Alec organized the meetings and was the lead contact with Coffin. Another student did research. Someone else began contacting Yale student groups to see which ones would stand with them.

In addition to the committee's core group of nine, other students would show up for a meeting or two and take on a task that needed doing. At the end of January, posters appeared all over campus pushing the message of sex-blind admissions. One of them began with a 1970 quotation from U.S. vice president Spiro T. Agnew. It was the reason Agnew gave over May Day when he called for Brewster's dismissal:

I do not feel that the students of
Yale University can get a
fair impression of their country,

the poster said, quoting Agnew, and then it continued:

Maybe Spiro was right.
After all, Kingman,
Half the people out there are WOMEN.

Meanwhile, the Ad Hoc Committee sent out a detailed report on the merits of sex-blind admissions to every professor at Yale. "Full and equal coeducation at Yale is an idea whose time is now," the document began. "Both common sense and overwhelming student sentiment support the enactment of this idea."

The Ad Hoc Committee sought to dispel the various myths that seemed to stand in the way of progress. "We have information which strongly suggests that women alumnae can and do make significant financial contributions to their alma maters, that both married women and mothers are active participants in the career world, that open admissions will not turn Yale into a woman's school," its document continued.

The report, twenty-nine pages in all, came complete with multiple citations, statistics with decimal points, and appendices. The words *justice* and *equality* did not appear in the document; *discriminating* occurred only once. The sober tone was purposeful. "We had to bring everything back from radical," said Alec. "The change was radical, but the process couldn't be radical."

Up until then, the pressure for greater equity for Yale women had largely been led by those at the university's margins: the Sisterhood, Elga Wasserman, and the small group of women who dared to take on Mory's or sign their names to the sex complaints filed with HEW. But those on the edge created a solid space in the middle from which people like Alec could act without being branded as militant. That spot in the center was exactly where the Ad Hoc Committee wanted to be. It was the spot that had never been possible for Elga Wasserman, no matter how hard she sought to find it.

The group's members kept themselves anonymous and signed their report "The Ad Hoc Committee on Coeducation": no names, no other identification. When the *Yale Daily News* wrote about their efforts, it omitted their names from the story and explained that this was what the group had requested. Part of the reason for the anonymity was to keep the focus on the goal. "We don't want this to be about us," said Alec. But another part was self-preservation. It was scary going up against an institution as powerful as Yale. Kit McClure had felt it as a freshman when she took part in the alumni lunch protest. Two years had passed since then, but opposing Yale had gotten no easier. "We took our bravery from each other," said Alec. "We were all supporting each other."

The Ad Hoc Committee's January report was the first step in a daily drumroll of pressure targeted at Brewster. Every day, he heard from a new group who advocated for sex-blind admissions. February 1 was the deacons of Battell Chapel, February 3 was the Women's Center, and February 7 was the Black Student Alliance at Yale (BSAY)—ten formal statements of support in all, plus a deluge of individual letters. The plan was masterful, a model of how to roll out a message and build a constituency to support it. It was something a deft politician like Brewster would have appreciated had he still been the deft and confident leader *Time* had once featured on its cover. But Brewster was never the same after returning from his sabbatical, observed Jonathan Fanton, who took Sam Chauncey's place in the office next to Brewster's once Chauncey became the university secretary.

Brewster "ran on adrenaline that year after May Day," said Fanton, but during those six months in London, he had time to think, and the weight of all the criticism he had received from conservatives over his handling of May Day began to press down. He was, after all, a Republican. "The negative part of the criticism sank in," said Fanton, and Brewster lost some of the confidence he had been known for. "Whether that [was] just May Day, whether it [was] the fact that he had by then been in office for quite a long time, I'm not sure."

Meanwhile, Coffin had been talking to Brewster ever since he came back from London. The two men had been friends for years, and you could often find Brewster in his seat at Battell Chapel as Coffin preached the sermon on Sunday. Brewster listened when Yale's chaplain spoke. As Coffin once explained about his relationship with Brewster, "I let him talk and talk and talk until he's talked out. And then I suggest what we should do."

Time and again, when a challenge threatened to stall the work of the Ad Hoc Committee, Coffin would say in his deep, scratchy voice, "Don't worry, I got it. I'll go to Kingman." Yet alone, not even Coffin was powerful enough to force a change in Yale's policy. "Look, if we all work on this together," he told the students on the Ad Hoc Committee, "I think we can get Brewster to focus on it."

The momentum toward change kept building. On February 3, the Ad Hoc Committee called a meeting for any student who wanted to help, and that night the Branford College common room filled to overflowing with seventy-five new recruits. Like Alec's group, those in the room did not want the label *radical*. The ideas that they brainstormed that night were ones that Yale would find comfortable: dinnertime discussions with the residential college faculty fellows and an invitation to alumni to meet with students at the Yale Club in New York. Further efforts, however, proved unnecessary.

Brewster "was the ultimate pragmatist," said Chauncey, and with pressure now coming from nearly the entire student body, not to mention Yale chaplain William Sloane Coffin and Brewster's own admissions committee, Brewster could see that continued silence was no longer viable. On February 13, Brewster issued a statement. He would ask the Corporation to reconsider Yale's admissions policy on women and to vote on it no later than November 1972. It was not action but the promise of action nine months hence. In the interim, one more group of high school students would apply to Yale, and Yale would reject scores of them simply because they were not men. Even this promise of allowing the question to make the Corporation agenda was no guarantee of success. Twice before, in the first and second years of coeducation, the Corporation had considered student requests to end Yale's gender quota, and twice before it had denied them. But perhaps this next time would be different.

———

Kit McClure was no longer enrolled at Yale. There was just no time. Kit was twenty years old, and the all-women rock band she had been imagining since she was sixteen had a record contract. She knew where her priorities lay. Leaves of absence like the one Kit had taken were not unheard of at Yale: eighteen of the other women juniors took leaves that spring as well as forty-seven of the junior men. Kit filled out the paperwork required and handed it in to the dean's office. As long as she returned to Yale by January 1973, she could pick up where she left off and graduate a year and a half later. In the meantime, she was on her own financially. Kit's parents had paid her costs when she was a student, but now she needed a job. Some of her lesbian friends made their livings as New Haven school bus drivers, and they introduced Kit to their manager. It was easy for the students on Kit's route to spot their driver in the long line of yellow school buses. Theirs was the one with the curly red hair.

In the mornings, Kit picked up the kids and drove them to school, and then she stayed in the empty bus and practiced her trombone and sax until the last school bell rang and it was time to drive the kids home again. She got better and better with all that practice, and one morning in March, the eight women in the New Haven Women's Liberation Rock Band climbed into Virginia Blaisdell's Volkswagen Beetle convertible and one other car and headed north on the highway to Massachusetts. Naomi Weisstein and the Chicago band were on their way too. The recording studio that Rounder Records had booked for them awaited.

Rounder was as excited about the album as the women musicians. "We were all very young," said Marian Leighton Levy. "And very enthusiastic!" The group from New Haven met up with its Chicago counterpart in a town an hour west of Boston, where a New England farmhouse with a connected barn had recently been renovated into a professional sixteen-track recording studio. "It was a nice studio," said Kit, and soon the room filled with the excited sounds of fifteen women musicians tuning instruments and laughing and sharing ideas about how to approach various songs. No one was in charge. That was part of the philosophy—democratic with a small *d*. In the New Haven band, Kit and Rika Alper did much of the composing, "but it was a very communistic ideology about it," said Kit. "If there was music or lyrics, then we all did it, no matter who did it," and every song the group played on the album lists the same artist: New Haven Women's Liberation Rock Band.

Missing at the farmhouse recording sessions were Levy and her two Rounder Record partners. It wasn't that the record didn't matter to Rounder. It was the first album in its protest series and the most ambitious project the fledgling record label had ever undertaken: two different bands, fifteen musicians, and sixteen tracks that needed mixing. Rounder operated on a shoestring budget, even with Levy, Irwin, and Nowlin working for free and supporting themselves through other jobs. One failed record could put them under. Yet still, they stayed out of the studio. "It was part of the political point being made," said Levy. "Women can not only make their own music. They can also have creative control."

The New Haven band had five songs on its side of the album, some showing the trace of the band's history: "Abortion Song," "Sister Witch," and "Prison Song." An all-women rock band—who would have believed it? Yet there on the back of the album were the photos to prove it: Kit McClure playing saxophone, Judy Miller on drums, and other women playing bass and guitar and French horn. In her photo, Naomi Weisstein is just beaming. Marian Leighton Levy loved the title that the women chose for their album: *Mountain Moving Day*. It came from the 1911 poem of that name by Japanese feminist poet Yosano Akiko, which Weisstein had set to music for the album's title track. "The mountain moving day is coming," it began. "I say so, yet others doubt it." Levy liked that the song was inspirational, "like keeping you going through tough times. It gave you a sense that there is this movement, whether other people are aware of it or not."

———

Back in New Haven, Elga Wasserman was in her office on Grove Street, firing off memos. Indeed, she had been doing so all year. In September, Brewster adviser Jonathan Fanton had proposed that one way for Yale to save money was to trim the Coeducation Office budget. Wasserman shot back a memo—two single-spaced pages—skewering that idea. In November, frustrated over a faculty hiring system that "virtually precludes the appointment of women or minority members," Wasserman wrote Associate Provost George Langdon, calling for change. In April, Kingman Brewster was still not giving Wasserman the support that she needed, and once again, she sent a memo to ask for his help.

The work of leading coeducation at Yale carried with it a terrible sameness. Wasserman had to battle for each inch forward, and sometimes she even lost ground. But Elga Wasserman was a fighter, and even if the title at the bottom of her memos had not changed since 1969, she had increased her power at Yale and beyond. By the spring of 1972, Wasserman was one of the most prominent women college administrators in the country. In March, she had been interviewed by KABC Radio in Los Angeles about the changing attitudes toward women. April took her to Atlanta to speak before the American College Health Association. In between, she was a speaker at two different Massachusetts conferences on coeducation. Wasserman was on the Status of Women Committee of the Association of American Colleges and a part of a tight network of women administrators at Harvard, MIT, Brown, and other New England colleges. Across the country, those who wanted to understand the status of women on college campuses knew to ask Elga Wasserman what she thought.

At Yale, Wasserman provided support and inspiration for the women. "She was the most senior woman that we knew; she was our go-to person," said Connie Royster, "and she did anything and everything that she could for us." At a time when most Yale women employees were assigned invisible roles as secretaries and dining hall workers, Wasserman showed women an alternative. "She was a female leader in a place where there were few of them," said Linden Havemeyer. "We were proud of her and glad she was there."

That year, Wasserman was one of five members of the most prestigious committee at Yale, tasked by Brewster with "reinventing undergraduate education." He had set up the group to answer the long list of questions that he claimed Yale had to resolve before it could consider changing its gender ratio. But the committee's report, released to great fanfare in April and covered on the front page of the *Yale Daily News*, contained one answer that Brewster had not counted on: "Admission to Yale College should be granted on the basis of qualifications without regard to sex." And that recommendation for sex-blind admissions was backed by the heft of the five names on the committee: Professor Robert Dahl, Professor William Kessen, Professor Jonathan Spence, Special Assistant Elga Wasserman, and Yale College Dean Horace Taft, the grandson of U.S. president William Howard Taft, Yale class of 1878. It was a sweet moment for Elga Wasserman.

Other cracks appeared that spring in Yale's centuries-old edifice. Mory's lost its liquor license. It was still allowed to serve alcohol pending its appeal, but in the meantime, the club had spent so much money on the lawyers who were defending its right to turn away women that it billed each of its seventeen thousand members twenty dollars to cover its costs. The *Yale Alumni Magazine* was "inundated with carbon copies of angry letters" from alumni to Mory's over its no-woman policy, and more than three quarters of Mory's members did not pay the bill, despite Mory's note that failure to do so would forfeit their membership.

Women v. Connecticut won its appeal on the ruling that its plaintiffs had no standing, and after that, the women lawyers and plaintiffs succeeded in overturning Connecticut's antiabortion law. On April 18, 1972, a three-judge U.S. district court ruled 2 to 1 that Connecticut's law was unconstitutional. It violated the due process clause of the Fourteenth Amendment, the judges declared, and it represented an "over-reaching of police power" by the state that "trespasses unjustifiably on the personal privacy and liberty of its female citizenry." Nine months later, this opinion would inform the U.S. Supreme Court when it ruled on *Roe v. Wade*. The mountains all seemed to be moving.

Beyond Connecticut, the world had also shifted. The Boston Marathon allowed its first woman runner since its founding in 1897. Congress passed the Equal Rights Amendment (ERA), guaranteeing equality under the law for all Americans whether they were women or men. If three-fourths of state legislatures voted approval, the ERA would become the Constitution's Twenty-Seventh Amendment. And on June 23, 1972, Congresswomen Patsy Mink and Edith Green got the victory they had long worked for.

In one simple sentence, Title IX of the 1972 Educational Amendments to the Civil Rights Act prohibited the gender discrimination that was rampant in U.S. colleges and universities when the first women undergraduates came to Yale: "No person shall, on the basis of sex, be excluded from participation in, be denied the benefits of, or be subjected to discrimination under any educational program receiving Federal financial assistance."

No one paid much attention to Title IX at the time it was passed. Few yet understood the extent of gender bias against women in America's colleges and universities. But in the decades that followed, Title IX would halt the gender quotas in admissions that had robbed women of their place in the nation's top schools. It would end the discrimination against women athletes, who were given hand-me-down equipment while the men's teams dined on steak. It would be used to challenge colleges' indifference to the sexual harassment and assault of their women students. But not yet. And not ever, in the case of gender quotas in admissions, for colleges like Yale.

Title IX began with its one elegant sentence, but then it included a list of institutions that were exempt from its provisions. The Boy Scouts, the Girl Scouts, fraternities, sororities, existing single-sex colleges—none of them had to change their practices because of Title IX. But the very first exemption went as follows: "In regard to admissions to educational institutions, this section shall apply only to...public institutions of undergraduate higher education." In other words, *private* institutions of undergraduate higher education—Yale, for example—were exempt from Title IX's prohibition of discriminatory admissions policies.

Bernice Sandler, who worked as a member of Congresswoman Edith Green's staff in addition to her Executive Order 11246 activism, explained what had happened. "Dartmouth, Princeton, Yale, and Harvard...were able to get a narrowly worded exemption for private undergraduate admissions." The letters to Congress from these four powerful institutions, written in the fall of 1971 during the initial stages of the legislation's development, had succeeded. Perhaps some backroom conversations had helped too. At any rate, by the time Title IX passed in 1972, Congress had deferred to Yale's outrage over Edith Green's call for sex-blind admissions, and the final version of the law exempted Yale and the others from that one provision. The exemption still stands today.

Meanwhile, Executive Order 11246 had turned out to be just another BB gun. Sex discrimination complaints had been filed against 350 colleges,   and HEW reported that investigators were finding evidence of sex discrimination "at virtually every campus we visit." But that was as far as the federal government was willing to go. Of all those complaints, HEW had withheld funds from only five institutions: Columbia, Cornell, Duke, Harvard, and Michigan. "They just don't enforce the order," said a frustrated Bernice Sandler.   HEW had made five different visits to Yale over the course of the year following the sex discrimination complaint filed by Yale women, but still there was no letter of findings.

Mountains had moved that spring to be sure, but if Yale wanted to keep the gender quota through which it excluded qualified women applicants, the federal government was not going to stand in the way. On this battle, Yale women and the men who stood by them were on their own.

Two weeks before President Richard Nixon signed Title IX into law, Yale University celebrated its 271st commencement. Connie Royster, Betty Spahn, and Shirley Daniels received their diplomas on June 12 as members of the class of 1972. Connie's parents and sister were there, along with many others from her family. One of her teachers from high school came too. "Oh, yes, you know it was a big deal," said Connie. "Oh my God, yes."

Afterward, Connie's parents threw a big family party at their home out in Bethany. This was no small gathering—Connie's mother had seven brothers and sisters—but whenever anyone in Connie's family graduated from high school or college, the family threw a party to celebrate. This graduation was special, though. Connie was the first of her grandfather's descendants to ever graduate from Yale in all the years that her family had worked there. Connie's older cousins, her guardian angels at Yale, were working the parties in the York Street fraternities the day that she graduated, but they were there with the cousins and uncles and aunts who celebrated at Connie's parents' house later. Connie's graduation from Yale was an accomplishment for all of them.

The last year at Yale had been a good one for Connie. She had written her senior thesis on the African art that she studied on her trip to Ghana and Nigeria. She and Betty Spahn continued to meet over Chinese food at Blessings—Betty had finally mastered her chopsticks—and decided that at some point they would just have to move to China together and write a book on the best places to eat Szechuan. Connie continued to act in Yale plays and spend time with her friends in the theater. The *Yale Daily News* review of a satire in which she starred could not have been more complimentary: "Connie Royster is hilarious as the petulant Sweetums," the reviewer wrote, a rating one notch higher than the "adequate" that he bestowed the next year on one of the rising stars at Yale Drama School—Meryl Streep. (Other *News* reporters soon corrected that assessment of Streep—"Superb," said one. "A tour de force," said another—but the praise of Connie's talents stood.) Connie would not be going into a career in theater, however. The family's first Yale grad, her father insisted, would be a professional. So Connie decided to go into publishing. The field was close to the arts, and it clearly needed more women.

As Connie was spending her Yale senior year immersed in art and drama, Betty Spahn, for the very first time, was doing what she had come to Yale for: she was simply being a student. Betty read books. She wrote her senior thesis on suffragist Leonora O'Reilly and traveled to the Schlesinger Library at Radcliffe to do research. It was thrilling to read O'Reilly's letters recounting her efforts to organize New York City's women workers. Betty did not have to work so many hours her senior year, which left more time for her studies. She had earned a good bit of money working three jobs the summer before, and her boyfriend, who had graduated in 1971, was working full time and picked up a good part of their rent.

Betty was not active on campus that year. Even though she and Kit McClure had founded the Sisterhood, Betty, like Kit, had moved on. She thought of herself as the first marine on the beach: "Everybody's shooting at me. I hold the beachhead, more people come in, and as soon as there's a critical mass, I can leave...and rest and read books." After a while, the cycle would repeat, when a new injustice moved Betty to action. For the time being, however, Betty focused on her studies and on applying to law school. After four years on the East Coast, she was ready to go home to

Illinois, and that spring she got the letter she had hoped for. The University of Illinois Law School at Champaign-Urbana accepted three women students that year, and Betty Spahn was one of them. Before Betty started classes that fall, she and her boyfriend got married. At the wedding in Park Forest, Illinois, that June, Connie Royster was the maid of honor.

Like Betty, Shirley Daniels spent much of her last year at Yale immersed in research and writing. She was a research assistant for the new director of Afro-American studies, history professor John Blassingame, and some afternoons you could find her way, way up in the stacks of Sterling Library on the hunt for one document or another.

Shirley stepped down from her role in the BSAY, although she still went to the occasional BSAY lunch with Brewster adviser Sam Chauncey. Shirley was the experienced veteran of the group now, the most senior woman at the table, but like other Yale seniors, she also had her eye on life after college. By spring, Shirley had landed a job that would let her continue the work she had led at the BSAY: helping black students succeed in college. She had been hired as assistant director of Yale Upward Bound, which provided tutoring and an intensive summer program for junior high and high school students from three poverty-stricken schools in New Haven. But first came graduation.

In June 1972, Shirley received her bachelor's degree with the major she had come to Yale for: Afro-American studies. Shirley's father, who had been so proud to have his daughter at Yale, was not there to see her graduate. He had died of his lung cancer the previous summer. But at least he had known his daughter was a student at Yale, one of the first women undergraduates ever enrolled there. "Yale! My daughter's going to Yale!" he had shouted. Few fathers could have been prouder.

The fourth year of coeducation at Yale began on September 14, a Thursday. Peace marshal coordinator Kate Field was back. After her rape as a sophomore, she had spent a year on a small farming commune in Seymour, Connecticut, a half hour northwest of New Haven. It was called Skokorat, after the name of the street on which it was located. A group of Yale students, both women and men, had founded Skokorat in the summer of 1970. They were all Kate's age or a year or two older—"A nice group of people," said Kate, "and talented." The students raised all their own food. They had goats, a cow, and a big flock of chickens, as well as gardens that produced enough vegetables to fill an enormous freezer. They all played music together. And Kate healed.

Kate knew another woman in her class at Yale who had been raped around the same time that she was. "Hers was worse," said Kate. "She was actually abducted, and it was much, much worse." The two women talked about their experiences once, but Kate felt guilty after the conversation: "I knew I was recovering, and she was not." Of the many areas where equity for women moved forward during the first few years of coeducation, safety was the one that saw little progress. Attitudes toward rape did not begin to shift significantly in the United States until Susan Brownmiller wrote *Against Our Will* in 1975.

Colleges' tolerance of sexual harassment continued as well, long after the HEW investigators who visited New Haven in April 1971 first learned about the problem from the group of Yale women they met there. It would take five more years until the term *sexual harassment* became widely known and six before the courts declared in 1977 that sexual harassment was a form of discrimination. But the very first step in the battle to end sexual harassment was taken by those young women at Yale in April 1971 who, for the first time, gave a name to the problem. The term *sexual harassment* had never been used before then.   The fight to make campuses safe for women students, however, would need to continue far longer than Yale women ever imagined. In the meantime, students who were targeted by predators had to figure out how to move on from that experience on their own.

The student that Kate Field had spoken to who was not yet recovering was Christa Hansen, the sophomore who was gang-raped while walking back to her dorm room from the library. Christa was back at Yale too. She was active in the Yale Sisterhood, and she was writing her psychology thesis on the reasons Yale students took leaves of absence or dropped out. Christa called it "The Yale Experience." Yale supported her research. The Office of Institutional Research gave Christa funding and coached her on the methodology for her survey, and Christa's acknowledgments at the start of her paper listed more than twenty Yale faculty and administrators who helped her.

The paper itself was chock-full of statistics and charts, seventy-five pages in all, but Christa's voice came through in the opening. "We sometimes forget the pain," she wrote. "We do not see the empty places. Some of us have left Yale. Some of us have skipped out for a term or two to see foreign lands, to have great adventures...but some of us have fled Yale shouting curses, or crying or confused into silence."   Briefly, Christa talked about herself. "And me?" she asked. "I left Yale. I left at the same time as a friend of mine, who will never return to Yale. I almost didn't come back." Christa never mentioned why it was that she left. As with Kate, one marvels at the courage it took to return.

Sisterhood activist Barbara Deinhardt was also back at Yale that fall after spending a semester in Italy and Yugoslavia doing research for her senior thesis. Little seemed to have changed while she was gone. "There are simply not enough women students, simply not enough women faculty, simply not enough participation of women in the decision-making process at all levels," Barbara said in a speech that October. As she had the previous fall, Barbara served on the Coeducation Committee with Alec Haverstick and Carolyn Grillo, now both juniors. Yet this year was different. It was no longer Elga Wasserman's Coeducation Committee. It was the committee of a woman none of the students had ever met before: Mary Arnstein.

Wasserman had decided the previous spring to take a one-year leave from her job, her first break from Yale in the ten years she had worked there. She was in Europe on a Ford Foundation grant to study the status of academic women in England, Sweden, Germany, and Israel. In the meantime, Mary Arnstein was Acting Special Assistant to the President for the Education of Women, a title even more ridiculous than Wasserman's. Before leaving, Wasserman gave Brewster some names of women whom she thought qualified to fill her role while she was gone. Instead, Brewster appointed a woman who had no professional or academic qualifications. Mary Arnstein was the mother of four, an active volunteer in the community, and the wife of Brewster's Yale College classmate Bob Arnstein. But perhaps her most important qualification was this: "Mary was anything but a feminist," said Sam Chauncey.

The appointment did not go over well with many Yale women. Barbara Deinhardt missed Wasserman's fire and outrage. Residential college dean Brenda Jubin called Arnstein's appointment "a joke... She was no one to ever advocate for women." The contrast between Arnstein and Wasserman surprised Carolyn Grillo, who was in the Coeducation Office when Mary Arnstein first arrived there.

In addition to serving on the Coeducation Committee and the Human Sexuality Committee, Carolyn worked ten hours a week as a bursary student in the Coeducation Office. Mary Arnstein walked in the door on her first day wearing white gloves and a Chanel suit with a matching skirt and jacket. Arnstein was tiny, not much more than five feet tall, and "very soft-spoken, very gentle." She had brought her own china tea set to the Coeducation Office so she could serve tea to visitors who stopped by. Carolyn had one thought when she first saw Mary Arnstein: *Nooooo. What's going to happen to us?* If Mary Arnstein was now the lead spokesperson for women at Yale, Carolyn reasoned, then they had no spokesperson at all.

———

All through her first three years at Yale, Lawrie Mifflin had worked to create a women's field hockey team that received the same recognition as Yale's sports teams for men. In the fall of her senior year, she received a letter from Joni Barnett, director of women's activities, letting her know she had succeeded. "Dear Lawrie," it began. "My sincere congratulations to you." The field hockey team had been made varsity. Every woman on the team got the same letter from Barnett, and each would receive Yale's coveted varsity sweater, with the blue Yale *Y* on the front of it. "We are proud of you and the manner in which you represent Yale University," Barnett's letter concluded.

The new status was like winning the lottery. Yale bought the team uniforms, and the women field hockey players were "resplendent in royal-blue kilts, knee socks, and cleated shoes," Lawrie wrote in an article for the yearbook. They had new field hockey sticks and a full-time coach, a woman who had been a field hockey star

Yale field hockey player fights for the ball against Princeton in the team's first season as a varsity sport, November 1972.
Photo © Yale Banner Publications.

in Philadelphia. Save for one absence, the victory would have been perfect. Jane Curtis, who had started the team with Lawrie when they were freshmen, was no longer at Yale to celebrate with the rest of the field hockey players; she had graduated a year early.

A few days after learning about the field hockey team's new status, Lawrie walked over to the *Yale Daily News*. "Hey. We're a varsity sport," she said to the sports editors. "You said you weren't covering us because we weren't varsity. Well, now we are." The guys at the *News* were completely flustered. They told Lawrie they would get back to her. But every women's field hockey game was covered in the *News* that year, albeit by a new woman reporter.

None of the male sports reporters, it turned out, had wanted to cover a women's sport.

The field hockey team caused one more discomfort that year when it came time for the captain's photo. Yale used a professional photographer for the pictures, which were published in the yearbook and, if you were one of the men's varsity captains, displayed on the walls at Mory's. (Mory's would not display the photos of women's varsity captains until 1981.) The photos had used the same formula for decades, with the captain posed in front of a split-rail fence, wearing his team uniform and his Yale varsity sweater. Yale allowed its varsity sports teams only one captain, but the women's field hockey team had two: Lawrie and her teammate Sandy Morse.

The women field hockey players elected cocaptains for a reason. Lawrie was a forward, and Sandy played defense; Lawrie was a senior, and Sandy was a junior. Both women, said Lawrie, "were leaders in their own way," but Yale was not having it. "You just have to name one person as captain," declared the athletic office. Lawrie and Sandy refused. "The team elected us together, and you have to take us together," they said, and Yale, somewhat surprisingly, backed down. In the hundreds of photos taken over the years of sports team captains at Yale, there is only one where the leadership is pictured as not one person but two. You can find it if you look hard enough. Lawrie and Sandy are wearing their white varsity sweaters, each with a big blue Yale *Y* on the front. They hold their field hockey sticks, lean up against the wooden fence, and stare out at the camera together.

———

The women's field hockey team may have scored a victory that fall, but for Kingman Brewster, things were still going badly. "Where

has all the luster gone?"
asked one *Yale Daily News*
columnist. Nobody talked
anymore about Brewster
as a possible U.S. senator
or president. He seemed
to be stumbling enough
as the president of Yale. In
September, *Time* magazine
had raised questions of
competence when Brewster
announced that Yale's budget
estimates were $5 million
off. The prior year's deficit
turned out to be $1 million,
not the $6 million predicted
three months earlier. Few

**Lawrie Mifflin (left) with field
hockey cocaptain Sandy Morse.**
Photo © Yale Banner Publications.

of the 1,500 attendees at the American Council on Education's
October conference could have missed the dig at Brewster in the
keynote address delivered by Barnard president Margaret Peterson.
"Nothing much has been heard recently from those persons who
formerly could be counted on to speak out on important issues
in higher education—to lead," said Peterson. "Yale apologizes for a
smaller deficit than anticipated. But is that intellectual leadership?"

Brewster thus limped rather than strode into the fourth year of
coeducation. Eight months had passed since his February promise
to have the trustees vote in November on Yale's admissions policy
on women, yet Brewster announced on October 12 that he still had
not "put his own thoughts in order" on the matter. A week later, he
issued an analysis of three coeducation options—sex-blind admissions,

a fifty-fifty quota, or continuation of Yale's current quotas—but he made no recommendation. The man who had once been the leader of Yale had stepped off to the side, silent while the conversation continued around him.

The Sisterhood was one of the first to respond to Brewster's document, which was widely distributed at Yale. With Sisterhood members now back from time abroad or time off, the group had rediscovered its energy, and Christa Hansen was the Sisterhood member that the *News* quoted. Yale must "become fully coeducational" and move to a one-to-one male-female ratio, she argued. That approach involved a quota of sorts, even if it was 50 percent each for men and women, and most students took a different position and advocated for sex-blind admissions. If either gender exceeded 60 percent, they argued, repeating the stance of the Ad Hoc Committee on Coeducation, Yale should correct the imbalance by recruiting the gender that was in the minority. On November 10, the Human Sexuality Committee, which Alec Haverstick now chaired, weighed in with a letter to the editor. "It is both the moral and social responsibility of this university to provide quality education for both men and women," he wrote. Elga Wasserman could not have put it better.

The Yale Corporation met in New Haven that weekend, and it wanted to hear from students. The Corporation's subcommittee on admissions—which included new trustees Marian Wright Edelman, Lance Liebman, and William Beinecke in addition to Cyrus Vance and J. Richardson Dilworth—arrived a day early, and on Thursday evening, it met with Yale students at every residential college. "Students to Trustees: More Women Now," read the *Yale Daily News* headline on the gatherings. Just in case any doubt remained about students' opinion, the Yale College Council presented the Corporation with a petition calling for sex-blind admissions that had been signed by 3,016 students, three-fourths of the undergraduate student body.

On Friday morning, the five trustees on the Corporation sub-committee met with Admissions Dean Worth David, Yale College Dean Horace Taft, Acting Special Assistant to the President for the Education of Women Mary Arnstein...and Alec Haverstick. Alec walked into the room with his proposal for sex-blind admissions and realized, "Wait a minute. I went to grammar school with half these guys' sons... This is the world I come from." The realization worked both ways. Some of the Corporation's more conservative members may have been skeptical about a student in a corduroy suit whose hair was far longer than theirs, but once they understood who Alec Haverstick was, he went from a firebrand to one of their own. Quite a few of them, it turned out, knew his grandmother.

———

One more month passed as the Corporation waited to hear the views of Yale's alumni. Yet students who fretted that alumni would derail sex-blind admissions need not have been worried. Association of Yale Alumni (AYA) chairman Fred Rose had a daughter who had graduated five months earlier as a member of the class of 1972, and the AYA's twenty-seven-member governing board included another recent graduate from that class: Connie Royster. The group voted to end Yale's thousand-man quota, with a goal for Yale's student body of 60 percent men and 40 percent women—not quite sex-blind admissions, but close enough. "Everybody agrees that coeducation is the best thing that has happened to Yale in a long time," Rose told the *Yale Daily News*. Even alumni who did not have a daughter at Yale were not the foes of coeducation they'd been made out to be. As Brewster wrote to the president of Amherst that fall, the alumni response to coeducation was "almost uniform approval."

On December 9, the Yale Corporation voted to abolish the gender quota that had shaped the first four years of coeducation at Yale. The announcement came with a simple statement: "We believe that the gender of the applicant should not be the deciding factor in a candidate's admission." Within five years, the percentage of women at Yale more than doubled to 46 percent. Other battles, both at Yale and beyond, still remained. But all through that year, 1972, the mountains had moved. Someday, they would do so again.

EPILOGUE

WHEN I WAS FIFTY-EIGHT, I WAS AWARDED MY PHD.
My mom, eighty-one years old, flew up from Baltimore for my
graduation. My husband, daughter, and younger son were there too,
while my older son, sister, and Hazel cheered me on from afar. All
of them knew by then, however, that I wasn't done yet. The story of
Yale's first women undergraduates deserved a broader audience than
the hardy few willing to wade through my dissertation. I had never
written a book before but, as they say, better late than never. And so
I began. My husband's cooking, as ever, was perfect.

Fifty years have now passed since the first women undergraduates arrived at Yale and looked around them at the village of men
they had entered. Yale has changed since then, yet it has not come
as far or as fast as those first women might have hoped. Sexual
harassment and assault have not disappeared. Women are now
51 percent of Yale's undergraduate enrollment, but they make
up just 27 percent of the tenured faculty. And while the diversity
of Yale's student body has markedly increased, only 8 percent of
Yale students are black, compared with 14 percent of college-age

Americans. Yale has never had a woman or person of color as its president, unless you count acting president Hanna Gray, who learned several months into her interim role that Yale had decided against offering her the actual presidency.

Yale men still have lunch at Mory's sometimes. Yale women sometimes do too. Women have been members there since 1974, when the Connecticut Supreme Court upheld the State Liquor Commission's cancellation of Mory's liquor license. The Yale Whiffenpoofs faced no such legal challenge, however, and did not admit their first woman until 2018. The quality of the singing group's sound, I am told, has shown a marked improvement.

Across higher education as a whole, equality for women has not yet been reached. Nationally women represent just 33 percent of full professors and 30 percent of college and university presidents. One in five women students is sexually assaulted while at college. Despite this, women graduate at a higher rate than their male class-mates. Yet their college degree earns them just 74 cents on the dollar compared with what white male college graduates are paid, just 65 cents on the dollar if they are a black woman.

And so women and their allies continue to press for change. The Yale Women's Center founded by the Sisterhood and New Haven Women's Liberation is now one of the longest-standing women's centers in the country. And while the Sisterhood disbanded in 1973, women students, faculty, and administrators have been pushing Yale ever since to become a better version of itself.

In 1976, the Yale women's crew team, denied basic facilities, staged a naked protest in the athletic director's office, an event that ESPN dubbed "the Boston Tea Party of Title IX." Chris Ernst, the protest leader, had played field hockey as a freshman on Lawrie Mifflin's team.

In 1977, women graduates of Yale Law School worked with the Undergraduate Women's Caucus to file *Alexander v. Yale*, which established for the first time that sexual harassment was a violation of women's right to an equal education.

In 1989, two women professors presented a petition to Yale's president that called on the university to close the ongoing gap between the numbers of male and female professors. Twenty years after the first women undergraduates arrived, only 9 percent of Yale's tenured professors were women.

In 2011, sixteen Yale students and alumni filed a Title IX complaint with the federal government, alleging that Yale had allowed a hostile sexual environment to persist on campus. Five months had passed since a gang of fraternity brothers stood outside the freshman dorms at night chanting, "No means yes! Yes means anal!" Yet Yale had still not taken any disciplinary action.

Courage and tenacity, of course, are not unique to Yale women, and neither are the challenges they have faced. There are women who have gone first and women who have spoken out in every town and city in this country. The nation needs still more of them. The battle to make Yale and other colleges and workplaces safe and fair places for women is not yet done.

―――――

The five women students at the heart of this book went on to have rich and rewarding lives. After graduating from Yale, Shirley Daniels worked as assistant and then associate director of the Yale Upward Bound Program, where she helped middle and high school students gain the skills that they needed to succeed in college. When the federal government reorganized Upward Bound, Shirley went to law school at the University of Virginia and received her JD in 1977. After a career as a New York City lawyer, including serving as general counsel for Paragon Cable in Manhattan, Shirley enrolled in New York Theological Seminary and received her masters of divinity. She was ordained at Canaan Baptist Church of Christ in Harlem under Dr. Wyatt Tee Walker and is now a Baptist minister. The Black Student Alliance at Yale, to which Shirley gave so much of her time, continues to thrive at Yale, enhancing the lives of Yale students through political action, community service, and social events.

Like Shirley, Connie Royster worked for many years as a lawyer. She first went into publishing, but after two years at *Time*, decided that the gender discrimination in that field ran too deep. She enrolled at Rutgers Law School and lived with her aunt, Constance Baker Motley, during her years as a student there. After a federal clerkship, Connie worked at Paul, Weiss, Rifkind, Wharton & Garrison, and then as an assistant U.S. attorney before becoming a founding partner of Cooper, Liebowitz, Royster & Wright, a major minority- and women-owned New York law firm. In the 1990s, Connie moved into fundraising and ultimately became the director of development at Yale Divinity School. Throughout her life, Connie has given her time to numerous nonprofit boards. On John and Ericka Huggins's daughter, Connie says, "Ultimately, the baby ended up at the boarding school I went to. The school was familiar ground, and the family knew the school would watch out for her and take care of her."

Connie has remained close friends with Betty (now Elizabeth) Spahn, who became a lawyer as well and has spent her life as a scholar and activist. From 1978 to 2014, Betty was a professor at the New England School of Law in Boston, which she chose because she wanted to teach students who did not come from wealthy backgrounds like so many of the students Betty met at Yale. As a lawyer,

Betty litigated cases tied to reproductive freedom and economic justice. She continued to perfect her use of chopsticks and in 1999 made it to China for a year and a half, where she taught American Constitutional Law as a Fulbright professor at Peking University Law School in Beijing. Betty and Connie have not yet written their guidebook to Szechuan food, but there's still time for that. "Without Connie, I don't know that I would have made it through Yale, and I certainly would not have made it through my life as happily," says Betty. "I consider myself really blessed."

Lawrie Mifflin ended up in journalism, a path begun in large part because of the *Yale Daily News* and its aversion to covering women's sports. In January of her senior year, fed up with the absence of women from the paper's sports pages, Lawrie walked over to the *News* and offered to write stories on the women's teams for them. Over the next five months, she wrote twenty-three articles on women's basketball, squash, and lacrosse as well as stories on several men's teams. Following her graduation in 1973, Lawrie received a master's in journalism from Columbia University and was hired by the *New York Daily News* as its first woman sportswriter. She later moved to the *New York Times*, where she worked for thirty years as a reporter, editor, and executive. Lawrie currently serves as the managing editor of *The Hechinger Report*.

Lawrie's classmate Kit McClure returned to her studies at Yale after her leave of absence and graduated in 1975. Seven years later, Kit founded the Kit McClure Band, an all-women big band and jazz combo. The band caught the attention of jazz singer and bandleader Cab Calloway, and it toured with English singer-songwriter Robert Palmer for two years, playing to sold-out crowds at Radio City Music Hall and the Garden State Arts Center. Kit's band made eight tours in Japan and released four albums: *Some Like It Hot, Burning, The*

Sweethearts Project, and *Just the Thing*. In 1993, President Bill Clinton hired the Kit McClure Band to play at his inaugural ball, and Kit was there with her red curly hair and her saxophone. In 2005, the band received New York City's Excellence in Small Business Award from Mayor Michael Bloomberg. Throughout her life, Kit and her black sisters Emily Smoot (Borom) and Mary Jane Western (Johnson) have remained close. Emily died in 2016, but she had been there with Kit to celebrate the band's many accomplishments.

Although both the New Haven and Chicago Women's Liberation Rock Bands disbanded by 1975, Rounder Records went on to become one of the top independent record labels in the United States, with more than three thousand titles to its name. Cofounder Marian Leighton Levy, however, still remembers fondly the fourth record that Rounder ever issued: *Mountain Moving Day*. "I think it's a really important record," said Levy. "We were proud of it then, and we're just as proud of it now."

———

Like Shirley, Connie, Betty, Lawrie, and Kit, the other women in this story have continued to reshape the world around them. A number of years after asking President Brewster for the mic, Margaret (now Maggie) Coon received her masters of forestry from Yale. She devoted her career to conservation of natural resources and wild places, including twenty years of work at the Nature Conservancy. Today, she is an environmental activist in the rural Methow Valley in eastern Washington State.

Vera Wells, who organized The Black Woman seminar and conference, graduated in 1971 and served as an executive at NBC for twenty years. When the Afro-Am House fell into disrepair, Vera worked with other Yale graduates, both black and white, to raise the funds needed to renovate it. The Afro-Am House continues to serve as a refuge and source of stimulation for Yale's African heritage students today. Vera has remained an active alumna at Yale, and in 2007, she received the Yale Medal for her outstanding service to the university. Vera's and Shirley's mentor Sylvia Boone became the first African American woman to be granted tenure at Yale. A noted scholar of African art, Boone served on the Yale faculty from 1979 until her death in 1993. Vera is the executor of Boone's literary estate and has established both a scholarship and a prize at Yale in Boone's name.

The Sisterhood members went on to lead varied careers. Some went into law. Judy Berkan graduated from Harvard Law School in 1974 and now runs her own law firm in Puerto Rico. Dahlia Rudavsky works on employment discrimination cases at the law firm she cofounded in Boston. Barbara Deinhardt has spent her career in labor and employment law. Looking back on her work with the Sisterhood, Barbara says, "I think it made a difference… Yale had a lot of years of male dominance and intransigence and tradition to overcome. That's why the Sisterhood needed to be there."

Other Sisterhood members became academics. Anna Tsing Lowenhaupt (now Anna Tsing) is an anthropologist at the University of California. Peace marshal coordinator Kate Field developed an interest in biology during her year on the Skokorat commune and went on to receive her PhD. She is now an expert on water quality and a professor of microbiology at Oregon State University, where you can sometimes see her riding around campus on her red bicycle.

Betsy (now Elizabeth) Hartmann became a professor of development studies at Hampshire College in Massachusetts, and she and her roommate Patty Mintz have remained lifelong friends. Patty's career has focused on promoting health care access and included roles as an executive at Kaiser Permanente and as a consultant for the World Bank on Latin American health policy and finance. Sisterhood member Christa Hansen graduated in 1973 with a degree in psychology but died in June 1991 at age forty. The paper she wrote about Yale students who took leaves of absence or dropped out is still preserved in the Yale archives.

Other Yale women continued to break barriers after their graduation. Women doctors were a rarity in 1972, yet Los Angeles premed major Carol Storey (now Storey-Johnson) received her MD from Cornell University Medical School in 1977 and became a professor of clinical medicine at Weill Cornell Medical College in New York City, where she is now professor emerita. Carol remained lifelong friends with "Stop the Cops" activist Darial Sneed, who got her MBA from Harvard and worked in marketing, corporate finance, and investor relations for companies including Exxon, CBS, and J. P. Morgan. In 2011, Darial began a second career as a professional photographer and took hundreds of beautiful photos of plays, dance productions, and concerts. She died in 2018.

Like Carol Storey, Denise Maillet (now Main) became a doctor. She and Elliott, by then her husband, attended the University of Vermont Medical School together and started a sexuality course there for medical school students like the one that Phil and Lorna Sarrel offered at Yale. Both Denise and Elliott became ob-gyns specializing in maternal-fetal medicine. They have spent most of their professional careers working in the same practice at California Pacific Medical Center in San Francisco. In 2000, Denise cofounded the nonprofit Siempre Unidos, which is now the leading care provider for HIV-positive individuals in Honduras.

Women were not the only activists in this story. Alec Haverstick, who led the Ad Hoc Committee for Coeducation and was instrumental in the final effort to end Yale's gender quotas, graduated in 1974 and spent his career in the financial services industry. Alec is currently the principal and senior wealth adviser at Bessemer Trust. Looking back at his time at Yale, Alec says, "I think the formation of that ad hoc committee was the bravest thing I ever did. I've done more foolhardy things, but that was the bravest thing I ever did."

Alec was not the first male student, of course, to help make Yale a more equitable place for women. *Yale Daily News* editor Lanny Davis, who barraged Kingman Brewster with pro-coeducation editorials, graduated in 1967 and went on to become a lawyer. Coeducation advocate Derek Shearer graduated in 1968 and served as U.S. ambassador to Finland from 1994 to 1997. His sister Brooke, the subject of his "Please, Mr. Brewster" poster, went to college at Stanford. Derek is currently the director of the McKinnon Center for Global Affairs at Occidental College in Los Angeles. Coed Week organizer Avi Soifer graduated in 1969, got his JD from Yale Law School, and became a law school professor. From 2003 to 2020, he served as the dean of the William S. Richardson School of Law at the University of Hawaii at Manoa.

Yale women also benefited from allies within Yale's faculty and administration. Phil and Lorna Sarrel continued to run the Yale Sex Counseling Service and teach Topics in Human Sexuality for thirty years. The course became a model for similar classes taught at dozens of different colleges and universities, and *Sex and the Yale Student* went through five editions, with more than forty thousand copies distributed to Yale students by 1990. Students on the Human Sexuality

Committee wrote an extended version of the booklet for college students nationally, *The Student Guide to Sex on Campus*, and their book, which was published in 1971 by Signet, sold one hundred thousand copies. Today, the Sarrels continue to welcome their former Yale students to their lovely home in the woods outside New Haven.

Brewster adviser Sam Chauncey served as secretary of Yale University from 1971 to 1980 and in several other roles, including founder and CEO of New Haven's Science Park. "Sam was a wonderful mentor," Wasserman told an interviewer in 2007. "He didn't have the hang-ups [about women] that a lot of the other guys had. I mean, he wasn't threatened by them in any way. So he was very helpful." Chauncey retired in 2000 and splits his time between New Haven and Vermont.

John Wilkinson served as the undergraduate dean until 1974, when he became headmaster of the Hopkins School in New Haven. From 1981 to 1987, Wilkinson, like Chauncey before him, served as the secretary of Yale. Women undergraduates and administrators mention Wilkinson repeatedly as an ally of women during coeducation's early years. "He's really been a savior to so many of us, an unsung hero in some ways," remarked Connie Royster. Wilkinson has retired as well. He and his wife live in New Haven.

Elga Wasserman's Yale career did not end as well as either Chauncey's or Wilkinson's. Two months after the Yale Corporation adopted sex-blind admissions, she learned that she no longer had a job at Yale. Brewster terminated her special assistant position and gave all four of the new jobs she expressed interest in to others. Wasserman was left with nothing. "To be outspoken is to be damned at Yale," the Yale Faculty and Professional Women's Forum wrote in an outraged letter to the editor afterward. "Elga's fate is an object lesson to those of us who want to keep our jobs here." Yet once again, Wasserman proved resilient. She enrolled at Yale Law School and received her law degree in 1976 at age fifty-two. Wasserman practiced family law in New Haven for the rest of her career and in 2000 wrote her first book, *The Door in the Dream: Conversations with Eminent Women in Science*. She died in 2014.

Assistant Dean Elisabeth Thomas (now Betsy Peterson), one of the Admissions Committee members who criticized Yale's gender quotas, left Yale in 1975 to become a lawyer. She spent the rest of her career practicing law in Massachusetts, with roles including associate general counsel for Houghton Mifflin. Her book *Voices of Alzheimer's*, published in 2004, captures the experiences of those whose loved ones suffer from dementia, the disease that afflicted her husband for the last fourteen years of his life.

As for Kingman Brewster, he remained the president of Yale until 1977, when he resigned to become the U.S. ambassador to England. Yale trustee Cyrus Vance, who by then was the secretary of state, helped him get the job. Brewster spent the remainder of his life in England, save for a three-year stint in New York following his ambassadorship. He died in 1988.

While Brewster had only agreed reluctantly to admit women undergraduates to Yale, Yale's 1968 coeducation announcement (and Princeton's two months later) finally lifted the coeducation taboo among America's top colleges, and by 1973, the vast majority of elite all-male campuses had gone coed too. Over time, however, the voices of those first women students were lost, the sharp edges of this history sanded down. What was left was a sanitized tale of equity instantly achieved, as if all it took to transform these villages of men into places where women were treated as equals was the flip of an admissions switch. That is not what happened, though. Just ask the Yale women. They have some remarkable stories to tell.

ACKNOWLEDGMENTS

FIRST, THANKS GO TO THE FIVE WOMEN WHOSE stories form the backbone of this book: Shirley Daniels, Kit McClure, Lawrie Mifflin, Connie Royster, and Elizabeth Spahn. I am grateful for their unfailing patience with my numerous questions, their commitment to getting this story right, and their actions to help the women who followed them. I am also so very grateful to all of the fifty-one women and men whom I interviewed for this book and who took such care in reading over their transcripts and answering my many follow-up questions. Each of their names is included in the list of oral histories and interviews in this book. Without them, *Yale Needs Women* could never have been written.

A number of those whom I interviewed deserve particular mention. I am grateful to Margie Ferguson, Kate Field, Denise Maillet Main, and Lydia Temoshok for their many insights and their trust in sharing difficult stories. Judy Berkan, Barbara Deinhardt, Dahlia Rudavsky, and Marie Rudden were all wonderful teachers about the Sisterhood, as were Carolyn Grillo, Linden Havemeyer Wise, and Tricia Tunstall about the class of 1974. Sam Chauncey, Alec

Haverstick, Betsy Thomas Peterson, Phil and Lorna Sarrel, and John Wilkinson all provided critical perspectives and were generous with their time. I am also indebted to Debbie Bernick, Maggie Coon, Betsy Hartmann, Marian Leighton Levy, Patty Mintz, Hank Murray, Avi Soifer, Carol Storey-Johnson, and Vera Wells for their thoughtful comments. Thank you to Derek Shearer for sharing with me the stories of the remarkable women in his family and to Derek's brother-in-law Strobe Talbott for allowing me to have a copy of the photo of Brooke Shearer that was used in the "Please Mr. Brewster" poster.

This book also owes much to earlier historians. Julia Pimsleur was the first to have conducted oral histories of Yale's first women undergraduates and of Elga Wasserman. Her 1990 videotapes were invaluable. So too was Presca Ahn's video *Arrival* and the collection of first-person accounts compiled by Pamela Geismar, Eve Hart Rice, and Joan O'Meara Winant in their book *Fresh Women*. Geoffrey Kabaservice's oral histories and his book *The Guardians* were crucial as well. Ruth Rosen's *The World Split Open* was an irreplaceable resource on the U.S. women's movement, as was Jerome Karabel's *The Chosen*, on the long exclusion of African Americans, Jews, and working-class students at Harvard, Yale, and Princeton.

No historian can do her work without the help of skilled archivists and librarians, and I have been fortunate indeed to work with the dedicated staff at Yale Manuscripts and Archives. Thanks go in particular to Mike Lotstein and to Michael Frost, Jess Becker, Steve Ross, and Bill Landis. Those who funded the digitization of the *Yale Daily News* deserve special mention; that resource is a gift to researchers. The indefatigable interlibrary loan staff at UMass Boston's Healey Library also went above and beyond in obtaining the many obscure books and articles I requested.

I have also been graced in this work by the help of generous and wise experts in the field of higher education. Thanks above all to John Saltmarsh for his enthusiasm about my research and knack for knowing the exact question to ask to help me think more clearly about what I was finding. Linda Eisenmann, whose work I admired long before I met her, has been a wonderful mentor and generous in connecting me with other historians. Dwight Giles sharpened my thinking about change, and Sana Haroon taught me everything I know about conducting oral histories. My understanding of methodology and theory owes much to Gerardo Blanco. I am grateful as well to the other UMass Boston faculty who encouraged this effort and pushed my thinking about it: Jay Dee, Glenn Gabbard, Tara Parker, and Katalin Szelényi. I could not have completed my research without the financial support of UMass Boston's Zelda Gamson Fellowship, Doctoral Dissertation Research Grant program, and Kanter Travel Grant program. I also lucked into the best doctoral cohort ever. My profound thanks to Jenene Cook, John Drew, Cate Kaluzny, Erin Kelley, Melissa Quashie, and Mike Walker for all the laughter, intellectual challenge, and friendship.

The list of those who have supported this project extends still further. The Association for the Study of Higher Education (ASHE) and History of Education Society deserve special mention for their support of new scholars. I am grateful to have presented papers at their conferences and for the helpful feedback from reviewers and discussants. Winning ASHE's Bobby Wright Dissertation of the Year Award remains one of my greatest honors. My colleagues at the Massachusetts Department of Higher Education were terrific, with special thanks to Katy Abel. Amanda Miller's early contributions to this research were indispensable, and Nick Adolph was generous in connecting me with his wonderful aunts. Anna Weiss has offered support and advice since I began, and thanks also to my cousin Will

Scarlett for his coaching on agents and book proposals. And I can't forget the team at Boston's Audio Transcription Service, who were unfailingly professional in transcribing the hours of interviews I sent them, or Gene Buonaccorsi, my tour guide in the land of social media.

Before writing this book, I never understood what it was agents actually do. Now I get it. I am lucky to have found Laurie Abkemeier, who has provided her considerable editorial skills, taught me about the publishing process, looked out for my interests, and always responded with wise advice to the unending questions of a new author. I also could not have found a better home for *Yale Needs Women* than Sourcebooks, the largest woman-owned publisher in North America. My editor Anna Michels has been a delight, and her questions and comments have vastly improved the drafts I sent her. I am grateful as well to the many others at Sourcebooks who've provided their support and expertise along the way, with particular thanks to Margaret Coffee, Steve Geck, Liz Kelsch, Michael Leali, Lizzie Lewandowski, Erin McClary, Stefani Sloma, and Katie Stutz.

And where would I be without my friends and family? If it is true that gratitude makes us happy, then I am a happy woman indeed. I am so very grateful for the encouragement and help I've received on this project from my friends Dave and Sally Hess, David and Ginger Kendall, Patterson Lacy, Hazel Mills, Ann Mantil, Wells Obrecht, Colleen Pearce, Roy Ruderman, Kirsten Schlenger, and Betsy Williams. My wonderful family has been forgiving of my absences, ceaselessly supportive, and caring of me throughout. Thank you to my husband, Rick High; our children, Lily, Robby, and Mac Perkins-High; my sister, Ginny Perkins, and mother, Anne Scarlett Perkins, and to Sarah Brown, Hilary Burgin, and George and Shirley Scarlett. And a final thanks to Rick, of course, for the many cups of hot tea. I would never have gotten over the finish line without him.

ORAL HISTORIES AND INTERVIEWS

THE ORAL HISTORIES USED IN THIS BOOK WERE conducted by five individuals: the author plus four earlier interviewers. The transcripts of Geoffrey Kabaservice's oral histories are held in the Griswold-Brewster Oral History Project (RU217), Yale University Library (YUL). The transcripts of Florence Minnis's oral histories are held in the Oral Histories Documenting Yale University Women (RU1051), YUL. The transcript of Joel Krieger's interview is held in the May Day Rally and Yale Collection (RU86), Accession 1983-A-108, YUL.

The videotapes of Julia Pimsleur's oral histories are held in the Boola Boola Archive Project, Yale University Film Center. All author interviews were transcribed, with the transcriptions reviewed and approved by the interviewee. In cases where multiple interviews and follow-up emails took place, the date of the first interview is used.

Interviewee	Gender	Race	Role	Interviewer, Date
Joan Ausubel	W	White	Class of 1973	Author, 2016
Joni Barnett	W	White	Athletic administrator	Pimsleur, 1990
Judith Berkan	W	White	Class of 1971	Author, 2017
Deborah Bernick	W	White	Class of 1972	Author, 2016
Linda Bishop	W	White	Class of 1973	Pimsleur, 1990
John Blum	M	White	Faculty member	Kabaservice, 1992
Henry "Sam" Chauncey	M	White	Brewster adviser	Author, 2014
Carol Christ	W	White	Graduate student	Author, 2017
Inky Clark	M	White	Admissions dean	Kabaservice, 1993
Margaret Coon	W	White	Class of 1973	Author, 2018
Shirley Daniels	W	Black	Class of 1972	Author, 2017
Linda Darling	W	Black	Class of 1973	Pimsleur, 1990
Barbara Deinhardt	W	White	Class of 1973	Author, 2017
Kate Driscoll Coon	W	White	Class of 1973	Author, 2017
Hester Eisenstein	W	White	Faculty member	Krieger, 1971 Author, 2017
Kai Erikson	M	White	College master	Kabaservice, 1992
Jonathan Fanton	M	White	Brewster adviser	Kabaservice, 1992
William Farley	M	Black	Class of 1972	Kabaservice, 1991
Margie Ferguson	W	White	Graduate student	Author, 2017

(continued)

Interviewee	Gender	Race	Role	Interviewer, Date
Kate Field*	W	White	Class of 1973	Author, 2017
Alfred Fitt	M	White	Brewster adviser	Kabaservice, 1991
Barbara Fried*	W	White	Class of 1973	Author, 2017
Connie Gersick	W	White	Wasserman aide	Author, 2016
Hanna Gray	W	White	Trustee	Kabaservice, 1991
Carolyn Grillo	W	White	Class of 1974	Author, 2018
Betsy Hartmann	W	White	Class of 1973	Author, 2017
Heidi Hartmann	W	White	Graduate student	Author, 2018
Linden Havemeyer Wise	W	White	Class of 1974	Author, 2018
Alec Haverstick	M	White	Class of 1974	Author, 2018
Katharine Jelly	W	White	Class of 1971	Author, 2017
Brenda Jubin	W	White	Morse College dean	Author, 2017
Carolyn Kenady	W	White	Class of 1974	Author, 2018
Prudence Leib Gourguechon	W	White	Class of 1973	Author, 2018
Marian Leighton Levy	W	White	Rounder records	Author, 2018
Steven Lieberman	M	White	Class of 1972	Author, 2018
Lance Liebman	M	White	Yale trustee	Author, 2018
Charles Lindblom	M	White	Faculty member	Kabaservice, 1991

(continued)

Interviewee	Gender	Race	Role	Interviewer, Date
Denise Maillet Main	W	White	Class of 1972	Author, 2017
Kit McClure*	W	White	Class of 1973	Author, 2017
Lawrie Mifflin	W	White	Class of 1973	Pimsleur, 1990 Author, 2017
Patricia Mintz	W	White	Class of 1973	Author, 2017
Charlotte Morse	W	White	Faculty member	Minnis, 2008
Hank Murray	M	White	Class of 1971	Author, 2017
Rebecca Newman	W	White	Class of 1973	Author, 2017
Diane Polan	W	White	Class of 1973	Pimsleur, 1990
Eve Rice*	W	White	Class of 1973	Author, 2017
Edna Rostow	W	White	Wasserman friend	Kabaservice, 1992
Constance Royster	W	Black	Class of 1972	Author, 2016
Dahlia Rudavsky*	W	White	Class of 1973	Author, 2017
Marie Rudden	W	White	Class of 1973	Author, 2017
Cynthia Russett	W	White	Faculty member	Pimsleur, 1990
Bernice Sandler	W	White	Title IX activist	Author, 2018
Lorna Sarrel	W	White	Sex Counseling Service worker	Author, 2016
Philip Sarrel	M	White	Sex Counseling Service worker	Author, 2016

(continued)

Interviewee	Gender	Race	Role	Interviewer, Date
Kurt Schmoke	M	Black	Class of 1971	Kabaservice, 1992 Author, 2016
Darial Sneed	W	Black	Class of 1973	Pimsleur, 1990
Aviam Soifer	M	White	Class of 1969	Kabaservice, 1991
Amy Solomon	W	White	Class of 1973	Pimsleur, 1990
Elizabeth Spahn	W	White	Class of 1972	Author, 2017
Carol Storey-Johnson	W	Black	Class of 1973	Author, 2017
Charles Taylor	M	White	Provost	Kabaservice, 1992
Deborah Tedford	W	White	Class of 1972	Author, 2016
Lydia Temoshok	W	White	Class of 1972	Author, 2017
Elisabeth Thomas Peterson	W	White	Assistant dean	Author, 2016
Christine Traut	W	White	Class of 1973	Pimsleur, 1990
John Trinkaus	M	White	College master	Kabaservice, 1992
Tricia Tunstall	W	White	Class of 1974	Author, 2018
Elga Wasserman	W	White	Coeducation head	Pimsleur, 1990 Kabaservice, 1992 Minnis, 2007
Jacqueline Wei Mintz	W	Asian	Associate provost	Author, 2016
Vera Wells	W	Black	Class of 1971	Author, 2017

(continued)

Interviewee	Gender	Race	Role	Interviewer, Date
John Wilkinson	M	White	Associate dean	Kabaservice, 1992 Author, 2016
Susanne Wofford	W	White	Class of 1973	Pimsleur, 1990
Janet Yellen	W	White	Graduate student	Author, 2018
Philip Zaeder	M	White	Associate chaplain	Author, 2018

* Date shown is the class that the student entered with.

NOTES

ABBREVIATIONS

ARCHIVAL SOURCES ARE ABBREVIATED AS FOLLOWS:

The letters *b* and *f* are used to indicate box and folder. Manuscript and archival collections are identified by call number.

For example, b1.f18.RU95 is box 1, folder 18, of RU95, Yale College, Records of the Dean. The first reference for each collection includes its name and accession number.

NEWSPAPERS, MAGAZINES, AND OTHER PUBLICATIONS

ER	*Educational Record*
HC	*Harvard Crimson* (student newspaper)
NHR	*New Haven Register*
NJ	*New Journal* (student magazine)
NYT	*New York Times*

OC   *Old Campus* (freshman face book)

WP   *Washington Post*

YAM   *Yale Alumni Magazine*

YB   *Yale Banner* (yearbook)

YDN   *Yale Daily News* (student newspaper)

Copies of all Yale publications are held in the Yale University Library, Manuscripts and Archives. The *Yale Daily News* is also available through the archives online.

ORAL HISTORIES AND INTERVIEWS

Oral histories and interviews (OH) are abbreviated by last name. If an individual was interviewed more than once, the year of the interview is included. Interview transcript pages are provided when available—for example, Wasserman OH (1992), 7. See previous section for the full citation.

OTHER ABBREVIATIONS

AHCC   Ad Hoc Committee on Coeducation

CC   Coeducation Committee

HSC   Human Sexuality Committee

OIR   Office of Institutional Research, Yale University

OUA   Office of Undergraduate Admissions, Yale University

WAC   Women's Advisory Council

YFC   Yale Film Study Center

YNB   Yale News Bureau

YUL   Yale University Library, Manuscripts and Archives

PROLOGUE

"flashpoints": Margaret A. Nash, "Thoughts on the History of Women's Education, Theories of Power, and This Volume: An Introduction," in *Women's Higher Education in the United States: New Historical Perspectives*, ed. Margaret A. Nash (New York: Palgrave Macmillan, 2018), 6.

"Don't screw it up": Royster OH.

ONE: 268 YEARS OF MEN

Yale men were ready: On mixers, see "Conversations at a Yale Mixer," *YDN*, November 17, 1967; Pepper Schwartz and Janet Lever, "Fear and Loathing at a College Mixer," *Journal of Contemporary Ethnography* 4, no. 4 (1976): 413–431; Garry Trudeau, "Bull Tales" (comic strip), *YDN*, October 1968 to May 1970; Bernick OH; Gersick OH; Soifer OH, 16; Temoshok OH.

"white men in tweeds": Houston A. Baker, "On My First Acquaintance with Black Studies: A Yale Story," in *A Companion to African-American Studies*, ed. Lewis Gordon and Jane Gordon (Malden: Blackwell, 2006), 6.

Only two colleges in America: Noah Petersen and Mattie Clear, "100 Years of Coeducation at W&M," *William and Mary News and Media*, September 21, 2018, https://www.wm .edu/news/stories/2018/100-years-of-coeducation-at-wm.php; Helen Horowitz, "It's Complicated: 375 Years of Women at Harvard" (lecture, Cambridge, MA, April 23, 2012), https://www.radcliffe.harvard.edu/.

"piece of chattel": Bob Mascia, "Frosh Girls Least Preferred," *YDN*, September 23, 1969.

"Say, aren't you from California?": "Conversations," *YDN*, November 17, 1967.

"I know all about your room": "Conversations," *YDN*, November 17, 1967.

"Some girls that I've talked to": Douglas Derrer, "Making It at Yale," *YDN*, October 6, 1967.

Kingman Brewster Jr.: "The Ivy League," *Newsweek*, November 23, 1964; James Reston, "Washington: The Tragedy of the Republicans," *NYT*, June 12, 1966; Mitchel Levitas, "Present and Future of Kingman Brewster," *NYT*, February 12, 1967; "Universities: Anxiety behind the Façade," *Time*, June 23, 1967, 78–85; Geoffrey Kabaservice, *The Guardians: Kingman Brewster, His Circle, and the Rise of the Liberal Establishment* (New York: Henry Holt, 2004); Jerome Karabel, *The Chosen: The Hidden History of Admission and Exclusion at Harvard, Yale, and Princeton* (New York: Houghton Mifflin, 2005); Blum OH; Chauncey OH; Clark OH (May); Fanton OH; Lieberman OH; Schmoke OH (2016); Trinkaus OH.

determined to bring about change: Jeffrey Gordon, "Inky's Era," *YAM*, March 1970, 32–37; Karabel, *The Chosen*, 354; Thomas Meehannew, "The Yale Faculty Makes the Scene," *NYT*, February 7, 1971.

"King," his childhood nickname: Kabaservice, *The Guardians*, 36; Blum OH (February), 38; communication from George Pierson to Kingman Brewster, January 6, 1971, b22.f910, Office on the Education of Women, Yale University, Records (RU821), Accession 19ND-A-086, YUL (hereafter RU821A).

"an imposing figure": Farley OH, 8.

"Whatever 'it' is": Gray OH, 13.

"the assurance that came from": Blum OH (February), 7.

"a Yale man": John Back, Edward Coughlin, and Rudolph Kass, "Yale: For God, Country, and
     Success," *HC*, November 25, 1950.

"a very complex man": Schmoke OH (1992), 2.

"Next to myself": George Kannar, "SAB," *YDN*, February 4, 1969.

four thousand students rose: George Kannar, "Mass Meeting Splits Evenly on ROTC," *YDN*,
     May 2, 1969.

"Coeducation should now be": "Enter the 88th," editorial, *YDN*, January 26, 1966.

"Lanny beat the drums": "On the Advisability and Feasibility of Women at Yale," *YAM*, September/
     October 2009, https://yalealumnimagazine.com. See also Samuel Babbitt, "Coeducation
     Forum," *YDN*, May 5, 1966.

The News was one of the oldest: Jeff Greenfield, *No Peace, No Place: Excavations along the Generational
     Fault* (Garden City: Doubleday, 1973), 208; Levitas, "Present and Future of Kingman
     Brewster"; "Universities: Anxiety behind the Façade," 80.

25 percent…to 60 percent: Claudia Goldin and Lawrence Katz, "Putting the Co in Education: Timing,
     Reasons, and Consequences of College Coeducation from 1835 to the Present" (working
     paper no.16281, National Bureau of Economic Research, August 2010), 11.

Harvard president Charles Eliot: Thomas Woody, *A History of Women's Education in the United States*
     (New York: Science Press, 1929), 304–312.

the list of U.S. colleges: Anne G. Perkins, "Unescorted Guests: Yale's First Women Undergraduates and
     the Quest for Equity" (PhD diss., UMass Boston, May 2018), appendix A.

"In the minds of many": Wasserman, "Coeducation Comes," 143.

He was…its president: Kingman Brewster, *The Report of the President*, September 1968, b575.f5,
     Records (RU11), Series V, YUL (hereafter, RU11-V), 12.

"the faculty adored him": Blum OH (March), 23.

he had awarded King: "Thousands View 263rd Commencement," *YDN*, April 13, 1964.

students at Trinity College: Peter Knapp and Anne Knapp, *Trinity College in the Twentieth Century: A
     History* (Hartford: Trinity College, 2000), 341–353.

more than two hundred students: Karabel, *The Chosen*, 389.

two central questions: Brewster, *Report of the President*, 1.

The growing women's movement: Ruth Rosen, *The World Split Open: How the Modern Women's
     Movement Changed America* (New York: Penguin, 2000); Sarah M. Evans, "Sons, Daughters,
     and Patriarchy: Gender and the 1968 Generation," *American Historical Review* 114, no. 2
     (2009): 331–347.

Derek Shearer: Shearer's emails to author, September 21, 2017, and October 28, 2018.

Yale students and their views: "The Coeducation White Paper," *YDN*, October 31, 1968; "It's Not
     about Home Economics: Q&A with Avi Soifer," *YAM*, September 8, 2009; Mark Zanger,
     "Women Now. Talk Later," *YDN*, October 4, 1969.

prep school boys who had long formed the majority: Gordon, "Inky's Era," 32–37.

"Complete and immediate coeducation": Kannar, "SAB."

"Kingman was not comfortable": Chauncey OH, emphasis in original. On Chauncey's relationship with Brewster, see Wilkinson OH; Fanton OH, 47; Greenfield, *No Peace, No Place*, 204.

"believed in change": Chauncey OH.

Mary Louise Phillips: Kabaservice, *The Guardians*, 88–89; "Mary Phillips Engaged," *NYT*, January 25, 1942.

"Kingman knew girls": Wilkinson OH.

"widely viewed as the training grounds": Karabel, *The Chosen*, 18.

"We are a national institution": Joseph Soares, *The Power of Privilege: Yale and America's Elite Colleges* (Stanford: Stanford University Press, 2007), 82.

"make the hunchy judgment": communication from Brewster to John Muyskens, March 15, 1967, b1.f8.RU821A.

all fifty of the state governors: Center for Women in American Politics, "History of Women Governors," 2019, https://www.cawp.rutgers.edu/history-women-governors; and "History of Women in the US Congress," 2019, https://www.cawp.rutgers.edu/history-women-us-congress.

the possibility of a sister school: Michael Rosenhouse and Avi Soifer, "Vassar Turns Down Merger; Yale May Start Girls' School," *YDN*, November 21, 1967.

$30 million: Ray Warman, "$30 Million Needed to Adopt Coed Plan," *YDN*, September 30, 1968.

"Please, Mr. Brewster": Kannar, "SAB."

2 tenured women: Mary B. Arnstein, *Coeducation 1972–73*, July 1973, b1.f5.RU821, Accession 2006-A-213 (hereafter RU821B), appendix VI, table 6.

Just 4 percent: Ann Sutherland Harris, "The Second Sex in Academe," *AAUP Bulletin* 56, no. 3 (September 1970): 290. See also U. of Michigan, "Trailblazing Women," 2019, http://umich.edu/~whimse/bckgd.html; U. of California, "The university should admit women," 2019, https://150.berkeley.edu/

Invisible is the word: Janet Lever and Pepper Schwartz, *Women at Yale: Liberating a College Campus* (Indianapolis: Bobbs-Merrill, 1971), 1.

less than 10 percent: YNB, "Press Release #316," April 13, 1969, b1.f5.RU821B.

Yale's treatment of women: Charles Hillinger, "For the Athlete, It's a Bit of Heaven," *Los Angeles Times*, December 30, 1985; "Gym to Go Coed," *YDN*, February 13, 1969; Jeffrey Gordon and Eric Rosenberg, "Wasserman Heads Coed Office," *YDN*, November 21, 1968; Christ OH; Jubin OH; Russett OH; Lorna Sarrel OH. The Elizabethan Club changed its rules on women in 1969.

discrimination against women: Bernice Sandler, "Title IX: How We Got It and What a Difference It Made," *Cleveland State Law Review* 55, no. 4 (2007): 475; Reed v. Reed, 404 U.S. 71 (1971).

"Speaking strictly": Karabel, *The Chosen*, 420.

The numbers did not look good: OUA, "Yield Figures—Classes of 1967–1976," September 25, 1972, b1.f15.RU821A, table I; Jeffrey Gordon, "Pressures on Admissions," *YDN*, April 4, 1969; Karabel, *The Chosen*, 416.

"vital to Princeton's future": Gardner Patterson, "The Education of Women at Princeton," *Princeton Alumni Weekly* 69, no. 1 (1968): 21, b1.f4.RU821B, 6.

a second choice to Yale: Karabel, *The Chosen*, 420.

"sense of competitive rivalry": YNB, "Press Release #158," November 14, 1968, b258.f5.RU11, Series II (hereafter RU-II).

"loss of first-rate students": Kingman Brewster, "Higher Education for Women at Yale," September 23, 1968, b10.f107, Yale College Records Concerning the Education of Women (RU578), Accession 1988-A-009, YUL (hereafter RU578A).

1,500 students: Brewster, "Higher Education for Women."

$575 million: "Universities in Ferment," *Newsweek*, June 15, 1970, 70.

"It was a bogus issue": Clark OH (May), 29.

"So Where Are the Women?": "So Where Are the Women?," *YDN*, September 23, 1968.

"Women Now. Talk Later": Zanger, "Women Now. Talk Later."

Avi Soifer: Soifer OH, 1, 16–17; Avi Soifer, "Vassar Study Committee Appointed by Brewster," *YDN*, January 25, 1967.

"Coeducation Week": Avi Soifer, "Coed Week: A Response," *YDN*, October 23, 1968; "Coed Events," *YDN*, November 4, 1968; William Borders, "Elie Joins Eli for Coeducation Week at Yale," *NYT*, November 5, 1968; John Coots, "Yale Coeds Register," *YDN*, November 5, 1968; Chauncey OH; Soifer OH, 5–20; Soifer email to author, September 19, 2017.

"under more natural conditions": Soifer, "Coed Week."

"we may go ahead anyway": Soifer OH, 12.

"All over the campus": Jody Adams, "I, a Yale Coed," *HC*, December 2, 1968.

"Women are people too": "It's Not about Home Economics."

"All of them consisted": Jody Adams, "Fortas Flicks Excite Coed Week Audience," *YDN*, November 5, 1968; Laura Kalman, *Yale Law School and the Sixties* (Chapel Hill: University of North Carolina Press, 2005), 194.

"There I was at Yale": Adams, "I, a Yale Coed."

"Give us a date!": Jeffrey Stern, "Coed Rally Meets Brewster at Home," *YDN*, November 7, 1968.

"a very smart political act": Trinkaus OH, 32.

Brewster called a meeting: Jeff Gordon, "On Coeducation: Hold Secret Parley," *YDN*, November 8, 1968.

"the quality of admission at Yale": Karabel, *The Chosen*, 418. On Corporation meeting, see YNB, "Press Release #158"; Taylor OH, 59.

200:1 in favor: Ray Warman, "Brewster Offers Coeducation Plan," *YDN*, November 15, 1968.

George Pierson: Kabaservice, *The Guardians*, 191.

"Yale Going Coed": William Borders, "Yale Going Coed," *NYT*, November 15, 1968.

"This is a crash program": Warman, "Brewster Offers Coeducation."

eight hundred letters…four thousand applied: William Borders, "Yale Beseiged by Female Applicants," *NYT*, November 24, 1968; Nancy Weiss Malkiel, *"Keep the Damned Women Out": The Struggle for Coeducation* (Princeton: Princeton University Press, 2016), 139.

"with the least disruption": Planning Committee on Coeducation, "Plans for Housing Women at
    Yale for 1969–70," January 31, 1969, b22.f908.RU821A.

TWO: SUPERWOMEN

Kit McClure: McClure OH; *OC Class of 1973* (New Haven: Yale Banner Publications, 1969);
    "Passaic Valley Regional Yearbooks," Little Falls Public Library, 1969, https://www
    .littlefallslibrary.org/pvyearbooks.asp.

Shirley Daniels: Daniels OH; Edward Gellman, ed., *Transfers 1972: A Supplement to the OC Volume*
    XXV (New Haven: Yale Banner Publications, 1969); *The 1972 YB* (New Haven: Yale
    Banner Publications, 1972).

"Why don't you apply?": Daniels OH.

Connie Royster: Royster OH; *Transfers 1972; The 1972 YB;* "Black Pioneer Motley Remembered at
    Yale Law School," *NHR,* December 14, 2005; "Eunice Royster," obituary, *NHR,* October
    5, 2014; "Miss Royster Is Trustee of Wykeham Rise," *NHR,* August 10, 1969.

Betty Spahn: Spahn OH; *Transfers 1972;* Todd Tubutis, "Park Forest, IL," *Encyclopedia of Chicago,* 2005,
    http://www.encyclopedia.chicagohistory.org; Zillow, "Homes for Sale," 201 Blackhawk
    Drive, Park Forest, IL, https://www.zillow.com/.

"Dear Miss Spahn": communication from John Muyskens to women transfer students, March 6,
    1969, in author's possession with thanks to Connie Royster.

an eleven-page article: Jonathan Lear, "The Great Admissions Sweepstakes: How Yale Selected Her
    First Coeds," *NYT,* April 13, 1969.

"the female versions…superwomen": Lear, "The Great Admissions Sweepstakes."

"one of those superwomen": Anonymous, "No Easy Answers," in *Fresh Women: Reflections on Coeducation*
    and Life after Yale, 1969, 1989, 2009, ed. Pamela Geismar, Eve Hart Rice, and Joan O'Meara
    Winant (self-pub., Yale Printing and Publishing Services, 2010), 105. See also Barbara
    Deinhardt, "'Mother of Men'?," in *Women in Higher Education,* ed. W. Todd Furniss and
    Patricia A. Graham (Washington, DC: American Council on Education, 1974), 66–69; Kate
    Driscoll Coon, "Rich Soil, Messy Stuff," in *Fresh Women,* 43; Havemeyer Wise OH; Marie
    Rudden, "A Woman's Place," in *Fresh Women,* 47.

Lawrie Mifflin: Mifflin OH (2017); *OC Class of 1973; The 1973 YB* (New Haven: Yale Banner
    Publications, 1973); Zillow, "Homes for Sale," 419 Drew Avenue, Swarthmore, PA,
    https://www.zillow.com/.

"Yale University announces": *The 1971 YB* (New Haven: Yale Banner Publications, 1971), 122.

The acceptances: Edward Gellman, ed., *Transfers 1971: A Supplement to the OC Volume XXIV* (New
    Haven: Yale Banner Publications, 1969); *Transfers 1972; OC Class of 1973.*

"We can't afford this": McClure OH.

one in twelve: Dartmouth College, *An Analysis of the Impact of Coeducation at Princeton and Yale*
    Universities (New York: Cresap, McCormick, and Paget, November 1971), D.C. Hist
    LC1601.A53 1971, v–4.

Even among alumni kids: Dartmouth College, *An Analysis of the Impact.*

"Ever since you've been two": "Coeds on Coeducation: A Discussion," *YAM,* April 1970, 34, italics in original. See also Bernick OH; Daniels OH; Jelly OH; Royster OH; Spahn OH; Tedford OH; Temoshok OH; Wells OH.

"Yale! Yale! My daughter's going": Daniels OH.

"a kind of reclaiming": Royster OH.

firing off memos: communication from Wasserman to Beach, September 2, 1969, b19.f888. RU821B; communication from Wasserman to Brewster, September 4, 1969, b1.f13. RU821A. Sections in italics are paraphrased.

Deans of women: Robert Schwartz, "Reconceptualizing the Leadership Roles of Women in Higher Education: A Brief History on the Importance of Deans of Women," *Journal of Higher Education* 68, no. 5 (September/October 1997): 517.

Ninety-five percent: Ruth M. Oltman, "Campus 1970: Where Do Women Stand?" (Washington, DC: American Association of University Women, January 1970), 14.

"The higher the fewer": Ann Sutherland Harris, "The Second Sex in Academe," *AAUP Bulletin* 56, no. 3 (September 1970): 284.

"You son of a bitch": Chauncey OH.

Brewster wanted a woman…inside of Yale: Chauncey OH. For a list of Brewster's hires who were Yale alumni, see Anne G. Perkins, "Unescorted Guests: Yale's First Women Undergraduates and the Quest for Equity" (PhD diss., UMass Boston, May 2018), 263, table 5.

fifty-three of Yale's top fifty-four: "Offices of Administration," *Yale University Catalogue 1968–69,* b4.f1, Yale University Corporation Records (RU164), Accession 1994-A-077.

Elga Wasserman: Wasserman OH (1990, 1992, 2007); "In Memoriam: Elga R. Wasserman," *YaleNews,* November 14, 2014, https://news.yale.edu/; Rebecca Davis, "Elga Ruth Wasserman," Jewish Women's Archive, March 2009, http://jwa.org/encyclopedia/article/wasserman-elga-ruth.

"a housewife": "Elga Wasserman to Head Planning for Coeducation," *YAM,* December 1968.

"sort of the ornaments": Wasserman OH (1992), 2.

"I don't think he knew": Wasserman OH (2007), 54.

"It was an hour and twenty-five minutes": Bernick OH.

575 women undergraduates: OUA, "Female Enrollment to Date," August 27, 1970, b1.f10.RU821A.

the racial and ethnic diversity: For black women students, see communication from John Muyskens to Elga Wasserman, June 8, 1970, b1.f.10.RU821A. Yale did not count the numbers of Asian and Latina students until 1971. I identified them through membership in the Asian American, Chicana, or Puerto Rican student group and/or last name.

"Oh, you're a Yale woman!": Wasserman OH (1990), emphasis in original. See also Anonymous, "No Easy Answers," in *Fresh Women,* 105; Darling OH; Betsy Hartmann OH; Wofford OH.

Few…would have described themselves: Darling OH; Deinhardt OH; Virginia Dominguez, "Scholar of the House," in *Fresh Women,* 33; Gersick OH; Jelly OH; Rudden, "A Woman's Place," 50; Russett OH; Sneed OH; Solomon OH; Spahn OH; Tedford OH; Traut OH; Wei Mintz OH; Wofford OH.

"Most people didn't experience": Julian Barnes, *The Sense of an Ending* (New York: Vintage International, 2012), 41.

She and Sam Chauncey: communication from George Langdon to Kingman Brewster, Charles Taylor, Elga Wasserman, and Sam Chauncey, February 25, 1969, b1.f13.RU821B; Chauncey OH; Wasserman OH (2007), 58.

two ground rules: communication from Kingman Brewster to residential college masters, November 18, 1968, b258.f6.RU11-II; Wasserman OH (1990).

Yale's twelve residential colleges: Lucy Eddy, "No Ruffles and Lace for Girls at Yale," *Hartford Courant,* November 30, 1969, b58.f388, Records (RU19), Series II, YUL (hereafter RU19-II); Havemeyer Wise OH; Janet Lever and Pepper Schwartz, *Women at Yale: Liberating a College Campus* (Indianapolis: Bobbs-Merrill, 1971), 1–71; Rudavsky OH; Temoshok OH; Elga Wasserman, "Coeducation Comes to Yale College," *ER* 51, no. 2 (Spring 1970): 145; Wilkinson OH (1992), 11; "Yale University Undergraduate Regulations," 1969, b8.f1048, Records of Elisabeth M. Thomas, Assistant Dean of Yale College (RU575), Accession 1988-A-001, YUL (hereafter, RU575), 24.

"a small isolated minority": communication from Brewster to residential college masters, November 18, 1968.

"to prevent a spring riot": Tim Bates, "Yale or Male?," *YDN,* February 13, 1969.

Wasserman fought the decision: Wasserman OH (2007), 59.

"at least 1,500": communication from Wasserman to women of the Yale College classes of 1973, 1972, and 1971, August 1969, b22.f908.RU821A.

"There was something hard-edged": Grillo OH. See also Ferguson OH.

"a really brilliant gal": Lear, "The Great Admissions Sweepstakes."

"strident" or "aggressive" or "difficult": Wasserman OH (1992), 28, 64; Chauncey OH; Wilkinson OH.

"safe middle ground": Wasserman OH (2007), 64.

Yale could be a leader: Elga Wasserman, "Proposal for Meeting the Special Needs of Women Students in a Coeducational Institution," October 29, 1969, b10.f154, Yale College Records of the Dean (RU126), Accession 1980-A-017, YUL (hereafter RU126).

"an insane title": Wasserman OH (2007), 60.

"Associate Dean of Yale College": communication from Wasserman to Brewster, May 12, 1969, b1.f13.RU821B.

Brewster said no: Wasserman OH (1992), 33; Rachel Donadio, "Interview with Elga Wasserman," in *Different Voices: A Journal Commemorating 25 Years of Coeducation at Yale College,* ed. Rachel Donadio (New Haven: Yale University Press, 1995), 22.

Out in the Vanderbilt courtyard: Paul Taylor, "Yale Officially Begins Era of Coeducation," *YDN,* September 15, 1969; Laurie Frank, "Second Thoughts on Being 'First,'" *Baltimore Sun,* September 8, 1995.

"Oh! I lived here": Presca Ahn, *Arrival: Women at Yale College,* video, 24:11, posted on July 26, 2010, https://vimeo.com/13664639.

the $3,600 it cost: "Yale University Undergraduate Regulations," 1969, b8.f1048.RU575, 29.
The MSRP price of a VW Beetle was $1,699. See Adclassix.com, "1968 Volkswagen
Beetle," 2016, http://www.adclassix.com/ads/68vwbeetlelivebelow.htm.

nearly five thousand women: Elga Wasserman, *Coeducation 1969–1970,* November 1970, b1.f5.
RU821B (hereafter *CC Report 1970*), appendix A, chart 1.

long-standing anti-Semitism: Clark OH (April), 37; Jerome Karabel, *The Chosen: The Hidden History
of Admission and Exclusion at Harvard, Yale, and Princeton* (New York: Houghton Mifflin,
2005), 1, 110–115; Dan Oren, *Joining the Club: A History of Jews and Yale* (New Haven: Yale
University Press, 1985), 196; Wilkinson OH (1992), 17–18.

"fine citizens": Karabel, *The Chosen,* 135, 366.

"a source of personality disorder": Lindblom OH, 15.

Yale's admissions process: communication from R. Inslee Clark to members of the Committee on
Admission, February 18, 1970, b1.f5.RU821A; communication from Bob Sternberg
to Sam Chauncey, September 3, 1971, b1.f8.RU821A; Admissions Office Annual
Report, 1971–1972, b3.f113, Secretary's Office, Yale University, Records (RU52),
Accession 1978-A-008, YUL (hereafter RU52B), table 6; Chauncey OH.

"no point in taking a timid woman": Chauncey OH.

THREE: A THOUSAND MALE LEADERS

field hockey: Mifflin OH (1990, 2017); Lawrie Mifflin, "The Two B's," in *Fresh Women: Reflections
on Coeducation and Life after Yale, 1969, 1989, 2009,* ed. Pamela Geismar, Eve Hart Rice,
and Joan O'Meara Winant (self-pub., Yale Printing and Publishing Services, 2010),
76–81; Lawrie Mifflin, "Women's Sports," *The 1973 YB* (New Haven: Yale Banner
Publications, 1973), 59–75; "On the Advisability," *YAM,* September/October 2009,
https://yalealumnimagazine.com. Field hockey accounts throughout the book are based
on these five sources.

"Being a member of a team": Liz Farquhar and Kaitlin Miller, "Constance Applebee: 'The Apple'
Stands Alone," *NCAA Field Hockey,* April 25, 2013.

Yale's orientation week: "Calendar for the Opening Days of the College: Class of 1973,"
September 15, 1969, b31.f998.RU821A.

"Where do I sign up": Mifflin OH (1990).

Athletic girls…a few options: Barnett OH; Rudden OH; communication from James Brandi
to Elga Wasserman, April 1, 1969, b24.f927.RU821A; communication from Bruce
Volpe to Elga Wasserman, February 18, 1969, b24.f927.RU821A; Christopher Luce,
"Cheerleaders Elect Four Yale Women," *YDN,* September 26, 1969.

"We don't want rah-rah": Jeffrey Gordon, "Coed Cheerleading Hits Snag," *YDN,* September 23,
1969.

The Yale Daily News: "Attention Women!," *YDN,* September 18, 1969; author review of *YDN*
bylines, September 1969 to May 1970.

"an inferior sound": Thomas Linden, "Militant Yale Coeds Irk 'Blues,'" *The Spokesman Review,*
March 2, 1970. See also Darling OH; Rachael Nevins, "Old Blue for Girls: Women's
Singing Groups," in *Different Voices: A Journal Commemorating 25 Years of Coeducation at Yale
College,* ed. Rachel Donadio (New Haven: Yale University Press, 1995), 46; Anonymous,
"Being a Yale Man," in *Fresh Women,* 85; Danielle Ward-Griffen, "Reforming Old Blue:
Female Voices, Coeducation at Yale, and the New Blue," *Yale A Cappella Project,* 2012,
http://yaleacappellaproject.wordpress.com/.

Not all student organizations: Royster OH; communication from Alan Mandl to Elga Wasserman,
February 14, 1969; Doug Grimes, February 19, 1969; communication from Joseph
Golden to Wasserman, March 8, 1969; communication from Alan Vomacka to
Wasserman, April 13, 1969. All communications in b24.f927.RU821A.

Girls were still barred: The 1970 YB (New Haven: Yale Banner Publications, 1970), 102–103;
communication from John Wilkinson to Elga Wasserman, October 14, 1970, b24.
f927.RU821A; Barnett OH; Mifflin, "Women's Sports," 62–63.

"Sounds OK": communication from Wasserman to Chauncey, January 20, 1969, b24.f927.
RU821A. See also communication from Chauncey to Keith Wilson, January 15, 1969,
b24.f927.RU821A.

"Pressure should not": CC minutes, February 14, 1969, b10.f152.RU126.

"Damn it": "On the Advisability."

"Anybody want to play": Mifflin OH (2017).

"I must do this": "On the Advisability."

"Doing what you're told": Farquhar and Miller, "Constance Applebee."

For $3.95: communication from Isaac A. Yedid to class of 1973, April 9, 1969, b8.f1044.RU575;
OC Class of 1973 (New Haven: Yale Banner Publications, 1969).

"I think every man": Courtney Pannell, "Forty Years of Women at Yale," *YDN,* September 21, 2009.
See also Driscoll Coon OH; Anonymous, "No Easy Answers," in *Fresh Women,* 104.

"Pardon me": "Coeds on Coeducation: A Discussion," *YAM,* April 1970, 37.

"268 years of celibacy": Paul Taylor, "Yale Officially Begins Era of Coeducation," *YDN,* September
15, 1969.

The sexual revolution: "Sex and Change," *Time,* March 20, 1972, 57; Susan Douglas, *Where the Girls
Are: Growing Up Female with the Mass Media* (New York: Random House, 1995), 65; Sarah
M. Evans, "Sons, Daughters, and Patriarchy: Gender and the 1968 Generation," *American
Historical Review* 114, no. 2 (2009): 332–343; Ruth Rosen, *The World Split Open: How the
Modern Women's Movement Changed America* (New York: Penguin, 2000), 51; Bernick OH;
Betsy Hartmann OH; Temoshok OH.

girls at Yale "will have to obey": Jonathan Lear, "The Great Admissions Sweepstakes: How Yale
Selected Her First Coeds," *NYT,* April 13, 1969. See also communication from Robert
Cavanaugh to Henry Chauncey, November 21, 1967, b32.f1001.RU821A; Student
Advisory Board, "Report on Parietal Restrictions," January 24, 1968, b32.f1001.

RU821A; Kelly C. Sartorius, *Deans of Women and the Feminist Movement: Emily Taylor's Activism* (New York: Palgrave Macmillan, 2014), 79–89.

offenses that were "of particular concern": Elisabeth M. Thomas, "Yale University Undergraduate Regulations," 1969, b8.f1048, RU575, 17. See also Yale College Dean's Office, "Yale College Visiting Hours," sign, Fall 1969, b32.f1001.RU821A.

No one enforced: Darling OH; Havemeyer Wise OH; Janet Lever and Pepper Schwartz, *Women at Yale: Liberating a College Campus* (Indianapolis: Bobbs-Merrill, 1971), 172–173; Sneed OH.

"Yale is a contemporary urban university": communication from Wasserman to parents of women of the Yale College classes of 1973, 1972, and 1971, August 1969, b22.f908.RU821A. See also Wasserman OH (1990).

birth control…was illegal: While *Griswold v. Connecticut* (381 US 479 [1965]) overturned Connecticut's ban on contraception for married couples, the ban on contraception for unmarried couples remained in place until *Eisenstadt v. Baird* (405 US 438 [1972]).

a sort of gentlemen's pact: "Connecticut Drinking Age," *NYT*, August 31, 1985; Abele v. Markle, 342 F. Supp. 800 (D. Conn. 1972); Houston A. Baker, "On My First Acquaintance with Black Studies: A Yale Story," in *A Companion to African-American Studies*, ed. Lewis Gordon and Jane Gordon (Malden: Blackwell, 2006), 7; Bernick OH; Chauncey OH; Betsy Hartmann OH; Rice OH; Phil Sarrel OH; Tedford OH.

"woman as princess": Wasserman OH (1990).

Philip Sarrel: Eleni Skevas and Eric Rosenberg, "DUH's New Gynecology Duo Discuss Sex Counseling Role," *YDN*, October 3, 1969, b2.f1, Philip M. and Lorna Sarrel Papers (MS 1922), YUL (hereafter MS1922); Judy Klemesrud, "Yale Students Have Own 'Masters and Johnson,'" *NYT*, April 28, 1971; Chauncey OH; Phil Sarrel OH; Lorna Sarrel OH.

"I don't come alone": Phil Sarrel OH.

No other college in the nation: Ruth M. Oltman, "Campus 1970: Where Do Women Stand?" (Washington, DC: American Association of University Women, January 1970), 11; John Hildebrand, "Casualties of Sexual Revolution," *Newsday*, March 20, 1980, b2.f1. MS1922; Zara Kessler, "Glorious. Consensual. Safe," *YDN*, January 26, 2012.

Arnstein…widely respected: Chauncey OH; Phil Sarrel OH.

"a whole anxious thing": Lorna Sarrel OH. See also Klemesrud, "Yale Students Have Own 'Masters and Johnson'"; CC minutes, February 14, 1969.

"What's going to happen": Lorna Sarrel OH. On pregnancies at other coed colleges, see CC minutes, October 10, 1969, b1.f7.RU575.

The committee voted to approve: CC minutes, February 14, 1969.

"You are urged": communication from John Wilkinson to women undergraduates, September 17, 1969, b31.f998.RU821A.

"present and future plans": communication from John Wilkinson to women undergraduates.

"very scary": Bishop OH. See also Skevas and Rosenberg, "DUH's New Gynecology Duo."

75 percent…were virgins: Philip M. Sarrel and Lorna J. Sarrel, "A Sex Counseling Service for College Students," report, 1970, b33.f1010.RU821A, 4.

as was half: Student Committee on Human Sexuality, *Sex and the Yale Student,* September 1970, b33.f1010.RU821A, 7.

"it was the dawn": Temoshok OH, emphasis in original.

"I was being very cool": Traut OH.

September 18: OC Class of 1973. All academic calendar dates in this book come from the calendars printed in the *OC* for the respective year.

"Hello, lady and gentlemen": Sneed OH.

87 percent…were men: CC Report 1970, appendix A, chart 1. On the hardships caused by women students' token status, see also Joseph Treaster, "Coeds Find Life at Yale Falls Short of Expectations," *NYT,* April 14, 1970; Deinhardt OH; Polan OH; WAC minutes, February 2, 1972, b35.f1035.RU821A; Wofford OH.

"The worst part": Traut OH. See also Dartmouth College, *An Analysis of the Impact of Coeducation at Princeton and Yale Universities* (New York: Cresap, McCormick, and Paget, November 1971), II-3; Elizabeth Davis, "Changing Identities: When Yale's 'First' Women Arrived," *YAM,* October 1979, 23; Ellen Keniston, "Eight Views (of a Phenomenon in Progress)," *YAM,* April 1970, 39; Tedford OH; "The Vanguard: Five of the First Coeds," *YAM,* October 1979, 24–27.

"the most precious right": Alice Miskimin, "Eight Views," *YAM,* 41.

"Everybody knew": Maillet Main OH.

The dining hall: Newman OH.

"a thousand male leaders": Tora Linden, "Students Discuss Coeducation at Silliman College Teach-In," *YDN,* November 7, 1968; see also Coed Week flier, November 8, 1968, b4.fWomen, May Day Rally and Yale Collection (RU86), Accession 1971-A-004, YUL (hereafter RU86A); Jeffrey Gordon, "Pressures on Admissions," *YDN,* April 4, 1969.

Kingman Brewster denied…every woman…assumed: Coeducation: The Year They Liberated Yale, directed by John Kennedy (New Haven: Yale Office of Public Information, YFC, 1970), DVD; Pamela Geismar, "Making Yale Less Male," in *Fresh Women,* 26; Grillo OH; Havemeyer Wise OH; Anonymous, "In a Man's World," in *Fresh Women,* 91; Leib Gourguechon OH; Polan OH; Rice OH.

"I remember that": Betsy Hartmann OH.

"and two hundred concubines": Ausubel OH.

the only one there: Anonymous, "Coming Back to Yale," in *Fresh Women,* 71; Lisa Getman, "From Conestoga to Career," in *Women in Higher Education,* ed. W. Todd Furniss and Patricia A. Graham (Washington, DC: American Council on Education, 1974), 65; Sneed OH.

the weight of proving: Virginia Dominguez, "Scholar of the House," in *Fresh Women,* 32; Maillet Main OH; Tedford OH.

"Not bad for a woman": "Coeducation Inside and Out," *YAM,* April 1970, 36.

as if the furniture: Anonymous, "Coming Back to Yale," in *Fresh Women,* 71. See also Dartmouth, *An Analysis of the Impact,* II-3.

"what is the woman's point of view": Chauncey OH. See also "Coeds on Coeducation," 35; Rachel Donadio, "Interview with Elga Wasserman," in *Different Voices*, 24; Newman OH; Rudavsky OH; Tedford OH; Wasserman OH (1990); Wofford OH.

most of the women had thought: Christa Hansen, "The Yale Experience," OIR Report 73R008, May 12, 1973, b2.f27.RU 173, Accession 1980-A-014, YUL.

"the smart girl": Rice OH. See also Tedford OH.

"Without fail": Lucy Eddy, "No Ruffles and Lace for Girls at Yale," *Hartford Courant*, November 30, 1969, b58.f388, RU19-II.

"an uncomfortable sense": Tedford OH.

"We do have the best girls": Lever and Schwartz, *Women at Yale*, 76.

"too quickly, too purposively": Davis, "Changing Identities," 23.

"How are you doing?": Royster OH.

"always been friends": Spahn OH.

a bursary job: Maillet Main OH; Marie Rudden, "A Woman's Place," in *Fresh Women*, 46; Wilkinson OH.

"I want to see you": Spahn OH.

"participatory democracy": Tom Warren, "Brewster Closes the Door on Participatory Democracy," *YDN*, September 26, 1969. See also John Darnton, "Yale Head Suggests a Limit to His Term," *NYT*, September 25, 1969.

64 percent of the men: OUA, "Yield Figures—Classes of 1967–1976," September 25, 1972, b1.f15. RU821A, table I. See also Kingman Brewster, *Yale University 1969–1970: Report of the President*, b580.f3.RU11-V, in which Brewster makes no mention of coeducation in his goals for the upcoming year.

"I could walk for blocks": Getman, "From Conestoga to Career," 63.

"It is virtually impossible": Lucy L. Eddy, "In the Blue: A Freshman Coed's Account of Her First Yale Year," *YAM*, April 1970, 25.

"The structure is...like living in a hotel": communication from Seymour Lustman to Wasserman, November 17, 1969, b258.f7.RU11-II. See also Wasserman's compilation of the comments that students made on their anonymous questionnaires: "Comments Taken from Transfer Questionnaire," November 21, 1969, b1.f5.RU821B; Bernick OH; Mintz OH; Polan OH; Rudden OH.

"If you didn't find a really close...friend": Mifflin OH (1990). See also Anonymous, "Being a Yale Man," 84; Bishop OH; CC minutes, November 14, 1969, b1.f7.RU575; "Coed Survey," *YDN*, November 17, 1969; Jelly OH; Michael Knight, "Yale's First Full Class of Women," *NYT*, June 3, 1973; Anonymous, "No Easy Answers," in *Fresh Women*, 106; Traut OH; Wasserman OH (1990); Wofford OH.

"antiwoman conditioning": Robin Alden, "First Outpourings Thinking about Yale" (unpublished essay, spring 1971), b1.f9.RU821B.

"Yale men see nothing wrong": Eddy, "In the Blue," 25.

"How is your daughter doing?": Coeducation: The Year.

black women were separated: OC Class of 1973; Edward Gellman, ed., *Transfers 1972: A Supplement to the OC Volume XXV* (New Haven: Yale Banner Publications, 1969); Edward Gellman, ed., *Transfers 1971: A Supplement to the OC Volume XXIV* (New Haven: Yale Banner Publications, 1969).

"There are no black women": Student Survey response, November 1969, b19.f889.RU821A, underline in original.

"the House": Wells OH. See also Pannell, "Forty Years of Women."

"It was a homey atmosphere": Wells OH. See also Pannell, "Forty Years of Women."

"It was a place where blacks": Daniels OH.

Black students...in sparse numbers: "Who Was the First African American Student at Yale?," *YAM,* May/June 2014; Joseph Soares, *The Power of Privilege: Yale and America's Elite Colleges* (Stanford: Stanford University Press, 2007), 112; Jerome Karabel, *The Chosen: The Hidden History of Admission and Exclusion at Harvard, Yale, and Princeton* (New York: Houghton Mifflin, 2005), 381; OUA, "Minority Groups," September 25, 1972, b1.f15.RU821A, table V.

"the blackest class": Henry Louis Gates Jr., "Joining the Black Overclass at Yale University," *Journal of Blacks in Higher Education,* no. 11 (Spring 1996): 95.

"I wouldn't sleep": Lever and Schwartz, *Women at Yale,* 76.

"They would sometimes look at me": Wells OH.

I'm not your experiment: Wells OH.

"We were searching": Geismar, Rice, and Winant, *Fresh Women,* 116.

"Bio for Poets": Mifflin OH (2017).

"Interactions...were awkward": Geismar, Rice, and Winant, *Fresh Women,* 116. See also Bernick OH; Deinhardt OH; Betsy Hartmann OH; Havemeyer Wise OH; Mintz OH.

"We didn't want to offend": Bernick OH.

"Shirley had a lot of leadership": Storey-Johnson OH.

"She was very bright": Chauncey OH.

"racial solidarity": Peniel E. Joseph, "The Black Power Movement: A State of the Field," *Journal of American History* 96, no. 3 (2009): 755. See also Joy Williamson, "In Defense of Themselves: The Black Student Struggle for Success and Recognition at Predominantly White Colleges and Universities," *Journal of Negro Education* (Winter 1999): 92–105.

"dreamed white dreams": Henry Louis Gates, Jr., "Through the Veil," *The 1973* YB, 145.

most of Yale divided by race: "Colleges Liberalize Social Transferring," *YDN,* November 3, 1969; Lever and Schwartz, *Women at Yale,* 77; Sneed OH; Storey-Johnson OH; Traut OH.

"we might be playing music": Storey-Johnson OH.

"If black students won't be friendly": Jeffrey Gordon, "Becoming Conscious Again," *YDN,* February 13, 1969. See also Wells OH.

"There is a comfort": Royster OH.

"economically disadvantaged": R. C. Burr and L. M. Noble, "Scholarship Changes—Economically Disadvantaged," Yale College Admissions Office (unpublished archival document, April 15, 1970), b48.f476.RU19-II. See also *CC Report 1970,* appendix A, chart 1, 18; Tedford OH.

"extraordinarily beautiful": Daniels OH.

FOUR: CONSCIOUSNESS

"had trouble putting the snap": Bob Small, "Huskies Stop Yale Comeback," *YDN*, September 29, 1969. See also Barnet Phillips, "Men Not Legends," *YDN*, October 13, 1969.

"You play what?": Mifflin OH (2017).

Yale Sex Counseling Service: Eleni Skevas and Eric Rosenberg, "DUH's New Gynecology Duo Discuss Sex Counseling Role," *YDN*, October 3, 1969, b2.f1, MS 1922; Philip M. Sarrel and Lorna J. Sarrel, "A Sex Counseling Service for College Students," report, 1970, b33. f1010.RU821A; Lorna Sarrel OH.

"Have you had intercourse?": Sarrel and Sarrel, "A Sex Counseling Service."

"pierced the fog...wonderful people": Havemeyer Wise OH.

"that a coeducational system...social pressure here": Skevas and Rosenberg, "DUH's New Gynecology Duo."

"This pressure": Skevas and Rosenberg, "DUH's New Gynecology Duo."

"The freshman guys": Mintz OH.

"There was so much pressure": Mintz OH. See also Daniels OH; Betsy Hartmann OH; Pamela Geismar, Eve Hart Rice, and Joan O'Meara Winant, eds., *Fresh Women: Reflections on Coeducation and Life after Yale, 1969, 1989, 2009* (self-pub., Yale Printing and Publishing Services, 2010), 102; Julia Preston, "What Is a Coeducation?," *NJ*, December 13, 1970, 8.

"absolutely entertaining": Storey-Johnson OH.

"deal constantly with questions": Zaeder OH.

"My boyfriend doesn't want me coming": Daniels OH.

"In those days": Daniels OH.

a threadbare budget: Gersick OH; communication from Wasserman to Fanton, September 28, 1971, b3.f1.RU821B.

Brewster did not attach: Chauncey OH.

"not what it should be": communication from Wasserman to Brewster, October 6, 1969, b258. f7.RU11-II. See also Wasserman OH (1992), 34; Wasserman, "Report of the Chairman of the Planning Committee on Coeducation, 1968–1969," b1.f13.RU821B, 5.

the Bulldog's third game: Tom Warren, "Eli Eleven Dumps Brown," *YDN*, October 13, 1969.

The previous Saturday: David Nix, "Elis 2nd Half Explosion Erases Colgate," *YDN*, October 6, 1969.

The band's reputation: Bernick OH; Daniels OH; Albert Shamash, "Colgate Halftime Performance," *YDN*, October 4, 1970; *The 1970 YB* (New Haven: Yale Banner Publications, 1970), 104; Lew Schwartz, "Invisible Band," *YDN*, October 12, 1971.

"Yes! We Have No Bananas": Courtney Pannell, "Forty Years of Women at Yale," *YDN*, September 21, 2009.

"Yale coeds make our fans' root": The 1970 YB, 104.

six out of ten Americans: "War Frustration Put at New High," *NYT*, October 5, 1969.

Vietnam Moratorium: "2 Antiwar Groups Join for Protest," *NYT*, October 5, 1969.

"Bronx G.I. Killed": "Bronx G.I. Killed in Vietnam," *NYT*, October 3, 1969; "Jerseyan Killed in Vietnam," *NYT*, October 1, 1969; "Suffolk G.I. Killed in Vietnam," *NYT*, October 9, 1969.

The war was ever present: Newman OH; "President's Draft Lottery Approved by Congress," in *CQ Almanac 1969*, 25th ed. (Washington, DC: Congressional Quarterly, 1970), 350–355.

"It really seemed like killing": Rice OH.

"Enough": Presca Ahn, *Arrival: Women at Yale College*, video, 24:11, posted on July 26, 2010, https://vimeo.com/13664639. See also Bernick OH; Jeffrey Gordon, "50,000 Mass at Convocation on Green," *YDN*, October 16, 1969; Bernard Weinraub, "Students Say 'Enough!' to War," *NYT*, October 16, 1969.

"old-style politicians": Anthony Lewis, "A Thoughtful Answer to Hard Questions," *NYT*, October 17, 1969.

"Our ability to keep the peace": Ahn, *Arrival*. See also Lewis, "A Thoughtful Answer."

"puny": Geismar, Rice, and Winant, *Fresh Women*, 69. See also Berkan OH; Jelly OH; Tedford OH; Wofford OH.

"With all due respect": Gordon, "50,000 Mass at Convocation." See also Tom Warren, "BSAY Head Halts Rally," *YDN*, October 16, 1969; Yohuru Williams, "No Haven: From Civil Rights to Black Power in New Haven, Connecticut," *The Black Scholar* 31, nos. 3–4 (2001): 59.

"Stop the Cops!": Marvin Olasky, "Black Students Disrupt Classes in Law School," *YDN*, October 21, 1969. See also communication from BSAY to Henry Chauncey, October 21, 1971, b3.f59.RU52, Accession 1977-A-008 (hereafter RU52A); Nick Perensovich, "Blacks Give Reply to Grievance Plan," *YDN*, October 21, 1969; Tom Warren and John Coots, "Law Dean Recommends Mild Rebuke for Blacks," *YDN*, October 30, 1969; Daniels OH; Sneed OH.

"It just brought": Sneed OH.

not *"political enough":* Sneed OH.

"We will not tolerate this!": Olasky, "Black Students Disrupt."

"We're going to shut down": Daniels OH.

"weekend women": Sneed OH. See also Randall Ganett, "Coed Normality," letter to the editor, *YDN*, November 20, 1969; Grillo OH; Havemeyer Wise OH; Tedford OH; Traut OH; Wofford OH.

"Hey, I'd like you to meet": Dori Zaleznik, "How Should Coeds Act?," *YDN*, November 3, 1969. See also Gersick OH; Traut OH; Wei Mintz OH.

"The weekly invasion": Zaleznik, "How Should Coeds Act?"

"What's your name?": Anonymous, "Vigils for Peace," in *Fresh Women*, 63.

still not a safe place: "Girls Face Problem of Town Intruders," *YDN*, October 29, 1969; WAC minutes, October 8, 1969, b35.f1032.RU821A; CC minutes, October 31, 1969, b1.f7. RU575; communication from J. Thorburn to P. Tveskov, November 18, 1969, b8.f1060. RU575; communication from Elisabeth Thomas to Daniel Sullivan, January 30, 1970, b8.f1060.RU575; Chauncey OH; Wasserman OH (1992), 34; Wilkinson OH.

"summary of action": communication from Thorburn to Thomas, October 31, 1969, b8.f1060. RU575.

"As you know": communication from Wasserman to Brewster, November 5, 1969, b1.f7.RU575.

Brewster responded: CC minutes, November 14, 1969, b22.f908.RU821A.

"Many thanks": communication from Wasserman to Thorburn, November 18, 1969, b258.
      f7.RU11-II.

"just didn't like": Chauncey OH.

the group decided to stage: For the Wright Hall sit-in, see communication from Charles Taylor
      to John Wilkinson, November 4, 1969, b34.f1016.RU821A; communication from
      suspended students to Yale community, November 7, 1969, b34.f1016.RU821A;
      Douglas Hallett and John Coots, "Scenario Faces Challenges," *YDN*, November 10,
      1969; Yale College Executive Committee, announcement, November 10, 1969, b34.
      f1016.RU821A; Marvin Olasky, "Committee Readmits Suspended Students," *YDN*,
      November 11, 1969; Spahn OH.

"We should leave": Spahn OH.

"We were being the conscience": Newman OH. See also Jeffrey Gordon, "Washington Peace Rally
      Biggest Ever," *YDN*, November 17, 1969; Ausubel OH; Bernick OH; Lieberman OH.

"ran a post pattern": Barnet Phillips, "Yale's Defense Squelches Tiger Attack," *YDN*, November 17,
      1969.

"Be quiet now, hear": Lydia Temoshok, diary entry, November 17, 1969. See also Temoshok OH;
      Temoshok email to author, July 5, 2018; "'L'Infidelte Delusa' Is a Lively Success," *YDN*,
      November 18, 1969; "Colleges Put Locks on Girls' Bathrooms," *YDN*, December 9, 1969.
      Lydia Temoshok went by the name Linda while at Yale.

The rest of November: Michael Goodman, "Blue Gridders Gain Third Straight Ivy Crown with
      7–0 Victory over Harvard," *YDN*, November 24, 1969; John Coots, "Brewster Answers
      Blacks' Proposals," *YDN*, October 24, 1969; Scott Herhold, "Campus Policemen Stay
      Cool," *YDN*, November 24, 1969; "Colleges Put Locks on Girls' Bathrooms," *YDN*,
      December 9, 1969; WAC minutes, January 22, 1970, b35.f1032.RU821A.

"Many of the new feminists": "The New Feminists: Revolt against 'Sexism,'" *Time*, November
      21, 1969, 53. See also Ruth Rosen, *The World Split Open: How the Modern Women's
      Movement Changed America* (New York: Penguin, 2000), 303, 338.

"furious…militant…radical…the angries": "The New Feminists," 53, 54, 56.

7 percent: "The New Feminists," 54.

"promises to grow": Henry Luce, "A Letter from the Publisher," *Time*, November 21, 1969.

FIVE: SEX-BLIND

"Betty the Red": Royster OH.

"bourgeois ideology": Stuart Rosow, "Students Secede from SDS," *YDN*, December 12, 1969.

"No, I haven't read": Royster OH.

"It was my way": Royster OH.

The Dramat...an unusual island: George Chauncey, "Gay at Yale," *YAM*, July 2009; Field OH; Royster OH; Rudavsky OH.

"Is her whole family . . . ?": McClure OH. See also "Madeline McClure," obituary, *Star-Ledger* (Somerville, NJ), July 6, 2018.

"How do you find . . . ?": McClure OH.

"Well, she's got to learn": McClure OH.

Changes to the draft law: "President's Draft Lottery," in *CQ Almanac 1969*, 350–355; Nicholas Perensovich, "First Draft Lottery since 1942," *YDN*, December 2, 1969.

"They either had": Newman OH.

its final editorial: "But Dink Remains," *YDN*, January 21, 1970.

two different women's groups: Barbara Packer and Karen Waggoner, "Yale and the New Sisterhood," *YAM*, April 1970, 28; Judith Plaskow, "Intersections," in *The Coming of Lilith: Essays on Feminism, Judaism, and Sexual Ethics,* eds. Judith Plaskow and Donna Berman (Boston: Beacon Press, 2005), 7; Ferguson OH; Laura Kalman, *Yale Law School and the Sixties* (Chapel Hill: University of North Carolina Press, 2005), 195; *Yale Break*, April 6, 1970, b.58.f388.RU19-II, 8.

New Haven Women's Liberation: Amy Vita Kesselman, "Women's Liberation and the Left in New Haven, Connecticut, 1968–1972," *Radical History Review* 81, no. 1 (2001): 18–19; Christine Pattee, "Chronology, New Haven Women's Liberation," 1973, b1.f1, Christine Pattee Papers on the New Haven Women's Liberation Movement (MS 1985), YUL (hereafter MS1985).

The Graduate Women's Alliance: Lenore Weitzman, Frances Pitlick, and Margie Ferguson, "Women on the Yale Faculty" (Washington, DC: U.S. Department of Education, Education Resources Information Center, ERIC ED056636, March 2, 1971); "Graduate Women's Survey," *Sex Discrimination at Yale: A Document of Indictment*, May 10, 1971, b280.f991.RU19, Series III; Ferguson OH.

"There is something about": "Graduate Women's Survey."

a women's book section: C. Roysce Smith, "The Opinionated Man: Women, Women, Everywhere," *Publishers Weekly*, March 30, 1970, 50–51, b4.f Women.RU86.

"Let me assure you": Smith, "The Opinionated Man," 50.

walked over to Mory's: "Women's Liberation Enters Male Mory's," *YDN*, February 9, 1970; Thomas Kent, "Up from Under," *YDN*, March 6, 1970; Kalman, *Yale Law School*, 197.

barring women from clubs: Georgina Hickey, "Barred from the Barroom: Second Wave Feminists and Public Accommodations in US Cities," *Feminist Studies* 34, no. 3 (2008): 382–384; Kent, "Up from Under"; Royster OH.

"executive hours": Hickey, "Barred from the Barroom," 384.

Mory's was the place: Daphna Renan, "'To the Tables Down at Mory's': Equality as Membership and Leadership in Places of Public Accommodations," *Yale Journal of Law and Feminism* 16, no. 2 (2004): 241–245, http://digitalcommons.law.yale.edu/; Clark OH (May), 13;

Marie Rudden, "A Woman's Place," in *Fresh Women*, 49; Arthur Greenfield, "The People vs. Mory's," *YAM*, June 1973, 25.

the Free Women Conference: "Free Women Conference," flier, February 1970, b4.f Women. RU86; Kalman, *Yale Law School*, 195; Packer and Waggoner, "Yale and the New Sisterhood," 27–31; Plaskow, "Intersections," 6–7; *Yale Break*, April 6, 1970, 6.

"Come to the conference": McClure OH.

Women's Advisory Council: communication from Wasserman to freshman counselors, September 10, 1969, b35.f1032.RU821A; communication from Wasserman to WAC members, January 5, 1970, b35.f1032.RU821A; Wasserman OH (1990).

"The problem of security": WAC minutes, January 22, 1970, b35.f1032.RU821A.

University Committee on Coeducation: CC minutes, May 26, 1970, b1.f7.RU575.

concerned about security: CC minutes, October 31, 1969, b258.f7.RU11-II; CC minutes, November 14, 1969, b1.f7.RU575; WAC minutes, October 8, 1969, and January 22, 1970, b35.f1032.RU821A.

the term sexual harassment: Ruth Rosen, *The World Split Open: How the Modern Women's Movement Changed America* (New York: Penguin, 2000), 186–187.

"There were many inappropriate": Jamie Stern Connelly, interview in Presca Ahn, *Arrival: Women at Yale College*, video, 15:54, posted on July 26, 2010, https://vimeo.com/13664639. See also Courtney Pannell, "Forty Years of Women at Yale," *YDN*, September 21, 2009; Sherrie Selwyn, "The Social Scene in 1969," in *Different Voices: A Journal Commemorating 25 Years of Coeducation at Yale College*, ed. Rachel Donadio (New Haven: Yale University Press, 1995), 17.

"Now don't you have something else": "The Adventures of Jane Smith at Yale University," in *Sex Discrimination at Yale*, May 10, 1971.

"demanded that I perform perversions": "The Adventures of Jane Smith."

"He doesn't seem to learn": "Graduate Women's Survey," May 10, 1971.

A fourth: "The Adventures of Jane Smith."

A fifth: "Graduate Women's Survey."

a sixth was propositioned: Ferguson OH.

"he seemed kind of ashamed": Ferguson OH.

the professor lunged at her: Field OH.

"The professor would call": Maillet Main OH.

he tried to rape her: Maillet Main OH.

"Nice girls did not tell": Joan Roberts, "Women's Right to Choose, or Men's Right to Dominate," in *Women in Higher Education*, ed. W. Todd Furniss and Patricia A. Graham (Washington, DC: American Council on Education, 1974), 51.

"It was very clear": Morse OH, 126. See also Ferguson OH; Jubin OH; Anne E. Simon, "Alexander v. Yale University: An Informal History," in *Directions in Sexual Harassment Law*, ed. Catharine MacKinnon and Reva Siegel (New Haven: Yale University Press, 2004), 51–59.

Stanford's dean of women: Kathryn Tuttle, "What Became of the Dean of Women? Changing Roles for Women Administrators in American Higher Education, 1940–1980" (PhD diss., University of Kansas, 1996), 338.

"mostly you just changed advisers": Connelly in Ahn, *Arrival.*

the media had moved on: "Mademoiselle Magazine," *YDN,* October 21, 1969; Darling OH.

Word was out: Erikson OH, 58. See also Bishop OH; Chauncey OH; Darling OH; Leib Gourguechon OH; Mifflin OH (2017); Russett OH; Wasserman OH (1990); Rachel Donadio, "Interview with Elga Wasserman," in *Different Voices,* 23; Wofford OH.

"feeling of isolation": WAC minutes, February 12, 1970, b35.f1032.RU821A.

Their friends at Yale were almost all men: Bishop OH; Darling OH; Driscoll Coon OH; Mintz OH; Anonymous, "New Old Blue," in *Fresh Women: Reflections on Coeducation and Life after Yale, 1969, 1989, 2009,* ed. Pamela Geismar, Eve Hart Rice, and Joan O'Meara Winant (self-pub., Yale Printing and Publishing Services, 2010), 111; Anonymous, "No Easy Answers," in *Fresh Women,* 106; Maillet Main OH; Polan OH; Tedford OH; Temoshok OH; Traut OH.

"Admit more women!": WAC minutes, January 29, 1970.

"likely to blame women": WAC minutes, January 29, 1970.

She went to a lot of meetings: communication from Wasserman to Brewster, May 21, 1970, b3.f1. RU821B.

a roster of the powerful: CC Report 1970.

Women in a Male Society: "New College Seminars," *YDN,* January 9, 1970. On residential college seminars, see Erikson OH, 54; CC minutes, December 12, 1969, b10.f154.RU126.

Yale was one of just ten U.S. colleges: Elaine Hedges, "Looking Back," *Women's Studies Quarterly* 25, nos. 1–2 (1997): 6.

Wasserman asked…Sue Hilles: communication from Wasserman to Hilles, February 15, 1973, b1.f3.RU821B; Moritz to May, October 14, 1970, b10.f156.RU126.

"You had no right": Wasserman OH (2007), 22.

Wasserman used the grant: communication from Wasserman to Hilles, February 15, 1973, and August 11, 1972, b258.f3.RU11-II.

"I would not like to see": Elga Wasserman, "Coeducation Comes to Yale College," *ER* 51, no. 2 (Spring 1970): 146.

Yale Sex Counseling Service: Philip M. Sarrel and Lorna J. Sarrel, "A Sex Counseling Service for College Students," report, 1970, b33.f1010.RU821A, 3.

"We wanted a boyfriend": Daniels OH.

"If you had a boyfriend": Havemeyer Wise OH. See also Mintz OH; Julia Preston, "What Is a Coeducation?," *NJ,* December 13, 1970, 8; Rudden OH; Wofford OH.

did not mean…wanted to lose her virginity: Student Committee on Human Sexuality, *Sex and the Yale Student,* September 1970, b33.f1010.RU821A, 7; WAC minutes, May 3, 1972; Bernick OH; Driscoll Coon OH.

Less than 10 percent: Don Letourneau, "Sarrel's Study," *YDN,* April 7, 1970. See also Phil Sarrel, letter to the editor, *YDN,* April 21, 1970.

"I heard a lot of the talk": Maillet Main OH.

Abortion was illegal: Amy Kesselman, "Women versus Connecticut: Conducting a Statewide Hearing on Abortion," in *Abortion Wars: A Half Century of Struggle, 1950–2000*, ed. Rickie Solinger (Berkeley: University of California Press, 1998), 44.

Yale opted: Lorna Sarrel OH; Phil Sarrel OH.

"If you made a mistake": Maillet Main OH.

"There was this feeling": Betsy Hartmann OH.

"remarkable…You were nineteen": Leib Gourguechon OH. See also Havemeyer Wise OH; Jelly OH; Maillet Main OH; Newman OH.

"We are trying to help": Eleni Skevas and Eric Rosenberg, "DUH's New Gynecology Duo Discuss Sex Counseling Role," *YDN*, October 3, 1969, b2.f1, MS 1922.

"It was the hot ticket": Rice OH. See also Eric Rosenberg, "New Sexuality Course," *YDN*, December 5, 1969; Shelley Fisher, "Sex Education: Record Number Enroll," *YDN*, January 29, 1970; Philip Sarrel and Haskell Coplin, "A Course in Human Sexuality for the College Student" (paper presented at the American Public Health Association annual meeting, Houston, TX, October 1970), b33.f1010.RU821A.

"You were more accustomed to": Bernick OH.

Human Sexuality Committee: Phil Sarrel OH; Bernick OH; communication from HSC to fellow student, November 1969, b10.f156.RU126; Sarrel, letter to the editor.

Everything You Don't Want: "D.U.H. Faces Pill and Bunny Surplus," *YDN*, October 17, 1970, emphasis added. This was a spoof issue.

"True or False?": HSC, "Sex Knowledge and Attitude Test," 1970, b33.f1010.RU821A.

gay sex was still a felony: William Eskridge, *Dishonorable Passions: Sodomy Laws in America, 1861–2003* (New York: Penguin, 2008), appendix.

The American Psychiatric Association: Neel Burton, "When Homosexuality Stopped Being a Mental Disorder," *Psychology Today*, September 18, 2015.

"sexual aberration": David Reuben, *Everything You Always Wanted to Know about Sex but Were Afraid to Ask* (New York: David McKay and Company, 1969), 3.

"Homosexuals…thrive on danger": Reuben, *Everything You Always Wanted to Know*, 134.

"pens, pencils, lipsticks": Reuben, *Everything You Always Wanted to Know*, 149.

"The majority of prostitutes are female homosexuals": Reuben, *Everything You Always Wanted to Know*, 217.

"was all very hush-hush": Grillo OH.

"We all knew": Royster OH.

"marked fear of homosexuality": Janet Lever and Pepper Schwartz, *Women at Yale: Liberating a College Campus* (Indianapolis: Bobbs-Merrill, 1971), 167, italics in original.

"painful and difficult": "Sexuality Discussion Tonight," *YDN*, October 30, 1969.

"To find a gay woman": McClure OH.

SIX: MARGARET ASKS FOR THE MIC

Alumni Day: "Annual Yale Medal, New Becton Center Highlight Alumni Day," *YDN*, February 20, 1970; "Yale Coeds Invade Alumni Fete to Protest Male Dominance," *NYT*, February 22, 1970.

Henry P. Becton: "Henry Prentiss Becton," obituary, *Bangor [ME] Daily News*, October 28, 2009; "Becton Dickinson Historical Development," 2019, http://www.companieshistory .com/becton-dickinson/; "Fortune 500 1955–2005: A Database of 50 Years of Fortune's List of America's Largest Companies," 1970, *Fortune Magazine*, 2019, http://archive.fortune .com/magazines/fortune/fortune500_archive/full/1970/; "Photographs by Jeffery Becton," Bates College Museum of Art, 2015, http://www.bates.edu/museum/traveling /photographs-by-jeffery-becton/.

"Sons of Eli": Charles F. Smith (bandleader), C. W. O'Connor, Julian Arnold, Henry P. Becton, A. M. Hirsh, S. P. Friedman, "Boola Boola; Down the Field; Glory for Yale," recorded December 4, 1937, U.S. Decca, 1938.

Cynthia and her roommate: Arty Pomerantz, "Protest to Have Women Admitted to Yale University," *New York Post*, February 24, 1970; see image and caption on Getty Images, https://www.gettyimages.com/license/540063392; Margaret Coon, "Our Call for True Education," in *Reflections on Coeducation*, ed. Emily Hoffman and Isobel Polon (2010), 26–27; Coon OH.

first women undergraduates: Tedford OH. See also Asef Bayat, *Life as Politics: How Ordinary People Change the Middle East* (Stanford: Stanford University Press, 2013), 4–5, 14–20.

"End Women's Oppression": "Yale Coeds Invade Alumni Fete." On the alumni lunch protest, see also "Margaret Coon," *YDN*, February 22, 1970; Coon, "Our Call," 26–27; Coon OH; Kit McClure, diary entry, May 1970; McClure OH.

"Mr. Brewster, I'd like to address": Coon OH.

"There are not enough of us": "Yale Coeds Invade Alumni Fete."

"To accept 1,000 'male leaders'": Thomas Linden, "Militant Yale Coeds Irk 'Blues,'" *The Spokesman Review* [Spokane, WA], March 2, 1970.

"Limit the Class of 1974": Richard Fuchs, "Girls Demand Fewer Men, More Women," *YDN*, February 23, 1970.

"harassment...After having been wedded": Fuchs, "Girls Demand Fewer."

Brewster was right to be concerned about the alumni: Nancy Weiss Malkiel, *"Keep the Damned Women Out": The Struggle for Coeducation* (Princeton: Princeton University Press, 2016), 268–270; Jerome Karabel, *The Chosen: The Hidden History of Admission and Exclusion at Harvard, Yale, and Princeton* (New York: Houghton Mifflin, 2005), 362, 453–454, 638n94; Joseph Soares, *The Power of Privilege: Yale and America's Elite Colleges* (Stanford: Stanford University Press, 2007), 86.

$4.6 million: Joseph Treaster, "Donating to Yale at Record Level," *NYT*, July 26, 1970. See also Dartmouth College, *An Analysis of the Impact of Coeducation at Princeton and Yale Universities* (New York: Cresap, McCormick, and Paget, November 1971), II-10.

entirely of his own making: Ray Warman, "Coeds' Housing under Review," *YDN*, November 18, 1968; CC minutes, October 13, 1970, b4.f80.RU52A; Mark Singer, "Trustees Vote to Increase the Number of Women," *YAM*, January 1973, 30.

"accountability to alumni": Fuchs, "Girls Demand Fewer." See also Chauncey remarks, CC minutes, October 13, 1970, b4.f80.RU52A.

"a terrific success": "Yale Coeds Invade Alumni Fete."

"much too small band": Fuchs, "Girls Demand Fewer."

"We can't give them women": Fuchs, "Girls Demand Fewer."

"We listened to the speaker": "The Vanguard: Five of the First Coeds," *YAM*, October 1979, 26.

"Women felt respected in the BSAY": Storey-Johnson OH.

"weren't given a speaking role": Berkan OH.

women in the BSAY: The 1972 YB (New Haven: Yale Banner Publications, 1972); Jeffrey Gordon, "Pressures on Admissions," *YDN*, April 4, 1969; communication from Sam Chauncey to Carl Banyard et al., February 18, 1972, and May 4, 1972, b3.f59.RU52A; Chauncey OH; Daniels OH.

the BSAY's priorities: Wei Mintz OH; Schmoke OH.

"because a lot of times": Daniels OH.

U.S. wage statistics: "Who's Come a Long Way, Baby?," Time, August 31, 1970, 17.

Vera Wells: Wells OH; Vera F. Wells, "The Life and Work of Sylvia Ardyn Boone" (lecture, Women of Yale Lecture series, New Haven, CT, February 28, 2017).

"It just seemed so strange": Wells OH.

only five were black women: Wells's email to author, December 8, 2018.

missing from Yale's curriculum: Ellen Keniston, "Women in a Male Society," syllabus, Spring 1970, b12.f137.RU578A; Wells OH.

The Black Woman: "Enrollment in Women's Studies Courses, 1970–71," Fall 1971, b12.f137. RU578A; Wells, "The Life and Work"; Wells OH.

"It was a very 'un-Yale' thing": Janet Lever and Pepper Schwartz, *Women at Yale: Liberating a College Campus* (Indianapolis: Bobbs-Merrill, 1971), 253.

Elga Wasserman was horrified: WAC minutes, March 5, 1970, b35.f1032.RU821A.

"They should have taken this matter": "Coeds Invade Alumni Luncheon, Call for Enrollment Reduction," *YDN*, February 23, 1970.

"radical elements": WAC minutes, March 5, 1970, b35.f1032.RU821A.

"We were not bomb throwers": Lieberman OH.

"About 40...stunned guests": "Yale Coeds Invade Alumni Fete."

"militant...pretty freshman": Linden, "Militant Yale Coeds."

"Their demands are reasonable": "Coeds Invade," *YDN*, February 23, 1970.

The alumni had applauded: "Yale Coeds." See also Chauncey OH.

"He was a very nice man": Coon OH.

"a bit presumptuous": "Coeds Invade."

"No wonder you're feminists": McClure, diary entry, May 1970.

"Take her torch": "Dinner Drama," *YDN*, February 25, 1970.

five hundred women: "Free Women at Yale," *Yale Break*, April 6, 1970, 6; Thomas Kent, "Up from Under," *YDN*, March 6, 1970.

Kate Millett: "Free Women at Yale," 6; Maggie Doherty, "What Kate Did: Today's Most Heated Literary Arguments Uphold the Legacy of Kate Millett's 'Sexual Politics,'" *The New Republic*, March 23, 2016.

Betty Friedan had given in a speech: "What's Happening?," *YDN*, February 18, 1970.

"We have 53 percent…Right on!": Lydia Temoshok, diary entry, February 27, 1970.

Naomi Weisstein: Barbara Packer and Karen Waggoner, "Yale and the New Sisterhood," *YAM*, April 1970, 28; "Free Women at Yale"; Jesse Lemisch and Naomi Weisstein, "Remarks on Naomi Weisstein," Chicago Women's Liberation Union Herstory Project, 1997, https://www.cwluherstory.org/text-memoirs-articles/remarks-on-naomi -weisstein?rq=Remarks%20on%20Naomi%20Weisstein; Ann Medina, "A Women's Liberation Timeline 1960–1977," 2019, Chicago Women's Liberation Union Herstory Project, https://www.cwluherstory.org/supplemental-writings/a-womens-liberation -timeline-1960-1977?rq=timeline; Marcia B. Kline, "Lamont Will Open to Cliffies after Twenty Celibate Years," *HC*, December 8, 1966; Leila McNeill, "This Feminist Psychologist-Turned-Rock-Star Led a Full Life of Resistance," *The Smithsonian*, April 7, 2017.

"Changes in social structures": Judith Plaskow, "Intersections," in *The Coming of Lilith: Essays on Feminism, Judaism, and Sexual Ethics*, ed. Judith Plaskow and Donna Berman (Boston: Beacon Press, 2005), 7.

"To me, what you do": Temoshok OH. See also Barbara Deinhardt, "Interview," August 5, 1973, b1.f1.MS1985; Lever and Schwartz, *Women at Yale*, 213; Anonymous, "No Easy Answers," in *Fresh Women: Reflections on Coeducation and Life after Yale, 1969, 1989, 2009*, ed. Pamela Geismar, Eve Hart Rice, and Joan O'Meara Winant (self-pub., Yale Printing and Publishing Services, 2010), 106; Russett OH; Sneed OH; Traut OH.

Just make your way: Mifflin OH (2017).

"felt like a generosity": Storey-Johnson OH.

"women felt so grateful": Rachel Donadio, "Interview with Elga Wasserman," in *Different Voices: A Journal Commemorating 25 Years of Coeducation at Yale College*, ed. Rachel Donadio (New Haven: Yale University Press, 1995), 23. See also Jubin OH; Cynthia Margolin Brill, interview in Presca Ahn, *Arrival: Women at Yale College*, video, 4:00, posted on July 26, 2010, https://vimeo.com/13664639.

Let me just get through this: Darling OH. See also Royster OH.

"We were all as different": Anonymous, "Radically Altered Expectations," in *Fresh Women*, 119. See also Anonymous, "Being a Yale Man," in *Fresh Women*, 84; Bishop OH; "Coeds on Coeducation: A Discussion," *YAM*, April 1970, 39; Driscoll Coon OH; Jelly OH; Mintz OH; Polan OH; Solomon OH; Temoshok OH.

"Unofficial Proposals for Equality": A Number of Yale Women, "Unofficial Proposals for Equality," February 29, 1970, b4.fWomen.RU86.

For Kit McClure: McClure OH; Kit McClure, handwritten notes on personal copy of "Unofficial Proposals," February 29, 1970, in author's possession with thanks to Kit McClure; Virginia Blaisdell, "The Birth and Death of the New Haven Women's Liberation Rock Band," *Sister*, February 1976, 1.

"come and hash things out": "Free Women Conference," flier, February 1970.

"Russ Meyer is coming": Richard Schickel, "Porn and Man at Yale," *Harper's Magazine*, July 1970, 34. On the Russ Meyer Film Festival, see also Kent, "Up from Under"; Packer and Waggoner, "Yale and the New Sisterhood," 27; Schickel, "Porn and Man," 34–38.

"beautiful, bosomy broads": The 1971 YB (New Haven: Yale Banner Publications, 1971), 168.

"three go-go Watusi dancers": Twentieth Century Fox, "Yale Law School Film Society Sets Russ Meyer Film Festival," press release, February 24, 1970.

"the last great undiscovered talent": Schickel, "Porn and Man," 34.

"not healthy": Jeffrey Gordon, "Inky's Era," *YAM*, March 1970, 34.

the Yale Corporation meeting: Richard Fuchs, "Trustees Reaffirm Endorsement of Coeducation by Expansion," *YDN*, March 9, 1970; Lieberman OH; Yale University, "Former Trustees," 2019, https://www.yale.edu/board-trustees/former-trustees.

Women and Men for a Better Yale presented its petition: Joseph Treaster, "Coeds Find Life at Yale Falls Short of Expectations," *NYT*, April 14, 1970.

"I had thought": McClure, diary entry, May 1970.

SEVEN: THE SISTERHOOD

Women and Men for a Better Yale: Lieberman OH; author's review of *YDN* articles, 1969–73.

Meeting for Yale Women: Spahn OH. On Sisterhood founding, see also Berkan OH; Field OH; Betsy Hartmann OH; Mintz OH; Kit McClure, diary entry, May 1970; Rudden OH.

"We'll walk you through it": McClure OH.

"just tough as nails": Spahn OH.

"What did they have": Spahn OH.

"this incredible lift": Lucy L. Eddy, "In the Blue: A Freshman Coed's Account of Her First Yale Year," *YAM*, April 1970, 39.

"There was such a feeling": Rudden OH.

No black women: McClure OH. On the separate activism of white and black Yale women, see Diane Polan, "Black Women and Women's Liberation: Is There a Connection?," January 1971, b12.f132.RU578A; Myown Hymer, "My Blue Heaven," *YDN Magazine*, February 14, 1973; Daniels OH; Spahn OH; Wells OH.

"I'm not sure": Spahn OH.

"consciousness-raising": Amy Vita Kesselman, "Women's Liberation and the Left in New Haven, Connecticut, 1968–1972," *Radical History Review* 81, no. 1 (2001): 22; Simon Hall, *American*

Patriotism, American Protest: Social Movements since the Sixties (Philadelphia: University of Pennsylvania Press, 2011), 63–64; Spahn OH; "Who's Come a Long Way, Baby?," *Time*, August 31, 1970, 16–21.

"the importance of having boobs": Kesselman, "Women's Liberation and the Left," 22.

It Ain't Me, Babe: Hall, *American Patriotism*, 64.

"I had been reading": Kesselman, "Women's Liberation and the Left," 22.

"We need a name": Spahn OH.

"there should be no reduction": Leonard Doob, "Report of the President's Committee on the Freshman Year," Yale University Historic Documents and Reference Material, April 13, 1962, 12, https://www.yale.edu/about-yale.

Yale's Admissions Committee: "Admissions Committee Members" (unpublished document, February 5, 1970), RU821A.b25.f231; communication from Clark to Admissions Committee members, February 18, 1970, b1.f5.RU821A; Admissions Office Annual Report, 1971–1972, b3.f113, RU52B, table 6.

"hunchy judgment": communication from Brewster to Muyskens, March 15, 1967, b1.f8.RU821A.

"Dear President Brewster": communication from Thomson to Brewster, March 26, 1970, b1.f8. RU821A, underlines in original.

Yale was not alone: Patricia Cross, "The Woman Student," in *Women in Higher Education*, ed. W. Todd Furniss and Patricia A. Graham (Washington, DC: American Council on Education, 1974), 34. Cross's study was based on 1969 data from the College Entrance Examination Board.

Yale put its policy right out there: Richard Fuchs, "Trustees Reaffirm Endorsement of Coeducation by Expansion," *YDN*, March 9, 1970; *CC Report 1970*, appendix A, chart 1.

"gratitude and commitment": communication from Johnson to Brewster, March 27, 1970, b1.f8. RU821A.

"You have received": communication from Wasserman to Brewster, April 6, 1970, b1.f13.RU821B.

a front-page story: "Coeds' Marks Top Men's," *YDN*, April 1, 1970.

"Of course we're smarter": Tedford OH.

Honors…in 31 percent: "Coeds' Marks."

"wrong sort of seriousness": Mary McCarthy, "Portrait of the Intellectual as a Yale Man," in *The Company She Keeps* (New York: Harcourt, 1967), 169. See also "The Vanguard: Five of the First Coeds," *YAM*, October 1979, 27; Jerome Karabel, *The Chosen: The Hidden History of Admission and Exclusion at Harvard, Yale, and Princeton* (New York: Houghton Mifflin, 2005), 20, 201–203; Wilmarth Lewis, *One Man's Education* (New York: Alfred A. Knopf, 1967), 102–103.

"We were all very much involved": Jelly OH.

"I loved studying": Mintz OH.

"Science…was an area": Storey-Johnson OH.

"The official tradition here": Lindblom OH, 16.

"To those of you who received honors": Dana Milbank, "Bush Embraces Yale in Graduation Speech," *WP*, May 22, 2001.

"music, music, music": McClure OH. See also Kit McClure 1975 Yale College transcript, copy in author's possession with thanks to Kit McClure.

"We had so much fun": Field OH.

Women's Liberation Rock Band: Virginia Blaisdell, "The Birth and Death of the New Haven Women's Liberation Rock Band," *Sister*, February 1976, 1–2; Field OH; McClure OH; Chicago Women's Liberation Rock Band and New Haven Women's Liberation Rock Band, *Mountain Moving Day*, recorded 1972, Rounder Records, vinyl.

"barely knew how to play": Leighton Levy OH.

"Well, close enough": McClure OH.

"I thought I just wasn't": Spahn OH.

"normal to be a woman student": Rudden OH.

"I had no idea": Spahn OH.

"Sexual assault and rape": Lorna Sarrel OH. See also "Yale Sex Counselors at YHC Offer Unique Student Service," *YDN*, September 28, 1971.

The term date rape: Ruth Rosen, *The World Split Open: How the Modern Women's Movement Changed America* (New York: Penguin, 2000), 184.

"Things like everyone": Tunstall OH. See also Spahn OH.

"bull sessions": See, for example, Fred Gants, letter to the editor, *YDN*, April 3, 1970; Scott Herhold, "Panther Supporters Meet," *YDN*, April 17, 1970.

"mother, lover, sister, confidante": Barbara Deinhardt, "'Mother of Men'?," in *Women in Higher Education*, 68.

"They would get up the nerve": Wofford OH.

"kind of stumbled in": Spahn OH.

"Divided We Fall": Yale Break, April 6, 1970, 1. See also Dori Saleznik, "Yale Women Voice Opinion," *YDN*, January 14, 1970.

three hundred acceptance letters: Bill Robbins, "Size Restrictions Keep Out Many Qualified Women," *YDN*, April 6, 1970.

"We desperately need more girls": Eddy, "In the Blue," 25.

"was frustrated over turning away": Joseph Treaster, "Coeds Find Life at Yale Falls Short of Expectations," *NYT*, April 14, 1970.

"A general campaign": Treaster, "Coeds Find Life."

"At long last": Paul Goldberger, "Girls at Yale," *Today's Education* 59, no. 7 (October 1970): 51.

A high-profile trial: Stuart Rosow, "Black Women: Panthers to Rally on Jail Conditions," *YDN*, November 3, 1969; Paul Bass and Doug Rae, "The Panther and the Bulldog: The Story of May Day 1970," *YAM*, July 2006.

Many on the left: Geoffrey Kabaservice, *The Guardians: Kingman Brewster, His Circle, and the Rise of the Liberal Establishment* (New York: Henry Holt, 2004), 2, 403; "Panther Aid Group Meets," *YDN*, November 3, 1969; "Over 150 Hear Wald Speak," *YDN*, December 19, 1969; Thomas Kent, "White Group Aids Panthers Here," *YDN*, April 6, 197. On the FBI campaign against the Panthers, see Yohuru Williams, "No Haven: From Civil Rights to Black Power in New Haven, Connecticut," *The Black Scholar* 31, nos. 3–4 (2001): 60–61; Garrett Duncan, "Black Panther Party," *Encyclopedia Britannica*, August 2018, https://www.britannica.com/topic/Black-Panther-Party.

April 14: William Bulkeley, "The Strike: Crisis at Yale," *YDN*, June 1, 1970; Farley OH, 29; Jeff Greenfield, *No Peace, No Place: Excavations along the Generational Fault* (Garden City: Doubleday, 1973), 212, 226–227; Kabaservice, *The Guardians*, 404–405.

"There was a particular spirit": Sneed OH. See also Daniels OH; Darling OH; Driscoll Coon OH; Farley OH, 21–22; Pamela Geismar, Eve Hart Rice, and Joan O'Meara Winant, eds., *Fresh Women: Reflections on Coeducation and Life after Yale, 1969, 1989, 2009* (self-pub., Yale Printing and Publishing Services, 2010), 116; Maillet Main OH; McClure OH; Mifflin OH; Mintz OH; Solomon OH; *The 1973 YB* (New Haven: Yale Banner Publications, 1973).

Columbia, Penn, and Harvard: Stefan M. Bradley, *Harlem vs. Columbia University: Black Student Power in the Late 1960s* (Chicago: University of Illinois Press, 2009), 136–146.

A series of mass meetings: Bass and Rae, "The Panther and the Bulldog"; Bulkeley, "The Strike"; Greenfield, *No Peace, No Place*, 220; Sneed OH; Joseph Treaster, "Attendance at Yale Is Cut '50% to 75%' by Pickets Supporting Black Panthers," *NYT*, April 23, 1970.

"May Day": John Geesman, "Residential Colleges Announce College Weekend Cancellations," *YDN*, April 22, 1970.

a four-hour riot at Harvard: Bass and Rae, "The Panther and the Bulldog"; Garrett Epps, "Rioting Devastates Harvard Square," *HC*, April 16, 1970.

"When Harvard was trashed": Wilkinson OH.

"biggest riot in history": Greenfield, *No Peace, No Place*, 212.

Columbia and Harvard: Kabaservice, *The Guardians*, 352, 405–406; Bass and Rae, "The Panther and the Bulldog."

Thirty thousand protesters: Joseph Treaster, "Yale Student Petition Supports Brewster's Stand on Panthers," *NYT*, April 30, 1970; Bulkeley, "The Strike."

intent on doing Yale harm: Bass and Rae, "The Panther and the Bulldog"; Kabaservice, *The Guardians*, 404–405; Laura Kalman, *Yale Law School and the Sixties* (Chapel Hill: University of North Carolina Press, 2005), 204; Henry "Sam" Chauncey, John Hill, and Thomas Strong, *May Day at Yale, 1970: Recollections* (Westport: Prospecta Press, 2016), 28, 112–115.

a new approach: Kabaservice, *The Guardians*, 3–9, 405–406; Bass and Rae, "The Panther and the Bulldog."

"an approaching hurricane": Bart Whiteman, "Yale University: Spring of 1970," *The Chatanoogan* (TN), November 26, 2005. See also Bulkeley, "The Strike"; Greenfield, *No Peace, No Place*, 205, 260; Joseph Treaster, "Brewster Doubts Fair Black Trials," *NYT*, April 25, 1970; Joseph Treaster, "National Guard Alerted for Panther Rally Duty," *NYT*, April 29, 1970; Treaster, "Yale Student Petition"; Wasserman OH (1990).

hordes of reporters: Greenfield, *No Peace, No Place*, 205, 240, 260.

"I am skeptical": Treaster, "Brewster Doubts."

"a more mature and responsible": "Universities in Ferment," *Newsweek,* June 15, 1970, 68.

Students admired Brewster: Field OH; Gersick OH; Betsy Hartmann OH; Mintz OH; Sneed OH; Temoshok OH; Treaster, "Yale Student Petition."

Yale's more conservative alumni: Fanton OH, 18; M.A. Farber, "Brewster Tells Friendly but Questioning Yale Alumni He Cannot Be 'Personally Neutral' on Public Issues," *NYT,* June 14, 1970; Schmoke OH (1992), 2, 12.

"There was word spreading": Storey-Johnson OH.

"You could stay": Rice OH.

"I felt personally threatened": Bishop OH.

"Our generation": Mifflin OH (2017).

the imprisoned Black Panther women: Rosow, "Black Women."

"The kids didn't know": Daniels OH. See also Robert Brustein, "When the Panther Came to Yale," *NYT,* June 2, 1970.

"You can't be doing this": Daniels OH. See also Treaster, "National Guard Alerted."

four hundred...National Guard troops: Bass and Rae, "The Panther and the Bulldog."

"Kiss him on the cheek": Spahn OH. On peace marshals, see also Field OH; Greenfield, *No Peace, No Place,* 224; Murray Schumach, "'Marshals' Seek Calm in New Haven," *NYT,* May 3, 1970; Sam Swartz, "Graduate Groups Give Strike Limited Support," *YDN,* April 29, 1970; Tedford OH; Wilkinson OH.

"very accomplished": Zaeder OH.

"No guns...we hung firm": Spahn OH.

"Black Celebration": Brustein, "When the Panther Came"; Farley OH, 31; Royster OH. Swartz, "Graduate Groups Give Strike."

the Black Panther Party: Williams, "No Haven," 54, 59, 61; Duncan, "Black Panther Party."

John Huggins: Gay Miller, "Black Panthers Promote 'Survival' at Huggins Free Health Clinic," *YDN,* June 26, 1972; Kabaservice, *The Guardians,* 402; Royster OH.

"the right thing to do": Royster OH.

two thousand army paratroopers: Homer Bigart, "US Troops Flown in for Panther Rally," *NYT,* May 1, 1970.

National Guard tanks: Schmoke OH (2016); Tedford OH.

Yale stuck with Brewster's plan: Betsy Hartmann OH; Mintz OH; Schmoke OH (2016); Tedford OH; Treaster, "National Guard Alerted."

the afternoon of May 1: Daniels OH; Bass and Rae, "The Panther and the Bulldog"; Kabaservice, *The Guardians,* 411; Michael Sherman, "Rally Hits Racism," *YDN,* May 2, 1970.

"Fuck Brewster! Fuck Yale!": Greenfield, *No Peace, No Place,* 258. See also Homer Bigart, "New Haven Police Set off Tear Gas at Panther Rally," *NYT,* May 2, 1970; Tom Warren, "Evening Outbursts Follow Peaceful Rally," *YDN,* May 2, 1970; Schumach, "'Marshals' Seek Calm"; John Darnton, "New Haven Panthers Preached Calm," *NYT,* May 4, 1970; "May Day Mixes Many Moods," *YDN,* May 4, 1970; Brustein, "When the Panther Came"; Field OH; Greenfield, *No Peace, No Place,* 256–260.

crowds were half the size: Homer Bigart, "New Haven Rally Ends a Day Early," *NYT*, May 3, 1970.

"Why are they doing that?": Mifflin OH (2017). See also William Bulkeley and Michael Sherman, "Weekend of Demonstration Ends with Second Night of Disorder," *YDN*, May 4, 1970; Thomas Kent and Tom Warren, "Gas Slows Protesters," *YDN*, May 4, 1970; Bass and Rae, "The Panther and the Bulldog"; Field OH; Kit Hadsel, "Sophomore," *The 1972 YB* (New Haven: Yale Banner Publications, 1972).

"What do we do?": McClure OH.

"The entire campus was saturated": Whiteman, "Yale University."

"Why are we getting tear gassed?": Spahn OH.

"Shock, like when wild rock": Lydia Temoshok, diary entry, May 3, 1970. On May 3, see also William Bulkeley, "Brewster Opposed: Yale Strike to Continue," *YDN*, May 5, 1970.

448 campuses across the nation: William W. Scranton, *The Report of the President's Commission on Campus Unrest* (Washington, DC: U.S. Government Printing Office, 1970), 18.

"a complete shambles": Eisenstein OH (2017). See also Bulkeley, "Brewster Opposed"; "Dean May's Directive," *YDN*, May 5, 1970; "Freshman Year," *The 1973 YB* (New Haven: Yale Banner Publications, 1973), 3–27; Fanton OH, 29; Solomon OH.

Elga Wasserman thought: Wasserman OH (1990).

"May Day sucked the oxygen": Berkan OH.

EIGHT: BREAKING THE RULES

Wasserman had been as engaged: Schmoke OH (1971), 8; Wasserman OH (1990).

Wasserman included some calculations: "Comparison of Male and Female Applicants" (unpublished document, April 15, 1970), b22.f908.RU821A.

"intellectually indefensible...Irrational": CC minutes, April 21, 1970, b10.f156.RU126.

Only three committee members: CC minutes, May 5, 1970, b21.f905.RU821A.

Wasserman was preparing to issue: communication from Wasserman to Brewster, July 26, 1972, b22.f911.RU821A.

For the Class of 1975: CC minutes, May 5, 1970.

"often, women simply are not": WAC minutes, March 5, 1970, b35.f1032.RU821A.

Confidential...RE: Administrative Structures: communication from Wasserman to Brewster, May 11, 1970, b3.f1.RU821B, underline in original.

Brewster was in Washington: Richard Fuchs, "Brewster Leads Anti-war Delegation to Washington," *YDN*, May 7, 1970.

Brewster was basking in widespread praise: "Universities in Ferment," *Newsweek*, June 15, 1970, 60, 68–69.

Brewster denied Wasserman's request: CC Report 1972, cover.

Jock Whitney had donated: CC minutes, May 26, 1970, b1.f6.RU575; Chuck Critchlow, "Yale Gets Funds to House 600," *YDN*, September 14, 1970.

"urgent"…vote was unanimous: CC minutes, May 26, 1970.

Two days later, Wasserman: communication from Wasserman to Brewster, May 28, 1970, b1.f13. RU821B.

"mind-numbing": Rice OH. On other summer jobs, see Mintz OH; Tedford OH; Spahn OH.

"had just been so crazy": Field OH.

"Something had been missing": Barbara Deinhardt, "'Mother of Men'?," in Women in Higher Education, ed. W. Todd Furniss and Patricia A. Graham (Washington, DC: American Council on Education, 1974), 67. See also Janet Lever and Pepper Schwartz, Women at Yale: Liberating a College Campus (Indianapolis: Bobbs-Merrill, 1971), 197; Solomon OH.

"Something needed to shift": Mintz OH.

"Betsy, you need to become": Betsy Hartmann OH.

The need…was enormous: David Reuben, Everything You Always Wanted to Know about Sex but Were Afraid to Ask (New York: David McKay and Company, 1969); "About Our Bodies, Ourselves," Our Bodies, Ourselves, 2019, https://www.ourbodiesourselves.org/; Nicholas Perensovich, "Sex Pamphlet: National Publication," YDN, October 4, 1970.

Sex and the Yale Student: Perensovich, "Sex Pamphlet"; Phil Sarrel OH.

"gave us a very good sense": Bernick OH.

Sarrel had always been careful: Phil Sarrel OH.

On page 7, "alot": Student Committee on Human Sexuality, The Ins and Outs of Sex at Yale, September 1970, b33.f1010.RU821A. As part of the editing process, the title changed to Sex and the Yale Student.

Students needed good information: communication from Elaine Fox to Elga Wasserman, August 24, 1970, b33.f1010.RU821A; communication from students on Human Sexuality Committee to Yale administrators, September 1970, b33.f1010.RU821A.

two charts: CC Report 1972, appendix E.

"Yale cannot legislate": communication from Sam Chauncey to Ann Freedman, February 24, 1970, b10.f156.RU126.

Yale was supporting discrimination: CC minutes, February 13, 1970, b1.f6.RU575. See also CC minutes, January 30, 1970; February 24, 1970; March 31, 1970; May 26, 1970; all in b1.f6.RU575.

In March: CC minutes, March 31, 1970.

In May: communication from Chauncey to deans, directors, and chairmen, May 21, 1970, b10. f156.RU126.

Trotman advised Wasserman: CC minutes, May 26, 1970.

"Dear Faculty member": Wasserman to Yale Faculty, June 1970, b10.f156.RU126.

A few letters back in support: communication from Burton Clark to Wasserman, June 11, 1970, b1.f11. RU821B; communication from Sidney Mintz to Wasserman, July 4, 1970, b1.f11.RU821B.

"I wonder whether": communication from Pierson to Wasserman, June 23, 1970, b1.f11.RU821B.

"Pierson" was an important name: Marie Arana, "'Cheerful Money' by Tad Friend," *WP*, October 11, 2009.

"If my tone": communication from Wasserman to Pierson, July 1, 1970, b1.f11.RU821B.

a sister band: Naomi Weisstein, "The Chicago Women's Liberation Rock Band, 1970–1973," *New Politics*, Summer 2014, http://www.newpol.org; McClure OH.

"a hippy version": Weisstein, "The Chicago Women's Liberation Rock Band."

their first public performance: Virginia Blaisdell, "The Birth and Death of the New Haven Women's Liberation Rock Band," *Sister*, February 1976, 1; McClure OH; Christine Pattee, "Chronology, New Haven Women's Liberation," 1973, b1.f1.MS1985.

Women's Strike for Equality: Ruth Rosen, *The World Split Open: How the Modern Women's Movement Changed America* (New York: Penguin, 2000), 92; "Women's Liberation Day," flier, August 1970, b4.fWomen.RU86.

Edith Green: U.S. House of Representatives, "Edith Starrett Green, 1910–1987," *Women in Congress*, 2019, http://history.house.gov/People/; "Congressional Committees," *CQ Almanac*, June 1, 1970; Bernice Sandler, "Title IX: How We Got It and What a Difference It Made," *Cleveland State Law Review* 55, no. 4 (2007): 477.

"Let us not deceive ourselves": Susan Tolchin, *Women in Congress* (Washington, DC: U.S. Government Printing Office, 1976), 32.

receiving millions: "Universities: Anxiety behind the Façade," *Time*, June 3, 1967, 79; Nancy Gruchow, "Discrimination: Women Charge Universities, Colleges with Bias," *Science* 168, no. 3931 (May 1, 1970): 559–561.

"Coeducational institutions that receive federal funds": Stacey Jones, "Dynamic Social Norms and the Unexpected Transformation of Women's Higher Education, 1965–1975," *Social Science History* 33, no. 3 (2009): 268.

1,261 pages: U.S. House of Representatives, *Discrimination against Women: Hearings before the Special Subcommittee on Education of the Committee on Education and Labor*, Section 805 of HR 16908, 91st Congress, 2nd Session (Washington, DC: U.S. Government Printing Office, 1970 for Part 1, 1971 for Part 2).

Women's Strike for Equality: Rosen, *The World Split Open*, 92; Simon Hall, *American Patriotism, American Protest: Social Movements since the Sixties* (Philadelphia: University of Pennsylvania Press, 2011), 51; Linda Charlton, "Women March Down Fifth in Equality Drive," *NYT*, August 27, 1970.

"At last, we have a movement": Hall, *American Patriotism*, 52.

"A Standing Ovulation": Blaisdell, "The Birth and Death," 1. On George Bush at Delta Kappa Epsilon, see Jonathan Lear, "No Intervention for Fraternities," *YDN*, November 7, 1967.

"Who's come a long way, baby?": "Who's Come a Long Way, Baby?," *Time*, August 31, 1970, 16. See also Hal Weinstein, "How an Agency Builds a Brand: The Virginia Slims Story," American Association of Advertising Agencies Eastern Annual Conference, October 1969, https://industrydocuments.library.ucsf.edu/.

NINE: THE OPPOSITION

Yale now had 800 women undergraduates: CC Report 1970, appendix A, chart 1; Elga Wasserman, *Coeducation, 1970–71*, August 1971, b1.f5.RU821B (hereafter *CC Report 1971*), appendix IV, table 1.

ten thousand copies: Nicholas Perensovich, "Sex Pamphlet: National Publication," *YDN*, October 4, 1970; communication from Elaine Fox to Elga Wasserman, August 24, 1970, b33. f1010.RU821A.

"Your interest in Yale's new sex booklet": communication from Wasserman to William Allen, September 25, 1970, b33.f1010.RU821A.

Vanderbilt Lounge, September 21: Lee Fleming and Joanne Lawless, "'Raise Consciousness': Women's Lib," *YDN*, September 28, 1970; Mintz OH; Spahn OH.

"a huge number": Mintz OH.

"coeducation is something": Julia Preston, "What Is a Coeducation?," *NJ*, December 13, 1970, 8.

"Look, we can do this": Mifflin OH (1990).

"was really a nice person": Mifflin OH (2017).

"ragtag": Mifflin OH (1990).

The Political Union: Bishop OH. On political union size, see communication from Ralph Gerson to Elga Wasserman, June 27, 1969, b24.f927.RU821A.

Yale Daily News: "1971–72 NEWS Board," *YDN*, November 24, 1970.

The Yale Dramat: communication from Mark Wheeler to Elga Wasserman, December 3 1970, b24.f927.RU821A.

"Norma was no cook": Royster OH.

"I know how to use chopsticks": Royster OH.

"I need to go out": Royster OH.

"Could you get me a job": Spahn OH. See also Berkan OH; Royster OH.

"That book just blew my mind": Rudavsky OH.

"Fuck off, you male chauvinist pigs!": Pamela Geismar, Eve Hart Rice, and Joan O'Meara Winant, eds., *Fresh Women: Reflections on Coeducation and Life after Yale, 1969, 1989, 2009* (self-pub., Yale Printing and Publishing Services, 2010), 83.

women students were outshining: CC Report 1971, appendix IV, table 6.

porn pictures on the music stands: Jubin OH.

never award a girl a high grade: Mifflin OH (2017).

"Wo"—Women: communication from Wasserman to Ken Wilberg, February 8, 1971, b10.f160. RU126.

professors who went out of their way: Daniels OH; Virginia Dominguez, "Scholar of the House," in *Fresh Women*, 34; Betsy Hartmann OH; Mintz OH; Rice OH; Wells OH.

What happens when you fuse: McClure OH. See also "Edgar J. Boell," obituary, *NYT*, December 1, 1996.

"she was just an extraordinary woman": Daniels OH.

Sylvia Boone: Vera F. Wells, "The Life and Work of Sylvia Ardyn Boone" (lecture, Women of Yale Lecture series, New Haven, CT, February 28, 2017); Bruce Lambert, "Sylvia A. Boone," obituary *NYT*, May 1, 1993.

"always focused on you": Wells OH.

Sociological Perspectives on Women: "Enrollment in Women's Studies Courses," abstracts of Yale student papers on women's issues, "Achievement" to "Marriage," 1972–1976, b12.f131.RU578A.

It was like a door opening: Lisa Getman, "From Conestoga to Career," in *Women in Higher Education,* ed. W. Todd Furniss and Patricia A. Graham (Washington, DC: American Council on Education, 1974), 65; Mintz OH; Spahn OH.

"blur of these old white men": Spahn OH.

"absurd…Why not a history": Russett OH. See also Spahn OH; Wasserman OH (2007), 61.

On October 15: communication from May to Brewster, December 3, 1970, b10.f158.RU126; communication from Wasserman to May, October 20, 1970, b4.f80.RU52A.

levers of power: Kingman Brewster, *Report of the President,* September 1968, 8–9, 12.

"The campaign for full coeducation": Kit McClure, diary entry, May 1970.

On Thanksgiving…December 3: Thomas Kent, "Rape, 2 Attempts Reported," *YDN*, December 10, 1970.

Christa Hansen: Class of 1973 OC; Christa Hansen, "The Yale Experience," OIR Report 73R008, May 12, 1973, b2.f27.RU173, Accession 1980-A-014, YUL; YNB, "Christa Hansen," photograph, September 15, 1969, b15.f252, Yale events and activities photographs, 1852–2003 (inclusive), RU0690, Series I, YUL.

She was gang raped: Ferguson OH; Field OH; Fried OH; Jubin OH; Betsy Hartmann OH; Kent, "Rape."

"utterly distraught": Ferguson OH.

"How could you": Jubin OH.

"safety precautions": Kent, "Rape."

"we do live in a city": Kent, "Rape."

"Many women students at Yale": Master's Council minutes, January 22, 1971, b18.f607, Council of Masters, Yale University, Minutes of Meetings (RU299), Series I, YUL.

documented four rapes: Yale University Police Department, "Annual Report: July 1972 to June, 1973," b10.f6.4.RU52B, 25–26. See also Betsy Hartmann OH; Judy Klemesrud, "Yale Students Have Own 'Masters and Johnson,'" *NYT*, April 28, 1971; Wilkinson OH.

almost certainly low: Ruth Rosen, *The World Split Open: How the Modern Women's Movement Changed America* (New York: Penguin, 2000), 181–182. Rapes continue to be significantly underreported today.

"asked for it": Rosen, *The World Split Open,* 181. See also Lorna Sarrel OH; Thomas Peterson OH.

"Yale wasn't going out it of its way": Grillo OH. See also Jubin OH; Thomas Peterson OH.

"I don't think I did": Ferguson OH. On women graduate assistants, see CC minutes, February 24, 1970, b1.f6.RU575.

Yale had nothing in place: Ferguson OH; Thomas Peterson OH.

"Could you let me have": communication from Wasserman to Brewster, October 29,1970, b22. f910.RU821A.

"There is widespread sentiment": communication from Wasserman to Brewster, December 4, 1970, in *CC Report 1970,* 34.

"She grated on him": Chauncey OH.

"Elga was very good": Wei Mintz OH.

"She was an advocate": Coon OH.

"She went to bat": Field OH.

Leon Higginbotham: "First Black Named University Trustee," *YDN,* Summer 1970.

"No more thousand male leaders!": Mintz OH. See also William Bulkeley, "Rally Demands Full Co-education," *YDN,* December 14, 1970; Ausubel OH, Betsy Hartmann OH, Polan OH.

Prestigious private colleges: Gardner Patterson, "The Education of Women at Princeton," report, *Princeton Alumni Weekly* 69, no. 1 (1968), b1.f4.RU821B, 21.

"Mrs. Wasserman's Committee": Kingman Brewster, "Memorandum in Response to Report of Mrs. Wasserman's Committee," December 11, 1970, b58.f388.RU19-II.

"if I had not been able": Brewster, "Memorandum in Response."

"Kingman, come off it": Wasserman OH (2007), 65–71. Trustee Bill Horowitz served on the Corporation from 1965 to 1971, and at the time of the statement, he was the acting master of Yale's Branford College. See also Joseph Treaster, "Trustees Praise Brewster's Rule," *YDN,* September 28, 1970.

1,930 signatures: Bulkeley, "Rally Demands."

"We stormed the Yale Corporation": Mintz OH.

"We went in and disrupted": Betsy Hartmann OH.

"a present to the Corporation": Bulkeley, "Rally Demands."

Conference on the Black Woman: Thomas Johnson, "Yale Conference Studies Role of Black Women," *NYT,* December 14, 1970; Carole Parks, "Today's Black Woman Examines Her Role with Black Men," *Jet,* January 14, 1971, 24–27; "To Analyze the Roles of the Black Woman in Society," *YAM,* January 1971, 38; Wells, "The Life and Work"; Wells OH.

"Statuesque": Wells OH.

"No good": Johnson, "Yale Conference Studies."

"Committee Urges More Coeducation": Charles Cuneo, "Committee Urges More Coeducation," *YDN,* December 16, 1970.

TEN: REINFORCEMENTS

For the first time: Nancy Gruchow, "Discrimination: Women Charge Universities, Colleges with Bias," *Science* 168, no. 3931 (May 1, 1970): 559–561; "Sex Discrimination: Campuses Face Contract Loss over HEW Demands," *Science* 170, no. 3960 (November 20, 1970): 834–835; "HEW Acts to Check Sex Discrimination," *HC,* January 8, 1971.

"What the hell difference": Morse OH, 142.

Executive Order 11246: Lyndon B. Johnson, Exec. Order No. 11246, 30 Fed. Reg. 12319, 12935, 3 C.F.R. (September 24, 1965): 339; Lyndon B. Johnson, Exec. Order No. 11375, amendment to Exec. Order No. 11246, 32 Fed. Reg. 14303, 3 C.F.R. (October 13, 1967): 684.

Bernice Sandler read about it: Gruchow, "Discrimination," 559; Bernice Sandler, "Title IX: How We Got It and What a Difference It Made," *Cleveland State Law Review* 55, no. 4 (2007): 474–475; "Sex Discrimination," 834.

"came on too strong": Sandler, "Title IX," 474.

"not really a professional": Sandler, "Title IX," 474.

more than two hundred U.S. campuses: "Sex Discrimination," 834.

On January 29, 1971: communication from Marcia L. Keller to James Hodgson, January 29, 1971, in *Sex Discrimination at Yale: A Document of Indictment,* May 10, 1971, b280.f991.RU19, Series III; communication from Arlyce Currie to James Hodgson, January 29, 1971, in *Sex Discrimination at Yale;* "HEW to Examine Sex Discrimination," *YDN,* April 15, 1970.

Sandler knew Elga Wasserman: Sandler OH.

"Out of a faculty of 839": communication from Sandler to Elliot Richardson, February 1, 1971, in author's possession with thanks to Margie Ferguson, underline and capitalization in original. See also Sandler, "Title IX," 476.

"exciting…There was a sense": Ferguson OH.

"a prod from Uncle Sam": Phyllis Orrick, "US Order Attacks Sex Bias in University Hiring Policy," *YDN,* January 25, 1972.

"Everything about entering Yale": Havemeyer Wise OH.

Alec Haverstick: OC Class of 1974 (New Haven: Yale Banner Publications, 1970); Haverstick OH; "Iola Stetson Haverstick," obituary, *NYT,* April 5, 2002.

"pretty much…a women's libber": Haverstick OH.

antiwar movement had been dormant: Richard Schwartz and Thomas Kent, "2500 'Bear Witness' at Woolsey Hall Rally," *YDN,* February 23, 1971.

antiwar activism: Leib Gourguechon OH; Maillet Main OH; Tunstall OH.

In October: Thomas Kent, "Feminists Picket Mory's," *YDN,* October 13, 1970.

In November: communication from Goldstein to William Daley, November 23, 1970, b1.f11. RU821B.

"Are you a racist": Heidi Hartmann OH.

"He was a highly ethical": Yellen OH.

"We cannot accept": communication from Marianne Hill, K. Burke Dillon, Floria Behlen, Laurie Nisonoff, Janet Yellen, Francine Weiskopf, Heidi Hartmann, Margaret D. Howard, Susan Tepper, Charlotte Stiglitz, Jenifer K [illegible], Marsha Goldfarb, Cheryl Ann Cook, and Lucinda Lewis to the faculty of the economics department, February 23, 1971, b1.f11. RU821B.

A few days later: Arthur Greenfield, "The People vs. Mory's," *YAM,* June 1973, 26.

four women's studies courses: Elga Wasserman, "Enrollment in Women's Studies Courses, 1970–71," Fall 1971, b12.f137.RU578A.

"raising flags and marching": Royster OH. See also Connie Royster, "The Great Dupe: Women and the Media," Spring 1971, abstracts of Yale student papers on women's issues, "Marriage" to "Work," 1972–76, b12.f131.RU578A.

Women v. Connecticut: Laura Kalman, *Yale Law School and the Sixties* (Chapel Hill: University of North Carolina Press, 2005), 197; Amy Kesselman, "Women versus Connecticut: Conducting a Statewide Hearing on Abortion," in *Abortion Wars: A Half Century of Struggle, 1950–2000,* ed. Rickie Solinger (Berkeley: University of California Press, 1998), 42–67; Allen Ramsey, "Historical Note," RG 009:006, *Abele v. Markle,* Finding Aid, Connecticut State Library, 2010; *Women v. Connecticut,* organizing pamphlet, circa November 1970, http://www.historyisaweapon.com/defcon1/womenvsconnecticut.html.

"Call the police!": Spahn OH.

about twenty undergraduates: Philip and Lorna Sarrel, "Annual Report: Sex Counseling and Ob/Gyn," June 1973, b9.f56.RU52B.

"It was like women": Rice OH.

Women "were the experts": Kesselman, "Women versus Connecticut," 48.

4 percent of U.S. lawyers: Kesselman, "Women versus Connecticut," 54.

Sisterhood members: Berkan OH; Rudavsky OH; Spahn OH.

858 women plaintiffs: Ramsey, "Historical Note."

Women's Center: Lise Goldberg, "Durfee to House Women's Center," *YDN,* December 7, 1970; Student Committee on Human Sexuality, *Sex and the Yale Student,* September 1970, b33. f1010.RU821A, 53; Bernick OH; Deinhardt OH; Ferguson OH; Newman OH; Spahn OH; Tunstall OH.

"could just drop in": Spahn OH.

"Scruffy": Tunstall OH.

"We hope that everyone": Goldberg, "Durfee to House."

"Ask yourselves the question": Tunstall OH. On Kate Millett at Yale, see also "Schedule for Kate Millett," March 1971, b1.f33, Chubb Fellowship Program, Yale University, Records (RU855), Accession 2014-A-065, YUL; Cookie Polan and Beverly Wagstaff, "Kate Millett: The Politics of Women's Liberation," *YDN,* April 1, 1971.

"sort of disappeared": Spahn OH.

"I had other things": McClure OH. See also Lee Fleming and Joanne Lawless, "'Raise Consciousness': Women's Lib," *YDN,* September 28, 1970.

"It was hard at first": New Haven Women's Liberation Movement, "A Gay-Straight Dialogue," June 23, 1972, MS1985.b1.f1. See also McClure OH; Berkan OH; Field OH.

Mostly the band played: McClure OH; Christine Pattee, photo, circa 1971, in author's possession with thanks to Christine Pattee; Naomi Weisstein, "The Chicago Women's Liberation Rock Band, 1970–1973," *New Politics,* Summer 2014, http://www.newpol.org.

"Soon there were more dancers": Virginia Blaisdell, "The Birth and Death of the New Haven Women's Liberation Rock Band," *Sister,* February 1976, 2.

"You must stop": Blaisdell, "The Birth and Death," italics in original.

"watching faces smile": "Women's Band Rocks Niantic Prison," *Modern Times,* circa January 1971, in
    author's possession with thanks to Kit McClure.

"He was just so kind": Field OH. See also Driscoll Coon OH.

On April 16: "Policy Meeting with HEW Investigative Team," in *Sex Discrimination at Yale;* "HEW to
    Examine"; Jim Liebman, "Women Meet HEW Examiners," *YDN,* April 18, 1971.

"form a strong affirmative action": Debra Herman and Ann Gilmore, "Undergraduate Women at Yale,"
    in *Sex Discrimination at Yale.*

1,973 students: Herman and Gilmore, "Undergraduate Women."

"a new idea": Liebman, "Women Meet HEW Examiners."

"had the feeling": Maillet Main OH.

six hundred of Yale's eight hundred women: Judy Klemesrud, "Yale Students Have Own 'Masters and
    Johnson,'" *NYT,* April 28, 1971.

"were wonderful": Newman OH.

"Oh, I went to see": Maillet Main OH.

another new couple: Havemeyer Wise OH; Haverstick OH.

"were so together": Haverstick OH.

workers went on strike: Cookie Polan, "Where Has All the Money Gone?," *NJ,* November 1, 1970,
    13; "Yale Students Take Workers' Demands to Brewster Home," *NYT,* May 2, 1971; Kathy
    Smith, "Freshman Year," *The 1974 YB* (New Haven: Yale Banner Publications, 1974), 14–26;
    Maillet Main OH; Rudavsky OH; Tedford OH.

the Black Panther trials: Jeffrey Mayer, "Charges Dropped against Seal, Huggins," *YDN,* May 26, 1971.

Wasserman hired five of them: communication from Elga Wasserman to Richard Carroll, October 5,
    1971, b34.f1017.RU821A; communication from Chauncey to John Muyskens, July 20,
    1971, b1.f6.RU821A; Berkan OH; Barbara Deinhardt, "'Mother of Men'?," in *Women
    in Higher Education,* ed. W. Todd Furniss and Patricia A. Graham (Washington, DC:
    American Council on Education, 1974), 68; Deinhardt OH; Royster OH; Spahn OH.

"Without participation": communication from Wasserman to Brewster, March 12, 1971, b3.f1.
    RU821B.

"I continue to feel": communication from Wasserman to Brewster, May 21, 1971, cited in Nancy
    Weiss Malkiel, *"Keep the Damned Women Out": The Struggle for Coeducation* (Princeton:
    Princeton University Press, 2016), 278.

the Yale Corporation's insularity: Charles Sprague, "Brewster Announces Creation of Governance
    Steering Group," *YDN,* May 21, 1969; Michael Spencer, "Closed Corporation Examined,"
    YDN, April 20, 1971; "First Woman Overseer," *HC,* September 29, 1989; Vanessa Snowdon,
    "History of Women at Princeton University," *Seeley Mudd Manuscript Library Blog,*
    November 5, 2014, https://blogs.princeton.edu/mudd/2014/11; "New Trustees Include
    'Firsts,'" *YDN,* June 30, 1971; Liebman OH.

William Beinecke: "New Trustees"; Ben Casselman, "William Beinecke Dies at 103," *NYT,* April 13,
    2018; *The 1971 YB* (New Haven: Yale Banner Publications, 1971).

pleased by the progress: communication from Wasserman to Carroll, October 5, 1971; *SHE: Information for Women at Yale, 1971–72,* in author's possession with thanks to Barbara Deinhardt; Judy Berkan, Barbara Deinhardt, Debra Herman, Connie Royster, and Elizabeth Spahn, "Women's Center Project," Summer 1971, b20.f427.RU52A; communication from Judy Berkan, Barbara Deinhardt, Debra Herman, Connie Royster, and Elizabeth Spahn to incoming freshmen women, August 11, 1971, b34.f1017.RU821A; communication from Barbara Deinhardt and Debra Herman to John Muyskens, August 2, 1971, b1.f8. RU821A; Barbara Deinhardt and Debra Herman, "Report on Admissions: The Position of Women," October 20, 1971, b1.f8.RU821A; Deinhardt OH; Russett OH; Spahn OH.

"was like she was speaking": Spahn OH.

"Many students never meet": CC Report 1971, 2.

"How could you have": Wasserman OH (1992), 46.

Kathryn Emmett…filed a petition: "Mory's 'Poor Little Sheep' Face Dry Future over Sex Bias Charge," *NYT,* February 1, 1972.

$10,000: Daphna Renan, "'To the Tables Down at Mory's': Equality as Membership and Leadership in Places of Public Accommodations," *Yale Journal of Law and Feminism* 16, no. 2 (2004): 251.

"Yale's pervasive maleness": CC Report 1971, 6.

ELEVEN: TANKS VERSUS BB GUNS

Brewster was in London: Scott Herhold, "A Talk with President Brewster upon His Return," *YAM,* March 1972, 30–31; Joseph Treaster, "Trustees Praise Brewster's Rule," *YDN,* September 28, 1970.

investigators had started: Gay Miller, "Mintz Will Survey Hiring of Women," *YDN,* June 26, 1972.

"going to have to realize": Michael Knight, "Town-Gown Struggle Intensifies in New Haven," *NYT,* November 30, 1973.

Cyrus Vance: Gay Miller, "Yale Corporation to Convene," *YDN,* April 7, 1972; Brad Graham, "Corporation to Preview Plans for Two More College Units," *YDN,* May 5, 1972.

"Where has all the money gone?": Cookie Polan, "Where Has All the Money Gone?," *NJ,* November 1, 1970, 11–13. See also "Yale Halts Hiring in Face of Deficit," *NYT,* September 12, 1970; Frederick Hechinger, "Financial Woes of Colleges Getting Critical," *NYT,* October 25, 1970; John Geesman, "Deficit of $5.7 Million Predicted by Ecklund," *YDN,* November 23, 1971.

"in a state of financial shock": Hechinger, "Financial Woes of Colleges."

"splendid": Blum OH (March), 23. See *CC Report 1970,* appendix E, for increases in numbers of professors.

"set out to make": Blum OH (April), 10. See also Taylor OH, 32.

"aglitter with famous names": Thomas Meehannew, "The Yale Faculty Makes the Scene," *NYT*, February 7, 1971.

"Suddenly, things are different": Meehannew, "The Yale Faculty."

$4.4 million in deficits: John Ecklund, "Yale's Financial Status," *YDN*, November 23, 1971. Ecklund was Yale's treasurer.

Yale netted $2.1 million: Dartmouth College, *An Analysis of the Impact of Coeducation at Princeton and Yale Universities* (New York: Cresap, McCormick, and Paget, November 1971), II-9, and Exhibit 38; communication from George Langdon to Brewster, February 25, 1969, b1.f13. RU821B. Dartmouth calculated Yale's profit at $800,000 based on numbers it received from Yale. These numbers omit income from a $500,000 Ford Foundation grant that paid for renovation costs and include $850,000 that Yale billed the coeducation budget in "general support" despite the fact that Yale had no marginal costs to account for. The size of the faculty actually declined in the first year of coeducation. I therefore added the $500,000 and $850,000 to Dartmouth's total to reach $2.1 million.

deficit...projected at $6.5 million: communication from Brewster to Officers, Deans, and those responsible for budgetary units, June 22, 1971, b16.f323.RU52A.

$5,000 that year to coach: Joni Barnett, "History of Yale Women's Athletics," in *A Celebration of Women's Athletics, Then and Now*, program, February 4, 1994, b11.f423; Yale University Department of Athletics, Records (RU507), Accession 2006-A-242, YUL; "Preliminary Report on Budget Savings in the Department of Athletics," September 16, 1971, b2.f54; Yale University Department of Athletics, Records of the Athletic Director (RU983), Accession 1992-A-049, YUL.

seventeen varsity teams: The 1972 YB (New Haven: Yale Banner Publications, 1972).

"to prove they were serious": Barnett OH.

an ambitious schedule: Phyllis Orrick, "Field Hockey Squad Loses to Radcliffe," *YDN*, November 23, 1971.

"You should be covering": Mifflin OH (2017).

Patsy Mink: U.S. House of Representatives, "Patsy Takemoto Mink," 2019, http://history.house.gov/People/detail/18329.

"the most powerful woman": American Civil Liberties Union, "Title IX: The Nine," 2012, https://www.aclu.org/other/title-ix-nine?redirect=womens-rights/title-ix-nine.

"Maybe you ought to": Fitt OH, 7.

"One of Kingman's lackeys": Eisenstein OH (1971), 45. On Fitt's role, see also Fitt OH, 8–13; Wasserman OH (2007), 75; Wei Mintz OH.

a bill voted out: David Rosenbaum, "No Strings Funds for Colleges Are Backed by House Committee," *NYT*, October 1, 1971.

topped $30 million: Ecklund, "Yale's Financial Status."

on October 14: Michael Spencer, "Legislation May Prohibit Sex Bias in Admissions," *YDN*, October 21, 1971; U.S. House of Representatives, "Patsy Takemoto Mink"; Sandler OH.

"offended...trust Yale": Spencer, "Legislation May Prohibit."

Yale had used its muscle: I owe this account of Yale's earlier discrimination to Jerome Karabel. See
 Karabel, *The Chosen: The Hidden History of Admission and Exclusion at Harvard, Yale, and
 Princeton* (New York: Houghton Mifflin, 2005), 112–115, 211–212.

"personality and character": Karabel, *The Chosen*, 115.

"would create a serious threat": Erlenborn, remarks, *Congressional Record*, 92nd Congress, 1st session,
 vol. 117, pt. 29, extensions of remarks, November 1, 1971, 38639. For the letters from the
 five colleges, see pages 38639–38641.

"establish an undesirable degree": communication from Charles Kidd to Erlenborn, October 29, 1971,
 Congressional Record, vol. 117, pt. 29, November 1, 1971, 38641.

"from exercising its own": communication from Fitt to John Erlenborn, October 28, 1971, *Congressional
 Record*, vol. 117, pt. 29, November 1, 1971, 38640.

an ambitious agenda: communication from Carl Mullis to freshmen counselors, October 28, 1971,
 b22.f914.RU821A; communication from HSC to fellow student, Winter 1972, b2.f91.
 RU575; HSC, "Report," December 1971, b22.f914.RU821A; Grillo OH.

"were really very gifted": Zaeder OH.

the Coeducation Committee: CC Report 1970.

"would meet and discuss": Haverstick OH. See also Jubin OH.

"just furious": Jelly OH.

"Elga had a hell of a time": Rostow OH, 12. On the two women's friendship, see Gersick OH.

"beaten…I can't win": Haverstick OH.

"They were tears of frustration": Haverstick OH.

"We felt brave": Thomas Peterson OH.

"We write to you": communication from Robert Chambers, Paula Johnson, Steven Scher, Elisabeth
 Thomas, and Keith Thomson to Taylor, November 3, 1971, b32.f1006.RU821A.

Elisabeth Thomas: OC Class of 1975 (New Haven: Yale Banner Publications, 1971); Chauncey OH;
 Wilkinson OH.

"deeply disturbing…anguishing": communication from Chambers et al. to Taylor, November 3, 1971.

"How assertive can you be": Thomas Peterson OH.

"the maximum desirable enrollment": "Admissions Group Protests Present Sex Quotas," *YAM*, January
 1972, 31.

the field hockey team's record: Orrick, "Field Hockey Squad Loses."

"See this?": Mifflin OH (2017). On Princeton game, see also Barnett OH; Mifflin OH (1990);
 Mifflin, *The 1973 YB* (New Haven: Yale Banner Publications, 1973), 59–75; Orrick, "Field
 Hockey Squad Loses."

"Can we borrow your kilts?": Mifflin OH (2017). See also Barnett OH.

The band had changed: "Yale Band," *The 1971 YB* (New Haven: Yale Banner Publications, 1971);
 Daniels OH.

"like the Vietnam War": Susan Klebanoff, "Economic Perspectives of Women Discussed in Feminist
 Meeting," *YDN*, November 15, 2018.

"It just seemed like": Spahn OH.

Abele v. Markle: Amy Kesselman, "Women versus Connecticut: Conducting a Statewide Hearing on Abortion," in *Abortion Wars: A Half Century of Struggle, 1950–2000,* ed. Rickie Solinger (Berkeley: University of California Press, 1998), 49, 52.

the Sisterhood itself: "U-Notes," *YDN,* October 1, 1971; Berkan OH; Polan OH; Ausubel OH; Hartmann OH; Patty Mintz OH; McClure OH; Rudavsky OH; Fried OH; Field OH; Rudden OH; Christa Hansen, "The Yale Experience," OIR Report 73R008, May 12, 1973, b2.f27.RU173, Accession 1980-A-014, YUL.

"pretty alienated": Rudavsky OH.

"a very bright and able girl": communication from Wasserman to Hilles, April 20, 1971, b1.f2.RU821B.

"We felt hostility": Barbara Deinhardt, "'Mother of Men'?," in *Women in Higher Education,* 68.

"Developing a Feminist Economics": Heidi Hartmann OH; Tunstall OH; "Developing a Feminist Economics," flier, in author's possession with thanks to Heidi Hartmann.

"Oh, wow, they were great": Tunstall OH.

"What does she do?": McClure OH. See also Christine Pattee, "Chronology, New Haven Women's Liberation," 1973, b1.f1.MS1985.

They had a gig there: McClure OH; Pattee, "Chronology"; "Foes and Backers of Abortion Laws March in Three Cities," *NYT,* November 21, 1971.

"Power to the Women!": "Foes and Backers."

In Cambridge, Massachusetts, the women's center: Leighton Levy OH; Jane Gould, "Personal Reflections on Building a Women's Center in a Women's College," *Women's Studies Quarterly* 25, nos. 1–2 (1997): 110; The 888 Women's History Project, *Left on Pearl,* 2019, http://leftonpearl.org/background-history.html.

"a void in the record bins": "Rounder Records Owners Bio," Rounder Records, December 16, 2011, https://www.rounder.com/2011/12/rounder-records-owners-bio/. On Rounder records, see also Leighton Levy OH; Anne Gibson, "Rounder Records Founder Celebrates a Life in Music," Clark University News and Stories, April 26, 2010, http://www.clarku.edu/blog/rounder-records-founder-celebrates-life-music; "Rounder Records: A Loss for Massachusetts," *Boston Globe,* October 21, 2013; Jessica Nicholson, "45 Years of Rounder Records," *Music Row,* December 21, 2015, https://musicrow.com/2015/12/exclusive-45-years-of-rounder-records/.

"For that matter": Leighton Levy OH.

On December 10: "U-Notes," *YDN,* December 8, 1971; Richard Hall, "Gay Blacks Face Cultural Pressures," *YDN,* February 10, 1972; McClure OH; George Chauncey, "Gay at Yale," *YAM,* July 2009.

"We'd like to record you": McClure OH.

"The idea was preposterous": Virginia Blaisdell, "The Birth and Death of the New Haven Women's Liberation Rock Band," *Sister,* February 1976, 3.

"A great deal of talk": HSC, "Report," December 1971.

"Alec Haverstick stepped up to organize": HSC, "Report"; Haverstick OH; Chris Waterman email
    to author, October 13, 2018; Havemeyer Wise OH.

"Alec belonged": Grillo OH.

"I was a preppy": Haverstick OH.

Alec quickly assembled a team: Steve Hiller, "Students Organize Drive; Full Coeducation Is
    Goal," *YDN*, February 4, 1972; communication from AHCC to "The Readers of
    This Packet," January 24, 1972, b32.f1006.RU821A; Haverstick OH.

"It was always full": Grillo OH. On Coffin, see also Warren Goldstein, *William Sloane Coffin*
    Jr.: A Holy Impatience (New Haven: Yale University Press, 2005), 244–245, 270–271;
    Geoffrey Kabaservice, *The Guardians: Kingman Brewster, His Circle, and the Rise of the*
    Liberal Establishment (New York: Henry Holt, 2004), 172–173, 322; Haverstick OH;
    Phil Sarrel OH.

"I've been told": Haverstick OH.

"If you want a radical result": Haverstick OH.

"a very strong feminist": Zaeder OH. See also "Coffin, Yale's Chaplain, to Wed Harriet Gibney,"
    NYT, May 31, 1969; "Harriet Harvey," obituary, *The Lincoln County News* (ME),
    March 31, 2007.

"the kind of person": Zaeder OH. See also Lucy L. Eddy, "In the Blue: A Freshman Coed's
    Account of Her First Yale Year," *YAM*, April 1970, 25.

"The morality of justice": William Sloane Coffin Jr., "Whom the Lord Loves He Chastens,"
    November 21, 1971, in AHCC, "Report for Full Coeducation," January 24, 1972,
    appendix C, b1.5.RU821B.

TWELVE: MOUNTAIN MOVING DAY

Kingman Brewster returned: Scott Herhold, "A Talk with President Brewster upon His Return," *YAM*,
    March 1972, 30–31.

he used the word militant: Alan Pifer, "Women in Higher Education" (speech to the Southern Association
    of Colleges and Schools, Miami, Florida, November 29, 1971, ERIC ED058844), 2, 44–45.
    On Pifer, see Wolfgang Saxon, "Alan Pifer," obituary, *NYT*, November 5, 2005.

Yale's ninety thousand alumni: YNB, "Press Release #129," December 10, 1972, b258.f1.RU11-II.

"deeply disturbing": "Admissions Group," *YAM*, January 1972, 31.

All through December: communication from AHCC to "The Readers of This Packet," January
    24, 1972; Haverstick OH. On Brewster in London, see Geoffrey Kabaservice, *The*
    Guardians: Kingman Brewster, His Circle, and the Rise of the Liberal Establishment (New
    York: Henry Holt, 2004), 429.

"We weren't going to stop": Haverstick OH.

"How do we get this done?": Haverstick OH.

"I do not feel": "Scientific Fact," caption and photograph, *YDN*, February 1, 1972.

The report, twenty-nine pages in all: "Report for Full Coeducation," January 24, 1972, b1.f5. RU821B.

kept themselves anonymous: "Report for Full Coeducation," January 24, 1972; Steve Hiller, "Students Organize Drive; Full Coeducation Is Goal," *YDN*, February 4, 1972; Haverstick OH.

daily drumroll of pressure: AHCC, "Postulated Strategy," January 1972, b32.f1006.RU821A.

"ran on adrenaline": Fanton OH, 18. See also Blum OH (March), 73–74; Schmoke OH (2016).

"I let him talk": Haverstick OH. On Coffin's relationship with Brewster, see also Phil Sarrel OH; Kabaservice, *The Guardians*, 321–322.

On February 3: Hiller, "Students Organize Drive."

did not want the label radical: Hiller, "Students Organize Drive." See also Haverstick OH.

"ultimate pragmatist": Chauncey OH. See also Kabaservice, *The Guardians*, 25; Haverstick OH.

On February 13: Phyllis Orrick, "Brewster Vows Reassessment of Sex Ratio Next Fall," *YDN*, December 14, 1971.

Kit McClure was no longer enrolled: McClure transcript; McClure OH.

Leaves of absence: Elga Wasserman, *Coeducation 1971–1972*, July 1972, b1.f5.RU821B, appendix 3, table 1; Executive Committee minutes, January 4, 1972, b1.f18, Undergraduate Affairs, Yale College, Records of the Dean (RU95), Accession 1976-A-007.

The recording studio…awaited: Virginia Blaisdell 1972 datebook; Leighton Levy OH; McClure OH; Chicago Women's Liberation Rock Band and New Haven Women's Liberation Rock Band, *Mountain Moving Day*, recorded 1972, Rounder Records, vinyl; Jesse Henderson, "Aengus Studios," *The Music Museum of New England*, 2018, http://mmone.org/aengus-studios/.

"We were all very young": Leighton Levy OH.

"It was a nice studio": McClure OH.

"The mountain moving day": Chicago Women's Liberation Rock Band and New Haven Women's Liberation Rock Band, *Mountain Moving Day*.

Wasserman shot back a memo: communication from Wasserman to Fanton, September 28, 1971, b3.f1. RU821B.

"virtually precludes the appointment": communication from Wasserman to Langdon, November 3, 1971, b3.f1.RU821B.

In April: communication from Wasserman to Brewster, April 14, 1972, b3.f1.RU821B.

one of the most prominent women: "Report from Elga Wasserman to President Brewster," May 1972, b3.f1.RU821B; Wei Mintz OH; Nancy Diamond and Stacey Farnum, "Guide to the Higher Education Resource Services (HERS) Records, 1969–1999," finding aid, Special Collections and Archives, Penrose Library, University of Denver, 2003.

"She was the most senior woman": Royster OH.

"She was a female leader": Havemeyer Wise OH.

"reinventing undergraduate education": Nathaniel Zelinsky, "In Memory of Dahl," *YDN*, February 7, 2014. See also "Report of the Study Group on Yale College," The Dahl Report, April 1972,

ERIC ED067024; Brad Graham, "Dahl Committee Reaffirms Basic Yale Principles," *YDN*, April 7, 1972.

"Admission to Yale College": "Report of the Study Group," 49. For committee members, see page 8. See also "New Yale College Dean: Horace Taft," *NYT*, February 6, 1971.

Mory's lost its liquor license: Arthur Greenfield, "The People vs. Mory's," *YAM*, June 1973, 27–28; "Mory's," February 1, 1972.

"inundated with carbon copies": "More on Mory's," *YAM*, May 1972, 33.

Women v. Connecticut won: Amy Kesselman, "Women versus Connecticut: Conducting a Statewide Hearing on Abortion," in *Abortion Wars: A Half Century of Struggle, 1950–2000*, ed. Rickie Solinger (Berkeley: University of California Press, 1998), 53–55; Allen Ramsey, "Historical Note," RG 009:006, *Abele v. Markle*, Finding Aid, Connecticut State Library, 2010.

"over-reaching of police power": Kesselman, "Women versus Connecticut," 55.

The Boston Marathon: Boston Athletic Association, "History of the Marathon," 2018, http://www.baa.org/races/boston-marathon/boston-marathon-history.aspx.

"No person shall": Education Amendments of 1972, Public Law 92–318, *US Statutes at Large* 86 (June 23, 1972): 235, codified at *US Code* 20, 1681–1688.

No one paid much attention: U.S. House of Representatives, "Patsy Takemoto Mink," http://history.house.gov/People/detail/18329; Bernice Sandler, "Title IX: How We Got It and What a Difference It Made," *Cleveland State Law Review* 55, no. 4 (2007): 478–480.

"In regard to admissions": "Title IX of the Education Amendments of 1972," U.S. Department of Justice, updated August 6, 2015, https://www.justice.gov/crt/title-ix-education-amendments-1972; Title IX did not take effect until July 21, 1975.

"Dartmouth, Princeton, Yale, and Harvard": Sandler, "Title IX," 477–478; Sandler OH.

complaints had been filed against 350 colleges: Pifer, "Women in Higher Education," 30; "University Women's Rights: Whose Feet Are Dragging?," *Science* 175, no. 4018 (January 14, 1972): 152–154.

"at virtually every campus": "University Women's Rights," 152.

"They just don't enforce": "University Women's Rights," 153.

HEW had made…visits to Yale: Phyllis Orrick, "US Order Attacks Sex Bias in University Hiring Policy," *YDN*, January 25, 1972; Gay Miller, "Black Panthers Promote 'Survival' at Huggins Free Health Clinic," *YDN*, June 26, 1972.

"Oh, yes, you know": Royster OH.

"Royster is hilarious": Henry Wiencek, "Satire at Cabaret," *YDN*, February 12, 1971. For Meryl Streep reviews, see Wiencek, "Two New Plays," *YDN*, March 9, 1973; Laurel Graeber, "'Karamazov' Plays Pure Literary Havoc," *YDN*, November 4, 1974; Jon Weiner, "Yale Rep's 'Shaft' Pops Soap Bubbles," *YDN*, April 1, 1975.

"Everybody's shooting at me": Spahn OH.

Shirley Daniels spent much: Daniels OH; *The 1972 YB* (New Haven: Yale Banner Publications, 1972); communication from Sam Chauncey to Carl Banyard et al., February 18, 1972, and May 4 1972, b3.f59.RU52A.

"A nice group of people": Field OH.

Attitudes toward rape: Ruth Rosen, *The World Split Open: How the Modern Women's Movement Changed America* (New York: Penguin, 2000), 184.

Colleges' tolerance of sexual harassment: N. Davis, "Sexual Harassment in the University," in *Women in Higher Education: A Feminist Perspective*, ed. Judith Glazer, Estela Bensimon, and Barbara Townsend (Needham Heights, MA: Ginn Press, 1993), 241–257; Alexander v. Yale, 549 F. Supp. 1 (D. Conn 1977).

The term sexual harassment had never been used: Ruth Rosen's exhaustive history of the modern women's movement states that women at Cornell University "coined the term 'sexual harassment'" in 1975 (Rosen, *The World Split Open*, 186–187), yet Yale women used the term *sexual harassment* four years earlier, in 1971. See Jim Liebman, "Women Meet HEW Examiners," *YDN*, April 18, 1971; "The Adventures of Jane Smith," in *Sex Discrimination at Yale*, May 10, 1971.

"The Yale Experience": Christa Hansen, "The Yale Experience," OIR Report 73R008, May 12, 1973, b2.f27.RU173, Accession 1980-A-014, YUL.

"We sometimes forget": Hansen, "The Yale Experience."

"There are simply not enough": Barbara Deinhardt, "'Mother of Men'?," in *Women in Higher Education*, 69.

a one-year leave: communication from Elga Wasserman to Bob Arnstein, July 28, 1972, b22.f911. RU821A; Don Letourneau, "Arnstein to Fill Wasserman's Job," *YDN*, September 11, 1972.

Wasserman gave Brewster some names: communication from Wasserman to Brewster, April 14, 1972, b3.f1.RU821B.

Mary Arnstein: "Mary Arnstein," obituary, *NHR*, September 9, 2012.

"Mary was anything but": Chauncey OH.

"a joke": Jubin OH. See also Deinhardt OH.

"very soft-spoken": Grillo OH.

Nooooo: Grillo OH.

"Dear Lawrie": communication from Barnett to Mifflin, November 29, 1972, in author's possession with thanks to Lawrie Mifflin.

"resplendent in royal-blue kilts": Mifflin, *The 1973 YB* (New Haven: Yale Banner Publications, 1973), 68. See also pages 62 and 73; Mifflin OH (2017).

"Hey. We're a varsity sport": Mifflin OH (2017). Articles on the field hockey team, written by Kate Moore, ran in the *YDN* between October 13 and November 29, 1972.

the captain's photo: The *1973 YB*; Mifflin OH (2017).

Mory's would not display: Marcia Synnott, "A Friendly Rivalry: Yale and Princeton Pursue Parallel Paths to Coeducation," in *Going Coed: Women's Experiences in Formerly Men's Colleges and*

Universities, 1950–2000, ed. Leslie Miller-Bernal and Susan Poulson (Nashville:Vanderbilt University Press, 2004), 130.

"were leaders": Mifflin OH (2017).

"Where has all the luster gone?": Chet Cobb, "The Yale Administration: Where Has All the Luster Gone?," op-ed, *YDN*, October 6, 1972.

questions of competence: John Geesman, "The Deficit Controversy," *YDN*, September 15, 1972.

Few of the 1,500 attendees: W.Todd Furniss and Patricia A. Graham, eds., "Preface," *Women in Higher Education* (Washington, DC:American Council on Education, 1974), xiii.

"Nothing much has been heard": Martha E. Peterson, "Women, Autonomy, and Accountability in Higher Education," in *Women in Higher Education*, ed. W. Todd Furniss and Patricia A. Graham, 5.

"put his own thoughts in order": Bradley Graham, "Trustees to Eye Cooper Study," *YDN*, October 13, 1972, 1.

an analysis of three coeducation options: Kingman Brewster, "Background Memorandum on Coeducation Admissions Policy," October 18, 1972, b258.f1.RU11-II.

"become fully coeducational": "Sisterhood Issues Statement: Admit 50% Women by Next Fall," *YDN*, October 27, 1972.

"It is both the moral": HSC, letter to the editor, *YDN*, November 10, 1972.

"Students to Trustees": Robert Sullwold, "Students to Trustees: More Women Now," *YDN*, November 10, 1972.

signed by 3,016 students: Bradley Graham, "Corporation to Pronounce Final Say on Coeducation," *YDN*, November 10, 1972.

On Friday morning, the five trustees: Graham, "Corporation to Pronounce Final Say"; Bradley Graham, "Trustees Postpone Decision," *YDN*, November 13, 1972.

"Wait a minute": Haverstick OH.

Quite a few of them: Haverstick OH.

One more month passed: Graham, "Trustees Postpone Decision."

Association of Yale Alumni: The 1972 YB; Royster OH; Frederick P. Rose, "News from the Association of Yale Alumni," *YAM*, April 1973, 73.

The group voted: John Yandell, "AYA Endorses 60–40," *YDN*, December 7, 1972.

"Everybody agrees that coeducation": John Yandell, "AYA: Plasma for Blues," *YDN*, November 17, 1972.

"almost uniform approval": communication from Brewster to John Ward, November 17, 1972, b258.f1.RU11-II.

"We believe that the gender": Robert Sullwold, "Trustees Eliminate Sex Quota," *YDN*, December 11, 1972.

more than doubled to 46 percent: Jerome Karabel, *The Chosen: The Hidden History of Admission and Exclusion at Harvard, Yale, and Princeton* (New York: Houghton Mifflin, 2005), 426.

EPILOGUE

Data on pages 288–289 are for the most recent year available as of December 2020.

Sexual harassment and assault: National Center for Education Statistics (NCES), "Yale University: Campus Security, 2017 Crime Statistics," accessed 2020, https://nces.ed.gov/globallocator/col_info_popup.asp?ID=130794.

51 percent of Yale's undergraduate enrollment: NCES, "Yale University: Enrollment, Fall 2019 Undergraduate Enrollment," accessed 2020, https://nces.ed.gov/globallocator/col_info_popup.asp?ID=130794.

27 percent of the tenured faculty: Yale OIR, "Ladder Faculty by Gender, 2020–2021," accessed 2020, author calculation based on headcount, https://oir.yale.edu/sites/default/files/w056_fac_u_tenterm_gen_2019_0.pdf.

8 percent of Yale's students are black: NCES, "Yale University: Enrollment."

14 percent of college-age Americans: NCES, "Status and Trends in the Education of Racial and Ethnic Groups," figure 1.4, February 2019, https://nces.ed.gov/programs/raceindicators/indicator_RAA.asp.

still have lunch at Mory's: Daphna Renan, "'To the Tables Down at Mory's': Equality as Membership and Leadership in Places of Public Accommodations," *Yale Journal of Law and Feminism* 16, no. 2 (2004): 251–253.

The Yale Whiffenpoofs faced: David Shimer, "Yale's Famed Whiffenpoofs Singing Group Admits First Woman," *NYT*, February 20, 2018.

33 percent of full professors: NCES, *Characteristics of Postsecondary Faculty,* Figure 2, fall 2018, accessed 2020, https://nces.ed.gov/programs/coe/indicator_csc.asp; https://nces.ed.gov/programs/digest/d17/tables/dt17_315.20.asp.

30 percent of college and university presidents: Lee Gardner, "What Happens When Women Run Colleges," *Chronicle of Higher Education,* June 30, 2019.

One in five women students: White House Task Force to Protect Students from Sexual Assault, *Not Alone,* April 2014, https://www.justice.gov/ovw/page/file/905942/download. The Association of American Universities's fall 2019 survey of students at thirty-three colleges found that 26 percent of undergraduate women, almost one in four, had experienced sexual assault (nonconsensual sexual contact by force or inability to consent) since arriving at college. See *Report on the AAU Campus Climate Survey on Sexual Assault and Misconduct,* October 2019, p. xi, https://www.aau.edu/key-issues/campus-climate-and-safety/aau-campus-climate-survey-2019.

graduate at a higher rate: National Center for Education Statistics (NCES), *Digest of Education Statistics,* table 301.10, enrollment, staff, and degrees/certificates conferred in 2015–2016, accessed 2019, https://nces.ed.gov/programs/digest/d16/tables/dt16_301.10.asp.

74 cents on the dollar: American Association of University of Women, "The Simple Truth about the Gender Pay Gap, 2020 update," 5, https://www.aauw.org/app/uploads/2020/12/SimpleTruth_2.1.pdf. Calculation based on U.S. Bureau of Labor Statistics 2019 salary data.

The Yale Women's Center: Rhea Hirshman, "A Decade of (Women's) Liberation," *New Haven Advocate*, October 22, 1980, b1.f3.MS1985.

"the Boston Tea Party": Steve Wulf, "Title IX: 37 Words That Changed Everything," ESPN, April 29, 2012.

Alexander v. Yale: Ann Olivarius, "Title IX: Taking Yale to Court," *NJ*, April 18, 2011; Anne E. Simon, "Alexander v. Yale University: An Informal History," in *Directions in Sexual Harassment Law*, ed. Catharine MacKinnon and Reva Siegel (New Haven: Yale University Press, 2004), 55–56.

two women professors: Micole Sudberg, "Coeducation at Yale: A Brief Chronology," in *Different Voices: A Journal Commemorating 25 Years of Coeducation at Yale College*, ed. Rachel Donadio (New Haven: Yale University Press, 1995), 71.

only 9 percent: Bruce Fellman, "Time of Arrival," *YAM*, May 1999.

"No means yes!": Gavan Gideon and Caroline Tan, "Department of Education Ends Title IX Investigation," *YDN*, June 15, 2012.; Margaret Clark email to author, December 28, 2019.

The five women students: Unless otherwise noted, the accounts of individuals that follow rely on interviews and curriculum vitae, as well as previously cited and publicly available sources.

Christa Hansen: "In Memoriam," Yale Class of 1973, https://alumninet.yale.edu/classes/yc1973/; Christa Hansen, "The Yale Experience," OIR Report 73R008, May 12, 1973, b2.f27. RU173, Accession 1980-A-014, YUL.

Darial Sneed: "Darial Sneed Photography: Showcasing the Best in the Performing Arts," https://www.darialsneedphotography.com/.

"Sam was a wonderful mentor": Wasserman OH (2007), 58.

"He's really been a savior": Royster OH. See also Deinhardt OH; Jubin OH; Thomas Peterson OH; Wells OH; Wei Mintz OH.

Elga Wasserman's Yale career: "Wasserman Loses Position," *YDN*, February 21, 1973; Wasserman memo to file, May 22, 1973, b3.f1.RU821B; communication from Wasserman to Brewster, February 13, 1973, b3.f1.RU821B; Yale College Dean's Office, "Annual Report," August 31, 1973, b8.f52.RU52B, 11; Wei Mintz OH; Wilkinson OH; Wasserman OH (2007), 70.

"To be outspoken": Yale Faculty and Professional Women's Forum, "Wasserman," letter to the editor, *YDN*, March 6, 1973.

Kingman Brewster: Eric Pace, "Kingman Brewster Jr.," obituary, *NYT*, November 9, 1988; Liebman OH.

INDEX

AAU. *See* Association of American Universities

Abele v. Markle, 222–224, 252, 272

Abod, Jennifer, 146–147, 190, 227

Abod, Susan, 190

abortion, 112, 124, 272

    and Yale students, 222–224, 229

Ad Hoc Committee on Coeducation, 259–261, 263–268, 285

Admissions Committee, 154–157, 247–249, 263

    and gender quota, 163–164

African Americans. *See* blacks

Afro-America House, 75, 79, 136–137, 293–294

Afro-American studies, 5, 27–28, 78, 139

Agnew, Spiro T., 168, 264

Alexander v. Yale, 290

all-male education

    college tradition of, 8–9

    and drop in Yale admissions, 17–18

    men's dislike of, 11–12, 15

    at private high schools, 12

Alper, Rika, 227, 269

alumni

    children favored in Yale admissions, 33, 120, 134, 212

    and coeducation, 134–135, 212, 286–287

    and gender quota, 120, 132–135, 141, 286–287

    opinion of Brewster, 134, 168

Alumni Day protest, 130–135, 139–142

Angelou, Maya, 213–214

anti-Semitism, 52, 244

Applebee, Constance, 54, 57

Arnstein, Mary, 280–281, 286

Arnstein, Robert, 61–62, 121, 179, 186

arts

    dance, 104

    music, 27, 56–58

    theater, 28, 56, 104–105, 198–199,
        275–276

Association of American Universities
    (AAU), 245

Association of Yale Alumni (AYA),
    286–287

athletics. *See* sports

Ausubel, Joan, 252

AYA. *See* Association of Yale Alumni

Barbieri, Arthur, 239

Barnard College, 219

Barnett, Joni, 249–250, 281

Battell Chapel, 266

Becton, Cynthia, 131–132, 141

Becton, Henry P., 130–131, 141

Becton Engineering and Applied
    Science Center, 130

Beinecke, Frances, 235

Beinecke, William, 235, 285

Berkan, Judy, 136, 151–152, 161, 177,
    224, 234, 294

Bernick, Debbie, 185

birth control, 60–61, 123, 232

Black Panthers, 164–166, 169–172, 234

Black Power movement, 78, 213–214

blacks. *See also* Yale undergraduate men:
    black: Yale undergraduate women:
    black

    as administrators, 137

    enrollment numbers, 91, 137

    as faculty, 138–139, 294

    student ratio of, 75–76, 288–289

    students, 74–80, 84, 90–92,
        136–138

Black Student Alliance at Yale (BSAY),
    78, 90–92, 98, 104, 136–138, 169–
    170, 266, 277, 291

    and May Day rally, 174

Black Woman: Yesterday and Today, The
    (course), 139, 203–204, 213

Blaisdell, Virginia, 146–147, 160, 190,
    226–228, 257

Blassingame, John, 277

Blum, John, 240

Boell, Edgar J., 202–203

Boone, Sylvia, 139, 203–204, 213, 294

Brewster, Kingman, Jr., 5–11, 101

    and admissions, 155–157

    and campus security, 94–95

    and coeducation, 7–8, 12–15,
        17–19, 23–25, 45–47, 211–212,
        284–286

criticism of, 134, 168, 266, 284

faculty opinion of, 9

and gender quota, 134–135, 205–206, 210–212, 262–263, 266–267

later career, 298

and May Day rally, 174, 181, 266

and Mory's, 188–190

political views, 7, 72–73, 134

power of, 9, 120, 206

in the press, 6, 167–168, 284

prominence of, 5–6

racial views, 5, 7, 167–168, 244

student opinion of, 7, 168

on Vietnam War, 90

views on women, 7–8, 13, 86

and Yale finances, 239–240, 284

Brooks, Gwendolyn, 214

Brown College, 86–88

Brustein, Norma, 198–199

BSAY. *See* Black Student Alliance at Yale

Bush, George W., 159

Cambodia, invasion of, 172–173

Candy (cook), 80

Cap and Gown Eating Club, 250–251

Chauncey, Sam, 8, 23, 37, 45, 77–78, 137, 174, 267, 277, 280, 297

and admissions, 52, 53, 154

and campus security, 94–95

on extracurricular activities, 56–57

influence on Brewster, 12–13

and Mory's, 188

cheerleading, 55, 81

Chicago Women's Liberation Rock Band, 190, 268–269, 293

Chisholm, Shirley, 191

Christ, Carol, 14, 16–17

Chubb Fellowship, 213

Civil Rights Act of 1964

Title IV, 17

Title VII, 17

Title IX, 17, 273–274, 290

civil rights movement, 76–77, 105–106

Clark, Russell Inslee "Inky," 12, 164

and admissions, 155

on coeducation, 17, 19

on gender quota, 149

Clarke, John Henrik, 214

Clinton, Hillary Rodham, 14

clubs, exclusion of women, 7, 16–17, 110–112, 188–190, 220–222. *See also* Mory's

coeducation

Brewster's opinion of, 7–8, 12–15, 17–19, 23–25, 73

financial implications of, 8, 19, 240

history of, 8

lack of, and Yale admissions, 17–18

at public high schools, 12, 20, 131

sexual aspect of, 62–63

women administrators of, 36–37

Yale approval of, 24

Yale as lifting taboo, 298

at Yale Graduate School, 16

Yale men's views on, 11–12, 15

Yale preparation for, 24–25, 45

Coeducation Committee. *See*
University Committee on
Coeducation

Coeducation Office, 45, 240, 270, 281

coeducation report, 179–180, 181–182,
187–188, 194, 237

Brewster's lack of response to,
205–206, 209–210

recommendations of, 211

and Yale Corporation, 210–213,
214

Coeducation Week, 19–23

Coffin, Harriet, 260–261

Coffin, William Sloane, 97, 259–261,
263, 266–267

College of William and Mary, 2

Columbia University, 10, 165, 167, 239

Concord Academy, 74, 218, 219, 259

Conference on the Black Woman,
213–214

Connecticut State Liquor Commission,
237, 252, 289

consciousness-raising, 107–108, 153–
154, 160–161, 195–196, 225

Coon, Margaret, 131–134, 140–141,
210, 293

Cooper, Sam, 27

Cornell University, 107

crew team, 289

Curtis, Jane, 57, 82, 197, 241, 282

Dahl, Robert, 272

Daniels, Shirley, 27–28, 34, 40–41, 75,
76, 77–78, 79–80, 85, 90–91, 92, 123,
135–138, 203–204, 234

graduation, 275, 277

later career, 290–291

and May Day rally, 169–170

dating, 58–59, 116, 123–124, 161–162

David, Worth, 286

Davis, Lanny, 8, 296

Dawson, Ralph, 90–91

DeChabert, Glenn, 90–91

Deinhardt, Barbara, 225, 234, 253, 279–
280, 294

Dempsey, John, 172

Department of Health, Education, and
Welfare (HEW), 217, 230, 238, 274,
278

DePradines, Emerante, 104

"Developing a Feminist Economics" conference, 254

Dilworth, J. Richardson, 285

dining halls, 65, 70–72, 80, 95–96

discrimination

in college admissions, 8, 14, 154–157, 242–245

gender, 11–12, 14, 17, 90, 136, 137–139, 144, 154–157, 188–190, 191–192, 215, 220–222, 242, 243–245, 262–268, 273–274

legality of, 17

legislation against, 191–192, 215–216, 243–245, 273–274

racial, 90–92, 137–139, 164–166, 221, 244

religious, 244

Dixwell Congregational Church, 104

draft, 89, 108–109

drama. See arts

Dramat. See Yale Dramatic Association

Du Bois, Shirley Graham, 214

Durfee Hall, 224–225

Ebert, Roger, 148

Edelman, Marian Wright, 14, 235, 285

Eisenstein, Hester, 243

Eliot, Charles, 8

Elizabethan Club, 16–17

Emmett, Kathryn, 237

Equal Pay Act of 1963, 17

Equal Rights Amendment (ERA), 191, 272–273

Ernst, Chris, 289

Executive Order 11246, 215–216, 274

extracurricular activities, 197–199

exclusion of women, 54–58, 105, 159

importance of, 159

faculty. See also blacks: as faculty; women: as faculty

and coeducation, 24

discrimination by, 66, 202

and gender quota, 154–155, 178

gender ratio, 187–188, 237, 288, 289

mentoring by, 202–204

and sexual harassment, 114–118

Falk, Gail, 222–223

Fanton, Jonathan, 266, 270

feminism, 10–11, 44, 101–102, 105–108, 183–184

study of, 222

at Yale, 109–113, 148–149, 153, 201

Ferguson, Margie, 208–209, 217

Field, Kate, 115, 159–160, 170–171, 175, 183, 210, 228–229, 253, 278, 294

field hockey, 54–55, 57, 81–82, 197–
    198, 240–242, 249–251
    as varsity sport, 281–283
financial aid, 5, 70, 79, 200, 240
Fitt, Al, 242–245
football, 81, 86–88, 92, 99, 100–101,
    197
Fourteenth Amendment, 17, 272
Free Women Conference, 112–113,
    142–147, 148, 151–152
Fried, Barbara, 253

Gates, Henry Louis "Skip," 76, 77, 78
gay men, 127–128
George Washington University, 29, 30
Giamatti, Bart, 215
Goldstein, Abe, 220
Gordon, Jeff, 79
governance, student, 72, 120
graduate students, 109–110
    gender ratio, 16
    housing, 16
    and sexual harassment, 114–115
Graduate Women's Alliance, 109, 110,
    112, 150
Gray, Hanna, 235
Green, Edith, 191–192, 242, 243–245,
    273, 274
Grillo, Carolyn, 258, 260, 280–281
Grove Street Cemetery, 115

Guida, Bart, 239
gynecology services, 25, 61–62

Hansen, Christa, 207–209, 253, 279,
    285, 295
Hartmann, Betsy, 183–184, 213, 252,
    294–295
Hartmann, Heidi, 220, 221
Harvard College, 2, 165, 166, 167, 235
    rivalry with, 17–18, 239–240
Harvard Crimson, 6, 240
Havemeyer, Linden, 218, 232–233, 246,
    258, 271
Haverstick, Alec, 218–219, 232–233,
    246, 247, 258–261, 263–266, 285, 286
    later career, 296
Hersey, John, 94, 121, 179
HEW. See Department of Health,
    Education, and Welfare
Higginbotham, Leon, 210
high schools
    private, 12
    public, 12, 20, 131
Hill, Ann, 222–223
Hilles, Susan, 122, 234, 253
Hillhouse High School, 169, 171
Hodgson, James, 216
Hoffman, Abbie, 166
homosexuality, 127–129. See also gay
    men; lesbians

Homosexuality Discussion Group, 257

House, the. *See* Afro-America House

House Education and Labor
  Committee, 243

housing, 73, 218. *See also* residential
  colleges; Vanderbilt Hall
    new residential colleges, 181–182,
      206, 238–239, 262
    off-campus, 228
    for women, 16, 25, 36, 45–47

Howard University, 138

Huggins, Ericka, 164–166, 172, 176,
  226–228, 234, 291

Huggins, John, 171–172, 291

Human Sexuality Committee, 126–
  128, 184–186, 195, 232–233, 246,
  285, 296–297
    and gender quota, 258–259

human sexuality course. *See* Topics in
  Human Sexuality

Irwin, Ken, 256–257, 269

Jackson, Sheila, 136–137

Jackson State University, 176

John Huggins Free Health Clinic, 171

Johnson, Lyndon B., 6, 215–216

Johnson, Paula, 155, 157, 247–248

Jubin, Brenda, 280

Judy Miller, 270

Karabel, Jerome, 13

Kent State University, 176

Kerry, John, 220

Kessen, William, 272

King, Martin Luther, Jr., 9, 76–77

Kit McClure Band, 292–293

Langdon, George, 121, 270

Laos, invasion of, 220

lesbians, 128–129, 226

Levy, Marian Leighton, 256–257, 269,
  270, 293

Liebman, Lance, 235, 285

Lindblom, Ed, 52–53, 158–159

Local 35 union, 233

Lowenhaupt, Anna Tsing, 152, 159–
  160, 224, 294

Maillet, Denise, 115–117, 230–231,
  232, 233, 295

marching band. *See* Yale Precision
  Marching Band

Massey, Joe, 81

May, Georges, 24–25, 121, 179

May Day rally, 164–177, 266
    peace marshals, 170–171, 174, 175
    Yale response to, 172–176

McCarthy, Mary, 158

McClure, Kit, 26–27, 33, 51, 112–113,
  123, 128–129, 143, 184, 202–203,

225–228, 252–253

  and Alumni Day protest, 133,
    141–142

  and feminism, 105–108, 149, 150–
    154, 206

  later career, 292–293

  and marching band, 56–58, 87–88

  and May Day rally, 169, 175–176

  and rock band, 146–147, 159–160,
    190, 192, 226–228, 254–255,
    257, 268–270

McDaniel, Cecelia, 139

Mendenhall, Thomas, 245

Meyer, Russ, 147–148

Mifflin, Lawrie, 32–33, 51, 73, 77

  and field hockey, 54–55, 57, 81–
    82, 144–145, 197–198, 240–
    242, 249–251, 281–283

  later career, 292

  and May Day rally, 168–169, 175

Miller, Irwin, 24

Miller, John Perry, 39

Miller, Judy, 147

Millett, Kate, 142–143, 148–149, 193,
    225

Mink, Patsy, 192, 242, 243–245, 273

Mintz, Jackie, 210

Mintz, Patty, 84, 158, 183–184, 195,
    196, 212–213, 252, 295

mixers, 1–5, 20, 92–93, 131

Moratorium March on Washington, 99

Moratorium to End the War in
    Vietnam, 72–73, 89–90

Morgan, Edmund, 178, 179

Morse, Charlotte, 215

Morse, Sandy, 251, 283

Mory's, 110–112, 188–190, 220–222,
    237, 252, 272, 283

  admission of women members, 289

Motley, Constance Baker, 29, 111, 291

music. *See* under arts

National Association for the
    Advancement of Colored People
    (NAACP), 29

National Guard, 170, 172–176

National Organization for Women
    (NOW), 10, 101

National Women's Studies
    Clearinghouse, 235–236

New Blue, 56

New Haven Board of Aldermen, 239

New Haven Green, as protest site, 90,
    164–165, 170, 174–175, 192

New Haven Women's Liberation, 109,
    110, 112, 153, 169, 184, 220

New Haven Women's Liberation Rock
    Band, 146–147, 159–160, 190–191,
    192, 226–228, 253–257, 268–270,
    293

Newman, Becky, 232

New York Times

on Black Woman conference, 214

on college finances, 239

on May Day rally, 167–168

on student morality, 59

on student protests, 140–141

on Yale coeducation, 22, 24

on Yale faculty, 240

on Yale gender quota, 163–164

on Yale undergraduate women, 31

Niantic Women's Prison, 226–228

Nixon, Richard, 172–173

NOW. See National Organization for Women

Nowlin, Bill, 256–257, 269

O'Connor, Dottie, 241

Old Campus face book, 58–59

"Operation Coeducation," 15, 19–20

Ostrom, John, 163

Passaic Valley Regional High School, 26, 27, 106

Percy, Chuck, 200

Peters, Ellen, 14, 121, 179

Peterson, Margaret, 284

Pierson, George, 24, 189, 205

Pifer, Alan, 262–263

Pillsbury, Sarah, 163, 261

Polan, Cookie, 252

Political Union, 198

pornographic films, 22–23, 147–148

pregnancy, 60–61, 63, 223

Princeton College, 235, 239

and coeducation, 18, 23, 298

rivalry with, 18, 99

protests, 9–10, 90–92, 96–99. See also student petitions; individual protests

antiracism, 165

antisexism, 130–135, 139–142, 148, 164, 191, 192, 211

antiwar, 72–73, 89–90, 99, 176, 220

pro-abortion rights, 255–256

sit-ins, 96–98, 136, 188

student strikes, 165, 166, 176–177

union strikes, 233

racial integration, 2, 5, 77, 91, 221

Rackley, Alex, 164, 172

Radcliffe College, 2, 18, 122

rape, 206–209, 228–229, 278–279

Rape of Yale, The, 134

residential colleges, 45–47, 73–74

additional wanted for women, 181–182, 206, 238–239, 262

residential college seminars, 121–122, 139, 204–205, 222

Robinson, W. C., 137

rock bands, 88, 113, 146–147, 256–257.

Rodham, Hillary. *See* Clinton, Hillary
    Rodham

Roe v. Wade, 272

Roraback, Katie, 224

Rose, Fred, 286

Rounder Records, 256–257, 268–270,
    293

Royster, Connie, 28–29, 34–35, 68–70,
    76, 77, 103–105, 171–172, 234, 236–
    237, 271, 286, 297
    arrival at Yale, 42–43
    graduation, 275–276
    later career, 291
    and May Day rally, 168
    on race, 79
    and theater, 56, 198–200
    and women's studies, 222

Rudavsky, Dahlia, 161, 201, 205, 213,
    253, 294

Rudden, Marie, 152, 161, 253

Russett, Cynthia, 235–236

Russ Meyer Film Festival, 147–148

Sandler, Bernice, 216–217, 274

Sarrel, Lorna, 61, 62, 83–84, 125–128,
    161, 184–186, 231–233, 246, 258,
    296–297

Sarrel, Philip, 61–64, 83–84, 125–
    128, 184–186, 231–233, 246, 258,
    296–297

Sayre, Jessie, 59

Schmoke, Kurt, 6, 121

SDS. *See* Students for a Democratic
    Society

Seale, Bobby, 164–166, 234

senior ("secret") societies, 56, 260

sex, 4, 83–85, 123–129

Sex and the Yale Student, 185–186, 194–
    195, 233, 246, 296–297

sex counseling. *See* Yale Sex
    Counseling Service

sex education, 62, 83, 125–128,
    184–186

sexual assault, 70–72, 95–96, 99–100,
    117, 161–162, 206–209, 228–229,
    230–231. *See also* rape
    lack of support for victims, 209
    statistics, 289

sexual harassment, 113–118, 230–231,
    278–279, 290

sexual revolution, 59, 63–64

SHE, 235

Shearer, Brooke, 11, 296

Shearer, Derek, 11, 12, 15, 19–20, 296

Silliman College dining hall, 70–72,
    95–96

Simmons College, 27, 34, 169

singing groups, 56. *See also* individual
    groups

sisterhood. *See* Yale Sisterhood

sister schools, 2, 9. *See also* individual schools

proposed for Yale, 14–15, 18

Skokorat commune, 278

Skull and Bones, 260

Smith College, 245

Smoot, Emily, 105–107, 293

Sneed, Darial, 64–65, 91–92, 165, 295

Sociological Perspectives on Women (course), 204

Soifer, Avi, 19–22, 23, 296

Southern Connecticut College, 250

Spahn, Betty, 29–31, 34, 69–72, 95–98, 103–104, 123, 136, 161, 182, 199–201, 224, 234, 276–277

arrival at Yale, 43–44

and feminism, 150–154

graduation, 275

later career, 291–292

and May Day rally, 169, 170–171, 176

and women's studies, 204–205, 222, 236

Spence, Jonathan, 272

sports. *See also* individual sports

men's, 54, 81, 241

women's, 54–55, 57, 81–82, 197–198, 240–242, 249–251, 281–283, 289, 292

Sterling Library, 236, 277

Stop the Cops protest, 91–92, 169

Storey, Carol, 77, 78, 84, 136, 145, 158, 168, 202, 295

Student Guide to Sex on Campus, The, 297

student petitions, 118, 120, 149, 211, 212–213, 230, 285–286

Students for a Democratic Society (SDS), 19, 96–98, 103, 107, 136, 176

Student Strike Steering Committee, 170–171

"superwomen" label, 31–32, 35

Swarthmore High School, 32, 33

Taft, Horace, 272, 286

Taylor, Charles, 96–97, 248–249

Temoshok, Lydia, 99–100, 176

theater. *See* under arts

Thomas, Elisabeth, 94, 155, 179, 186, 248, 298

Thomson, Keith, 154, 156–157, 247–248

Thorburn, James, 94, 95, 99, 101

thousand-man quota, 65–66, 113, 118, 120, 135, 157, 180, 212

end of, 287

Time, 101–102, 138, 193

Title IX. *See* Civil Rights Act of 1964

Tobin, James, 221

Topics in Human Sexuality (course), 62, 125–128, 184, 233, 296

Trinity College, 9–10

Trotman, Stanley, 188–189

Tucker, Larry, 251

tuition, 8, 24, 33, 34, 51–52, 70, 200

Tunstall, Tricia, 254

University Committee on
   Coeducation, 113–114, 121–122,
   205–206, 218, 246–247, 280
      Brewster's views on, 211–212
      and gender quota, 178–180, 181–
         182, 194
      and Mory's, 188–190
      recommendations of, 181–182
      and women faculty, 187–188, 194

University of Michigan, 215–216

University of Pennsylvania, 165

"Unofficial Proposals for Equality,"
   145–146

Vance, Cyrus, 239, 260, 262, 285

Vanderbilt Hall, 25, 45, 46, 195–196
      men's access to, 60

Vassar College, 15, 20

Vietnam War, 10, 44, 72–73, 89–90, 99,
   108–109, 171, 220

Wasserman, Elga, 36–40, 45, 47–49, 57,
   118, 120–122, 140, 177, 178–182,
   194–195, 205–209, 211, 235–237,
   280–281

accumulation of power, 121,
   270–271

and admissions, 52, 53, 154, 155

budget for, 122, 270

and campus security, 86, 93–95,
   113–114

later career, 297–298

position of, 85–86, 179, 180–181,
   218, 246–247

pressure on Brewster, 157,
   178–182, 209–210, 234–235,
   271–272

progressiveness of, 60–64, 186

public support of Brewster, 120,
   122

seen as "difficult," 122, 210

titles of, 39, 49, 180–181, 234–
   235, 238

women faculty report, 187–188, 217

women's opinion of, 210, 271

Wasserman, Harry, 38

Weisstein, Naomi, 142, 143–144, 190,
   268, 270

Wells, Vera, 75, 76, 85, 138–139, 203,
   213, 293–294

Western, Mary Jane, 105–107, 293

Wheaton College, 28, 34–35

Whiffenpoofs. See Yale Whiffenpoofs

Whitney, Jock, 181–182

Wilkinson, John, 13, 166, 186, 225, 297

William and Mary. *See* College of
William and Mary

Williams, Colia, 96, 98

Wilson, Keith, 56–57, 58

women

as administrators, 36–37, 94, 181,
271

and Black Power movement,
213–214

as faculty, 16, 110, 187–188, 270,
290, 294

in government, 14, 101, 191, 242

as graduate students, 16–17, 20,
109–110

leadership potential of, 14

limitations on, at work, 48, 144,
180

as trustees, 235

Women and Men for a Better Yale,
132–134, 135, 139–142, 149, 150

Women and the Law (course), 222

Women in a Male Society (course),
121–122

Women's Advisory Council, 113–114,
118, 120, 140

women's history course, 236

women's movement, 10–11, 44, 101–
102, 107–108, 148–149, 190–193

and blacks, 152–153

at Yale, 109–113, 150–154, 201

Women's National Abortion Action
Coalition, 255

women's sports. *See* sports

Women's Strike for Equality, 191, 192

women's studies, 121–122, 196, 203–
205, 222, 235–236

Women v. Connecticut. *See* Abele v.
Markle

Yale Alumni Fund, 135

Yale Alumni Magazine, 37–38, 52, 149,
163, 261, 263, 272

Yale Alumni Office, 130

Yale Athletic Department, 197, 241, 283

Yale Break, 163

Yale College

admissions, 12, 13–14, 52–53, 133,
134–135, 149

admissions, drop in, 17–18

admissions, process, 52–53,
154–155

as all-male, 2, 9, 12

campus, 40, 73, 79, 195

enrollment numbers, 41

as "establishment," 166

federal funding for, 215, 243–245

finances, 239–240, 284

gender quota, 65–66, 109, 118,
120, 134–135, 149, 154, 157,
163–164, 180

gender quota, end of, 287

gender ratio, 45, 65, 93, 118, 131, 164, 194, 238, 258, 288

loss of students to rivals, 17–18

mission of, 13–14, 135

as producing leaders, 13–14, 52–53, 158–159

security at, 86, 93–95, 99–100, 113–114, 279

and sex discrimination legislation, 243–245, 274

sex regulations, 59–60

student demographics, 65, 75–76

women administrators, 36–37

women applicants, 25, 26–36

women faculty, 16, 187–188, 270, 290, 294

Yale College Council, 285–286

Yale Corporation, 24, 235

and gender quota, 149, 206, 210–213, 214, 267–268, 285–287

and May Day rally, 166, 168

Yale Daily News, 55–56, 59, 198, 265

on admissions discrimination, 163

on gender quota, 109, 113, 135, 214, 285

as pro-coeducation, 8, 19

on sexual assault, 206, 207, 208

sports coverage, 81, 242, 282–283, 292

theater reviews, 275–276

on Vietnam War, 89

on women's academic performance, 157–158

on women's movement, 148–149

Yale Drama School, 171

Yale Dramatic Association, 56, 104–105, 198

Yale Economics Department, 222, 254

Yale Gay Alliance, 257

Yale Graduate School, 16, 39

Yale Health Center, 25, 45, 223

Yale Health Service, 16, 61–62, 229

Yale Law School, 91–92, 220, 254, 290

Yale Law School Film Society, 22–23, 147–148

Yale Law Women Association, 109, 110–112, 150

Yale Precision Marching Band, 56–58, 87–88, 251

Yale Sex Counseling Service, 63, 64, 83, 123, 125, 161, 231–233, 296

Yale Sisterhood, 150–154, 159, 160–163, 170–171, 183–184, 195–196, 201, 204–205, 212–213, 224–225, 252–253, 276, 285, 289, 294–295

Yale undergraduate men

academic performance, 157–158

approaches to women, 1–5, 49–51, 58–59, 123

black, 74–76, 84, 85, 136–138

and dating, 123–124

and sex, 4, 84, 85, 232

and Vietnam War, 89

and women's appearances, 3

Yale undergraduate women

academic performance, 52, 157–158, 202

admissions standards, 53, 163–164

arrival on campus, 40–44, 49–52

black, 74–80, 84, 85, 136–138, 152–153

as conspicuous, 64–68

and dating, 123–124

demographics of, 41

diversity of, 51–52

divided between residential colleges, 45–47

and loneliness, 73–74, 118

media coverage of, 41–42, 67, 118

men's attention to, 65, 67–68, 123, 161

reasons for leaving Yale, 223, 229, 279

seen as gender representatives, 66–67, 76, 131

and sex, 83–85

and sexual harassment, 114, 115–117

social pressure on, 67–68, 83–85, 93

Yale Upward Bound, 277, 290

Yale Whiffenpoofs, 56, 111, 116, 189–190

women singers in, 289

Yale Women's Center, 224–225, 266, 289

Yellen, Janet, 14, 221, 222

Yippies, 166

Zaeder, Phil, 170, 185, 246, 259, 260

Zaleznik, Dori, 93

Zanger, Mark, 19

ABOUT THE AUTHOR

Anne Gardiner Perkins is an award-winning historian and expert in higher education. She graduated from Yale University, where she won the Porter Prize in history and was elected the first woman editor in chief of the *Yale Daily News*. Perkins is a Rhodes Scholar who received her PhD in higher education from the University of Massachusetts Boston and her master's in public administration from Harvard, where she won the Littauer Award for academic excellence and served as a teaching fellow in education policy. She has presented papers on the history of higher education at leading academic conferences and been a visiting scholar at the New England Resource Center for Higher Education. Perkins lives with her husband in Boston and Harvard, Massachusetts. This is her first book.

ANNEGARDINERPERKINS.COM